THE HISTORY OF
AMERICAN CATHOLIC WOMEN

THE HISTORY OF
AMERICAN CATHOLIC WOMEN

James J. Kenneally

CROSSROAD • NEW YORK

1990

The Crossroad Publishing Company
370 Lexington Avenue, New York, NY 10017

Printed in the United States of America

Library of Congress Cataloging-in-Publication Data

Kenneally, James Joseph, 1929-
    The history of American Catholic women / James J. Kenneally.
      p.   cm.
    Includes bibliographical references.
    ISBN 0-8245-1009-7
    1. Women in the Catholic Church—United States—History.
2. Women, Catholic—United States—History. 3. Catholic Church—
United States—History. 4. United States—Church history.
I. Title.
BX1407.W65K43   1990
282'.082—dc20   89-77880
                                                                CIP

For Louise, Ann, Jo, Judy, and the two Stephanies,
Catholic women all

CONTENTS

INTRODUCTION

It took half a century before historians responded to the 1922 appeal of Arthur M. Schlesinger to include women in their research. Scholars of American Catholicism, however, have not really met that challenge, although narratives of today are much more balanced than those of even a decade ago. There have been some efforts, with varying degrees of success, to incorporate women into traditional Catholic history, such as James Hennesey's *American Catholics: A History of the Roman Catholic Community in the United States* (New York, 1981) and Jay P. Dolan's *The American Catholic Experience: A History from Colonial Times to the Present* (Garden City, N.Y., 1985).

Other encouraging signs are the special "Women in the Catholic Community" issue of the *U.S. Catholic Historian* (Summer/Fall 1986) and the series of essays in Karen Kennelly's *American Catholic Women: A Historical Exploration* (New York, 1989). Mary Jo Weaver's *The New Catholic Woman: A Contemporary Challenge to Traditional Religious Authority* (New York, 1985), a study of women activists in the post–Vatican II church, devotes considerable attention to historical perspective, and Mary Ewens has done pioneering work on the history of nuns, particularly in the nineteenth century (*The Role of the Nun in Nineteenth Century America* [New York, 1978]). Nevertheless, for the most part contributions of Catholic women to American life and their relationship to church and society have remained unexplored by historians. This neglect jeopardizes the relationship of contemporary women with their church by ignoring their past and overlooking the lengthy struggle of women to reconcile faith and feminism.

This survey of the history of Catholic women from the colonial era to the beginning of the feminist movement of the 1960s demonstrates that many Catholic women of the past, like their contemporaries today, have not been inhibited by the traditions of a male-dominated church. Some found independence and self-esteem in the sisterhood of religious orders, where they contested hierarchical dictates and enjoyed the company of a community of women. Others drew strength from the church even as they followed a life-style that was in sharp contradistinction to the reticence that institution expected of them. Many seemed to compartmentalize faith and action with little relationship between the two — closet feminists unaware that their daily activities challenged traditional church norms. As a result, they often had little sympathy for radicals who directly defied religious convention.

The lives of these women demonstrate clearly that the thrust for equality in church and state by Catholic females from the 1960s to the present is merely a new phase of an enduring struggle. The post–Vatican II rebel is the natural product of two hundred years of Catholic experience — an exciting saga of gains and setbacks that until recently has been ignored by historians of religion.

Many people have assisted in the preparation of this narrative, among them Ed Hynes and Janice Schuster, whose good nature and efficient cooperation in the interlibrary loan section of the Stonehill College Library made it a delight to impose on them. The services of the following archivists even exceeded those that one has come to expect from such a generous profession: Rosalie McQuaide of the Sisters of St. Joseph of Peace, Charlotte P. Seeley of the National Archives, Warren Willis of the U.S. Catholic Conference, Patricia Harpole of the Minnesota Historical Society, Christine Krosel of the Cleveland Diocese, and Caroline Gimpl of the Sisters of the Holy Name of Jesus and Mary. Answering inquiries and sharing their experiences with me were Dorothy Shipley Granger, founder of the St. Joan Society, Julia Mack, founder of the American Lithuanian Roman Catholic Women's Alliance, Mary Fitzgerald Phaneuf of the Frances Sweeney Committee, and the following scholars: Ann Allen, Nelson J. Callahan, Ellen Marie Kuznicki, and William Wolkovich. Peggy Karp cheerfully struggled with my handwriting, and my wife, Louise, has willingly shared me with an interesting variety of Catholic women over the past several years.

Chapter 1

TENUOUS TRADITIONS: WOMEN AND THE CHURCH IN BRITISH AND REVOLUTIONARY AMERICA

The English colonies in North America, although established in part as a refuge for dissenters, reflected the religious xenophobia of the day and rarely extended tolerance to other sects. This attitude was especially true in the case of Catholics, whose religion appeared inimical to the traditions that established limited monarchy and representative government in England. Furthermore, Catholics were suspected of collaborating with fellow Romanists in the French and Spanish settlements by challenging English hegemony in the New World. Legal disabilities were imposed upon them, and every colony apparently disfranchised Catholics by the end of the seventeenth century. Even Maryland, the most Catholic of settlements, yielding to Protestant domination, established the Church of England and proscribed public Catholic worship: services were confined to private homes.[1]

For the handful of adherents of this bedeviled faith in a frontier society, there was no parish organization. By necessity the exercise of religion became a very personal matter. Consequently it is difficult to identify individual Catholic men and their role in the colonial world. It is even more difficult to discover the colonial Catholic woman. The conventional theology from St. Paul to St. Augustine to St. Thomas that English Catholics brought to the colonies subordinated woman to man and confined her to a restricted sphere of activity centering in

1

the home, the children, and the church. Contributions in these realms were frequently overlooked by notetakers.

These traditions of subservience were reinforced by available literature. Catholic devotional books were not published in the English settlements until after the French and Indian War, when the danger from external Catholic aggression was virtually eliminated. Nevertheless, books of advice for girls were available. In 1759 Abbé d'Ancourt's manual, designed especially for Catholic ladies, intertwined religious values and ladylike demeanor. Females were warned that every thought and deed should be directed not only toward their ultimate end, salvation, but toward their temporal destiny, marriage. Thus girls should excel in modesty, exercise reserve with young men (who are "always ready to take more than you ought to allow them"), and never forget that public affairs and the character of public persons are improper subjects for conversation.[2]

Between the Treaty of Paris (1763) and the outbreak of the American Revolution (1776), three books of a specifically religious nature were published for a Catholic audience: *A Manual of Catholic Prayers* and Bishop Richard Challoner's *The Catholic Christian Instructed* and *The Garden of the Soul*. These works remained popular for about a century. Challoner, who was bishop of London and therefore of North America from 1758 to 1781 (and coadjutor since 1741), reenforced the precepts in the lady's guide and reemphasized the church's historical image of women by stressing marriage as their rightful vocation and by underscoring the scriptural mandate of Paul, Peter, Titus, and Tobias that wives were to be subject to their husbands.[3]

Evidently, however, Catholic women had begun to defy the church's strictures on motherhood, pregnancy, and conception. To assist in the examination of conscience in preparation for confession, Challoner, in a section headed "The Sixth Commandment" and dealing with "pollution of the marriage bed," reminded women of the sinful nature of "irregularity" in order to prevent pregnancy. Furthermore, both the bishop and the *Manual of Catholic Prayer* admonished those who committed serious sin and violated the Fifth Commandment by inducing a miscarriage. Challoner also warned of the sin of aiding or assisting one to miscarry or even thinking of such an action. Instead he suggested as reparation for sin the daily recitation of the prayer, "I accept whatever I have to go through in childbearing."[4] This teaching, of course, was not unique to the colonies. The *Catechism of the Council of Trent* stated that married persons who "have recourse to medicine" to prevent conception or procure abortion are guilty of "nothing less than murder."[5] The *Manual* also warned Catholic women of the sinful nature of eating hot meat or drinking hot wine to incite lust. As one might expect from a patriarchal church, the section intended for men listed neither these sins nor any pertaining to miscarriage or "irregularities." Even before the Revolution, it appears that "American" women had begun to ignore the sexual teachings of the institutional church — a defiance that would grow in intensity into the twentieth century.

Moreover, in the few cases where one can identify Catholic women, it appears that the leveling influence of a primitive society, the process of immigration wherein only the adventuresome, self-confident, or desperate crossed the Atlantic, and the personal relationship between men and women in a relatively church-free society had begun to erode the traditional roles assigned by religion. It was most likely at the instigation of his wife that the first Lord Baltimore, after his unsuccessful attempt to found a colony at Newfoundland, applied to the king for a new charter at Chesapeake Bay.[6]

From that time on, to the amazement of many, women continued to play prominent roles in Maryland and in the church. Most surprised were the clergy, who for the next two centuries would be astonished at the initiative, courage, and self-esteem of Catholic women. In writing of the death in 1638 of a "noble matron," who accompanied the first settlers and set an example in prayer, charity, and nurturing, a Jesuit observed with typical male hauteur that she "with more than a woman's courage bore all her difficulties and inconveniences."[7] Shared decision making was reflected twenty years later when William Bretton, with the "hearty liking of my dearly beloved wife," Temperance, donated land for a church and Catholic center and when Jerome Hawley, who had come with the first settlers as commissioner to assist the governor of the colony, refused a political post in Virginia, as the capital at St. Mary's would lose the influence of his wife.[8]

Most unusual was Margaret Brent (c. 1601–c. 1671), for whom a Catholic woman suffrage society was named in 1918. One of the largest landowners in Maryland and a shrewd businesswoman as well, she and her sister had received adjoining land grants from Baltimore. Margaret paid for the transportation of ten men to increase the size of her holding and also was deeded additional land by her brother, Giles. As executor of the estate of Governor Leonard Calvert, no one in the colony was more powerful than she. Her leadership in preventing a mutiny by soldiers who had been hired from Virginia to fight rebellious Protestants was acknowledged. The assembly publicly asserted that Calvert's estate was "better for the colony in her hands than in any man's else in the whole province."

Yet, despite her accomplishments, the assembly refused Brent's demand for the vote. (Actually she petitioned for two: one as a freeholder, and one as Calvert's executor.) Foreshadowing the stance of American women two centuries later, she then "protested against all proceedings" of that body. Although little is known about her, it does not appear as if Brent abandoned her femininity in the pursuit of power or in the exercise of her proprietorship. She adopted and raised the daughter of an Indian chief, who later married her nephew. Furthermore, one historian has interpreted the assembly's use of the words "civility and respect" in describing the soldier's demeanor toward her during the revolutionary crisis as resulting from Brent's "womanliness" as well as her strength.[9]

Shortly after Brent left Maryland for a new life in Virginia, a successful Puritan revolution ushered in a century of religious turmoil in the colony. By the end of the century Maryland was a royal province with an established Anglican church. Catholics were barred from office and allowed to worship only on the condition their meetings be held in private homes. Thus the challenge of preserving the faith was primarily woman's. As the chief religious instructor for children and as the cook and meal planner, it was she who assumed responsibility for observing the round of feasts and fasts.[10] To circumvent the law preventing Catholic schools, French seamstresses were hired in the 1760s ostensibly to instruct in weaving and needlework in sewing schools but actually to teach religion. Probably the first mass in Pennsylvania was in the improvised chapel of Elizabeth McGauley in 1708.[11] It took courage to adhere to the faith, for routine practices such as marriage ceremonies and baptisms defied conventional norms and resulted in opprobrium.[12]

In their reports Jesuits in Maryland frequently omitted names or changed them because of intolerance, thus making it even harder to trace female achievements.[13] Nevertheless, daring men and women preserved their religious heritage. In 1756 Bishop Challoner estimated there were from five thousand to seven thousand Catholics in Maryland, about two thousand in Pennsylvania and a handful in the rest of the colonies.[14] In New England, and probably the other settlements as well, it was impossible to enumerate Catholics, if there were any; despised by the community and left without priests, they had ignored or disguised their religious duties.[15]

Colonial women participated in the American Revolution, boycotting imported goods, establishing antitea leagues, and joining the Daughters of Liberty, who along with the Sons, held massive urban rallies, distributed revolutionary propaganda, and intimidated tax collectors into resigning. Furthermore, they encouraged men to enlist, provided supplies for the army, in some cases acted more directly as spies or saboteurs, and even joined troops in the field. There is no indication these activities were restricted to Protestant women, as the necessity for unity against the British enemy and the alliance with his Most Catholic Majesty, the king of France, resulted in greater colonial acceptance of Catholics. Only a few names of these patriotic women have been preserved, however, and not much is known even of these. Probably the most noted Catholic females of this period were Sarah McCalla, who provided intelligence information to American forces; Mary Digges Lee (1745–1805), who raised money for the revolutionary forces; Catherine Meade FitzSimons (d. 1810) whose husband was a captain in Pennsylvania's militia; the nurse Mary Waters (fl. 1770–99); and Margaret Sharpe Gaston (1755–1824), who was as renowned for her son's achievements as for anything she did.

McCalla, a cousin of the revolutionary hero General Anthony Wayne, followed her soldier-husband into the field and tended the wounded at the battle of Brandywine. Three years later her spouse was captured in South Carolina. She discovered his whereabouts, implored the British to exchange him because he was ill, and for six months while running the farm, crossed enemy lines to visit him in prison. She raised the morale of all the incarcerated, for she had borrowed money to supply them with clothes and provisions and during her visits also provided latest news of the war. Furthermore, on each of these trips McCalla gathered information on the British forces for the American revolutionaries.[16]

Mary Digges ignored the reservations of her devout father and married a non-Catholic, Thomas Sim Lee, who promised to raise their children in their mother's faith. Lee not only honored his pledge but became a convert himself, and when his wife was dangerously ill built a church that he named St. Mary's in her honor. Both were dedicated patriots. She mobilized the women of Maryland behind the patriot cause and received the thanks of General George Washington for raising funds for his army. Her husband served as governor of Maryland (1779–83), delegate to the Continental Congress (1783–84), and again as governor (1792–94), declining a nomination for a fourth term at his wife's request.[17]

Little is known of Catherine Meade FitzSimons, the daughter of a wealthy Irishman born in Limerick who helped build St. Mary's in Philadelphia. She exploited her husband's revolutionary reputation and used the patriot financier Robert Morris as intermediary to request from George Washington a pardon for a deserter.[18]

More direct were the contributions of Dublin-born Mary Waters to the revolutionary cause. An emigrant to the colonies in 1776, Waters was described in the Philadelphia City Directory as a doctoress and an apothecary. Convinced by her pastor that her's was a special skill by which she "might merit heaven," Waters rejected the temptation to abandon her nursing career. All during the War for Independence she served in military hospitals, adding to her reputation for charitable endeavors a renown for skill and devotion to duty.[19]

Margaret Sharpe was born in England and educated in a convent in France. She visited her brother in the colonies, where she met and married the Huguenot Dr. Alexander Gaston in May 1775. Despite her entreaties, Gaston, a member of the Committee of Public Safety in North Carolina, was shot by Tories while attempting to flee from the British by crossing a river. His enraged wife ignored remonstrances from the murderers and courageously retrieved his body from the drifting skiff.

Widowed and alone at age twenty-six (her brother had also died), Gaston was the sole support of her two small children, whom she was determined to raise as exemplary Catholics. She sent William at age twelve to Philadelphia to prepare for college, then to Georgetown and finally Princeton. This son, at one time described as "the greatest lay Catholic in America," helped to establish the church in the Carolinas and Georgia and successfully campaigned to remove restrictions against Catholics in the North Carolina constitution.[20] After serving eleven terms in the state legislature and then in the United States House of Representatives from 1813 to 1817, he earned a reputation as an outstanding jurist by his contributions on the North Carolina Supreme Court. Like his mother, he was not an advocate of slavery. He called upon students at the state university to aid in its elimination and supported the right of free blacks to vote. Repeatedly and publicly Gaston acknowledged his mother's influence on him and asserted that he owed everything to her and the many virtuous lessons she had taught him.

Rather typically, little is known of his sister. She received a straight-laced upbringing, not being allowed, for example, to look in mirrors or let her shoulders touch the back of a chair in her mother's presence. At age seventeen she married a twenty-six-year-old lawyer and apparently submerged herself in his career.

Mrs. Gaston wore widow's black for thirty years and earned a reputation as a devout woman, visiting the poor and sick and keeping a place for worship in her house. She was publicly praised by Bishop John England of Charleston for her piety, intelligence, and attachment to religion. Most important, for over a generation this self-effacing woman was hailed as the exemplar of Catholic motherhood.[21]

The return of peace initiated a new era in religious liberty, for although some states retained their established churches, penal laws were swept away. As early as 1779 John Carroll (1735–1815), who later became the first American bishop, described the nation as having the fullest measure of toleration, with Catholics eligible to hold civil, military, and other posts in state, local, and national government.[22]

Shortly after Carroll's consecration as bishop (1790), four nuns from the English community of Carmelites in Hoogstraet, Belgium, arrived in Maryland to open the nation's first convent. Although Carroll probably would have preferred a teaching order to this contemplative band, he could hardly deny them permission to establish a house in the United States. His cousin, Anna Louisa Mills, was a member of that community, and three of the sisters, including the superior Mother Bernadine of St. Joseph, were Americans. As their existence in Belgium was threatened by Napoleon's suppression of Carmelite houses in the Low Countries, Father Ignatius Matthews, Bernadine's brother, had urged them to come to the United States, and their confessor, Father Charles Neal, an old classmate of Carroll's, had presented them with a farm at Port Tobacco.[23] One week after establishing themselves, the nuns accepted their first postulant, forty-nine-year-old Elizabeth Carberry (1745–1814). Carberry had waited twenty years to fulfill her dream, for her father, a prosperous Maryland farmer, had refused her permission to leave the colonies to enter a European convent. During that period she had taught children in Newton, Maryland, and managed the family plantation when three of her brothers served in the revolutionary army.[24]

With the cessation of hostilities the number of Catholics and parishes multiplied rapidly. In the twenty-five years after 1775 many Catholic immigrants from southern Ireland and Germany came to the United States and established churches in cities such as New York and Philadelphia. By 1808 there were four new dioceses: Boston, New York, Philadelphia, and Bardstown, Kentucky. In these areas undeveloped ecclesiastical organization fostered lay initiative.[25] In Boston Mrs. Mary Connell Lobb, the daughter of a sea captain, was instrumental in forming a congregation and obtaining quarters for the church.[26]

In addition to immigration and a high birth rate, converts from older established families added substantially to the influence and prestige of the church, as they did all during the nineteenth century. Among the most significant recruits of this time were Charlotte Melmouth (1749–1823), one of Ireland's leading actresses, whose final years were spent tutoring children in Brooklyn; Fanny Allen (1785–c. 1819), the daughter of Ethan Allen of Green Mountain Boys Revolutionary War fame, who became a Hospital Sister of St. Joseph in Canada; and Jerusha Barber (1789–1821), the wife of an Episcopal clergyman in Boston, who entered the Visitandine Community so that her husband could become a priest (her daughters, three of whom became Ursuline nuns, boarded at the Georgetown Academy, where she taught).[27] But the most influential convert, male or female, in the history of the American church was the widow Elizabeth Bayley Seton (1774–1821), the founder of the parochial school system in the United States. In 1806 she opened a girl's school in Baltimore, where she was joined the following spring by two of her sisters-in-law who also had become converts. A few years later they followed Seton in taking religious vows in her newly formed community the Sisters of Charity of Emmitsburg.[28]

As the church was becoming established along the coast, it was also spreading into Kentucky and the Mississippi Valley, for families from Virginia and Maryland had begun the trek westward. Father Stephen Badin, a conservative émigré from the French Revolution who ministered to Catholics in Kentucky, praised women pioneers for their virtue and influential role in promoting religious life. What was probably the first elementary school in that state was opened for emigrant children by Mrs. William Coomes (fl. 1770s and 1780s) of Maryland, who was also one of the first settlers to engage in salt making.[29] A Maryland woman who had attended the Visitandine Academy in Washington, Mary Rhodes (1782?–1853) opened a girl's school southeast of Bardstown. There with the guidance of Father Charles Nerinckx, a Belgian exiled during the French Revolution, she founded a teaching community, the Sisters of Loretto at the Foot of the Cross, the first native American sisterhood without foreign affiliation.[30]

Less than a year later, in 1813, another teaching order was established in that state, the Sisters of Charity of Nazareth, headed by Catherine Spalding (1793–1858) who had migrated from Maryland with her parents.[31] These were probably the first two academies for girls in Kentucky to receive state recognition.[32] The piety of these settlers, however, did not prevent them from trying to influence church policy. Women from Louisville remonstrated with Benedict Flaget (1763–1850), bishop of Bardstown, over his choice of a coadjutor.[33]

Although the religious devotion of frontier women was noted repeatedly, churchmen seemed to be excessively concerned with the effect of dancing — on females particularly. The first missionary in Kentucky, an Irish Franciscan, tried unsuccessfully to stop the custom, which had spread even into the Catholic community of St. Louis. Father Nerinckx refused to prepare girls over fourteen for first communion if they attended dances.[34] In 1812 a synod was held in Bardstown to deal with the major problems faced by the church: (1) the administration of confirmation, (2) marriage to non-Catholics, and (3) dancing on Saturday evening, the pernicious effects of which interfered with night prayers, Sunday mass, and "pure morals." Consequently, the synod decreed that "although it was possible that a lady could so conduct herself that there would be no approximate danger of mortal sin, nevertheless as this case was rare, the good of souls demands that dances should be absolutely forbidden and the Sacraments refused to those who would be obstinate in their disobedience."[35]

John Carroll, the nation's first bishop, also was concerned about women's fondness for dancing and about their "incredible eagerness" to read novels. Chastity of mind and body were endangered by these practices and by the "free conduct" between the sexes, an American characteristic.[36] Carroll was further troubled about marriages to nonbelievers, a particularly pressing problem due to the scarcity of Catholics and their daily contact with Protestants. To bar intermarriage, he asserted, would reduce many of the faithful to celibacy; to approve, would often result in children being reared outside the church. To resolve the dilemma, Carroll requested permission to allow marriage to first cousins.[37]

Even when both partners were Catholic, however, the faith was jeopardized in this Protestant nation. Referring to the marriage of one of his relatives, Carroll wrote, "Terrifying is the idea of a young woman being seated down in a hotbed of presbyterianism, at least 100 miles from a Catholic church or clergyman.... No worldly advantage... can make compensation" for this event.[38]

As these dangers could be reduced substantially by sound religious training, Carroll encouraged European communities of nuns to establish houses in the United States and promoted the organization of American foundations. He was adamant in advocating that the sisters undertake educational missions, not only to strengthen the faith but to support themselves, because contemplative orders would have no means of support in the United States. Consequently, he urged that only those religious who knew English be sent to America, that constitutions be changed so that contemplatives could undertake instructional duties, and that requirements on fasting and prayer be modified so as not to interfere with teaching duties. In expressing his indignation about Carmelites who were reluctant to change their rule, he was but the precursor of nineteenth-century bishops who would attempt to subvert the independence of women's religious communities by bending their rules to serve diocesan needs.[39]

With his encouragement women religious established schools throughout the nation. Among the earliest were those of the Visitation Nuns at Georgetown (1799), Sisters of Charity at Emmitsburg (1809), and in Kentucky the Sisters of Charity of Nazareth at St. Joseph's farm near Bardstown (1813) and Sisters of Loretto at Hardin's Creek (1812). The Ursulines established an academy in New Orleans (1727), which became part of the United States with the Louisiana Purchase, and attempted one in New York City (1812–15).[40] These institutions were dedicated to religious instruction, leading students to salvation, and fostering ladylike qualities, including a gentle and easy deportment. To the nuns and the Catholic community at large, all three were inextricably linked. Among other practices Ursulines required their pupils to wear "gloves, hats, or coifs or muffs" when they appeared in public and were so successful in their objectives that the bishop of New Orleans viewed their training as the reason that girls were "less vicious than the other sex."[41]

Despite an increasing self-assertiveness on the part of American women, clerical conventions and Catholic ideals remained unchanged and severely circumscribed the activities and opportunities for females. The attitude of the most renowned Catholic patriot of the period, Charles Carroll of Carrollton, was probably typical. Although some correspondence with the women in his family touched upon politics and military affairs, he extolled the pleasures of household tasks to his granddaughter and urged her to cultivate the feminine virtues: piety, modesty, sweetness of manner, affability, and dignity. Furthermore, he reminded her that it was necessary to study only those subjects that would polish these refinements.[42] To Carroll, as to most males of his generation, homemaking tasks clearly belonged to those of the other sex. He himself loathed infants and relegated their care to his harried wife. By age twenty-five this rather frail woman had had at least five pregnancies in six years and suffered from "female complaint." Three more children undermined her health and helped to account for her reliance on laudanum and opium.[43]

Despite her commitment to education for women, even Mother Seton expressed conventional, orthodox views. To a former pupil who married shortly after completing her schooling at St. Joseph's Academy Emmitsburg, she wrote, "I wish very much to know if you make a *good obedient wife* studying the happiness of your husband, as you wish him to study yours, and as a *true Christian* setting him the first example of a humble heart, and forbearing temper...prepare yourself to become a happy mother of souls you will bring up to God, by the faithful discharge of every domestic virtue."[44]

As in the colonial period, religious handbooks helped to shape these perceptions. Bishop François Fénelon's *Treatise on the Education of Daughters*, which first appeared in France in 1688, was published in the United States in 1806 and again in 1821. Fénelon emphasized that girls should not be "ridiculously learned," since their minds (like their bodies) were weaker than those of men. Furthermore, as they were destined to be "the ornament and comfort of the home" and were born with a desire to please, their education should be but a preparation for their role as wife and mother.[45]

Chastity, modesty, and evenness of temper were stressed in Abbé René Houdet's *Treatise of Morality*, which also warned against self-love, coquettish dress, excessive fashion, gross adulation (from foul flatterers), and too much freedom. Furthermore, Houdet directed women to attend to domestic affairs as they had been assigned by nature and to be sincerely attached to their husbands and warned each wife that the "limit of her desire [should be] to please him." Although Houdet's study promoted traditional perceptions, it foreshadowed the means of liberation for generations of Catholic women with its far-reaching views on education. Woman's responsibility as ruler of the home and her function to entertain her husband required learning. Education formed the heart and judgment and thereby enriched understanding, enabled conversation with a well-informed man, made mutual intercourse more pleasant, and enabled her to inspire and teach her children, the "most indispensable of her duties."[46]

Carroll was not as enlightened as Houdet, for although the bishop wanted educated women and viewed nuns as the instrument to achieve this end, he had reservations even about the abilities of these chosen women. To his friend Charles Plowden he confided, "Female missioners are not much to my taste! But I hope I shall not be blind to the wonderful works of God, if He chuses [*sic*] to make use of such instruments for the salvation of the world."[47] Carroll's views were in keeping with those of Rome. Permission for a confraternity of the Scapulars in Baltimore was denied by church authorities, as any such organization among religious women would "produce an intercourse with seculars, occasioning thereby dissipation, and relaxation of religious discipline."[48] This restrictive perception of female religious resulted in the American hierarchy's intruding into the question of governance rather than letting communities rule themselves; in short, it treated women like children.

Mother Seton, who was described as a saint by Carroll, was not immune to such management.[49] Her frequent struggles with male superiors, who allegedly knew what was best for her sisters, nearly resulted in her expulsion. On the verge of demoralization she wrote, "Rules, prudence, subjection, opinions, etc. dreadful walls to a burning soul wild as mine.... For me I am like a fiery horse I had when a girl which they tried to break by making him drag a heavy cart, and the poor beast was so humbled that he could never more be inspired by whips or caresses and wasted a skeleton until he died."[50] However, like many women, religious and lay, Seton tended to blame herself when assertiveness contravened male leadership, for she informed Carroll that she was "illy qualified" for her responsibilities, as she did not have "a pliancy of character."[51]

By the time of Carroll's death in 1815, the relationship between the institutional church and American women had begun to assume the form it would take for the next 150 years. For the clergy there was an unearthly vision of women wherein females were viewed either as daughters of Eve (prone to sin and needing guidance), or as children of Mary (pure, fragile, delicate, and needing protection). In an unending struggle for dignity and independence, women — lay and religious — frequently defied such concepts, while others adapted these very ideas to turn them against their male protagonists.

Chapter 2

THE CATHOLIC LADY:
A CONCEPT FURTHER REFINED

Historians have disagreed over the effects of the Revolution on American women. Some assert that it offered opportunities for females to assume male tasks during the war and that the ideology it spawned required improved education for women. Much of their postwar domestic responsibility assumed a public guise, for the new nation required mothers to raise republican sons. As this task served a social and political purpose, it drew women's sphere closer to the world of men. On the other hand, some historians contend that progress was illusory. The role of republican motherhood, according to them, was only a refinement of traditional concepts. Furthermore, industrialization and urbanization accompanying the conflict resulted in a loss of status in the household and introduced a class distinction among women: leisured ladies and mill girls.[1]

There is little dispute, however, that the conservative period following the War for Independence ushered in a new era of proscriptive pronouncements on women, emphasizing traditional demeanor and asserting that the ideal woman possessed four cardinal virtues: piety, purity, submissiveness, and domesticity.[2] Catholicism was no different. Building on its colonial tradition, it too stressed these qualities. However, it clung to this unrealistic perception long after most of its Protestant confreres had adopted more reasonable sentiments.

Catholic notions were explicated at length in the essays of Robert Walsh, one of that era's greatest Catholic intellectuals. A Georgetown graduate and father of twelve children, Walsh was editor of the *American Review of History and Politics* (1811–12, the first American quarterly), the Philadelphia *National Gazette* (1820–36), and the

13

American Quarterly (1821–36). Walsh also authored several books, including the highly praised and popular two-volume treatise on manners and behavior, *Didactics*.[3]

Dismissing the feminism of Fanny Wright and Mary Wollstonecraft as "rotten stuff," Walsh maintained that happiness for all could be found in industry, temperance, frugality, and domesticity. He affirmed that females were naturally more pious than males. According to him that quality, the crowning grace of womanhood, should be developed fully. Moreover, he asserted, women had received from the Creator a specific moral character — chastity — both internal and external, leading to delicacy in social intercourse.[4]

Women's "knowledge and general-tone and cast of character," he alleged, should be developed in relationship to their "unavoidable sphere" — the home. A major familial responsibility was the education of children, which necessitated that mothers themselves be learned and even have some theoretical acquaintance with politics. However, the practical Walsh advocated that their education differ from that of males. Classical learning was unnecessary; it was not relevant to the duties of wives. Instead "the morals and numberless delicacies and graces which adorn the female character" should be nurtured. And if, perchance, a wife was intellectually superior to her mate, "externally she ought to be a woman," pleasing, loving, and seeking support.[5] Advocacy of this type of subordination lasted late into the century. An 1897 guide exhorted wives to make the home pleasant for their spouses, advising them to keep quiet even when their husbands insisted on views known to be wrong, were angry, or were not in their "sober senses."[6]

Walsh's teaching, like that of most American Catholic moralists of the nineteenth century, contained not only contradictions but the seeds of its own destruction. Haunted by the account of Eve in Genesis, Walsh emphasized the relative weakness of female nature and its susceptibility to temptation. On the other hand, when these penchants were overcome, woman partook of the qualities of Mary and, although "inferior to man," became "near to angels." Then she possessed a kind of moral supremacy, for the sum of her virtue exceeded that of man. The pragmatic Walsh, realizing that society would be the loser if this feminine excellence was strictly confined, wrote, "Religion of the cloister may be admired, as it divorces the spirit from matter.... Still where there is the most usefulness, we must acknowledge the most dignity."[7] That notion was advanced even further at the end of the century, when many women and priests charged that as society at large was little more than an extended family, females had a mission to share their moral excellence with the world of families about them.

Catholic moralists continued to write along the lines of Walsh even after the Civil War, when many ministers had begun to endorse the feminist movement and an ever-increasing number of women were entering the work force. After stressing that woman's proper place was in the home, Father Jean Landriot in *The Valiant Woman* contended she would find happiness by serving her family and adoring her husband with "unvarying amiability." Like Walsh, Landriot emphasized her weakness, cautioning her against "effeminate idleness," "effeminate manner," and "effeminate beauty," characteristics that addressed themselves to the senses. Nevertheless, like other commentators, he claimed a moral superiority for women, for they could refine and polish men's character merely by allowing contact with their finer nature.[8]

In the very popular *The Mirror of True Womanhood; and True Men as We Need Them* (1881), Father Bernard O'Reilly bluntly declared, "The head of society is man; its restoration and salvation must be through a woman."[9] Nevertheless, no woman, animated by the spirit of baptism, would ever fancy any activity other than that of homemaker, her God-appointed duty. Though it would mean self-sacrifice, she was to make everyone in the home happy, but especially her man, whom she was to please, soothe, and captivate. Inspired by true love, she would think of a thousand new devices each day to brighten his leisure. The tavern and intoxication, O'Reilly warned, were the results of her failure to be loving and devoted.[10] *The Mission Book for the Married* even proclaimed that a wife should be fond of housework, for not only was it honorable, but it made her healthy and cheerful.[11]

It was further assumed that household tasks were the normal lot for every woman, including religious. When Father Edward Sorin, the founder of Notre Dame University, solicited nuns to come to Indiana to conduct a girls' academy, he took it for granted that they would "look after the laundry and infirmary" of the priests and students — even though the nuns might have to walk six miles.[12] His expectations that nuns would cook, sew, wash, mend, and nurse priests and students (that is, perform duties that fathers and sons expected from female family members) was typical of many male religious. Nuns frequently were assigned as domestics in seminaries, and Pope Pius IX suggested that Mercy Sisters could support themselves without a dowry by earning an income as laundresses.[13]

Women's submissiveness to men had become such a part of Catholic tradition that a respected marriage manual taught brides-to-be that from the very day of marriage their husband was to exercise command. Consequently the first week of the honeymoon was most important in establishing a proper relationship. There, even if his desires were against her wishes, his will was to be done without his having to resort to flattery and remonstrances to achieve concessions from her.[14]

One of the best summaries of Catholic perceptions of this nature is found in the writing of John Boyle O'Reilly (1844–90). An essayist, poet, editor, and reformer, O'Reilly was at one time hailed as the most distinguished Irishman in America. An outspoken advocate of improved working conditions and wages, of black rights, of Irish peasants — of justice for all the oppressed — he was, nevertheless, one of the strongest critics of women's rights. Feminism could not be reconciled with the proper image of women as elucidated in his vignette "A Lady."

A lady is simply the highest type of woman. She will be gentle and modest, mistress of temper and curiosity.... She will know and honor her own place in the social order, as the divinely appointed moulder, teacher, and refiner of men; and out of this beautiful and noble place she will not seek to move. To fit herself for her place, she will cultivate body and mind, the body in health and vigor that she may take her share of burdens and be cheerful under them, and that her work in the world shall be as fairly done as her hands can do it; and the mind in knowledge, accomplishment and taste, that she may be a delight and a help in her home.... A lady is always natural; and calm self-respect and respect for others are two of the unseen but real shields that protect ladies even in associations which must surely stain or injure natures of lower culture or less poise.... There is a lady hidden in every woman, as there is a gentleman in every man; and no matter how far the actual may be from the possible, one thing is certain, that a true lady or a true gentleman is always recognized and acknowledged by this secret nobility in the human heart.[15]

The subservient position of women also was a major part of authoritative church teaching. The *Catechism of the Council of Trent*, which governed Americans from its publication in 1829 to 1884, when the Baltimore Catechism appeared, the *Mission Book of 1853*, designed to preserve the fruits of a religious revival, and the 1883 *Mission Book for the Married* asserted that a wife, in all things not inconsistent with Christian piety, owed her husband, as the *Mission Book* described it, a "willing and obsequious obedience." Underscoring the sacredness of the family and the nature of woman's salvation through childbearing, these volumes stressed the sinfulness of limiting the number of children by preventing conception or "destroying the fruit of the womb." The *Mission Book* warned that God would inflict temporal as well as eternal punishment on those who engaged in the detestable practice of birth control. Unlike some earlier manuals, these admonished both sexes as well as physicians about this heinous crime and reminded all that it was a matter for confession.[16]

Virginity was extolled as one of female's "most precious treasures," and the Second Plenary Council of Baltimore declared it even more pleasing to God than the married state. So glorified was celibacy that an 1881 marriage manual incongruously devoted about one-third of its nearly three hundred pages to praising the single state as superior to married life.[17] Closely akin to virginity was the virtue of purity, which in 1893 Archbishop John Ireland (1838–1918) of St. Paul claimed was the source of woman's "power for good."[18] John Hughes (1797–1864), bishop of New York, even questioned the possibility of reforming a young woman if she "lost the glory of her womanhood."[19] Although it was asserted that females were naturally pious, young women were cautioned that virginity and purity were fragile and needed protection and that as Christian heroines they should fight to the death to preserve these virtues. Nuns, even more so than lay women, had to be on guard. Bishop Francis P. Kenrick (1796–1863) of Philadelphia pointed out that as "flowers that decorated the garden of the Church," they were special targets for the "wiles and assaults of Satan . . . the serpent [who] seduced Eve."[20] One of the threats to this treasure and a violation of the Sixth Commandment stemmed from womanly weakness, namely, a "passion for dress. . . . Many females adorned with gold and precious stones have lost their only true ornament, the gem of female virtue."[21]

This confusion of churchmen over the dual nature of women (children of both Eve and Mary) was further reflected in their views of that sex's enticing effect on innocent males. Although purer and nobler than men, the mere presence of women was a sexual temptation. The *Mission Book* flatly counseled young men "to avoid as much as possible the society of females." One guide offered the example of King Roger; for three years he never looked a woman in the face in order to avoid an occasion of sin. The Diocesan Synod of Philadelphia in 1842 even enacted special regulations for the confession of women and girls.[22]

The concept of the traditional woman's role was so powerful that even as females succeeded in endeavors outside the home, the assumptions of many Christian observers remained unshaken. When John England (1786–1842) sailed from Cork, Ireland, in 1820 to assume his position as bishop of Charleston, South Carolina, his young sister, Joanna (1800–1827), accompanied him. Until her untimely death from yellow fever seven years later, she assisted him in the work of the diocese, committing her small fortune to the development of the church and for all practical purposes editing the *Catholic Miscellany*, the first Catholic paper in the nation. Equally important, she was able to persuade England to be less abrasive in his writings. At the time of her death, the bishop described her as "a sensible companion, a great literary aid...she did more by the sacrifice of her money and of her comforts to establish the Diocese than was done by any other means I know."[23]

Yet despite her contributions, when England promulgated a constitution for the governance of churches in his diocese (Georgia and North and South Carolina), membership in vestries and in state and regional conventions was confined to men. Women and children were "incapable of being united in the association" and could not be "considered a member of the Roman Catholic Church."[24] His successor, Bishop Ignatius Reynolds (1798–1855), at least allowed women to participate in fund-raising activities, albeit with some reservations. "The ladies who preside over tables, and their assistants, should be of such an age and manners, as to combine with their amiableness a certain dignity, becoming the Christian lady engaged in a work of charity for which she overcomes the timidity of her sex."[25]

Precisely such a view of women helped make the church attractive to one of the century's leading converts and renowned intellectuals, Orestes Brownson. Although he was a friend of the feminist reformer Fanny Wright, he was unable to support women's rights even in his salad days.[26] In 1844 he completed his religious odyssey from radicalism to Catholicism, entered the church, and began *Brownson's Quarterly Review*. This journal, pressed into service on behalf of the church, was used to instruct the faithful, reconcile Catholicism with Americanism, and twit Protestantism.[27] Until Brownson's death in 1876, the *Review* was an outspoken champion of male superiority (woman "was made for him [man] and in herself is only an inchoate man"), except in the home, where woman reigned supreme. Repeatedly Brownson attacked supporters of women's rights, accusing them of trying to reverse the laws of nature through a "silly" effort. Furthermore, the whole woman suffrage campaign, he claimed, was merely "a free love movement" that contributed to the curse of the age — femininity." Reforms allowing brides to retain a portion of their property after marriage were anathema to him. Brownson asserted such laws would lead to a separation of interests and were not only incompatible with the true nature of marriage but "odious and immoral...[and] anti Christian." As one might expect, he denounced divorce and offered the Virgin, the exemplar of humility, piety, and sweetness, as the model for Catholic women.[28]

To preserve these ideals he championed the spread of Catholic education and advocated Protestant attendance at Catholic schools. Those institutions taught "maidenly modesty and reserve, and wives and mothers due submission to their husbands." They trained them "to be contented to be women, and not aspire to men, or to usurp the function of men and to bid them to stay at home and not be gadding abroad, running over the country and spouting nonsense, free love, infidelity and blasphemy at suffrage conventions."[29]

Catholic schools shared Brownson's objectives. One of their goals, unlike secular institutions, it was thought, was to promote the very values that some critics feared might be undermined by education — the true function of women.[30] Their first task was to strengthen the faith and its handmaids — Catholic housekeeping and social grace. The prospectus of St. Joseph's Academy, Emmitsburg, in 1832 proclaimed its intent "to cultivate the seeds of virtue which had been planted in their [student] breasts under the paternal roof, and to give them the genteel and easy deportment which is so essential in their intercourse with society." In 1849, two years after its establishment, the Academy of Mount St. Vincent, at the request of Bishop Hughes of New York, introduced into the curriculum "the science of housekeeping."[31]

The *Manual of 1840,* designed for girls educated at Ursuline convents, declared that religious instruction prevented vanity, levity, and undirected lives, all of which accompanied liberal education. Furthermore, a proper program of studies would offset the extravagance and passion for pleasure to which young girls are especially attracted and instead would cultivate humility and meekness.[32] In 1854 the superior of the School Sisters of Notre Dame predicted her community's educational mission in the United States would be a success because it would prepare young women to be mothers. As late as 1897 the *Mission Book for the Married* advised parents to provide for their daughter "an ordinary school education," seeing to it that she was taught cooking, washing, ironing, sewing, and baking.[33] These same skills were emphasized by the black Order of Oblate Sisters of Providence, whose task in 1839 was to train black girls of Baltimore to become either mothers or servants.[34] The aims of the Sacred Heart nuns to prepare pupils "as Christian homemakers, Catholic wives and mothers" remained unchanged for the better part of a century. In 1922 their plan of studies was still designed to fit "our children" for their destiny as "wives and mothers of families."[35] So successful were the schools in these endeavors that they attracted many Protestant parents who wanted their children prepared for "the cult of true womanhood." On the other hand, these institutions were criticized by social reformers for keeping students ignorant by maintaining "showy" requirements (needlework, music, drawing, foreign languages) rather than developing their mental prowess.[36]

In theory the Catholic perception of the feminine role inhibited the educational development of confident, independent, and curious women and also discouraged females from becoming wage earners. Repeated emphasis on a God-designed domesticity, which really was applicable only to the middle class, ignored working women as an abnormality.[37] When job opportunities mushroomed in the Civil War era, religious writers, for the first time, expressed interest in the plight of the working girl. However, they assumed she was single (a good Catholic woman would leave employment with marriage), and they seemed to be concerned only with the temptations that factory work presented to purity; din, danger, and dirt appeared irrelevant.[38]

Furthermore, the very concept of reticent and submissive Catholic "ladies" contributed to exploitation in the workplace. A commentator in the Catholic World in 1867 declared that abominable working conditions for women could lead to an appreciation of the divine institution of industry as a means of sanctification and the creation of a spirit of godliness. The popular guide for Catholic working girls, first published in 1868, advised them to accept gratefully the wages and conditions of employment as the will of God, who had given them the life of "continued labor... a very great favor of his love." The guide asserted that the lot of employers, with their pressing responsibilities, was harder than that of employees, whose major obligation was merely to please the Creator by working hard and complying with the scriptural injunction of loyalty and obedience to masters.[39] Not until the end of the century did moralists begin to advocate the amelioration of working conditions for women, and even then their justification was based on the contention that mothers-to-be needed protection.

In the first seventy-five years of the nineteenth-century, the most prominent Catholic spokesperson for justice for wage-earning women was not a theologian but a publisher and an economist. Mathew Carey, an Irish immigrant and one of the founders of the Female Improvement Society of Philadelphia, demanded higher pay, lesser hours, and improved conditions and even advocated making day-care centers available to women workers. In so doing, Carey had not abandoned adherence to the traditional feminine role, for he was convinced that employment fostered habits of order and regularity, promoted public and private usefulness, and led to early marriage. As a matter of fact, he was still bound by the ideal of ladylike behavior. On two occasions when he championed higher wages for women, "from motives of delicacy" he omitted the names of those females who had prepared a report on inadequate wages.[40]

However, Catholic women were less given to delicacy than Carey thought. Many, both religious and lay, like their colonial counterparts, either interpreted the concept of Catholic ladylikeness to serve their ends, ignored it, or challenged it directly. Even those who promulgated the doctrine usually defied its tenets in their own life.

The career and writings of Eleanor C. Donnelly (1836–1917) seem to personify the Catholic lady. Her father, a Philadelphia physician, died when she was quite young, leaving six children to be raised and, in Eleanor's and her sister's case, educated by his Irish wife. However, as their home was the gathering place for authors and prominent visitors, Donnelly was more fortunate than those whose schooling was traditional. A member of the church choir and of the Third Order of St. Francis, she so expounded Catholic values in her essays, short stories, and over fifty volumes of poetry that she has been described as an ultra Catholic by one scholar and by a contemporary as the Poet of Pure Soul. Piety, purity, and the liturgy were the marks of her poetry, one volume of which, dealing primarily with the Virgin, was published to raise money for the statue of Mary on the dome of the University of Notre Dame. Often Donnelly also turned her hand to children's tales because she was convinced "that a good story book is for them the next best thing to the Catechism."[41]

In her essays this Philadelphian repeatedly stressed that women, who were subordinate to men, were supreme in the home, the sphere of activity designed by God for them. Rare exceptions with extraordinary missions, such as Joan of Arc or Isabella of Spain, were "females of masculine minds, of almost masculine physiques." Proof that these were exceptions was found in the life of Mary, who instead of obtaining so-called rights for her sex, remained at home setting an example in humility, obedience, and chastity. Naturally Donnelly was opposed to the feminist movement, contemptuously dismissing it with the words, "Eve was content with one of Adam's ribs. Her daughter of to-day wants (what the Irishman called) 'his entire system.'"[42] As one might expect from a lady, she turned to a male for assistance in starting her career. She asked her brother, who was rapidly gaining fame in Minnesota, to get her poetry published and promised not to disgrace him.[43]

Nevertheless, Donnelly was not a shy, clinging, frail domestic. Not only was she self-supporting, but even in a priestly dominated church she assumed a vigorous role — praising its glories, celebrating its feasts, and hobnobbing with one of its bishops, Eugene O'Connell (1815–91), of Grass Valley, California, an old friend who spent a month with her in Philadelphia.[44] Even more revealing, she interpreted the moral goodness of woman as a type of female superiority that could elevate men and mold and form public opinion. She was even willing to allow queenly women to step from their "royal dais" and engage in social reform as long as they were careful not to soil their white sandals or bedraggle the splendor of their robes. It was precisely these qualities that made woman suffrage, at best, irrelevant. Women, according to Donnelly, could use their wisdom and piety to train future voters and to influence society by example. There was no reason children of Mary should not learn statutes or statistics, but there was every reason they should not vote.[45]

The most significant insight into Donnelly's closet feminism is found in her will, in which she left no money to male relatives.

> Knowing from long observation and experience how much more difficult it is for a woman than for a man to earn a proper and profitable livelihood, and being convinced that my nephews are good, industrious men and can always maintain themselves unaided by me, my sympathies are naturally enlisted in behalf of those females who are nearest kin or who are endeared to me by special services to my family.[46]

When a woman as conservative and as dedicated to traditional concepts as Donnelly was unable to adhere completely to the precepts expected of Catholic ladies, it is obvious that beneath the charade of ideal Catholic woman there were restless females who had more in common with women of the 1970s than with churchmen of the 1870s.

Chapter 3

"LADY" NOVELISTS: UNWITTING INNOVATORS OF THE NINETEENTH CENTURY

Despite the restraints imposed on women by the idea of being a "lady," it was still possible for a bright ambitious female, without abandoning domesticity, to find an outlet for her intelligence and, if necessary, to earn money. She could write. And many nineteenth-century women did just that. Although their names are hardly house-hold words today, authors such as Catherine Sedgwick, Fanny Fern, Maria Cummins, Emma D. Southworth and Augusta Evans Wilson so dominated the literary field that an embittered Nathaniel Hawthorne in 1855 complained to his publisher that "America is now wholly given over to a d—— mob of scribbling women...the public taste is occupied with trash." More pungent were the observations of an English visitor to a Catholic critic, "In America people do two things: the men expectorate and women write novels."[1]

Catholic women were no different. From 1835, when the first novel by a Catholic woman appeared (Mrs. Mary Hughs, *The Two Schools: A Moral Tale*), until well into the twentieth century, a whole spate of novels dealing with religious themes were produced by Catholic females from a wide variety of backgrounds. The works, which often appeared first as serials, and their authors can be divided into four categories: (1) those by middle-class Anglo-Catholic descendants of early settlers, who wrote chiefly for sympathetic Protestants and Catholics of their own class; (2) converts who directed their efforts at Protestants in an effort to counter nativism and win additional converts or who aimed their novels at fellow Catholics to engender

23

greater tolerance for Protestants; (3) newer arrivals, who tended to be quite critical of Protestantism and whose readers consisted primarily of immigrant or first-generation women (by midcentury about 75 percent of all Irish immigrants were literate and were described as having a love of reading and the habit of buying books); and (4) authors at the end of the century who, no longer concerned that a struggling Catholicism would be swamped by an aggressive Protestantism but fearful that their faith would be diluted by a creeping secularism, addressed a middle-class constituency with tales permeated with Catholic principles rather than expositions on Catholic dogma.[2]

Although directed to different audiences and written by women of varied backgrounds, all of these stories had certain common features. The tales were amazingly complex, the plots were contrived with an overriding reliance on coincidence, and for the most part, they were poorly written. On occasion these works were even criticized by contemporaries for these characteristics.[3] Although lacking aesthetic merit, the novels certainly were not without value. All of them were didactic, designed to strengthen the Catholic faith, preserve immigrant traditions, disarm Protestant critics, and illustrate the dangers of dissolute living and the rewards of adhering to moral values. On the surface they upheld the traditional view of woman: her homelike nature, religious temperament, and purity of soul and body. If females yielded to passions, they were punished, but more likely these women characters had no sexual desires and were able to repress their emotions in the name of a purer and nobler love. Katherine Conway (1853–1927) — novelist, essayist, arbiter of manners, and editor of the *Boston Pilot* — even wrote of one of her heroines, "Not for the world would she have been so wanting in matronly dignity as to kiss him [her husband] before the children."[4] To Conway one of the functions of literature was to uphold marriage and lawful love. Only works that promoted moral and spiritual values were worthy of immortality.[5]

Catholic authors sought this type of immortality, often announcing that intention in their introduction. Anna H. Dorsey (1815–90), who has been described as a pioneer of Catholic literature in the United States and whose works were praised by Cardinal James Gibbons (1834–1921) of Baltimore, wrote that the object of her novel *The Oriental Pearl; or, The Catholic Emigrants* (1843) was "to eulogize and assist in sustaining the great Catholic truth, that confidence in the wisdom and mercy of God is the best preservation from temptation and despair." Placing her book "under the patronage of the Blessed Virgin Mary, the authoress dedicates it to the Society of the Archconfraternity of the Immaculate Heart of Mary; praying, that at least some soul fainting beneath its cross may find an incentive to encouragement and new hope in its simple pages."[6] *The Sister of Charity* (1848), also written under the patronage of Mary, was designed by Dorsey to provide the Catholic community with a type of mental recreation that would lead the reader to the conclusion that true and lasting happiness could be found only in religion and morality.

Others had similar goals. To instruct the young to appreciate the contemplation of beauty, the holiness of religion, and the faith and fortitude the church expected during trials and difficulties was the stated purpose of Mary L. Meaney in *Grace Morton; or, The Inheritance* (1864).[7] Even one of the most nontraditional of these women, Mary C. Smith (1849–1918, pseudonym Christian Faber), wrote *Ambition's Contest; or, Faith and Intellect* (1896) under the auspices of Mary to aid in the training of Catholic youth. Both Madeline V. Dahlgren (1825–98), a Washington socialite, and Lelia H. Bugg (d. 193?), who was educated by Ursulines and raised under the care of Dubuque's future bishop, the Reverend John Hennessy (1875–1960), asserted that the purpose of their works was to show the force of a moral life.[8] The most prolific and the most popular of these novelists, Mary A. Sadlier (Mrs. James A., 1820–1903), penned *Aunt Honor's Keepsakes: A Chapter from Life* (1866) "to please the Divine Master" by alerting readers to the proselytizing of Catholic orphans and to convince her public of the need for organizations such as the Society for the Protection of Destitute Catholic Children, her favorite charity. In a lengthy introduction to her widely read *The Blakes and the Flanagans: A Tale Illustrative of Irish Life in the United States* (1873), she declared:

> The world is... divided into two great classes, believers and nonbelievers; the children of the one true Church, and the children of the world. It is needless to say that all of my writings are dedicated to the one grand object; the illustration of our holy faith, by means of tales or stories.... I do not profess to write novels — I cannot afford to waste time pandering merely to the imagination, or fostering that maudlin sentimentality, which is the ruin of youth both male and female. No conscientious Catholic can write a story wherein the interest depends on the workings of passion. One who has Eternity ever in view, cannot write mere love-tales; but simple practical stories embodying grave truths, will be read by man, who would not read pious books. Such then is the Blakes and the Flanagans.

It was for this very reason, "to root" her son more effectively in his religion, that the mother of Maurice Egan, one of Catholicism's leading intellectuals at the end of the century, presented her young son with a copy of this book.[9]

These novels often taught dogma by means of lengthy disputations between a Catholic and a Protestant. Usually the Catholic was young, sometimes a religious, and always well versed in Scripture and apologetics. Through wit and wisdom the Catholic would triumph over Protestant objections to the real presence, confession, fasting, or the role of Mary and in the process would win the opponent to the faith. This was a favorite device of Dorsey, who included quotations, references, and footnotes to actual studies on the church. In her *Student of Blenheim Forest* (1867), a young man becomes a Catholic despite the offer of land and slaves if he remains loyal to Protestantism. Moreover, lengthy liturgical discussions result in six conversions, including that of the hero's father. By means of prayer, example, and footnoted disputations in *Sister of Charity*, a shipwrecked nun and a visiting priest at a southern mansion convert everyone, including the local ministers and plantation slaves. (Twenty-one pages on Catholic doctrine were used in justifying the conversion of one character.) The only nonconvert was a pleasant Baptist housekeeper who was forever blessing the Sister of Charity. Dorsey, who tended to view Protestants not as heretics but as separated brethren, mentioned her own conversion in The *Flemmings: A True Story* (1864). She asserted that most Protestants were attracted to the church but were prevented from entering it by circumstances of birth, education, and prejudice. Catholics then, because they possess the faith, should be charitable toward their persecutors, products of coarse and ignorant minds. In that novel Wolfert Flemming, an itinerant peddler of Irish origin, inspired nine non-Catholics "to seek the truth where alone it can be found" and thereby enter the church. One almost gets the impression from Dorsey that the more conversions, the better the novel.

As a means of instruction, conversion was also used by Mary I. Hoffman in *Agnes Hilton; or, Practical Views of Catholicity: A Tale of Trials and Triumphs* (1868) and in Sadlier's *Aunt Honor's Keepsake*. In Agnes Hilton, Becky Sharp discusses the sacramental system and marks of the church with her grandfather, causing him to embrace the faith. There are many didactic conversations in *Keepsake*, wherein well-educated Catholics answer questions explaining practices such as confession and veneration of the cross to sympathetic Protestants who in time change their creed.

The convert theme was used not only to teach the faith but to illustrate the exemplary effects of a good Catholic life. The major character in the first female Catholic novel, *Two Schools*, was so filled with goodness and sweetness because of the influence of nuns that she became a beacon leading others into the fold. Frances Tiernan (1846-1920, pseudonym Christian Reid), like many characters in her novels, was a convert, attracted by the beauty, majesty, and tradition of the church. Described by her biographer as one who "never wrote a line that could soil a Christian soul," Tiernan, in *A Woman of Fortune* (1896), depicted a female with manly attributes who was not humble enough to accept a woman's lot. With marriage and conversion to the church, however, she became more feminine and found true happiness. Tiernan's *Light of the Vision* (1911) was a little more typical of the convert novel. There a divorcée, after turning to Catholicism, realized her first marriage was forever and thus refused to marry her beloved. Instead she prayed for and nursed her former husband, who recovered from a near-fatal accident, became a Catholic, and remarried her in the church. In *Katherine* (serialized in the *Catholic World*, 1884–85, and published by Henry Holt in 1886 under the title *Whom God Hath Joined*), a novel by Elizabeth G. Martin (1837–1911), who was trained in a convent and was a normal-school graduate, lengthy religious conversations win adherents to the faith by demonstrating that the Catholic church is true because of its authority, order, beauty, and goodness. However, as Martin warned in *John Van Alstyne's Factory* (1887), the motive for conversion had to be spiritual; love for another was inadequate, but of course love of God was fitting and proper.

In addition to educating and inspiring audiences by means of conversion tales, these novels emphasized the threats pluralistic society posed for the faithful. Especially singled out were dangers from mixed marriage, public schools, worldly ambition, and longing for human respect. To some, Protestantism itself was the danger, the most odious feature of which was blandishments by those attempting to wean Catholic young from their faith. The first step in this nefarious scheme often was an effort to get the victim to break the law of abstinence by eating meat on Friday.[10] More critical of Protestants than her contemporaries was Sadlier, who used this device in *The Blakes and the Flanagans, Aunt Honor's Keepsake*, and *Confessions of an Apostate* (1868). So condemnatory was she that in *Con O'Regan; or, Emigrant Life in the New World* (1864), she described Protestantism as "a mere chaos... dark and void, and shapeless like the original nothing from which the world was founded." In that book, as in most of hers, churchgoing non-Catholics are cold, austere, and often given to bigotry. Moreover, in *The Blakes and the Flanagans* Sadlier maintained that strong-minded Catholic women who chose the high calling of a religious life of virtue and modesty, if raised as Protestants, would be merely strong-minded women wasting their time at public meetings, a far inferior life. Novel after novel reenforced the view that such displays were unnatural: the way to happiness for women not honored by a vocation was marriage. Dorsey's *Nora Brady's Vow* (1869) asserted that blissfulness could still be achieved in wedlock, despite poverty and travail. However, Meaney's *Grace Morton* warned that for true happiness the husband too must adhere to religious principles.

In two of her novels Tiernan emphasized that traditional femininity was essential to marital happiness. *The Man of the Family: A Novel* (1897) is the story of a young woman who runs a plantation and goes to Haiti, disguised as a boy, to retrieve her grandfather's fortune. Never worrying about her proper sphere, she "simply accepted tasks laid before her as countless women have done through the ages, before the clamor arose for woman's rights." In so doing, she demonstrated that bravery in a woman could be admirable, for it was not necessary to lose "the heart of a female" to exercise it. Because she was able to retain her femininity, she was able then to assign "her position as the man of the family" to her fiancé. In Tiernan's *Daughter of a Star* (1913), the reader encounters one of the nastiest females in this genre. An actress who compares herself with Nora in *Doll's House* clashes with her "old-fashioned husband" and daughter as she refuses to give up her career for motherhood. In time she lost her starring role, alienated the two men who loved her, and during an attempt to avenge herself on her innocent daughter, suffered heart failure as, "in a last effort to assert her impervious will, Violet Lestrange had met a Force stronger than herself, and the curtain had fallen forever in the play of life."

Tiernan also extolled the sanctity of marriage. The heroine in her *Far Away Princess* (1914) rejected advice from her friends and relatives and refused to divorce her amnesia-stricken, non-Catholic husband. After an accident his memory returned as he sorrowed for his flirtations and recited the act of contrition as he died in her arms. Other women writing for middle-class audiences at the turn of the century, when there was less need for Catholic apologetics, also assailed the evils of divorce. Madeline Dahlgren made it the center of two of her novels. That retribution must follow the violation of divine law was the theme of *Divorced: A Novel* (1887); in *A Washington Winter* (1884), an attack on the mores of the nouveau riche, she denounced divorce as the first step toward free love. Martin's *Katherine* is a convoluted narrative of marriage to a divorced man, wherein the newlyweds become Catholic and agree they must give each other up, since the husband's first wife is still alive. However, fate intervened as the first wife kills herself because of her earlier marriage irregularities.

The number of evils exposed in these novels was legion. Dorsey's *Warp and Woof* (1887) warned of the dangerous ideas of Kant and Spinoza; Dahlgren's *The Secret Directory: A Romance of Hidden History* (1896) attacked liberalism, public schools, coeducation, and Marxism and accused Masons of poisoning the minds of the young "to enlist women in this nefarious crusade against all that is holy in her sacred right as wife and mother, by sensuous and captivating appeals to the larger license of so-called freedom." Sadlier's "Iban Dempsey's Story" (1896) pointed out the foolishness of indulgent parents, while her *Blakes and the Flanagans* hammered public schools, where "un-Catholic training" results in a Catholicism "no more the faith of their fathers or mothers, than the vile brass ware displayed on street stalls is the pure gold of the jeweler."[11] Pride was the bête noire in Hoffman's *Agnes Hilton* and Donnelly's "A Lost Prima Donna" (1896).[12] In the latter a vocalist catches cold because of her low-cut dress, sings poorly, and collapses on stage in the realization that "my pride is justly punished." In *Hilton* saintly women impart the lesson that humility is the secret of happiness. However, the moral is repeated so frequently that even a sympathetic Brownson found the novel wearying.

Temptations to the faith of Catholic immigrants in the city were so powerful that two of the authors supported the ideals of the Catholic Colonization Society by urging immigrants to move to the West. In *Oriental Pearl* Dorsey contended that Catholicism flourished on the frontier, where people were hardy and simple and where each generation improved morally and physically. The entire novel *Con O'Regan* was given over to the same theme. Catholics should go west, according to Sadlier, to avoid bad company, overcrowding, poverty, drink, public schools, and the corrupting forces that threatened to make them Yankees.

For those who could not make the trek, however, novelists often promised happiness on this earth, as well as hereafter, if Catholic teachings and Old World traditions were followed. Dorsey's *Oriental Pearl* described how a German immigrant family, despite all of its troubles, avoided despair and found peace by complying with the Beatitudes and relying on God's mercy. Material success is achieved in *Nora Brady's Vow* through thrift, industry, honesty, and an upright life. Traditional values and customs (including the Irish wake) made the home a place of delight in Sadlier's *The Blakes and the*

Flanagans, a thinly disguised appeal to the immigrant community to resist the regimentation of Americanization. The purpose of Dorsey's *Nora Brady's Vow* was to show the generosity and devotion of Irish-American women, while her *Mona the Vestal* (1869), a narrative of Ireland in the age of St. Patrick, was intended to create popular interest in the history of that country before its subjugation by the English. Faber's *Carroll O'Donoghue: A Tale of the Irish Struggle of 1816 and of Recent Times* (1881) depicted the Irish virtues that were usually ignored by Americans: self-sacrifice, affability, and heroic and cheerful endurance of an unrectifiable wrong.

Although many of the novelists challenged American xenophobic attitudes toward immigrants and especially the Irish, they shared the nation's derogatory perception of blacks. Slavery in Hugh's *Two Schools* was alleged to have benefited blacks, while in Dahlgren's *Lights and Shadows of Life: A Novel* (1887), slaveowners are sympathetic gentlemen, deprived of the opportunity to learn humility and Christian forbearance because of that institution. In *Blenheim Forest* Dorsey described slavery as a "hereditary and necessary evil" and pointed out in *Sister of Charity* that the process of conversion would teach the slaves acceptance, discourage rebellion and indolence, and increase production. Her prejudiced attitude was revealed further in *Nora Brady's Vow,* where a black cook is described as course, ignorant, and wasteful, with "too good an opinion of herself" because of her rescue by the "Equal Rights and Southern Transportation." Tiernan in *Man of the Family* not only shows no sympathy whatsoever to a slave uprising, but her "good slave" dies while defending his white master. (Such incidents could reflect her conservatism as much as racial bias, for two of her volumes were criticisms of the French Revolution. Furthermore, her writings showed no sympathy for Irish rebels; in *Woman of Fortune* the Irish landlord is even depicted sympathetically.)

To Dorsey and Dahlgren the greatest social danger from the presence of blacks in the United States was miscegenation. The most depraved character in *Warp and Woof* was a quadroon who, suffering from the "stain of birth," planned to avenge the wrongs against his mother by revolting against nature and marrying a white. In those of "mixed race," according to Dorsey, "blood poison and other ills combine with time to bring on premature age and decay and extinguish the generation." Dahlgren apparently was afraid the generation of mulattoes would not be extinguished. According to her, the real motif of *Lights and Shadows* "is the distinctly American one of exhibiting, as it actually exists among us, that strong prejudice against

race intermixture which is essentially and peculiarly a national trait."
She wished "to present the question as it actually is." Dahlgren went
on to state her own view: "Is it not providential that this invincible
antagonism to social and race intermixture should stand as a mighty
barrier to preserve intact the purity and autonomy of that superior
race which has the directing influence in moulding the destiny of
our wonderful Republic?" In that novel a young woman, realizing
that "one drop of African blood is a misfortune," breaks her engagement when she discovers that her fiancé is part black. "When death
has washed out the stain, ask for me in eternity, and then I shall be
yours...until then, farewell."

Dahlgren's antipathy, like Tiernan's, was probably as much a reflection of class bias as negrophobia, for *Secret Diary* was replete with
anti-Semitism. There, insidious Jews were alleged to hold high office
in the despised and anti-Christian Masons, and an old, repugnant
Jew, the head of the "Universal Israelists Alliance," participates in a
mock marriage ceremony extolling divorce and suicide. Even Irishmen were not safe from her. *Washington Winter* contained a rather
ludicrous doorman, an "untrained son of Erin...the bog trotter."

In addition to trying to educate a mass audience through novels, some women writers used nonfiction to promulgate their ideas —
especially as to the proper function and role of Catholic ladies. In
Dahlgren's *Etiquette of Social Life in Washington* (5th ed., 1881) courtesy, good breeding, and the Golden Rule were depicted as essential
to a Christian life. The leveling tendency of American democracy was
sharply criticized, however, its genesis being attributed to President
Andrew Jackson who received all comers without any special rules.
Dahlgren expressed traditional views on marriage, urging a wife to
adopt the title of her husband and to be addressed as Mrs. Senator or
whatever the appropriate designation, for "when a woman captures a
President or other dignitary, she has won the right to claim the title
too." Dahlgren further asserted that it was pleasing to be the wife of a
powerful figure, to share authority without responsibility. Even more
traditional behavior was expounded on in "Liberties of Our Daughters," in the *Ladies Home Journal* (1890).[13] There Dahlgren asserted
that a mother's "first duty is to form our daughters in the true mold
that makes wise mothers," for "God given and sacred motherhood
was woman's great destiny, her highest vocation." To help achieve
this end a daughter's freedom must not be confused with license.
Mothers had the obligation to examine the letters of schoolgirls and
ensure that education would "exercise a proper influence on their
sphere of action."

Bugg's *Correct Thing for Catholics* (12th ed., 1891), dedicated to St. Joseph, and *A Lady: Manners and Social Usage* (1893) were as class conscious as Dahlgren's pieces. Her intent was to help produce "that noblest product of our civilization — an American gentlewoman." Consequently she railed against the "caste-levelling street car," where one cannot always avoid rough, dirty, tobacco-smelling men, and castigated women (not ladies) for attending public picnics or promiscuous assemblies. Furthermore, she warned against the evils of rouge, blondine, and immodest dress while describing the joys of a dutiful wife aiding and pleasing her husband. Unlike Dahlgren, Bugg was committed to social justice. In *The Correct Thing* she reminded Catholics they had an obligation to make their wedding an occasion to benefit the poor. It was immoral, she maintained, to have a trousseau sewn where it was the cheapest, with no thought of the suffering of underpaid seamstresses. One had an obligation to pay a dressmaker a fair wage.

Catholic men had no qualms about penning novels to inspire ladies to nobler lives or to reenforce the church's precepts on feminine behavior. *The Cross and the Shamrock; or, How to Defend the Faith: An Irish-Catholic Tale of Real Life* (1853), by "a missionary priest" (Hugh Quigley), was specifically designed to help male and female servants fight temptation and safeguard their religion. Apparently one of the dangers to faith was feminism, for Quigley censured bloomer women "and others of a diseased public mind," while blaming Protestantism for the woman's rights movement. The book, which also assailed Know-Nothings and the British, had lots of converts, lots of prayers, and lots of discussion on religion wherein the Catholic outsmarted the minister. In denouncing the proselytization of Catholic children, Quigley created one of the worst characters in this type of literature and must have fostered considerable loathing for Protestants among his readers. In order to get a young Catholic orphan to abandon his faith, a wily guardian, after starving, beating, and robbing the lad of his rosary, tied him up and left him exposed to the elements to die.

Directed more specifically at women were Con O'Leary's *Lost Rosary; or, Our Irish Girls: Their Trials, Temptations, and Triumphs* (1870) and John McElgun's *Annie Reilly; or, The Fortune of an Irish Girl in New York: A Tale Founded on Fact* (1877). Written at the request of the publisher Patrick Donahoe, *Lost Rosary* was to "profit" Irish girls and serve as an "antidote to the filthy and deadly poison that issues in streams from the immoral and indigenous press." It was the story of two virtuous and modest colleens. Faithful to their church and parents, the young women overcame adverse circumstances in New York City, preserved their chastity, and thereby grew in desirability. The book warned that poverty was better than the "unmixed evil" of mixed marriage, castigated woman suffrage, and contrasted its typical advocate, who was man hating, disappointed in love, a "loud mouthed...haughty...scandal monger," with sensitive, caring Irish lassies. *Annie Reilly* also exalted Irish girls, claiming that they outshone all other immigrants because of their religious training. This education is put to good use when Reilly, even though a humble servant, is able to resist the efforts of her Protestant employer to convert her, giving brilliant replies to his prejudiced inquiries.

The Watson Girls: A Washington Story (3d ed., 1900) was written at the request of a Sister of Charity by Maurice Francis Egan, a graduate of La Salle College. A professor at Notre Dame and Catholic universities and minister to Denmark (1907–18), Egan wrote five other books in the series, known as The Belinda Girls. One frequently encounters confession, prayer, and friendly priests in his pages, but Egan's chief characters are well-to-do girls whose major temptations are thoughtlessness and bad manners. These problems and the concern over Belinda's tendency to be a tomboy make clear that the purpose of the book is to encourage the development of Catholic young ladies. Egan's old fashioned chauvinism was revealed when he wrote, " 'Manly' meant 'womanly' in this case," after describing how Amelia, despite great provocation, refused to run away and instead cried. Like many female Catholic novelists, Egan's perception of blacks was distorted. The most sympathetic one in his pages was an old nanny who did not like Washington, D.C., because it was full of "educated niggers" who tried to be like white folks. Such ambition, according to her, was permitted for Methodists and Baptists, but not for good Catholics.

In novels by males, female characters were weak, those to whom things happened, creatures of circumstance. The most self-confident of any of these figures was the heroine in McElgun's *Annie Reilly*, who emigrated to the United States. Unlike most of her actual counterparts, however, relatives awaited her at the docks. Movers and shakers were men. However, in the writings of Catholic women, including those most supportive of the "cult of true womanhood," females were the stronger characters, frequently shaping their own destiny and in a way superior to base men whom they enabled and redeemed.

Bugg, who in fiction and prose repeatedly glorified gentility and propriety, offered alternatives to domesticity in *The Correct Thing* and in *The People of Our Parish: Being the Chronicle and Comment of Katherine Fitzgerald, Pew Holder in the Church of St. Paul the Apostle* (1901). Not only did she make it apparent that wage earning was acceptable for females, but she advocated equal pay with men. Her leading character in *Orchids: A Novel* (1894) was an independent and aggressive young woman. After discovering that much of her inherited wealth was due to fraudulent stock options, she made restitution, entered religious life, and journeyed to Colorado to work with Indians. Women are clearly superior to men in her "Prodigal's Daughter" (1898) and *People of Our Parish*.[14] One female's advice enables a male to acquire a fortune; other women keep the faith alive and lead their mates to salvation. Bugg even questioned the divine origin of male supremacy, since men were so inferior to women in meeting religious obligations.

Similar contradictions are found between Dahlgren's conservative ideology and her novel *Washington Winter*. Although she was the first major female opponent of woman suffrage, Dahlgren set her novel in the nation's capital and based it in part on her own experiences attempting to get a widow's pension for her husband's Civil War service. Many of her characters, drawn from real life, were friends of hers, such as President James Garfield and Orestes Brownson. In the novel, women exhibit considerable influence over men. Dinner parties succeed only when both sexes attend and engage in stimulating conversation. Yet Dahlgren makes it clear that the approved role for woman is that of homemaker.

Redemption was a favorite device of Dorsey. In "The Mad Penitent of Today" a wife's prayer, penance (including the wearing a hair shirt), and deathbed petition resulted in a change of heart by her dissolute husband and his eventual entrance into the Franciscans.[15] In *Blenheim Forest* Dorsey glorified women's love as "a spirit of endurance and devotion next akin to that eternal inspiration which exalts man to the angelic state." This same theme was used by Tiernan, who in *The Light of Vision* had a woman responsible for the salvation of two men through "the ideal of womanhood, which, after faith is the most elevating influence a man can possess."

Molly Elliot Seawell (1860–1916), although one of the most conservative of the Catholic writers, nevertheless employed the redemption motif also. Scion of an old Virginia family, grandniece of President John Tyler, and a Catholic since age eighteen, Seawell wrote to support her mother and sister after her father's death. However, for years she was so fearful of seeing her name in print that she used five different pseudonyms. In time she publicly attacked woman suffrage and submitted a statement to a congressional committee in opposition to it. She identified enfranchisement with divorce and asserted it would deny married women support from their husbands and endanger their property privileges. Additionally she charged that suffrage was part of a leveling movement that threatened the republic by watering down the quality of the electorate, already dangerously debased by the extension of the ballot to former slaves only a few generations removed from cannibalism. Suffragists, according to her, possessed socialistic and communistic tendencies and were antagonistic toward men. Furthermore, Seawell professed that feminine nature lacked the faculty for creative and abstract thinking and that woman's only inventive role was as homemaker.[16]

Her fiction reflected these views by contending that neither suffrage nor original thinking were necessary for women. Most of Seawell's novels were imbued with Catholic principles, wherein a young boy is elevated and purified because of his idealization of a girl.[17] One of her few historical novels dealing with American themes, *Despotism in Democracy: A Study in Washington Society and Politics* (1903), had an unusual setting for an author with her philosophy. Yet it reflected her ideology accurately in its assertion that a good wife was the best fortune a man could have. Its strongest figures were women who, with their "power to charm, to sustain, to lead forward," maneuvered and inspired "superior" men. Little wonder Seawell believed the vote was unnecessary for females.

Strong women, of course, could also be responsible for the downfall of men. In Sadlier's *Confessions of an Apostate* a young Irish immigrant leaves the church for a woman (appropriately named Eve), and years later when he sees his non-Catholic son participating in Know-Nothing riots contritely murmurs, "In and through her had I sinned, and in and through her was judgement to be inflicted on my guilty head." A warning to all Catholics was Eve's dying plea for forgiveness and admission to her husband that she had sinned in leading him "to sell your God for a wife." In contrast, Sadlier's *Bessy Conway; or, The Irish Girl in America* (1863) demonstrated that working girls can win respect and gain self-confidence by adhering to Catholic principles. Two of the most sympathetic male characters in her *Con O'Regan* recognized the "unlimited power of women," and Sadlier mentioned Cleopatra, Helen of Troy, and, surprisingly for a Catholic novelist, Elizabeth I as examples of such leadership.[18]

These strong female characters were but pale imitations of their creators, whose interests transcended the domesticity emphasized by their church. Anna Hanson, a convert in 1840 with her marriage to Lorenzo Dorsey, was the mother of five children and yet found time to publish nearly forty novels, receiving the University of Notre Dame's Laetare Medal for distinguished contributions to literature. Writing from her Washington home, she demonstrated a fervent patriotism both in *The Oriental Pearl* and especially in her literary support for the Civil War, which included a paean on the Sanitary Commission.[19]

The mother of six children, Sadlier produced nearly sixty volumes. As a result she was one of the most widely read Catholic authors and the mainstay of the publishing firm of D. and J. Sadlier, managed by her husband. She even had the audacity to edit the work of her chauvinistic friend Orestes Brownson, whom she persuaded to contribute to her husband's *Tablet* after the collapse of *Brownson's Review*. Her achievements were such that not only did she too win the Laetare Medal, but she was praised by the two major feminist papers of the day, the *Revolution* and the *Woman's Journal*.[20]

The most bizarre contrast between life and ideology was that of Dahlgren. After the death of her mother, for nearly twenty-five years she served her father, a Washington congressman, as companion and hostess. Completely at ease in the swirl of national politics, she was the friend of statesmen and literati, holding receptions at her home for diplomats, clergymen, and scholars. Although she vigorously campaigned against the extension of the ballot as inappropriate for ladies. she was not so reticent that she refrained from suggesting a cabinet appointment to her friend President James A. Garfield.[21]

Like Dahlgren, Frances Fisher (Christian Reid) turned to writing as a means of support as she was forced to be self-sufficient following the death of her father at the battle of Manassas. A North Carolinian convert and also a recipient of the Laetare Medal, she traveled throughout Europe and, after her marriage to James M. Tiernan, lived in Mexico for ten years. Widowed in 1898, Tiernan again turned to writing to support herself, producing over forty volumes before her death in 1920.

The novelist whose life and writing exhibited the most tension between the real and ideal of Catholic ladyhood was Mary E. Smith (1849–1918), who wrote under the name Christine Faber. A onetime schoolteacher, author of twelve novels and editor of *Redpath's Magazine*, she was also a close friend of the radical priest Edward McGlynn, whose advocacy of the single tax led to his excommunication. (McGlynn was guardian of his dead sister's children, whom Smith helped raise.) She was the advocate of another radical, the reform candidate for mayor of New York, Henry George, for whom she campaigned in 1886.[22]

Nevertheless, in the preface to *Ambition's Contest* Smith denounced those who would reject heavenly authority by encouraging women to ignore their first duties and move from their designated sphere. Although she depicted her female characters as physically weak and tender, they proved to be strong willed and, as in many other novels, played redemptive roles. In *Ambition's Contest* prayers and the exemplary life of a young woman whose "purity of thought which of itself must have rendered her womanhood beautiful" led her brother back to the church and the priesthood. Also touching on the theme of redemption was *The Guardian's Mystery; or, Rejected for Conscience's Sake* (1887). Smith's heroine, a graduate of Manhattanville, who fell in love with a non-Catholic, turned to the Virgin Mary and prayer to strengthen herself against the temptations of a mixed marriage. In time her boyfriend became a convert, and although he found her intransigence unfeminine and discovered that even in marriage she refused to acknowledge "his right to command her," they achieved happiness.

Smith's *Original Girl* (1901) was even more feminist. With the exception of Father Hammond, who was created as a means of defending McGlynn's ideas, all of the men as in *Ambition's Contest* are weak and often described by her as effeminate. In the novel Smith protested the subordination of women and their relegation to household tasks. Instead she portrayed them as instrumental in political reform and advocated the ballot be extended to them. " 'If only we had woman's suffrage,' sighed Miss Fairfax; 'just to think, those illiterate Italians, and semi-savage negroes that Herrick has employed purposely, can vote, and you and I, and a couple of hundred other intelligent women, are debarred just because we are women.' " Her point was made in an even more striking fashion when an antifeminist chairman of the schoolboard, although owing his office to his wife's skill, complained, "D—— the women; they're always trying to do what the creator never made 'em for — dictate to the man." When this arrogant character was forced to write his own speeches, rather than rely on his spouse, he became the laughingstock of the town.

Only one other author hinted at issues of social justice. Elizabeth Martin in *John Van Alstyne's Factory* claimed there was no social regeneration without religion and used Christianity to defend socialism. Furthermore, she advocated specific reforms such as profit sharing for employees.

Domesticity was also challenged when several authors upheld the right of women to work, even if not necessary, and suggested that employment was an honorable alternative to marriage. Bugg denied that wage earning degraded women and pointed out that work was never disdained by the Virgin Mary. Furthermore, she asserted, any type of employment was a thousand times better than an unhappy marriage. Guidelines for businesswomen were even developed by Bugg, who reminded those that worked for "pin money" of their obligation not to undercut the female wage structure by accepting less than a regular salary. Despite these strictures, she also reminded employees of their feminine obligation as children of Mary: they were to accept laborious duties "with a patient serenity which in time moves the hardest hearted employer to increase her salary, or give her a promotion." Ladylike decorum was the way to promotion and marriage.[23]

Also denying that marriage was the only goal for women were Dahlgren and Dorsey. The later, who suggested religious life as an alternative, had Eva in *The Flemmings* reject a proposal, saying, "It does not seem to me that marrying should be the sole end and aim of a woman's life." Dahlgren, probably reflecting the necessity of supporting herself, asserted that it was perfectly acceptable for women to be breadwinners. In "Liberties of Our Daughters" she reminded mothers not to teach their daughters to depend on marriage, even though bearing children was their destiny, for they may then make an "indiscreet alliance."

Martin's novels also reflected the competing forces that pulled at these women. A mother in *Katherine* taught her daughter to be passive, as St. Paul had advocated in his Epistles to the Corinthians. However, the girl followed her father's advice, became a tomboy, questioned everything, and converted to Catholicism in the process. Although Katherine was concerned about signing her own name for the last time before completely losing her identity, "as a woman must when she gives herself to a husband," she remained happy in marriage. Martin's heroine Zip in *John Van Alstyne's Factory* was similar to Katherine. As a result of her father's admonition to do something worthwhile with her life, Zip went away to school and became a teacher. An independent woman, she substituted silent prayer for Protestant Bible readings because of the sensibilities of her Catholic pupils. In time she became a Catholic herself, despite her mother's alarms over entering an idolatrous faith. Martin was obviously concerned about the family names of women, for the most reprehensible character in that novel was a male who believed the only reason that wives assumed their husband's names at marriage was convention. As a result he hyphenated his own name with that of his mother's family to prevent her name from dying out.

The only Catholic novelists of the period who were unabashedly feminist were Mary Agnes Tincker (1835–1907) and Kate O'Flaherty

Chopin (1851–1904), both of whom had difficulty reconciling their faith with their vision of women. Chopin drifted out of the church as she rejected inflexible legalisms. Her father, a daily communicant and well-to-do immigrant, was killed in a train accident when she was four. As a result Chopin was raised by independent women — her mother, her grandmother, and especially her great-grandmother, who taught her that only God could judge human behavior. In early years a devout Catholic, she was confirmed by Archbishop Peter Kenrick of St. Louis, a friend of her father's, and graduated from the Academy of the Sacred Heart. Her independence of spirit was shown, however, at an early age, when she was dubbed the Little Rebel because of her zealous support for the Confederacy.

In 1870 she married Oscar Chopin, a wealthy New Orleans merchant, and bore him six children, naming her only daughter Lelia, after a character created by George Sand. Although a devoted mother, she rejected traditional wifely subordination and domesticity. Apparently she heeded the advice of the notorious feminist Victoria Woodhull, who warned the young bride on her honeymoon about the degrading confinement of a typical marriage. To many, Chopin appeared outrageous: she smoked, wore unconventional clothing, and maintained an individuality that was respected by her loving husband.

After his death she administered their plantation and then returned to St. Louis an attractive thirty-two-year-old. Her major biographer states that she refused to remarry because she continued to love her deceased husband and feared that wedlock would jeopardize her independence and deny her the opportunity to write. Less than ten years after her return to St. Louis, she had published nearly one hundred stories, becoming known to a large portion of the public through her Louisiana Tales.

About the time she began writing professionally, she stopped practicing Catholicism. Influenced by her agnostic friend Dr. Frederick Kolbenheyer, she embraced the relativity of morals and denied the right of clergy to speak for her. However, she never openly renounced her faith and was buried from the church.[24] It is possible that although rejecting the institutional church, Chopin still considered herself Catholic. As late as 1895 she wrote for a Catholic periodical, and her stories frequently had Catholic settings, often being sympathetic with the fundamental principles of the church, although mindless ritualism and moral priggishness were derided.[25] The greatest difficulty in reconciling her writings and orthodoxy lay with her female characters, who not only were self-assured, emancipated, and unrestrained but were passionate in and out of marriage.

Even in her most controversial work, however, Chopin's women never resorted to divorce in order to maintain or recapture their independence. Her first publication, "Wiser than a God" (1889), was the tale of a pianist who rejected a desirable marriage for a career in which, contrary to nineteenth-century norm, she found happiness.[26] More controversial, yet still orthodox, was *At Fault*, her first novel (1890).[27] There the Catholic heroine forces the man she loves to remarry the alcoholic woman he had divorced. His wife slipped back into drunkenness, and although she died, leaving the couple free to marry, the new bride questions the value of absolute moral truths, which may prevent sin but create misery. Her short story "Madame Célestin's Divorce" (1893), which has been described as clearly reflecting Catholic principles, is the account of a Catholic wife whose repentant husband returns to her, ending her struggle between desire for a divorce and a wish to follow the teachings of the church.[28] A wife achieves a type of liberation from an unhappy marriage in "The Story of an Hour" (1894) when she is told her husband is dead. Even though the report is a mistake, she dies of happiness.[29]

Her most controversial work was *The Awakening* (1899), wherein a young married mother awakens to her sexuality, independence, and artistic talents. Willing to seek love outside her conventional, boring, middle-class marriage, she finds that she still is expected to be a subservient woman. The novel ends as she walks into the sea to find both sexual and spiritual freedom in an act of independence. Although it is possible to interpret her drowning as an accident rather than suicide, the novel was condemned from Boston to San Francisco and banned in the public library of Chopin's native St. Louis, where the Fine Arts Club refused her membership. Chopin, who was a devoted mother and had authored children's stories, was heartbroken and wrote seldom thereafter. Her last published story, "Charlie" (1900), was the tale of a tomboy who was sent to a seminary to learn to become a lady but who left school to manage the family plantation and care for an ill father, whose demands kept her from marrying.[30] Sex, love, independence, and marriage once again appeared impossible to reconcile for women.[31]

Tincker, who was probably more orthodox than Chopin, was criticized nearly as severely. She began teaching at age thirteen, became a convert at twenty, and served as a nurse during the Civil War. She then supported herself by writing and lived in Italy for fourteen years. In the 1890s she left the church, for some years, a step that surely did not surprise critics of her early novels, which had been serialized in the *Catholic World*.[32] Her *House of Yorke* (1872), an attack on Know-Nothings, dealt with the tarring and feathering of a Maine priest. As in Sadlier's writings, the eating of meat on Friday was prominent in the plot. Masters attempted to get their servants to violate church teachings by doing so, and one of the more dramatic events was the fearless refusal of a young girl to yield to such pressure. Her strongest characters by far were courageous women: females, not males, attempted to rescue the priest and fight the forest fire. Orestes Brownson was led by her depiction of these self-confident women to charge that "she is in reality one of the strong minded and is sadly deficient in feminine grace and delicacy." Even worse, he continued, Tincker was in need of conversion, for her soul was not yet Catholic.[33]

Brownson was even more critical of Tincker's next novel, *Grapes and Thorns; or, A Priest's Sacrifice* (1874), accusing her of revising the order of nature by having no strong male characters and subordinating men to women. Novels of this type, he charged, led to the woman's rights movement. A review in the *Catholic World* was equally as harsh, accusing Tincker of rejecting the highest ideals of her sex and failing to appreciate the lofty Christian teaching on conjugal love and marriage.[34] The work that provoked these reactions dealt with the inviolability of the seal of confession, revolving about the murder of a priest's mother and the false imprisonment of a warm-hearted and sympathetic Jew. Although he believed he was a better Christian than those who had imprisoned him, the Jew was inspired by the selflessness of women to become a convert. Tincker wrote, "It must be remembered that while man was made of the slime of the earth, woman was formed of the flesh; and that the material part which is the veil between her spirit and the outer world has felt twice the refining touch of the creator's hands."[35]

If she had been content to describe this type of moral superiority, *Grapes and Thorns* would not have been so severely criticized, but Tincker audaciously praised female bonding, contrasting it with heterosexual love. "How sweet is the friendship of one true woman for another: — sweeter than love, for it is untroubled, and has something of the calmness of heaven; deeper than love, for it is the sympathy of true natures which reflect each the entire being of the other; less selfish than love, for it asks no merging of another into itself; nobler than love, for it allows its object to have other sources of happiness than those it can furnish; more enduring than love, for it is a life and not a flame."[36]

Equally as threatening to traditional Catholic views was the criticism of the social contributions of nuns. Tincker claimed that as sisters were removed from the problems of the world, they seldom were found where heroes were needed but only looked with pity from their safe, screened cloister. "But it is not they who pierce their way through the rabble, with Veronica, to take the imprint of his misery onto their stainlessness, nor they who weep around his tomb through dews and darkness."[37] Tincker was hardly fair to nuns. They often acted courageously and exercised responsibilities to a greater degree than did many men, and in doing so not only challenged the stereotypes of women imposed by society but defied the influences of American bishops.

Nuns were like nineteenth-century women writers; on the surface they appeared to reinforce traditional values, but their very lives revealed another class of women who chafed under clerical conventions. Nuns were even more dangerous to the century's norms, but both groups of women betrayed their restlessness to thousands of others: authors to their readers, nuns to their pupils.

Chapter 4

"LADYLIKE" NUNS: NINETEENTH-CENTURY ACTIVISTS

In its treatment of nuns the Catholic church further applied the societal restraints that forced women to conform to masculine notions of ladylikeness. After all, why should sisters behave differently from other women? The deference a wife owed her husband logically should be replicated in the submission of nuns to male leadership.[1] By its refusal to ordain them to the priesthood, the patriarchal church sanctified the subordination of nuns to clerics and perpetuated a system that treated female religious as childlike. As late as 1931 spiritual directors of women's communities were warned that their charges were emotional beings rather than rational ones, distinguishing the essential from the accidental only with difficulty. Furthermore, it was asserted they lacked prudence, were shortsighted, and were apt to develop idiosyncrasies.[2]

Yet these were among the most liberated women in nineteenth-century America. They were self-supporting, owned property, were well educated, held administrative positions, lived in a community of women, and were free from the dominance of husbands and the responsibility of motherhood.[3] Often they were envied by their Protestant sisters for their independence and hailed by businessmen for their acumen, even though they sometimes embarrassed and discomforted them when transacting community affairs.[4]

As they built and administered schools, orphanages, and hospitals, these women ignored cholera epidemics, braved Indians, and defied Know-Nothings. Yet their greatest challenges were institutional: the

43

struggle with churchmen to preserve their independence and to adapt rules designed for medieval European communities to an American Protestant society — often under frontier conditions.

In the bull *Circa Pastoralis* (1566) Pius V compelled all nuns with solemn vows to live in enclosures, which meant they were not to go beyond the walls of the convent, nor were others to enter without the bishop's permission. Furthermore, a grating in the parlor was to separate the religious from her visitor, and the convent had to be proximate to the church so nuns could attend mass without leaving the grounds. If there was a school, it, too, had to be adjacent to the convent, and sisters were permitted to confer with parents and pastors only in the convent parlor or behind a grill. The whole concept was based on the assumption that limited contact with the world was necessary to protect these women, as they were weak and incapable of controlling their lives. On the other hand, most orders adopted ascetic practices that would tax the strength of the hardiest women: bare feet in the winter, manual labor, endless rounds of prayer, and various forms of mortification.[5]

Change was necessary if communities were to survive in America, where endowments and dowries were few and wealthy patrons were scarce. Survival meant teaching, and teaching required adaption of rules. The impossibility of reconciling the demands imposed by teaching with austere mortifications were exemplified by the first native American sisterhood, the Sisters of Loretto, a teaching community in Kentucky. Their founder, Charles S. Nerinckx (1761–1824), like most émigré priests a proponent of the European ideal, required the nuns to go barefoot, to sleep on straw or on the floor, to labor in the fields plowing, clearing land, cutting and hauling wood, to maintain silence except for an hour after dinner (a privilege withdrawn during Lent), and to begin their work day at 4:00 A.M. in the summer and 4:30 in the winter. The rule was so severe that fifteen of sixteen sisters under thirty years of age died of tuberculosis in one year. Their regimens, which hardly suited Kentucky winters, thoroughly drained teaching sisters. When the rules were modified in 1844 as a result of the intervention of Louisville's bishop, Benedict J. Flaget (1769–1850), an embittered Nerinckx left the state.[6]

Nerinckx, however, was an exception. Spiritual directors and bishops usually encouraged a revision of stringent practices, finding them inimical to the duties nuns were encouraged to undertake: administering schools and orphanages. (Sometimes the superior herself resisted the innovations proposed by the hierarchy.)[7] Equally important for the success of the American missions was the circumvention of the rules of enclosure. New foundations were "congregations" rather than "orders," and thus their members could take "simple" rather than "solemn" vows, leaving them free to act outside the cloister. As the United States was officially mission territory until 1908, there was greater flexibility and opportunity to flout these European conventions. But nuns in American communities until 1910 were not recognized as bona fide religious. Rome, which held to a different ideal, merely tolerated them as "pious ladies."[8]

Freedom from the cloister and the revision of rules enabled nuns to raise funds by teaching. Tuition and revenues obtained from private lessons in music and art supported poor schools, often in the church basement, and by the middle of the century a small-scale orphanage was common to all academies.[9]

Teaching had become so common by 1852 and simple vows so much the norm that the First Plenary Council of Baltimore exhorted bishops to establish schools in connection with all the churches in their dioceses. The plea was repeated even more strongly in 1884 at the Third Council, which also urged the establishment of normal schools to train sisters.[10]

Even more dramatic than the changes of rules and practices was the protracted struggle between bishops and women's religious communities. There were provisions for two types of congregations: diocesan approved, by the local ordinary, and pontifical approved, by authorities in Rome. If diocesan, the bishop exercised a great deal of jurisdiction over the group, including the power to veto the choice of a superior. However, even in diocesan orders, canon law reserved to female superiors authority in such matters as general relations of subject to superior, admission to the congregation, education, and formation. Nevertheless, bishops encroached in these areas, often viewing them as matters for their attention.[11]

The very qualities that made women religious instrumental in the growth of the church (understanding, openness to society, intelligence, and self-assurance) created sisters who asserted the right to make decisions about their life-style and institutions. As a result the century was marked by conflict with bishops, who even forced pontifical communities out of their sees and fashioned sisterhoods responsive to their own demands.[12] Typically, in 1829 when Bishop England established the Sisters of Our Lady of Mercy, he never wrote a constitution, for "I do not wish to make my institutions dependent upon Superiors over whom I have neither control or influence."[13] After seventy-five years attitudes had changed little, if at all. Bishop John Moore (1835–1901) of St. Augustine forced the separation of the Sisters of St. Joseph from their Le Puy motherhouse, writing to their Superior in France, "I see a necessity to have only sisters who are entirely diocesan, Sisters who obey the Bishops of the Diocese.... I repeat, I want Sisters who obey me like their Bishop and who are not in any manner subject to orders of a Superior in another country."[14]

In the face of such challenges dozens of American communities behaved in a non-"ladylike" fashion. They cooperated with one another in acquiring pontifical status in their search for freedom and independence from what one historian has described as idiosyncratic and aristocratic hierarchical authorities.[15] Even the first canonized American saint, Mother Frances Cabrini (1850–1917), encountered difficulties with New York's Archbishop Michael Corrigan (1839–1902), who at one point suggested she return to Italy. Little wonder that she advised superior generals to seek pontifical status for their congregations.[16] The attitude of bishops was creating a type of sisterhood far different from anything envisioned by the church.

Rare indeed was the congregation immune from clerical efforts to exercise power. Mother Seton, recognized as a saint in her own times, disclosed to Bishop Carroll discord with her spiritual director.[17] More significant and a threat to all communities were the Machiavellian tactics of New York's Bishop Hughes. When the Sisters of Charity refused to contravene their rules by administering a boy's orphanage, Hughes, although these nuns had been in his diocese since 1817, a period of twenty-nine years, ordered them to leave or to establish a new community under his tutelage — the Sisters of Charity of New York. About one-half (or thirty) of the nuns, including his sister, remained to form the new organization. Hughes's intentions were clear when shortly after their formation he began to exercise authority over them. He intervened in the election of a superior, and when the council informed Bishop William Walsh of Halifax that probably it would be two years before they could send nuns to establish a house there, Hughes overruled them and ordered immediate compliance.[18] The bishop also intervened in the affairs of the Sisters of Mercy, whom he brought from Ireland to care for homeless girls. Furthermore, he was so antagonistic to the Sisters of Holy Cross, who had opened an industrial school for girls in 1856, that they left the diocese. Hughes's distrust of nuns was rooted in his perceptions of authority. As he wrote to a fellow bishop, he could not approve of anyone in whom strict obedience was not a virtue, including "that wild-eyed girl of France," Joan of Arc, about whose "real merits" he had "serious doubts and misgivings."[19]

Undoubtedly Archbishop William G. McCloskey (1823–1909) of

Louisville shared Hughes's views. He tried to keep each community under his control and jurisdiction, even forcing mothers general to withdraw petitions to Rome seeking pontifical status. He intervened in elections of the School Sisters of Notre Dame, the Sisters of Loretto, and the Ursulines. At various times communities were placed under interdict, superiors were deposed, individual nuns were ordered out of the diocese, and the School Sisters of Notre Dame were driven away. Only a year and a half after McCloskey's consecration, an embittered superior of the Sisters of Charity, the Rev. Francis Chambige, wrote to Archbishop Martin J. Spalding (1810–1872), "It would fill pages to relate to you the unreasonable requisitions and persecutions that community has had to suffer from him." The passage of time did little to moderate his approach. Mother Dafrosa Smythe of the Sisters of Loretto, after a meeting with McCloskey in 1892, wrote in the council book: "The 18th of July — Day never to be forgotten. Oh! Oh! the reproachful lecture the Council got. . . . Traduced, Abused, I cannot write more. Oh! cruel man! May the Lord give the grace to forgive. Treated with the utmost contumely, and not permitted to say a word of explanation."[20] The sisters' complaints were not confined to the house journal, as they had the audacity to criticize McCloskey to his superiors. They appealed for relief to Cardinal Sebastiano Martinelli, the apostolic delegate, based on their "right to justice . . . even if the aggressor is a Bishop"; they later wrote to Martinelli denouncing the bishop's "petty persecutions." To the Dominican master general they described McCloskey as mentally affected.[21]

Much of the history of the Sisters of Mercy in the United States is an account of the heroic efforts of the American founder, Mary Francis Warde (1810–84), to preserve their independence. She defended her community against the trespasses of Bishop Michael O'Connor (1810–72), Pittsburgh, Michael Domenec (1816–78), Pittsburgh, and James F. Wood (1813–83), Philadelphia, who wanted separate motherhouses under diocesan control. After a prolonged conflict in Chicago during which the nuns had threatened to leave, a weak superior finally yielded their deed to Lake Shore property and made a low-interest loan to Bishop Anthony O'Regan (1795–1858).[22] Cincinnati was not much better. When Sisters of Mercy nuns threatened to withdraw from parochial schools rather than violate their rules, Bishop William H. Elder (1819–1904) refused to receive their vows or to appoint a confessor, angrily dismissing them as pious women who could go to confession in their own parish church.[23] Bishop James A. Healy (1830–1900) of Maine was probably the most contentious of all, interfering in the smallest details. He also diverted fifty thousand dollars donated for a convent to a school and reorganized his diocese in such a way that he would control the community.[24] All during these controversies Warde was opening new schools, orphanages, and hospitals and defying Know-Nothings in New England who tried to intimidate her nuns by threatening them, smashing windows, and harassing students.[25]

Irish-born Mother Austin Carroll (1835–1909) of the Mercy Sisters was also forced to defend community rules against the nuns' Redemptionist spiritual director and Bishop James X. Leray (1825–87) of New Orleans. Despite the distracting contentiousness Carroll was instrumental in establishing nearly sixty-five schools for blacks and whites in the South, took steps toward establishing a woman's college as early as 1887, and with her sisters tended prisoners, and trained immigrant women and widows to be self-sufficient.[26]

One of the bitterest and saddest of these disputes was that between Mother Theodore Guérin (1796–1856), the naturalized American founder of the Sisters of Providence of St. Mary-of-the-Woods, and Bishop Celestine de la Hailandière (1798–1882), who had recruited the nuns from Europe. While Guérin was in France raising money for the community, the bishop began a seven-year struggle and deposed her, for as the annalist recorded: "He understood his rights as bishop and Superior in a manner contrary to the spirit of our Rules, he regarded our opposition to his views as contempt of episcopal authority, an act of blackest ingratitude...he considered as criminal disobedience which we look upon as sacred obligation."[27] In this conflict over rules Hailandière excommunicated Guérin, denounced her at the Council of Baltimore, declared her rebellious, and expelled her from the community. As he informed the nuns, "To oppose the Bishop was to revolt against God himself"; the least priest in the diocese had more power over sisters than did their superior general.[28] The struggle was resolved in Guérin's favor by John S. Bazin (1796–1848), who succeeded to the see after the resignation of the truculent bishop. Threats from the non-Catholics of Terre Haute to burn the school must have seemed mild compared with the fulminations of the bishop, while the patience exhibited by Guérin must have contributed to the decision to declare her beatified.

Religious congregations affiliated with men's orders seemed to have even more difficulty. In 1830, eight years after a Dominican religious community was established in Kentucky, the new superior, Father Raphael Muños, ordered the nuns to sell their land, take off their garb, and return home, for they were not living a monastic life. Although the community was keeping matins and lauds, spinning and weaving flax, raising sheep and selling wool, felling trees and repairing fences, according to him they were too involved in a "foolish experiment" — running a girls' academy. The nuns defied Muños, by refusing to disband. Because of this "feminine insubordination" some of their lands were sold, and they were denied the Blessed Sacrament and told to attend their parish church. Until the appointment of a new Dominican master general, the nuns existed in abject poverty. Years later, however, they were again forced to assert their independence and, under the leadership of Mother Angela Sansbury, successfully resisted the efforts of Bishop Edward D. Fenwick, O.P. (1768–1832), Cincinnati, to send some of them to Ohio.[29]

The founder of the Sisters of Saint Benedict, Mother Benedicta Riepp (1825–62), had even greater difficulties remaining free from the dictates of Boniface Wimmer, who claimed that his jurisdiction over the Benedictines in America included nuns. He ousted Riepp from her Pennsylvania community, impounded donations of over $1,200, and twice deposed Mother Willibalda Scherbauer (1828–1914), who had been sent by Riepp to found a house at St. Cloud, Minnesota.

Determined not to endure "disobedient and undisciplined sisters whom he would teach who is master," he denounced both nuns as tramps. After Riepp appealed Wimmer's actions, he referred to her as audacious, self-willed, unruly, and lacking the "discretion belonging to the female sex." The power struggle continued with the new abbot, Rupert Seidenbusch, who deposed Willibranda and suppressed the convent. Relationships were clarified in 1859 when Riepp succeeded in getting Rome to place their houses under the jurisdiction of the local bishops. Later, however, this step led to additional problems, for the community in Racine urged the superior in San Jose to avoid dependence on local authority by obtaining pontifical status, and Dominicans in Reno struggled against the capricious exercise of power by Bishop O'Connell, who withheld absolution from the mother superior.[30]

Although the situation never deteriorated to the level of excommunicating the sisters of the Congregation of Holy Cross, Father Edward Sorin certainly exploited the community that was brought by him from Europe in 1842 to help his educational work. Sorin, the founder and president of Notre Dame, used his office as head of the men's congregation and a member of the council of St. Mary's (the academy run by the sisters) to advance the male institution and to direct sisters' lives. The protests of Mother Angela Gillespie (1824–80), the founder of the congregation in America, were ignored. When he found hired female domestics unsatisfactory at Notre Dame, he

established a novitiate for all nuns from the Wisconsin area at South
Bend, where they would be used for the exclusive benefit of the university community. For seventeen years there were two novitiates, one
only nominally under St. Mary's control. Furthermore, he used funds
from the women's school to help rebuild the university after a fire.
Although Gillespie served as the de facto editor of the monthly religious magazine *Ave Maria*, which was established primarily through
her endeavors, she was listed anonymously in the journal only as a
"religious assistant."[31] Humility of this type was to be expected from
ladies, particularly nuns, but of course was not in keeping with the
nature of men.

Other communities also shattered female stereotypes and defied
male trespasses. Bishop Kenrick of St. Louis opposed the "impudent
manner" of the Sisters of Charity of Emmitsburg in uniting with the
Daughters of Charity in France and as a result refused to yield his
right to appoint a confessor.[32] Catherine Spalding (1793–1858), the
first superior of the Sisters of Charity of Nazareth, successfully resisted Bishop Flaget's efforts to assume direct supervision over her
community.[33] The struggle with Richard P. Miles (1791–1860), bishop
of Nashville, was so severe that in 1851 many Sisters of Charity returned to Kentucky, while others fled to Kansas and formed the Sisters
of Charity of Leavenworth.[34] From 1833 to 1850 the Poor Clares
engaged in a protracted struggle with Bishop Frederick C. Résé (1791–
1871) of Detroit. After lawsuits, the withholding of sacraments, and
excommunications, the nuns left the country.[35]

Many other bishops also attempted to bring communities under
their jurisdiction. Mother Theresa of Jesus, superior general of the
School Sisters of Notre Dame, in 1851 protested to Rome the efforts
of Bishop John Henni (1805–81) of Milwaukee to separate her community from its European motherhouse "so he may have a free hand
in our affairs."[36] Bishop John J. Hennessy (1847–1920), Wichita,
caused "great suffering" for Mother Frances Streitel (1844–1911),
founder of the Sisters of Sorrowful Mother, and nearly destroyed
the community in an effort to separate it from Rome and bring it
under his jurisdiction.[37] The founder of the Society of the Sacred
Heart in America, Saint Rose Philippine Duchesne (1769–1852), was
refused absolution, communion, and public renewal of her vows because of her struggle to preserve the society's rules from male clerical
encroachment. Shortly after her death the community was embroiled
in another conflict, a two-year power struggle with Bishop Peter P.
Lefevre (1804–69) of Detroit. In an attempt to force the nuns to conform, he withdrew their chaplain and the Blessed Sacrament from

their chapel.[38] In 1860 the Sisters of St. Joseph of Carondelet found it necessary to defend their prerogatives against Bishops Thomas Grace (1814–97), St. Paul, and John Loughlin (1816–91), Brooklyn. The Sisters of Notre Dame de Namur, in order to teach poor children, successfully defied Bishops John B. Purcell (1800–83), Cincinnati, Archbishop John J. Williams (1822–1907), Boston, and John N. Neumann (1811–60), Philadelphia.[39] The fortitude displayed by Mother Caroline Friess (1824–92), School Sisters of Notre Dame, in protracted struggles with the hierarchy was such that in her eulogy she was described as a valiant woman "of a manly spirit."[40]

In their day-to-day work these religious often displayed still another aspect of the "male" virtue — courage. Many of these women left the familiar shores of Europe to sail to a strange land, often without a knowledge of English. Frequently the ocean trip was dangerous: sheltered women, alone in thronging port cities, embarked in the cheapest quarters for a long and often storm-tossed journey. Mother Mary Theresa of the School Sisters of Notre Dame wrote back to Europe on her arrival that she appeared ten years older, with "affected" eyes and loosened teeth and feeling that "this miserable machine is no longer of much use."[41] After disembarking in the United States or after entrance into a community, the women faced further ordeals: grinding poverty often resulting in hunger, inadequate shelter, snakes in Mississippi, Indians in the West, heat in the South, cold in the North, and even more dangerous treks to the frontiers. As Mother Duchesne explained to a candidate: "Inconvenience in everything, especially our lodging... food that is often disgusting... severe cold, prostrating heat, and practically no spring weather. God alone and the desire of His glory: nothing else matters."[42]

Religious communities were not even sure of a welcome from fellow Catholics once they arrived. Two sisters, Mothers Mary Magdalen and Mary Constance, founders of the American Order of Poor Clares, came to the United States from Italy in 1875 and were unable to find a diocese that would accept their group. For four years they wandered from city to city, searching for a place to open a convent before they were invited to Omaha by Bishop James O'Connor (1823–90). There, with the help of Mrs. John Creighton, they opened a monastery in 1882 and before long founded establishments in New Orleans, Evansville, Philadelphia, and Boston.[43] Once in place, in addition to their assigned duties, the sisters often were forced to support themselves by making flowers, vestments, or ornaments.

Many nuns faced threats from anti-Catholics and found it dangerous to travel unaccompanied or in religious garb. Others, fearful that their convents would be burned, fully expected to die for the faith in the cities of the Northeast. Yet it appears as if the self-assurance and self-confidence of these women contributed to these threats by unsettling their male protagonists.[44]

A different type of courage was shown by a large number of sisters who tended cholera and yellow fever victims in the United States. Nuns had begun nursing in private homes, then in almshouses, and between 1829 and 1860 opened about twenty-five hospitals.[45] The sisters nursed the stricken in alleys and lanes, wherever the sick were found, and unlike other medical practitioners, opened their hospitals to the victims. Many Americans considered these outbreaks a punishment from the Creator for sin and believed the ungodly and immoral were most susceptible to the diseases. Nevertheless, the willingness and eagerness of nuns to care for these neglected victims, sometimes at the cost of their lives, amazed onlookers. Their courage contrasted markedly with the pusillanimity of many panic-stricken physicians who fled and nurses who refused to tend victims. This bravery was often hailed by governmental agencies and even by the *Woman's Journal* and the *Revolution*, suffrage papers often critical of the church because of its conservative stance on women.[46]

In establishing religious communities, women showed leadership, administrative skills, organizational ability, and determination — attributes usually associated only with males. In addition to those already mentioned, many other nuns displayed these qualities, among them Mother Cornelia Connelly (1809–79), Philadelphia-born founder of the English Society of the Holy Child Jesus, and Mother Mary Frances Clarke (1803–87), the Irish originator of the Sisters of Charity of the Blessed Virgin Mary. Connelly and her husband, both converts to Catholicism, renounced their marriage vows and entered religious life. Pierce Connelly, however, changed his mind, spirited his children away from contact with their mother, tried to assume control of his wife's community, denounced his priestly vows, and sought (and ultimately failed) to restore his conjugal rights through court action. Connelly, whose cause for canonization was opened in 1959, withstood these assaults and continued her work as religious superior. Emphasizing the educational mission of her community, she established schools in England and Pennsylvania, one of which became Rosemont College in 1921.[47] After an adventurous voyage to the United States, Clarke and three companions founded her community in Philadelphia and with difficulty moved it to the primitive West in 1843, establishing the motherhouse in Dubuque, Iowa, where a teaching order was in great demand.[48]

The specific undertakings of some nuns called for unusual heroism and extreme self-confidence. Mother Marianne of Molokai (1836–1918) was the founder of the first American community to initiate mission work in a foreign land. Appeals were made to over fifty American societies before she and six other Franciscans left the United States for Hawaii to establish and staff a leper house for women. She also began a general hospital school for girls and took charge of Father Damien de Veuster's home after he died.[49] Mother Mary Amadeus (1846–1919) was known as Great-Chief-White-Woman by the Indians. Superior of all Ursuline houses in North America, she devoted her talents and those of many of her community to serve the Cheyennes in the western part of the United States and perform missionary activity in Alaska in areas where no white woman had previously been. At various times she was caught in blizzards and on one occasion saved a man from drowning while crossing a stream. Amadeus's activities never decreased, even though she was crippled the last twenty years of her life as a result of a train accident.[50]

There were specific sisterhoods of Indians, but they seldom lasted any length of time because of a lack of vocations. Usually native American Catholic women with a calling entered white religious communities. However, the Congregation of American Sisters did serve as nurses in the Spanish American War before their dispersement because of a lack of numbers. Among the most courageous Catholic Indian women was Louise Sighouin, the daughter of a Coeur d'Alene chief; she lived an exemplary life but was in danger, as her teaching of Christianity to the tribe undermined the authority of the medicine man.[51]

Mother Alphonsa Lathrop (1851–1926), the third daughter of Nathaniel Hawthorne and a successful writer in her own right, became a lay sister after the death of her husband, George. She opened her home to those stricken with incurable cancer and created her own sisterhood, the Dominican Congregation of St. Rose of Lima, to nurse these victims.[52] The onerous work and self-sacrifice involved in these endeavors was readily reconciled by Lathrop with the traditional role of women. She believed that women had a saving influence on the world because of their domesticity and that men admired those who imitated "the noblest, tenderest, most exalted" of her sex, Mary.[53]

An entirely different type of courage, revealing a behavior pattern that was also considered more masculine than feminine, was manifest by nuns who defied social norms and frequently violated the law by teaching black children. Even more defiant of contemporary mores were those women who established or joined black religious commu-

nities. Color difference exacerbated contests with authoritarian clergy
and engendered hostility from Protestant and even Catholic laity.

Among the earliest American communities was the Oblate Sisters of Providence, founded in Baltimore in 1829 by Father Nicholas
Joubert (a white Sulpician) and Mary Elizabeth Lange (1774–1882),
both of whom were émigrés from San Domingo. It was the first black
Catholic religious order in America. Only five years after the oblates
were established to educate slaves, there were twelve nuns (at least
three of whom had been slaves) and a girls' school offering courses
in "refined and useful education" as found in "well-regulated female
seminaries." Although every sister volunteered to tend those smitten
by cholera in the 1830s and although a resolution of thanks for their
service was enacted by the Bureau of the Poor, the community was
discriminated against by many Baltimorians and threatened by na-
tivists. Even more disheartening was the prejudicial myopia of many
clergy and, according to community tradition, Archbishop Samuel
Eccleston (1801–51), who wanted the order to disband because there
was a greater need for house servants than black nuns. Furthermore,
the church offered little material support. To feed themselves and
survive, the sisters took in washing, ironing, and mending, made and
sold clerical vestments, and served as domestics in the seminary. As
the community spread, it encountered problems in other areas of the
country. Even on those rare occasions when the price was fair, it was
difficult legally for Afro-Americans to acquire property. Moreover, as
their mission was financed by the religious community and not the
diocese, their institutions continually flirted with pecuniary disaster.
Nevertheless, because of the diligence, determination, and devotion
of the sisters, their many schools and orphanages survived and in
time even flourished.[54]

The second black congregation in the United States, Sisters of the
Holy Family, was founded in 1842 in New Orleans. Marie J. Aliquot
had pledged her services to Afro-Americans when a black risked his
life to rescue her from the Mississippi River when she had fallen from
a collapsing gangplank. After having three women train in France
for seven years, she established, with the aid of the bishop of New
Orleans, Anthony Blanc (1792–1860), an Afro-American community
to educate black girls and care for the aged. (As a white, Aliquot never
joined the order but lived with the nuns as an auxiliary.) Although
the sisters taught catechism to slaves and opened an old-age home
and a school within a year of their establishment, the community
did not flourish until the Civil War, when it opened orphanages and
academies in much of the South.[55]

The only pre-Civil War effort at an integrated community was undertaken by Nerinckx, who wanted a sisterhood to educate black females and administer a refuge for elderly and useless slaves. He brought black girls from farms to be trained and then admitted them to Loretto. They lived apart from the whites but shared community exercises. After Nerinckx left for Missouri in 1824, his successor, Bishop Guy Chabrat (1787–1868), administrator of the Bardstown diocese, released the women from their vows and sent them home, unconvinced of the practicality of Afro-American religious.[56]

Probably the most successful educational effort directed toward blacks was clandestine instruction after normal school hours by white teachers.[57] Formal institutions, even when staffed by whites, were usually short lived. Bishop England established the Sisters of Our Lady of Mercy to administer a school for Afro-Americans and provide religious instruction for female slaves. Because of the protests of Charlestonites, the school was closed in 1835 and reopened in 1841 with enrollment confined to free blacks. However, even with this restriction the school was forced to close a few years later.[58]

The School Sisters of Notre Dame were able to run a night school for black women in St. Louis for a few years, but the Sisters of St. Joseph were less fortunate. In 1845 in that city they began teaching catechism to slaves and a general curriculum to free Afro-Americans. However, the nuns yielded to the mayor's entreaty and closed the school after the police dispersed a mob that had surrounded the convent and tried to drive the inhabitants out.[59]

In the immediate post-Civil War period the only organized effort by the hierarchy specifically designed to educate former slaves was that of Bishop John M. Verot (1805–76) of Savannah. Verot recruited Sisters of St. Joseph from Europe to teach blacks in Georgia and Florida.[60] Sixteen years after the war, the Franciscan Sisters from Mill Hill, an English missionary community, came to the United States for the sole purpose of educating Afro-Americans, the only white community with such a mission. To assist these sisters the Mission Helpers of St. Joseph's Guild, whose fourth vow dedicated them to the salvation of the colored race, was founded in Baltimore in 1888. They established a school for two hundred black girls and a sewing school for children and visited blacks in jails, poorhouses, and hospitals.[61]

In 1888 Margaret Murphy (1833–1907), a San Antonio widow, began her own mission among the blacks, which resulted in the formation of the Sisters of the Holy Ghost, who took a special vow to tend Negro children. These sisters opened schools in Texas, Louisiana, and Mississippi.[62]

The most prominent woman in these endeavors was Mother Mary Katherine Drexel (1858–1955), founder of the Sisters of Blessed Sacrament for Indian and Colored People. Daughter of a prosperous banker, she turned her home into a mecca for the poor. Shortly after Pope Leo XIII responded to her appeal for missionaries to Indians and blacks with the words, "Why not you?" she established her community. Her sisters, who took a special vow "to be the mother and servant of the Indian and Negro races," established service houses, missions, and schools throughout the nation. The only Catholic college for blacks in the United States, Xavier University, New Orleans, was begun by Drexel in 1925. (Despite Pope Pius XI's 1929 encyclical against coeducation, the apostolic delegate gave Drexel special permission to retain coeducational instruction at Xavier.) On the occasion of Drexel's jubilee in 1936, Bishop Joseph M. Corrigan (1879–1942), rector of Catholic University, asserted that her sacrifice lessened the national shame of the "white man's" treatment of the blacks.[63]

One of the major functions of practically every community was the administration of schools and academies for females. Supported by the Provincial Councils, which saw them as a means of preserving the faith, and by the Third Plenary Council, which urged bishops to make Catholic school accessible to all, educational institutions spread rapidly. They even followed the paths of trailblazers along the very edge of the frontier. By 1852 there were over one hundred academies, seminaries, and institutions for females staffed by women's religious communities.[64] Their major object, the preservation of faith and morals, necessitated single-sex education, for during the nineteenth century coeducation was denounced as promiscuous, a threat to morality and womanly virtues. The 1875 warning from the Congregation of Propaganda of the dangers inherent in seating children of both sexes side by side in the classroom was really unnecessary.[65]

Single-sex education made it possible to develop specific goals for females — the preparation of young women to fulfill the duties of wives and mothers in a middle-class society and the nurturing of the attributes and virtues of a lady. An 1844 directory of a high school administered by the Madames of the Sacred Heart expressed these objectives in typical fashion: "The most uninterrupted attention is given to form the manners and principles of the young ladies, and to train them up to habits of order, neatness, and industry."[66] Curricula, then, tended to emphasize what some disparagingly referred to as ornamental studies: art, music, French (a polite accomplishment), dancing, manners, and at times even the graceful entering and withdrawing from a room.[67] According to Bishop England, "Education that...makes them [women] ornamental to society will prepare them for heaven."[68] Whether true or not, those qualities certainly made them desirable to middle-class men. Lestant Prudhomme, a young college graduate reading law in his native New Orleans, confided to his diary that he was "enchanted with the young ladies" from academies; "their conversation pleases me, they are charmingly mannered, they are altogether beautiful and lovely." Of course, he regretted that on their return to school from vacation they would be rebuked by nuns for having waltzed, even though their parents consented.[69]

Despite their emphasis on social graces the academies achieved a scholarly reputation and attracted numerous non-Catholics. Protestants often contributed generously to their support and sometimes welcomed nuns into a community, hoping that a school would follow soon.[70] So successful were these institutions that Sarah J. Hale, the noted editor of *American Ladies Magazine*, urged the spread of Protestant schools to offset the influence of Catholic schools; the educator Catherine Beecher established the Western Education Society to encourage Protestant teachers to emulate nuns by journeying west and establishing academies.[71]

Although one of their objectives was to develop Catholic ladies, nuns, like Catholic novelists, while attempting to foster typical feminine virtues, provided role models belying traditional life-styles. Furthermore, the preparation of good Catholic mothers was not compatible with the development of ladies, frequently undercutting the virtues of domesticity and submissiveness. As early as 1827 the prospectus of Georgetown Academy unintentionally but clearly exposed this contradiction: "To the care of ladies is entrusted the guardianship of society in its earliest age.... It is often in their power to refine the taste, and to whet the appetite for every virtuous and literary requirement."[72]

To be an effective Catholic mother, then, required a mastery of more than social graces. The result was a well-educated, stronger, confident female. As Mother Guérin wrote: "Woman in this country is only yet one-fourth of the family. I hope that, through the influence of religion and education, she will eventually become at least one-half — the better half."[73] A knowledge of the "masculine branches of learning" was deemed a necessity for the Catholic mother, according to Mother Mary Aloysia Hardey (1809–86) of the Sacred Heart. In order to prepare her nuns for the teaching of such subjects, Hardey required them to study Latin.[74] But the greatest internal danger to an educational system designed to produce "ladies" was an objective similar to that of Mother Gillespie. She wanted every St. Mary's graduate to be capable of pursuing studies "without the aid of a teacher."[75]

As a result, "non-ornamental" subjects such as math, bookkeeping, Latin, and science began to appear in the curriculum as early as the beginning of the nineteenth century.[76] Some Catholic commentators even openly advocated a course of studies similar to that of males. Brownson, certainly no feminist, claimed that in order to elevate and protect society, women must be thinking, reasoning beings, capable of rational discourse. Mother Mary Frances Clarke, whose community was to serve the church in the light of current social needs, charged that modern females had to be truly learned, which meant exposure to a wide range of thought and demanding teaching.[77]

Day-school students, who were usually from immigrant families and for whom the ladylike values of an academy were only a dream, were introduced to a "practical" curriculum by pragmatic nuns. But future mothers, who would have the responsibility of ensuring the education of their children, were also introduced to "liberal" studies.[78] Even more challenging to feminine stereotypes were the "industrial schools" opened during the antebellum period. Here young women were taught skills useful to society such as sewing, tailoring, and flower making. Sometimes these schools provided apprenticeships in the trades and residences for working girls.[79] Endeavors of this type became more common after 1866, when the Second Plenary Council of Baltimore urged bishops to provide industrial education for homeless or neglected teenagers in large cities. Sisters of Charity undertook the opening of many such institutions and in 1863 administered a school to save destitute girls from moral ruin by teaching them a trade.[80] The Sisters of Mercy, founded in Dublin to "reclaim intemperate females," came to the United States in 1841 to perform the same mission. They ran night school for adults, many of whom had been prostitutes, trained "wayward" girls to be self-supporting, and helped find positions for their students. Their renown in this area was such that Mother Mary Baptist Russell (1829–98), West Coast superior, was hailed at her death by the *San Francisco Bulletin* as the "best known charitable worker on the Pacific Coast."[81]

Nuns were really the force holding the church together. By the last half of the century they outnumbered male church workers in every diocese, were four times as numerous as priests, exercised the major influence on the growing immigrant population, and bore the economic brunt of selfless service — "Catholic serfs," according to one historian. In a sense no matter what their community, they were all Sisters of Charity.[82] Equally as significant, in following a life dedicated to the Beatitudes, they were subverting the ideal of the true Catholic woman — domestic, obedient, passive, timorously humble. The sisters provided an alternative role model, a tradition for Catholic female rebels, and an educational system that produced many women who would either ignore these ideals or directly challenge them.

Chapter 5

CONFORMITY AND REFRACTORINESS AMONG NINETEENTH-CENTURY "LADIES"

Although novelists and nuns appeared to conform to the Catholic perception of ladies while consciously or unconsciously undermining it, many women openly embraced the concept. Nevertheless they still exercised a considerable degree of freedom. The virtues of piety and domesticity allowed them to function outside the home by permitting them to devote their talents to church affairs or charitable endeavors. Indeed Bishop England, who had refused women the opportunity to participate in church governance, hailed a Mrs. Thompson for preserving the faith of a Georgia congregation that for over thirteen years had no priest and only occasional clerical visits for five years.[1] One of New York's leading Catholic gynecologists in the first half of the nineteenth century, Thomas Emmet, objected to political rights for women and to their participation in hospital administration, even in institutions founded by nuns. However, women made ideal nurses, according to him, and medical practice, he asserted, would be indebted to nurse Margaret Brennan, a devout Catholic, for her contributions to gynecology.[2]

Prior to the Civil War, parish groups, organized and administered by females, displayed "manly" skills in raising funds for hospitals, orphanages, schools, the aged, and the poor (endeavors that became even more common after the war). Ladies auxiliaries were established to aid sisters in running schools, "social service agencies," and

60

hospitals.[3] By midcentury a French Jesuit, who had spent forty years in Kentucky and New York, observed that lay communities of women had done more good than the clergy. They were esteemed and loved by the masses for their acts of charity and revered by their husbands and children. According to this chronicler, these honors so satisfied females that they had no need to meddle in politics or claim equality with men.[4]

Adèle Parmentier Bayer (1814–1892), the childless wife of a German-born merchant, joined her well-to-do widowed mother, Sylvia, in providing financial support for German Catholic pioneers. With her sister, Rosine, she aided Indian and Negro missions and raised money for a Catholic girl's high school in New York. Even more significant, Adèle Bayer, who has been described as one of the first Catholic welfare workers, ministered to merchant seamen in the Brooklyn navy yard, established a private allotment system for sailors during the Civil War, and was responsible for the appointment of the first Catholic naval chaplain. Little wonder she was dubbed the Guardian Angel of Sailors.[5]

Because her boundless vitality was considered unfeminine, the young, Irish-born widow Margaret Gaffney Haughery (1814–82) was described in later years by a clerical author as "always having a masculine energy in her character."[6] With money earned as a laundress she bought cows and, although probably illiterate, started a dairy business. These profits and the food she begged were used to establish and provision orphanages, a chapel, and a home and industrial school for working girls (probably the first in the South under Catholic auspices). Known as the Bread Woman of New Orleans, she also nursed yellow fever victims, tended flood casualties, fed Confederates imprisoned during the Union occupation of that city, and willed tens of thousands of dollars to the needy at her death. During the dedication of a statue to her, allegedly the first in the United States in honor of a woman, it was proclaimed that "the substance of her life was charity, the spirit of it, truth, the strength of it, religion, the end peace — then fame and immortality."[7] Her renown was such that nearly a decade after her death, encomiums to her still appeared in the suffrage paper the *Woman's Journal.*[8]

Some women undertook new obligations merely by donating money, but in so doing expressed interests that transcended the home. A graduate of Sacred Heart Academy, Manhattanville, Ellen Theresa Gavin (Mrs. Michael, d. 1922) was one of the founders of the Sacred Heart Convent, Boston, and a generous benefactor to the Jesuits, to Carney Hospital, and to foreign missions. Henrietta Agnes Crean

(d. 1873), wife of James Gordon Bennett of the *New York Herald* and a former music teacher, negotiated the release of American adventurers taken prisoner by Spain because of their activities in Spanish Cuba. She also raised money for various charities including needy students and wrote to James Buchanan congratulating him on his election as president.[9]

To prepare herself for marriage to the railroad magnate James J. Hill, Mary T. Mehegan (1846–1921) attended the Academy of the School Sisters of Notre Dame in Milwaukee, where she learned ladylike skills such as French and music. Mary Hill ran the home, supervising the moral and religious welfare of their nine children and entertaining a stream of clerical visitors, including Bishop Ireland of St. Paul. James Hill was a frequent contributor to Catholic causes and on the occasion of a gift to the seminary at St. Paul stated, "For nearly thirty years I have lived in a Roman Catholic household, and daily have had the earnest devotion, watchful care and Christian example of a Roman Catholic wife, of whom it may be said, 'Blessed are the pure in heart for they shall see God,' and on whose behalf I desire to present the seminary and its endowment."[10]

Old-line converts in midcentury were few in number. In 1860 they and their descendants accounted for less than 3 per cent of the Catholic population but with prestige and hauteur provided leadership to the laity. Their wealth endowed charitable institutions, and with their education and enthusiasm they became outspoken apologists for the church. Imbued with a zeal for their new faith, these women further crossed the bounds of accepted female behavior by their efforts to spread the "good news" or to apply it to the problems of society. Sophia Dana Ripley (1803–60) first learned about Catholics from Isaac Hecker, the founder of the Paulists. He himself was in the throes of conversion when he met her at the experimental commune Brook Farm, which had been founded by her husband. After studying Dante and the writings of the church fathers (in Greek), she became a Catholic, devoting much of her life to the poor. She recruited other women to assist her in caring for social outcasts such as hospitalized indigents, prisoners, and "fallen women." Shortly before her death from cancer much of her mission was assumed by the Sisters of the Good Shepherd.[11]

Sarah Worthington King Peter (1800–1877), the well-educated daughter of Thomas Worthington, United States senator and governor of Ohio, was attracted to Catholicism in part because of the opportunities it presented to women. After visiting a community of nuns during a European tour, she wrote, "Protestants fall so short of these true labors of love... bigots are justly chargeable for losing the good which our women might accomplish, if, like the Papists, they were allowed a fair field in which to exercise their faculties." A few years later, shortly before her conversion, in referring to the happiness of Sacred Heart nuns, she contended that "truly it is a gratification of any one favoring the idea of 'women's rights' to see how great a part these ladies have to perform, and accomplish their work so well."[12]

However, Peter did not have to take vows or even become a Catholic to enjoy being a reformer. While living in Philadelphia with her second husband, the British counsel William Peter, she joined with other females to establish a refuge for fallen women, founded an association to protect and advance female tailors, and taught design in her home, the forerunner of the Philadelphia School of Design for Women. In 1851–52 she toured Europe studying art and by then was so attracted to the church that she described herself as good a Catholic as any. She visited churches, the pope and the Holy Land. The following year she was widowed for the second time, returned to her native Cincinnati, and two years later became a Catholic.

From then on she dedicated her life to others, raising money for charitable endeavors, recruiting communities of nuns from Europe (Franciscans from Germany, Mercy from Ireland, Little Sisters of the Poor from France), and assisting them in their tasks of education, nursing, and care of the destitute. During the Civil War, Peter nursed on the battlefield, cared for those in hospitals and prisons, and in 1866 ministered to victims of the cholera plague. Long interested in prison reform, having studied it in Europe, she tended the city's female convicts. In time she established a Good Shepherd convent to assume this task and persuaded the city to place women prisoners under the administration of nuns. For ten years these sisters ran the jail, teaching skills to the women and making them self-supporting. In addition to all of these undertakings, Peter, who for many years lived the life of a semi-religious, continued her interest in art. She tried to elevate public taste through her presidency of the Cincinnati Academy of Fine Arts and by collecting copies of major paintings.

Peter had no difficulty reconciling her Catholicism and a type of feminism. Obviously she believed women had many talents and should exercise them, and as a result she advocated that there be no limitations upon their opportunities to learn. Furthermore, she advocated better employment opportunities and fairer property rights for women, attributing feminine failure to men who were responsible for keeping women weak and ignorant. Yet there were limitations upon Peter's feminism. Despite her friendship with the suffragist Thomas

Wentworth Higginson, she never advocated political equality and warned wives not to rival their husbands but to complement then instead.[13]

The services of Caroline Earle White (1833–1916), although quite different from Peter's, were like hers in that they also were partially the result of a devout faith from which she seemed to draw strength. The daughter of the drafter of the Pennsylvania Constitution, she became a convert at age twenty-one, two years after marrying the prominent Catholic attorney Richard White. Deeply concerned with the welfare of children, she was one of the organizers of the Philadelphia Society for the Prevention of Cruelty to Children and was instrumental in introducing "humane" educational methods into public and parochial schools. White, in what was considered an unusual achievement for a woman in 1867, founded the Pennsylvania Society for the Prevention of Cruelty to Animals. For forty-five years she was active in that organization and was a prime mover in the founding of the American Anti-Vivisection Society in Philadelphia in 1883. In addition for many years she was the chair of the Ladies Auxiliary of the American Catholic Historical Society.[14]

It was not a husband but an Irish hairdresser, Harriet Ryan, who first roused the interest of Emma Forbes Carey (1833–1916) in the church. A convert at age twenty-two, she began a lifelong interest in Catholic social agencies, especially the House of the Good Shepherd, a reformatory for wayward girls. Carey's sister was the wife of Harvard's Professor Louis Agassiz, one of the foremost figures in establishing Radcliffe College. To safeguard the spiritual interests of her coreligionists at that institution, Carey founded the Radcliffe Catholic Club, which met at her home to foster an interest in courtesy and kindness and promote "fears of liberality."[15] Thus guest lecturers were all conservative and spoke on noncontroversial subjects. The most daring activity was raising money for the poor.[16] Despite her commitment to ladylike values, for twenty-five years Carey was a member of the Massachusetts Prison Commission, where she became friends with her fellow commissioner Katherine Conway, another frequent contributor to Catholic periodicals.[17]

One of the more unusual converts was Mary Gove Nichols (1810–84), a woman's rights advocate and health reformer who, with her second husband, opened a school of life that encouraged the water cure and free love. Moved by the spirits of St. Francis and St. Ignatius, along with her husband and many followers she entered the church in 1857 and lectured on Catholicism and health until 1861, when she took up residence in England.[18]

When bright, aggressive women turned to the church as an outlet for their energies, the belief that women were naturally pious mushroomed. Many Catholic females, however, challenged the notion of subservience to clerical authority that was supposed to be a hallmark of this religiosity. Among the earliest examples of female assertiveness in church affairs was that of "Hoganism" or "trusteeism," triggered by the refusal of Reverend William V. Hogan to return to a parish rectory when ordered to do so by Bishop Henry Conwell (1784–1842) of Philadelphia. Hogan, who had been reported to the bishop because of sexual misconduct, had his faculties withdrawn when he refused to comply. Despite this censure and his pamphlets attacking the bishop and the local clergy, the lay trustees of St. Mary's, who claimed ownership of the church, appointed Hogan pastor. He continued serving in this capacity although excommunicated and ignored a decision by the Pennsylvania Supreme Court upholding Conwell's right to oust him. Bloody riots between the followers of Conwell and Hogan continued until the issue died out when the priest left Philadelphia and the bishops agreed to accept trustee recommendations.

All during this fray many female parishioners fervently supported the priest. When rebuffed in their demands to see Conwell, they publicly attacked his position and resolved not to recognize the authority of the new pastor. Conwell himself complained of the "contemptuous treatment" he received at their hands, and John Connolly, bishop of New York (1750–1825), expressed the hope to Conwell that the Almighty would "enlighten these poor deluded creatures."[19] The testimony of Hogan's female supporters was of considerable significance when a jury, after five minutes' deliberation, found him not guilty of assaulting a Mary Connell for resisting his advances.[20]

A half-century later, under somewhat similar circumstances, a disproportionate number of Catholic female parishioners and advocates of reform followed one of their favorite priests into excommunication. The Reverend Edward McGlynn, a theological liberal and political progressive, was excommunicated by New York's Archbishop Corrigan in 1887. The prelate also declared attendance at meetings of the Anti-Poverty Society a serious sin. This organization had been founded by McGlynn to spread the doctrine that poverty was the result of the abuse of private property. McGlynn, however, continued his campaign appealing to men and especially to women to join a crusade for social justice. Large numbers of females defied the bishop, attending society meetings at Cooper Union and organizing a boycott of the parish from which McGlynn had been ousted. On one occasion the women advocates of the priest occupied that church's basement and had to be ejected by police.

One of his champions was Sister Mary Francis Clare (Margaret T. Cusack), the Irish-born founder of the Sisters of Peace of St. Joseph, whose mission included the care of homeless and friendless girls. Cusack wrote a 187-page book on the McGlynn controversy, charging church dignitaries with ignoring the destitute (especially working-class women), forcing McGlynn into acts of rashness, and treating him in an unforgivable fashion. These accusations infuriated her ordinary, Archbishop Winand M. Wigger (1841–1901) of Newark, whose response helped drive Cusack from the church.[21]

The authoritarian and conservative Bishop McCloskey, who had been defied by nuns in his diocese, was also challenged by some of the lay women of Louisville in 1875. Forty females, contemptuously dismissed in the diocesan paper as "a few apostate old women," sent petitions to his ecclesiastical superior Archbishop John B. Purcell (1800–1883), Cincinnati, dissenting from McCloskey's policy of transferring and publicly lambasting their pastor because he had been uncooperative in the bishop's assessment system.[22]

On occasion even the humblest of Catholic women challenged the hierarchy. In 1863 Harriet Thompson, a free black, wrote to Pope Pius IX complaining that the education of blacks in the United States was neglected and imploring him to intervene. She charged that this neglect happened because most priests were Irish and thus opposed letting blacks mix with whites. Especially deplorable was the attitude of Archbishop Hughes, who, Thompson alleged, forced a Catholic school for blacks to close because he did not consider the "colored race" part of his flock.[23]

Thompson's charge about the Irish reflected the changing complexion of American Catholicism as its ranks were swelled by thousands of immigrants from the Emerald Isle. At the end of the Revolution there were less than twenty-five thousand American Catholics. But there were a half million by 1840 and three million by 1860, consisting primarily of wealthy Anglo-Americans along the border states, poor Germans in the rural areas, and many destitute Irish in the cities.[24]

As was true throughout the nineteenth century, a large percentage of Irish immigrants, more than that of any other nationality, were single females. According to one historian, their flight to the United States was part of an Irish Woman's Liberation Movement.[25] These women, who certainly were not the personification of the American virtue of submissiveness, frequently turned to domestic employment as they spoke English and were unskilled, single, and at liberty to live in. Free room offset the disadvantages of long and irregular hours and enabled them to avoid sweatshops and slums. The pay, albeit low, was adequate, so that by scrimping they could send money home to Ireland. It was often difficult for these women to adhere to church rules on fasting and attendance at mass, and sometimes their employers would pressure them to convert to Protestantism. Nevertheless, they earned a reputation as devout, virtuous, and pure.[26]

Those who were unable to find employment as domestics usually found work in the sewing trades, the second-highest category of employment for Irish women at the eve of the Civil War. These were unskilled, low-paying positions and because of poor working conditions and the necessity of living close to the factory were viewed by some as less desirable than domestic service.[27] Even Irish female immigrants had begun to divide into two classes: ladies and women.

Wages were also low for the Irish male, who was typically unskilled and had little choice but to work long hours away from home. As a result his wife was the dominant force in family life, handling the finances and often exercising a manipulative power over him. Occasionally, because of either necessity or ambition to climb the social order, mores were defied and a wife worked. Whenever possible, though, her employment was in the home, either sewing or running a boardinghouse.[28]

Sometimes because of a lack of opportunity, a demoralized husband fled, leaving his wife and children to fend for themselves. Thus, abandonment and the death of Irish males at an early age because of cholera or accidents in building railroads and canals left a large percentage of Irish-American households headed by females (18 percent in 1855).[29]

By the end of the Civil War these conditions that forced Catholic women to work led moralists to modify their perceptions of ladies' roles. Increasingly their attention was directed to working conditions rather than to efforts to persuade women that their place was in the home. But clerical suggestions concerning employment were frequently impractical. A popular guide for Catholic working girls first published in 1868 urged them not to rebel against their employers but to accept their wages as the will of God, a "favor of His love." If their earnings were low, they should remember that plain living is in keeping with God's will. Hard work, it was alleged, not only was in accord with scriptural injunctions but pleased both God and employers and led to promotions. Catholic women, however, were warned to avoid working in hotels and saloons or where gambling was present. This treatise, which went through at least thirty-one editions, assumed that wage-earning women were single and would quit their employment when married. The Sisters of Charity of New York were much more practical: in 1873 they opened a day nursery to care for children of working mothers.[30]

There was a rapid turnover of Irish domestics, for at an early age most left their employer to marry (usually an Irishman of similar background). By then these servants had become familiar with and influenced by middle-class life-styles and values. As early as 1843, an article in a Catholic journal had thought this knowledge a valuable by-product of such employment, hoping servants would be introduced to habits of neatness and order "with which they have hitherto not been properly disciplined."[31] It would appear that among the mores imitated by domestics was family limitation. Both Irish and German immigrant women who had experience as domestics (which includes also almost all Germans) averaged less than one child more than native-born women. Apparently many other Catholic women also attempted to limit the number of children.[32]

Churchmen expressed no real concern about contraception until after World War I but nevertheless found violations of sexual morality by Catholic women in the mid-nineteenth century shocking. Temptations stemming from poverty and low wages and the perils of the city drove many women into prostitution. Of two thousand harlots in New York in 1855, over one-third were Irish born, nearly half were Catholic, and 40 percent had been engaged in low-paying domestic service or needle trades. Brothels in Philadelphia during the same period were concentrated in the Irish district, and until the end of the century a large percentage of that city's prostitutes were daughters of the Emerald Isle.[33]

Despite the doubts of Bishop Hughes that fallen females could ever be redeemed (a view probably shared by other churchmen), religious communities of women, particularly the Sisters of Good Shepherd and Sisters of Mercy, began a special mission for them. By 1870 in every major city there were centers designed to reform these women by getting them to return to the sacraments, especially communion, teaching them a trade, and restoring their health, including the treatment of venereal problems. Reverend Thomas Preston, a convert, founded the Sisters of Divine Compassion, whose special task was to assist young girls who had lost their innocence. This order sought out these outcasts, provided them with shelter, prepared them for employment, placed then in jobs, and encouraged a religious vocation in those so inclined.[34] By 1893 the Good Shepherd Sisters were maintaining 150 houses, had cared for twenty thousand females, and had accepted many into their community.[35] The men and women engaged in these efforts probably manifested the qualities that Father Richard L. Burtsell, a New York pastor, believed necessary for these endeavors: men who were "good...pure minded, self confident, and not over nice" and women who would not look with sternness on another woman's crimes but would have sympathy for "unfortunates."[36]

Some religious communities attempted to prevent prostitution by assisting young Catholic women to cope with city life. In major urban areas, institutions were established to house young girls, to care for them, and to teach them trades. In 1846 Bishop Hughes established a home for newly arrived immigrant females where they were taught sewing or laundry work and then placed with an employer. In only five years over eight thousand immigrant women were assisted there. Mary Corbett and a handful of acquaintances founded a residence for sick and friendless servant girls in Boston. The organizers became nuns in time, and the residence the Working Girls' Home. Other cities also had religiously inspired women, especially the Sisters of Mercy, reaching out to the lonely and poor in efforts to keep them virtuous and pure.[37] This was also the objective of the Social Purity Movement, one of the early examples of ecumenism, as it was supported by numbers of the Catholic hierarchy, Protestant clergy, and nonsectarian leaders.[38]

Church efforts to prevent fornication were designed not merely to preserve female chastity but to prevent the even worse sins of abortion and infanticide. Although deliberately induced miscarriages were a serious sin according to confessional guides, prior to the Civil War Catholic publications seldom dealt with abortion. It was not until 1858 that a prominent church spokesman, Bishop John B. Fitzpatrick of Boston (1812–66), attacked the practice. Nevertheless, it became so widespread that ten years later churchmen began a concentrated effort against it by reprinting Bishop Martin Spalding's pastoral on the subject in diocesan papers throughout the country. Although the incidence of abortion among Catholic women may very well have been less than that of the populace at large, there is little doubt that Catholics, especially immigrants, engaged in it. A Chicago doctor urged the archbishop of Cashel, Ireland, to discourage the emigration of women to the United States, as abortion was "becoming common among Irish females...shockingly prevalent among Irish-Americans."[39]

One of the Catholic manuals at the end of the century even warned of the sin of indirect abortion — miscarriages caused by recklessness such as passion, long journeys, heavy lifting, jumping, dancing, and tight clothing. It concluded with the dire warning that "what has been said of riding in trains applies with redoubled force to the riding in the jerkey trolley-car, especially with women raised in the cities, where effeminacy, want of air and sun-light, variety of dress and sedentary habits conspire to make the young mother's womb an open grave."[40]

Apparently Catholics were also guilty of infanticide, as an 1871 New York study concluded that all races and creeds were answerable for the crime. To prevent the heinous offense religious orders opened foundling homes, often funded by laywomen. The center in New York reduced the number of infant killings from about 100 to 150 a month to between 10 and 15. By 1892 it was estimated that because of social services the crime was practically stamped out.[41] In Cleveland, too, the results of such homes were most gratifying. An early chronicler of St. Ann's Maternity Home and Infant Asylum wrote, "Rarely was it heard after the house was opened that infants were destroyed by their natural mothers, or others, to conceal a crime; thus adding to their first sin, a second of murder."[42]

The reduction of this type of offense was also attributable to the increased solicitude and understanding provided single pregnant women and the care rendered their newborns. As early as 1852 a hospital for unmarried mothers was founded under Catholic auspices in Buffalo. By the 1870s there was one in just about every diocese — including Cleveland, whose bishop, Richard Gilmour (1824–91), originally opposed such an institution, believing it an endorsement of unwed motherhood.[43] Gilmour was not the only one with trepidations. When Boston's Carney Hospital in 1870 set aside a ward for abandoned infants and single mothers, Carney's widow was infuriated and ceased her financial support, compelling Bishop Williams to purchase land and open St. Mary's Asylum to care for illegitimates.[44] In these hospitals the anonymity of mothers was protected as they received pre- and postnatal care while efforts were being made to place both the baby and the mother.[45]

Closely allied to this work was the opening of orphanages for youth left homeless — especially due to the ravages of cholera. Until about 1840 the care of orphans was almost incidental to the educational mission of the church. However, from 1840 to 1860 large numbers of men and women, including many nuns, at great sacrifice concentrated on founding and administering these homes. By the time of the Civil War nearly every diocese had an orphanage, and Catholics, aided in part by the Society for the Protection of Destitute Catholic Children, were succeeding in reducing the placement of Catholic waifs in Protestant homes.[46]

Church work, charitable endeavors, wage earning, and changing sexual mores had begun to erode the reality and in some cases the ideology of women's roles and virtues. Traditional lines were further blurred by women, lay and religious, trekking west and settling on the frontier. Occasionally Catholic women went alone to teach in frontier towns, to find a husband, or, armed with a shotgun, to follow the lonely path of the homesteader planting, plowing, and building.[47]

Usually, however, they went as part of a family. The decision to move was the husbands', and wives acquiesced in order to hold the family together, even when they had serious doubts about the wisdom of the journey. During the dangerous passage females continued to fulfill traditional roles, insisting upon having Sunday devotions, cooking meals, washing clothes, tending the children, and often riding in the wagons with their offspring. One observer encountering a caravan of Catholics on the way to St. John's, Nebraska, in 1856 described their evening encampment. "Tents were pitched, fires burning brightly, the *ladies* [italics mine] were preparing the evening meal, while their leige lords were enjoying their pipes and a social chat, and a score or more young paddies were making the woods reverberate with their childish sports."[48]

Regardless of efforts to maintain women's place, notions of their work and that of men increasingly overlapped. Women were expected to round up buffalo chips for fires, even if it meant wandering far from camp. They also assisted in pushing the wagons when mired down and walked beside them when it was necessary to conserve the strength of the animals. Women's sphere and place widened to the accompaniment of personal growth and a sense of self-assurance and self-worth.[49]

From 1841 to 1869, when the railroad was completed, 350,000 pioneers made their way to the Pacific Coast, crossing deserts, traversing mountains, and braving Indians. The first Irish Catholic party to enter California by blazing a path through the Sierra Nevadas was that of the Martin Murphys. Murphy, Sr., a widower, his sons, daughters, grandchildren, and other relatives had come from Canada to Missouri. Desiring an area more amenable to Catholics, they set out for Mexico (California). For eight months the party was baked by the sun or chilled by the cold. Frequently on the verge of starvation, they resorted to eating animal hides. During these trials Murphy's daughter-in-law, Mary (Bolger), was steadfast, leading and inspiring the other women. Once the family became established in southern California, she became renowned for her devotion to the church and established a reputation for supporting charities, especially education.[50]

The hardships of the Murphys paled into insignificance when compared with those Catholics who crossed the plains with the Donner Party in 1846. Included in that group were another Murphy family (probably Catholic) and Patrick Breen, with his wife, Elizabeth, and seven children. After crossing the Great Salt Lake Valley, the party, caught by early blizzards, was snowbound in mountain passes for seven months. Trapped with the Breens was thirteen-year-old Virginia Reed. When the girl was ill she was slipped extra food by Elizabeth Breen, who was responsible for doling out rations. After devouring their animals, then the hides that helped shelter them, the starving band, including the Breens and Murphys, resorted to cannibalism. They were among the forty-seven survivors of the original eighty-seven who had first camped in the valley. Reed was so impressed by the religious faith shown by the Breens during the ordeal that she became a convert to Catholicism.[51]

More typical were the experiences of the Medleys, a prosperous Catholic farming family lured to California by dreams of gold and a climate that would restore the wife's health. The mother, father, three daughters (ages ten to seven), and two sons (seven and four) waited three weeks to cross the Missouri River, where they joined with a team of twenty wagons progressing about twelve miles a day. The mother, described as "a religious woman, gentle, refined, and devoted to the family," died of cholera and was buried along the trail. The seven-year-old broke his leg falling from a wagon, and the four-year-old lost all of his hair to mountain fever. During the five-month trek to Sacramento, ten-year-old Mary in assuming much of the responsibility for the family fulfilled the function of a woman, not a child. It is little wonder that she was mature enough to marry at age fifteen.[52]

Surviving on the frontier was often as dangerous as crossing the Great Plains, for living conditions were no better. Many Catholic adventurers lived in isolated log cabins with mud-filled cracks, dirt floors, and greased paper windows. Others lived in sod houses. One Catholic family sold their land in Wisconsin, journeyed four hundred miles to homestead in snow-filled Missouri, only to have the mother and her newborn twins die in isolation.[53] On the other hand, a mother of five, Mary Ann Mahan, known as the Fearless Frontier Woman, had to be dissuaded by army guards from shooting two Indians who were being brought to Fort Dodge for hanging. When they escaped, an angry Mahan, armed with only a revolver, hunted them with dogs for several days before losing their trail.[54] Theresa O'Neill Campbell, a Sacred Heart graduate, trekked to Texas with her husband but in

1842 had to flee from Mexican forces. In subsequent years, even when Indians posed a danger, she was left to manage the ranch with only Indian women and a few slaves to assist her.[55] Even the wives of regular army officers adapted with difficulty, if at all. Mariquitta Coudray accompanied her husband, Jules Garesche, to his lonely post in Texas, where their four-month-old son died, leaving the mother lonely and disconsolate. On one occasion Garesche wrote to his mother-in-law that he was delighted with the necessity of leaving for a few days, as his nervous system was upset by the sight of his suffering wife and children. Intolerant of his spouse's weakness, he wrote to her, "I'm almost angry with you Mariquitta first, for your want of submission to Almighty God, and next, for your want of obedience, of respect, of affection for myself."[56]

In contrast to the devout if not always long-suffering Garesches was Sarah A. Bowman. When her husband enlisted during the Mexican War, Bowman followed his unit as a laundress and cook and even served meals during the seven-day shelling of Fort Brown. When she was refused a musket during the engagement at Buena Vista, she traversed the battlefield nursing the wounded. After the death of her husband she opened a restaurant in El Paso in 1849 and then one in Yuma, a town so wild that Bowman carried pistols for her own protection. For several years during this period she was sexually active with a variety of men. After her second marriage in 1860, however, she seemed to have returned to a more conventional life-style. In 1866 she was buried in the post cemetery at Yuma after Catholic rites at a military funeral.[57]

Nelly Cashman, an Irish immigrant, mixed adventure and piety. She supported her sister and her sister's five children, raising them when their mother died. The first white woman to penetrate the interior of British Columbia, she ran a boardinghouse for miners. With the proceeds she opened a restaurant in Tucson and two more in Tombstone, where she also established a hotel. Cashman wandered throughout the West, prospected in Alaska, where she founded the Midnight Sun Mining Company, and launched a cafe in Dawson City and a store in Fairbanks. She died at about age seventy-four in Alaska in 1925. A religious woman, Cashman was responsible for the erection of the first Catholic church in Tombstone, where she organized the Miner's Hospital Association and the Irish National League, of which she was treasurer. She raised money for the poor of both Tombstone and Dawson as well as gathering funds for a church and hospital in the latter city. She was so respected by miners that she was able to intervene and save the superintendent of mines at Tombstone from being kidnapped and hanged by strikers.[58]

In addition to the western migration of individual Catholics, there were concerted efforts to encourage groups of them to leave the crowded East. In the 1840s the inducement was to abandon cities ridden with Know-Nothings for the hospitable West, but in later years the stress was on escaping the poverty and sinfulness of urban life. Both Bishops John Ireland and John Lancaster Spalding (1840–1916), Peoria, champions of the Colonization Society, enthusiastically subscribed to the myth of the yeoman farmer as they encouraged coreligionists from Ireland and the United States to strike out for the land of opportunity.[59]

Discouraged by religious hostility, Catholics of Philadelphia and Baltimore in 1842 established the German Catholic Brotherhood, which sponsored the migration of twenty-five families to the wilderness of western Pennsylvania to found a prejudice-free colony.[60] Twenty-five other families who had fled to Iowa because of Know-Nothing opposition left that state in 1856 and trekked to Nebraska. There, one of the earliest arrivals, during a particularly horrible winter, gave birth unattended and shortly afterward died of exposure and fright from Indians.[61] In that same decade a large number of Catholics, sponsored by the Chicago Land Society, settled at New Ulm, Minnesota. When they were attacked by the Sioux in 1862, one woman, after her husband and hired hands had been murdered, hid for twelve days. During that time she lived on berries and, fearful her dog might reveal her position, strangled him with her apron.[62]

Inspired by Ireland's vision, four thousand families from the Emerald Isle and the East came west between 1875 and 1885, but even though buttressed by church groups, many settlements failed. John O'Neil, an army veteran supported by the *Irish World* and by Patrick Ford, that paper's editor, established the town of O'Neil with over one hundred men, women, and children. Inexperienced in agriculture, plagued by a drought, and denied the solace of a priest, the colony barely survived, for the young sought education and wealth elsewhere.[63] A similar fate awaited John Sweetman's experiment in Minnesota. Passage to America was financed; seed, food, and equipment were advanced; and a priest (both rare and overworked in the West) was found for the settlement. However, rural life was unappealing. Unmarried women flocked to the city to work as domestics, and in two years 34 percent of the families had abandoned the project. The experiment of an Irish Arcadia collapsed, and land was sold to anyone.[64]

In addition to the Irish, large numbers of Italians in search of a better life migrated westward — especially in the 1880s to the Southwest (Colorado, Utah, New Mexico, and Arizona). Italian women, who were among the European peoples most subservient to their men, often participated in the decision to migrate. To aid in adjusting to their new environment, they created a female network based on relatives, churches, or provincial origins. Traditional roles were further undermined by their leadership in Italian clubs and societies and by working for wages outside the home. But even in instances where well-to-do husbands maintained their traditional dominance, their daughters, unlike many Italian girls in the East, completed their education and thereby began a life less encumbered by domestic dominance.[65]

Women of other nationalities also gained independence as wage earners in the West, even if their vocation was found in such traditional female duties as teaching school, running a boardinghouse, or managing an inn.[66]

Among the successful adventurers was Ignatius Donnelly, who with his schoolteacher bride, Katherine McCaffrey, left his Philadelphia home in 1856 for Minnesota. In time he served his adopted state as governor, congressman, and senator and ran for vice-president of the United States in 1900 as a Populist, a reform party that he was instrumental in establishing. At the time of the Donnellys' arrival, Hastings, Minnesota, was a frontier community; homes were spartan, and hostile Indians hovered near by. Katherine, a profoundly religious woman, was disappointed to discover that the Catholic church was also in "pitiful" condition. To enrich religious life she established a Sunday school and a church choir, the first in Dakota country and perhaps the first in present-day Minnesota. She also undertook charitable campaigns including raising funds for the Baptist church. Ignatius, an agnostic, admired these initiatives. He also respected her advice on his political career and her assistance in preparing his speeches. Most likely she influenced his views on women and offset the hidebound conservatism of his sister Eleanor by reminding him of the injustice females suffered under the double standard.[67] Ignatius came to sympathize with woman's rights, believing females needed the vote to improve their working conditions and urged legislation to achieve this goal. Nevertheless, he still revered ladies as ennobling and superior to men. In his novel *The Golden Bottle*, Sophia represented the woman of the future: educated, intelligent, heroic, affectionate, and refined.[68] His views were shared by his wife as reflected in the valentine she composed for him:

Look on her, and behold your heart's delight
In the full bloom of tasting twenty-nine,
Your little hero of a hundred fights
Your wife, your charming Valentine.[69]

Even more than that of laywomen, settlement in the West by nuns
shattered shibboleths as those women traversed difficult terrain to
minister to Indians or to build schools, hospitals, and orphanages in
frontier towns. Sometimes they came directly from Europe (Ireland,
France, Germany, or Belgium), more often from the eastern parts
of the United States. Those who left the Old World usually booked
the cheapest passage, often on rat-infested, poorly constructed ves-
sels. Sometimes they sailed around Cape Horn or more likely crossed
the Isthmus of Panama by lake steamer or mule. Those that went
overland traveled by flatboat, steamboat, stagecoach, covered wagon,
muleback, or even sleigh, through boiling desert, icy mountains, and
flooded riverbanks. They were racked by cholera and plagued with
horseflies, wolves, mountain lions, mosquitoes, lice, and snakes. Suffering from a lack of bedding and a shortage of supplies, many ate
buffalo meat for the first time. One nun after crossing the desert was
so parched by thirst that her tongue was cracked and bleeding.[70]

Mother Mary Magdalen wrote to a schoolmate describing her trek
and that of five other nuns who left Loretto, Kentucky, for Santa Fe
in 1854. One of her companions died of cholera while sailing from
St. Louis to Independence, another was so seriously stricken that she
returned to the motherhouse, and Magdalen herself was "severely attacked by the dreadful scourge, but stopped, with the help of God,
at the gates of death." Nevertheless, she continued doggedly across
"immense plains with meandering creeks and rivers, those numberless ferocious looking animals...and fearful storms of wind, rain,
lightning, and thunder....But nothing frightened us more than the
Indians. For a time, we were surrounded by hundreds of those sons
of the forests."[71]

One group of nuns reported that males in their caravan were more
afraid than they, when going through Indian territory. Nevertheless,
sisters had every reason for fear. In 1865 four Sisters of Charity
opened a school in Santa Fe at the request of Bishop John B. Lamy
(1814–88). These nuns, the first to serve in that city, had arrived after a hazardous journey involving a boat to Omaha, stage through
Indian country, and open coach to their destination. Two years later,
after enlisting five more sisters, Lamy and the new recruits joined
a caravan of eighty wagons heading west. After a difficult crossing

of the Arkansas River, they fended off an attack by a small band of Indians. Shortly thereafter one nun died as cholera struck the pioneers. All were suffering from thirst when a large party of hundreds of Kiowas attacked. During the seven-hour battle one sister tended the wounded, but another, eighteen-year-old Sister Alphonse Thompson, died of fright. The men in the convoy had planned to kill the nuns if necessary, for as one sister related, death would be preferable to capture by Indians. After the battle the caravan continued, and the remaining three nuns went on to Santa Fe, where they opened an industrial school.[72]

When sisters reached their destination they usually found that women were extremely scarce, so much so that in some instances they received marriage proposals. Often, with but little help from males, the nuns proceeded to establish schools, frequently doing some of the carpentry themselves. Their institutions at first were designed to prepare girls for careers as housewives by teaching cooking, sewing, and serving, the same skills taught at Indian schools. Sometimes a vocational curriculum was introduced, but as towns grew, academies, similar to those in the East, were founded to prepare young ladies.[73]

The buildings, especially in the early years, were primitive. Sometimes they were made of sod or adobe or stone. Often they only had mud floors or mud roofs and failed to shut out the cold. Indian mission structures were the worst, usually poorly heated and sometimes the abode of rattlesnakes. Yet nuns were known to stay at these missions as long as fifty years.[74]

In 1829 Mother Matheron wrote to the Sacred Heart superior general from her frontier post: "When it rains, the kitchen is always flooded. And now sometimes, little mice awaken me by gnawing on my fingers. Not a bad morning call."[75] Frequently, the nuns were insufficiently clothed, had to haul their water great distances, and were forced to beg to survive. Furthermore, despite their religious garb, they never were really safe from frontier lawlessness. Those at Indian missions feared attacks from hostile tribes, while those in the area of "white civilization" were hardly safer. In 1852 in Brownsville, Texas, a Comanche slipped into a convent chapel and stole the sisters' cloaks. In Santa Fe, a few years later, a man forced his way into the academy and shot two students. On Christmas Eve 1865 a madman wounded one of the patients in the sisters' hospital there.[76]

Despite hardships, these religious followed the ever-moving frontier, performing their acts of mercy. They moved into the Southwest after the Mexican War and learned Spanish to enable them to serve the Catholic community. They by-passed the Great Plains to minister to those in the California goldfields and then followed the mining and ranching frontiers into the last wilderness. In so doing, they showed imagination and adaptability. Like communities of a century before, European nuns adjusted their rules on enclosure to survive in the ever-practical West. Teaching orders added nursing and care of orphans to their rules, and practically all nuns tended smallpox and cholera victims.[77] So successful were these missionaries that the Beecher family, the nation's most prominent educators and preachers, urged Protestant women to follow the example of nuns and go west to ensure the preservation of the American character in that area.[78]

To many sisters hardships were really a mark of God's favor, further enabling them to serve his will in religious life. Yet some must have shared the thoughts of Sister Catherine Mallon, who, despite toiling from 5:00 A.M. to 11:00 or 12:00 P.M. in primitive New Mexico, believed that her calling had saved her from a traditional woman's lot. When she met poor mothers of five or six children cooking for twenty to forty men at a mining camp, she wrote, "Oh! How often I thanked the good God for saving me from such a fate." She went on to relate how she met many a beautiful young woman who had left family and friends to share inconvenience and hardship with a man who might forsake and abuse her. She wished her fellow sisters could see these misguided females so "that they might the better realize the great gift bestowed by God in calling them to the religious state."[79]

The humility of these pioneering nuns led to anonymity; fortunately, however, accounts of the adventures of some have been preserved. About 1880 a graduate nurse and licensed pharmacist, Sister of Charity Mary de Sales Leheney (b. 1856), arrived in Santa Fe. In that city's St. Vincent's hospital she nursed and performed operations and in 1901 was granted a medical license. Leheney was the first certified physician in the territory of New Mexico.[80] Sister Joseph of the Sacred Heart (Esther Pariseau, 1823–1902), a Sister of Providence from Montreal, spent over five weeks to reach the Oregon Territory via the Isthmus of Panama route. Once there, despite being robbed while a passenger in a stagecoach, she continued to beg money in cities and mining camps, raising funds to construct a variety of charitable institutions. Having learned carpentry from her father, she worked as architect, contractor, and builder, often camping in the wilderness to construct or supervise the construction of her projects. By the time of her death in 1902, she had founded eleven hospitals, seven academies, five Indian schools, two orphanages, and an old-age home.[81]

In response to an appeal for nuns to serve in the West, Sister Mary Amadeus (Sarah Dunne, 1846–1919) left Ohio for Miles City, Montana, where she established both a boarding and a parish school. She then journeyed for four days to work with the Cheyenne at a mission considered so dangerous that the priests fled, leaving it to her and two other nuns. Known to the Indians as Great Holy White Chief Woman, Dunne also founded and taught at schools for the Blackfoot and Crow and raised money for them when the federal government withdrew funds for such education. Despite a railroad accident in 1910, which left her in constant pain and needing a cane to walk, Dunne sailed to Alaska to serve the Indians there. She established a mission and convent so deep in the wilderness it could be reached only by dogsled. This courageous and nontraditional woman was buried in Montana with the Indians she loved.[82]

One of the most interesting of these adventuresome nuns was the Italian-born Sister Blandina (Rosa Maria Segale, 1850–1941), who recorded her experiences in a journal for her sister (who, like Blandina, was a Sister of Charity). At age twenty-two Segale left Ohio for Trinidad, Colorado, where under primitive conditions she ran a public school. While there she intervened with the sheriff to prevent a lynching and tended a wounded member of Billy the Kid's gang. Allegedly from that time on, Billy always treated Sisters of Charity courteously. She later met Billy, who, in gratitude for her ministrations and in response to her appeal, changed his mind about shooting the Trinidad physician who had refused to remove a bullet from a gang member. In 1876 Segale went to Santa Fe, where she taught school, raised funds for a hospital and orphan asylum, and built an industrial school for Indian girls. She was recalled to her mother-house in Cincinnati in 1894 to care for immigrant Italians and was as successful in this endeavor as in those in the West. In Ohio much of her energy was spent in what today would be described as social work. Furthermore, she served as a probation officer with the juvenile court, initiated legal action against white slavers, and established three schools and four settlement houses for the Italian community.[83]

While these western women were displaying the "male" virtues of courage, innovation, and pragmatism, other women through their participation in the Civil War and in facing the problems of Reconstruction were also demonstrating that stereotypes of women had little relationship to reality.

Chapter 6

CIVIL WAR AND RECONSTRUCTION: A CHALLENGE TO "LADIES"

Even those who believed most steadfastly in the ideology of domesticity were willing to temper their convictions temporarily in the name of patriotism. Thus the Civil War not only provided opportunities for large numbers of women to assume responsibilities and tasks usually reserved for men but also led to a modification of stereotypical ideology as women were encouraged to break from traditional roles. (This reassessment was even more characteristic of World Wars I and II.)

During the struggle over slavery that had precipitated the conflict, however, the voices of Catholics were muted. Few if any Catholic women, or men for that matter, assumed a prominent position in the abolitionist controversy. Like the church itself, they tended to see the issue as political rather than religious and rejected the notion of the sinfulness of slave owners. (There was not one Catholic among the over three hundred officers in the American Anti-Slave Society from 1833 to 1840.)[1] Indeed religious communities of men and women owned slaves. Catholic owners, like other masters throughout the South, cannot be classified easily. There were those such as Mrs. Reese Cook, who must have been quite cruel. Her slaves ran away, then changed their minds and returned and murdered her. On the other hand, Catherine Minor of Mississippi was uncomfortable with the institution, writing: "I was always an abolitionist at heart, but I am afraid not a philanthropist. I did not know how to set [my slaves] free, without wretchedness to them, and utter ruin to myself."[2] Probably Mrs. Thomas Hutchinson was more typical. She had her

80

slaves (nearly four hundred in number) baptized and built a special chapel for them. A few years later she fled from the area. During the war the church was burned down and priests were not available, yet when discovered by missionaries in 1868, well over one hundred of her slaves had managed to cling to the faith.[3]

Although not prominent in the controversy preceding the war, Catholic women did not hesitate to join the struggle once the conflict had begun.[4] Sometimes their contributions were along traditional lines. In both the North and the South they rolled bandages, made clothing for soldiers, sewed flags for combat units, served in hospitals, encouraged their men to enlist, and established committees to care for families of soldiers and provide relief.[5] Catholic wives of military commanders applauded their husbands' exploits, while assuming the entire responsibility for their families. (Ellen Sherman even interceded with President Abraham Lincoln to further her husband's career.) However, confederate General P. T. Beauregard believed this type of "domestic" support was inadequate. His Creole wife was seriously ill in Union-occupied New Orleans for two years before her death in 1864. At that time the general noted, "I well know that her beautiful soul, her generous, and patriotic heart preferred the salvation of the country to the joy of seeing me." But after the South's defeat he refused permission for a sketch of her to appear in a book of prominent Confederate women. "I would accept with pleasure," he wrote, "if the one I loved so dearly had done more than to pray and suffer in silence for the success of our sacred cause."[6]

Catholic women from both sides of the Mason-Dixon Line did more than pray and suffer. They accompanied their husbands, sometimes into the conflict itself, nursing, cooking, laundering, and cheering the army on.[7] The wife of General James A. Mulligan accompanied her husband into battle and trailed him into a southern prisoner-of-war camp, where she remained until he was paroled.[8] One of the most famous of the camp followers was probably Catholic, Bridget Divers, "the Irish Biddy." Attaching herself to her husband's unit, the First Michigan Cavalry, she acted as chaplain, nurse, and supply steward and even rode into battle with the men, where two horses were shot from under her. She also scouted, raided, picketed, and twice rallied retreating troops.[9]

Other women participated even more directly. In 1862 an Irish-born female named Hodges enlisted under the pseudonym Albert D. J. Cashier and fought in several campaigns during the three years she served in the Union army. (Not until 1911, when she was injured in an automobile accident, was Cashier's sex revealed).[10] Loreta

Velazquez, the wife of a Confederate officer, passed herself off as Lieutenant Harry T. Bufort and, when her sex was discovered after being shot in battle, reenlisted as a private. After once again being wounded, discovered, and discharged, she spent the remainder of the war visiting Confederates in northern prisons.[11]

The South's most famous woman spy, Rose O'Neal Greenhow, had been active in James Buchanan's presidential campaign. The forty-four-year-old widowed aunt of Stephen A. Douglas used her political connections in Washington to gather intelligence for the Rebels. General George B. McClellan allegedly claimed, "She knows my plans better than Lincoln or the Cabinet and has four times compelled me to drop them." Placed under arrest with her eight-year-old daughter and guarded day and night, she still managed to transmit data to the Confederates. Brazenly she wrote to Secretary of State William H. Seward, defying him to imprison her soul. Yet she protested the denial of her religious rights and consequently was allowed to attend mass — but under armed escort. The Political Prisoners Commission was unsure how to handle "a lady" spy and therefore released Greenhow on the condition she not return to the North for the remainder of the war. Instead she went to France and England on diplomatic missions for the Confederacy. On her way back she was drowned and later was buried with full military honors.[12] Some southern women were even willing to flout church authority for their cause. According to the prominent convert and art authority Eliza A. Starr, parishioners behaved in a "dreadful way" in Baltimore when Bishop Francis P. Kenrick (1796–1863) had the priests of his diocese continue reciting prayers during mass for governing authorities, who were of course northern.[13]

Participation in the war by most Catholic women assumed more mundane forms. Large numbers in the North volunteered for fairs raising money for the Sanitary Commission, a civilian auxiliary to the medical corps. Madame Boileau, the sister of General John C. Freemont's wife and herself the wife of the French counsel, was active in the Commission. Starr believed that exertions on its behalf were demanded by "the honor of the Church." Defying her husband's disapproval of "ladies selling things over a table," Ellen E. Sherman, the wife of General William T. Sherman, took charge of the Catholic section at one of the largest sanitary fairs in the country.[14] Irish-born Mrs. Mary A. Brady in 1862 organized and was elected president of the Soldiers Aid Association of Philadelphia, which ministered to the sick and wounded by distributing clothing and medicine and raised money for widows. The exertions involved in traveling repeatedly to the front with supplies, assisting surgeons, and caring for the wounded were too much for her weakened heart. Brady died at age fifty-two, a casualty of the war as surely as any soldier.[15]

Many Catholic women from the poorer classes supported the conflict by flocking to the 100,000 new industrial jobs made available because of the labor shortage and wartime industrial expansion. In New York in 1865 the first known Catholic day nursery was established to assist those workers, and a Catholic judge, Charles P. Daly, helped institute the Workingwomen's Protective Union to advance their interests. At a public meeting of working females, Daly praised their intelligence, selflessness, and patriotism.[16]

The patriotism of other Catholic women, however, was questioned. Many females joined the mob of mostly Irish workers during the New York draft riots of 1863. Witnesses repeatedly described them as cheering and urging on the male demonstrators and as initiating the pillaging and looting. Although scanty, police records indicate a large proportion of women arrested were Irish and Catholic. On the other hand, it is asserted that it was a Catholic woman who intervened and persuaded Archbishop Hughes to issue a statement and to meet with the rioters, urging them to preserve the peace. (The use of federal troops was probably more effective than the bishop's plea in quelling the disturbance, which evolved into an antiblack outburst.)[17]

Southern "ladies" also rioted. The most serious incident was in Richmond, where about one thousand women armed with hatchets and revolvers pillaged stores for food and clothing. Apparently Catholics were involved, for many Protestants accused foreign-born Romanists of instigating the fracas.[18]

Less forgivable in southern eyes were the actions of a Mrs. Munro of Virginia. Mary Boykin Chestnut, acclaimed as the most brilliant diarist of the period, described Munro as not only a cultivated and enthusiastic Catholic but a violent abolitionist and Yankee sympathizer whose political views created rows worthy of a Donnybrook Fair. According to Chestnut, Munro had admired and trusted General Sherman because he was a Catholic but became disillusioned upon hearing that he had burned a convent in Columbia, South Carolina.[19]

Apparently Sherman's troops had disobeyed orders and torched and looted that city's Ursuline Convent. The religious superior, Madame Ursula, treated the general like one of her charges when he came to apologize. Making him appear awkward and nervous, according to one student, she "stood erect, like an injured princess dethroned... in the majesty of her sacred order, and her own grand womanhood." Refusing to accept his pleas for forgiveness, she used the occasion to get him to promise to protect the home of one of her benefactors.[20]

Ursula was not the only nun to challenge federal authority. Mother Anna Shannon of the Society of Sacred Heart at Union-occupied St. Michael's, Louisiana, refused to fly the stars and stripes, as it would offend the sensibilities of Confederate families. Moreover, at the request of a deputation of women, she wrote to General Benjamin Butler, the military commander in the area, to protest the pillaging of his soldiers and astutely stated that she knew such lack of behavior was without his approval and would cease (as it did) when called to his attention.[21]

Many nuns, both north and south, acted with equal if not greater courage. Prior to the Civil War there were no schools of nursing and but few hospitals, as home care was the usual treatment for those who were ill. Sisters were the only class of women with experience in nursing and hospital management, having established as many as twenty-eight hospitals by 1860. Even as late as 1868 a report of the American Medical Association recognized nuns as the only organized group that realized the importance of nursing.[22] Thus when military officials appealed for hospital volunteers, their entreaties were directed mainly to Catholic sisters. The response was overwhelming. Even though special efforts were made later in the war to increase the proportion of non-Catholic nurses, at least one-fifth of all military nurses were sisters — nearly six hundred volunteers from over twenty congregations.[23]

Sisters tended the wounded of both sides on many battlefields, they crossed enemy lines, and they advanced and retreated with the armies. They administered overcrowded military hospitals under adverse circumstances, including shortages of candles, food, and medical supplies. To ease the demand for beds they turned their academies into medical stations. Moreover they nursed prisoners of war, served on floating hospitals, and wrestled with smallpox and typhoid — and gave their lives in discharging these duties.[24]

As a result of their outstanding war record, sisters were asked to take over hospitals in Baltimore and in Washington and in Illinois at Alton and Cairo.[25] The competence and dedication of the nuns was praised by many observers, including some ordinarily hostile to Catholics. Their services, more so than those of laywomen or Protestant sisters, were welcomed by military officials. According to critics this reception was because nuns were conditioned to obedience and authority. However, there are many instances of their challenging doctors on the care of patients, and Surgeon General W.A. Hammond, a non-Catholic, praised their efficiency, faithfulness, and calm demeanor. It may very well be that some of the contemporary criticism can be attributable to jealously over their professionalism and their willingness to adapt to adverse circumstances.[26]

Although Catholic women had responded in large numbers to wartime needs, their assistance to the newly freed slaves was minor. This may have been in part because Catholics were once again deliberately keeping a low profile. They were probably chagrined when Mary Surratt (1820?–1865), a devout convert, was executed for conspiracy in the assassination of Abraham Lincoln.[27] A more likely reason however, is that Catholics in the South shared the same assumptions about race as did southern Protestants, while those in the North reflected the dominant Irish sentiment, which was antagonistic toward blacks. The Second Plenary Council of Baltimore (1866) actually deplored the haste of emancipation, which, it declared, should have been gradual in order to prepare for freedom those "multitudes with their peculiar disposition."[28] Furthermore, Catholic assistance was not welcomed by the Freedman's Aid Society. Wanting to inculcate middle-class values and Protestant morality, it criticized Catholic efforts to assist former slaves.[29]

Although sanctioned by the Baltimore Council, assistance for freedmen was limited and sustained primarily by local parishes or dioceses. Despite the pressing need, some white communities refused to assume this duty because of a lack of religious or because a diversion of funds would jeopardize other missions. As a result these efforts frequently collapsed. Nevertheless, black schools, and occasionally integrated educational institutions, were established. Special efforts were made to recruit black sisters to teach in these schools, for former slaves responded most enthusiastically to these women, demonstrating that race was more important than religion in reaching these unfortunates.[30]

Even though Catholic women were not leaders during Reconstruction, the Civil War era provided new role models for Catholic girls and fostered a sense of assertiveness and confidence for Catholic women in treating public issues. Ironically these qualities were first used to preserve traditional shibboleths. The proposal for woman suffrage at the Seneca Falls meeting, the most controversial plank of the 1848 indictment of male dominance, waxed and waned before the Civil War. It was put aside during that conflict but revived at its conclusion. When the Fourteenth Amendment included a clause for reducing representation in the United States Congress for denying the vote to male adults (and not all adults) and when the Fifteenth prohibited disfranchisement because of race but not sex, feminists demanded a Sixteenth — a woman suffrage amendment.

Catholic publications and churchmen found such a proposal dangerous and denounced it. The misogynist Orestes Brownson, who had condemned the reform since 1848, claimed its proponents were motivated by a desire to abolish marriage and substitute free love. The church, he asserted, had the obligation to redress these dangers, to teach maidenly modesty, and to train females to be content and not spout woman-suffrage nonsense. As Catholicism recognized that woman was subject to man, even requiring its female religious superiors to be subordinate to male clerics, Brownson believed the church the ideal teacher of these values.[31] One of the most vitriolic and outspoken clerical opponents was Bishop Joseph Machebeuf of Colorado (1812–99), who, in a series of sermons and lectures, some of which were distributed throughout the state, dismissed suffrage advocates as "spiritualists, divorced women, and free lovers...old maids disappointed in love...short-haired women and long-haired men."[32] By 1886 the nation's leading prelate, Cardinal Gibbons, accused not only the suffrage movement but the bloomer costume and women lecturers of endangering the home and motherhood. He appealed to American women to practice a "heroism of silent suffering" rather than "noisy action."[33] The *Catholic World* seemed to represent many Catholics when it asserted, "The curse of our age is femininity, its want of manliness, and its pruriency," all of which were aggravated by woman suffrage — feminists were not reformers but revolutionists.[34] By 1879 one of the leading suffragists, a Catholic sympathizer Thomas Wentworth Higginson, publicly referred to the "unanimous" opposition of Catholic priests to female enfranchisement.[35]

Although expressing admiration for nuns, the suffrage papers *Woman's Journal* and the more radical *Revolution* frequently criticized the church and clergy for their attitude on the rights of women.[36] But more disappointing to suffragists than clerical enmity was the opposition organized by two Catholic women. Ellen Ewing Sherman (1824–88) and Madeline Vinton Dahlgren (1825–98), both well known in Washington circles, circulated petitions asserting that enfranchisement was unscriptural and then submitted these memorials to the United States Senate on behalf of an antisuffrage organization they established. To her friend Congressman James A. Garfield, Dahlgren repeatedly forwarded antisuffrage petitions and tracts, including articles she had written. She also complained to him about the testimony of suffrage witnesses and their use of the Education and Labor Committee Room. Nevertheless, Dahlgren refused to debate enfranchisement at the national woman suffrage convention, for it would be a spectacle, a violation of "female modesty." However, the use of her pen to fight the cause was consistent with "home life and its duties." Consequently she wrote diatribes attacking the reform as an outcropping of socialistic and communistic schemes that would undermine Christian civilization by luring women from the home with a needless vote. The ballot was unnecessary, she contended, for it was mothers who formed the character of their sons, who were future voters, and it was wives who influenced their husbands. In time Dahlgren became less reticent. In 1878 she was the only remonstrant before the Senate Elections Committee as she defended the sanctity of the family from the assault of the suffragists.[37]

Like antifeminists for the next century Sherman and Dahlgren were enmeshed in a mass of contradictions, using political means to protect women from political burdens and assuming a public role to proclaim that the major responsibility of females lay in the privacy of their home. Moreover, neither woman was a traditional housewife adhering to the virtue of domesticity. Sherman, who believed that a "wife is part of a man's own self — his BETTER half and not his slave," had rejected her husband's advice in 1860 to invest in slaves, ignored his disapproval of ladies' selling at a Sanitary, undermined his Indian program by helping to establish the Ladies Catholic Indian Mission Association, and embarrassed him when he was commander of the armies by flying a papal flag with black crepe from their Washington home when Rome was besieged by the Italian state in 1870. To the complaints of the Italian ambassador, the general sheepishly replied that he only lived in that house.[38]

Dahlgren, twice widowed, supported herself and her children by writing novels and essays in which her conservative views on all aspects of life were publicized. Her home became a salon for the literary figures and intelligentsia of Washington. Young scholars, politicians (including her friend Garfield), members of the diplomatic corps, clergy, and writers gathered at her dinner parties for lively conversation — where often her political views were expounded before all.

None of these activities affected her opposition to suffrage. Dahlgren believed the uniqueness of woman made her superior to man morally and as such she was ordained by nature to ennoble the world about her. "Pray to God to assist us to reform whatever needs reform," she wrote, "to devise proper means to ameliorate the grief of our sisters of toil and our sisters of sin. So may we become truly, and within the limits prescribed by God himself, the ministering angels of humanity." (Dahlgren advocated equal wages with men, migration to the West, taxing bachelors, and dowries for the poor to achieve this reform.)[39]

By the end of the century such concepts were relatively common. Both Catholic and non-Catholic reformers were contending that one of the differences between the sexes was the moral superiority of women, which obliged them to reform society, an extension of the home. Consequently it became easier for Catholic females who believed in traditional values to move out of the so-called woman's sphere and demand political rights, while those who opposed the extension of suffrage contended females could improve the world about them without becoming involved in politics. Increasingly the difference between Catholic feminists and traditionalists became one of means not ends.

Chapter 7

STEREOTYPES ENDANGERED: MIDDLE-CLASS "LADIES" BECOME REFORMERS

As the nineteenth century drew to a close, Catholic women who wanted to expand their role in society began to receive support from the institutional church. To remedy the failure of the American political system, liberal churchmen assumed a leading role in efforts to purify voting and legislative practices by urging Catholics to participate fully in the electoral process. Furthermore, in a challenge to conservatives, whose response to societal ills was typically prayer and passivity, they proclaimed the necessity of Catholic involvement in solving social and economic problems.[1] Although liberals, like traditionalists, believed women were special because of their piety and purity, unlike conservatives they believed these virtues should not be confined to the home but should be applied to society at large. As Katherine Mullaney wrote in the *Catholic World*, it was "woman's mission to elevate, purify, ennoble, not only man but mankind.... If she will but exercise it beneficently, white winged Peace will hover over the land and the millennium of earthy happiness be come unto us."[2]

In a Catholic adaption of the Social Gospel movement, journals expounded on the notion of superior women reforming the world. Catholic women were exhorted to do social work, to teach, and to write. An article in the *American Catholic Quarterly Review* attacking schools whose goal was merely to produce ladies closed with the aphorism, "I live for the heavens above me and the good that I can do."[3] One of the most outspoken clerics in encouraging feminine reformers was Bishop John L. Spalding (1840–1919) of Peoria. Because woman was gentler and purer than man, he demanded that higher education be available to her so that she might better promote change in the world. This reasoning, of course, justified careers outside the home, for as Spalding wrote, "We degrade her when we consider her as little else than a candidate for matrimony."[4] Consequently the bishop was an exponent of equal rights, equal pay, and equal suffrage.[5]

Even liberal members of the hierarchy who feared equal suffrage were willing to redefine the role of women. The dean of American churchmen, Cardinal James Gibbons of Baltimore (1834–1921), albeit a suffrage critic, encouraged females to enter the field of medicine as doctors but did suggest separate anatomical departments for each sex and implied that the practice of women doctors should be limited to female patients.[6]

Bishop Ireland, unsure of the merits of suffrage, temporized. Nevertheless, he praised the independence of American females, their energy, spirit, and good sense. These qualities, he asserted, were producing a "new woman," whose sphere of activity was ever widening. Opportunities for higher education were necessary so that she could fulfill these new duties. According to Ireland, modern woman must be more than a graceful lady; she must be a cultured and accomplished scholar. Like other liberals, Ireland found these new obligations rooted in traditional concepts. To the World's Congress on Social Purity he declared that society had an obligation to aid unprotected and defenseless young women and to support the endeavors of Anthony Comstock to protect morality. "The hope of pure morals, the hope of high civilization, is woman ... and with the degradation of woman, civilization perishes."[7]

Changing attitudes were best reflected in Catholic congresses. In 1889 a general convention of laity met to deal with concerns of common religious interests. No women delegates were appointed by the hierarchy, no woman delivered papers at the gathering, and no women's issues were explored. The only mention of females was almost incidental: resolutions denounced easy-divorce laws for degrading females and condemned the employment of young men and women.[8] But only four years later at the World's Columbian Exposition of 1893, a world's fair to commemorate the four hundredth anniversary of the discovery of America, there was a Catholic pavilion with a woman's building, female delegates, and position papers prepared by women.[9]

Presentations at the fair were further manifestations of how the "new woman" was really the "traditional woman" applying feminine talents to society at large rather than confining them to the home. One of the best examples was the paper "Woman and Mammon," in which Rose Hawthorne Lathrap, a prominent convert, asserted the hour had come for women to prove their concern for the elevation of the nation as well as the protection of the home. It was time "to arise and defend your rights, your abilities for competition with men, in intellectual and professional endurance." But, she cautioned, one must still maintain the tender virtues of the female sex.[10]

Emma J. Carey, a vice-regent of Trinity College, one of the first Catholic Colleges for women, took pride that the basis of the woman's movement was in St. Paul's epistle proclaiming that in Christ Jesus there was neither male nor female. In her paper "Elevation of Womanhood" she contended that the church in carrying out this injunction was the major agent in the improvement of the status of women, who, as a result, were obliged to use their gifts in the world.[11]

No one was better fit for the mission of education, according to the paper of Mary Maher, than woman, whose "tender conscience, philosophy of love, and ability to inspire made her a helpful instructor in *every walk of life*."[12] The values of the traditional church and the social activism of Catholic gospelers was also reflected in the two papers of Mary J. Onahan, a Chicago newswoman. In "Catholic Women's Part in Philanthropy" she hailed the work of nuns and laywomen in reclaiming sinners, and in "Isabella the Catholic" she proclaimed that the queen of Spain, a model for Catholic women, was "a power, morally, socially, and intellectually." On the other hand, Onahan warned that the more common sphere for women was at home as wife and mother; although she may be man's equal, she is really his helpmate. Furthermore, she offered the ladylikeness of Isabella for all to emulate. According to her, the queen spurned the advice of her court and refused to require an act of homage on first meeting her betrothed, Ferdinand of Aragon, although his domain was inferior to hers. "She never forgot that she was a queen, and would not allow a sign of inferiority from one who was to be her husband."[13]

One of the most outspoken Catholics at the congress, a harbinger of the radical feminist Charlotte Perkins Gilman, was Alice T. Toomy. She claimed that every girl should be taught a profession, business, or trade, for inability to earn a living determined the marriage relationship by forcing dependent women to seek rich husbands. Only those fortunate enough to have developed a bread-winning capacity could obtain true marriage — "freedom of selection, untrammeled by mercenary motives."[14] Toomy contended that the congress demonstrated women's ability to help the needy and then urged Catholics to cooperate with the Women's Christian Temperance Union, as there was no equivalent Catholic organization.[15]

As a result of these changing perceptions, the congress resolved that Catholic societies should be formed for the "assistance, encouragement and protection" of young working girls. One of the most successful of these organizations was the Catholic Women's Association of Brooklyn. In order to train "young women to help themselves" to become "self-reliant and self-supporting," the association conducted classes in academic subjects, including English and mathematics, while maintaining a trade school and employment bureau. (This program was so successful that in 1900 the association was recognized as a University Extension Center of the state of New York.) A gym and library were also part of the institute, whose regular offerings included vocational courses for young girls and, most unusual, cooking for men.[16]

The delegates to the congress also established a Catholic Woman's League, with headquarters in Chicago under the honorary presidency of Starr. Its purpose was to advance and promote "the genuine good of humanity in accordance with the principles of the Catholic Church." To achieve this end the league established day nurseries, shelters for homeless girls, and an employment bureau as well as conducted industrial classes. More significantly, it even became a champion of equal suffrage as means of obtaining women's rights.[17]

Other Catholics at the turn of the century who championed women as reformers frequently urged educational modifications as a means to that end. A nun who contributed to the *Catholic World* sought funds to create a Catholic institute to prepare women for professions such as accounting, pharmacy, and nursing. However, the institute would also include courses in cooking, mending, and homemaking.[18] More radical was a Catholic teacher who insisted that convent schools stop impressing on their students that the only options for females were marriage or religion. Not all women were fitted for domestic duties, she claimed; some were called to be women "of affairs" such as physicians. The task of teachers was to develop natural gifts and skills. If girls then opted for a life of domesticity, not only would this be a free choice, but they would be better prepared for its responsibilities.[19] Some observers even criticized nuns for not being intellectually demanding and producing only pious ladies. They should prepare students to "go forth to elevate, to purify, to refine society" by raising educational standards to those of Protestant schools. If necessary, a Catholic Harvard Annex (Radcliffe) should be established.[20] Thomas E. Sherman, the Jesuit son of General and

Ellen Sherman, not only asserted that mothers needed trained minds but contended that cloistered nuns were a impediment to women's education, as they could not stay abreast of modern research. Furthermore, he claimed, women who were given to "billing and cooing" rather than intellectual development forfeited the respect of young men and became objects of contempt.[21]

Conservatives, however, fought such innovations, claiming that the object of education was the preservation of the faith, which included preparing girls for the duties of being wife and mother. To Father J. J. O'Connell, female colleges were vulgar, producing bold and forward women who rebelled against nature by becoming lawyers and physicians.[22] The Jesuit Nicholas Walsh claimed that higher studies were "an evil for the vast majority of girls" and that manual labor should be included in their education, for "idle-minded and idle-handed" subjects were worthless if not dangerous.[23] Traditionalists who accepted the inevitability of higher education emphasized that it must not endanger Catholic values by overemphasizing professional opportunities or intellectual activities. The unnaturalness of such a curriculum was evident, they claimed, for it strained women physically, thus unfitting them for domestic duties destined by God.[24] Thomas Shields, professor of psychology and education at Catholic University and one of the faith's most renowned educators during the first quarter of this century, was unremitting in exposing the dangers of the new philosophy. Female health was endangered by overwork in high school and college, he claimed. But more significant was the menace posed to society by any influence, including education, that made womanly duties less sacred. The aim of schooling, after all, was to prepare homemakers or nuns, the only acceptable choice for women — for according to him, females were by nature less fit than men, even for the teaching profession.[25]

These Cassandras were no more able to stop the evolution of a "new Catholic woman" than their secular counterparts were able to stem the tide of the "new woman."[26] Goals of secondary education were adjusted to reflect the reformers' vision. In Philadelphia, at century's end, the clerical superintendent of schools demanded that education adjust to the "emancipated woman" and, after overcoming opposition, established the first diocesan girls high school in 1911.[27] Mother Caroline Friess of the School Sisters of Notre Dame was hailed as a model educator by Bishop Spalding for promoting the necessity of a practical curriculum for girls.[28] A successful businesswoman alumna of the Sisters of Notre Dame de Namur remembered the nuns of that era as introducing the "startling proposition of females earning their own living" and impressing upon students their right to enter any profession. Ambition and competition became integral parts of the Notre Dame educational experience.[29]

One of the innovators preparing the "emancipated Catholic woman" was Mother Seraphine, superior of the Sisters of St. Joseph of Carondelet, and the sister of Archbishop Ireland. Seraphine, who opened thirty schools and founded the College of St. Catherine (Minnesota), adopted a manual for that community's schools calling for lessons that "show [the] application of what pupils have learned to [the] business of life." These ideas were also reflected in *Immortelles of Catholic Columbian Literature* (1897), a girls' school reader. Prepared by Ursuline nuns, the book was designed to display the versatility of American women writers and put "before the young public what brain-workers we have." Brief biographies of the sixty-three contributors to the anthology were designed to inspire young ladies to develop their talents. Several of the pieces dealt with the influence women could exercise on the world about them. Only one was a traditional, old-fashioned exposition, "Home, Woman's Sphere," but even this one acknowledged that "exceptional women have been born to exceptional vocations." Joan of Arc, Isabella of Spain, Catherine of Siena, and the Old Testament's Deborah, Judith, and Esther were offered as examples.[30]

The Ursuline text was a dramatic change from the older but popular *Young Ladies Reader* (1875) by Mary A. Sadlier. This reader had been designed to foster a taste for the beautiful and the noble, to reinforce the traditional submissive roles of women. As might be expected, the first lengthy selection in Sadlier concerned elocution and the reading of poetry.[31]

The new emphasis on secondary education was part of the emergence of a more self-assured church, more confident as a result of increased numbers and growing tolerance by the community. At the Third Plenary Council (1884) parishes were required to build schools and bishops tasked to take the initiative in providing teachers. Thus the practical necessity of training teachers for the mushrooming Catholic school system was added to the contention of liberals that higher education be made available to develop the full range of talents of Catholic women. Such expansion required a change in Catholic higher education, for although teaching was considered primarily a female profession, women were excluded from Catholic colleges and discouraged from attending secular institutions. Bishop Bernard J. McQuaid of Rochester (1868–1909) refused communion to Cornell coeds and their parents. (Consistent with society's double standard, McQuaid did not impose the same penalty on males.)[32]

Four-year colleges were established for women, beginning with Notre Dame of Maryland in 1896. But the capstone of women's education was to be Trinity College. The first Catholic institution for the higher education of women to be established as a college was located near the newly founded bishops' school, Catholic University, in Washington, D.C. Spalding, one of the leaders in creating Trinity, envisioned it as "a monumental witness to our faith in the *right* of a woman to uphold her being in its full stature, to learn whatever may be known, to do whatever right things she may find herself able to do."[33] On the other hand, the bishop still clung to traditional perceptions, for he believed "it is our duty to give the best educations to woman, for she, a mother, is the aboriginal God-appointed educator."[34]

Instrumental in starting Trinity was Sister Julia McGroarty (1827–1901) of the order of Notre Dame de Namur. Her dreams for the college were delayed four years because of conservatives who feared the consequences of higher education on woman's role and dreaded the deleterious effects of female students on the males at nearby Catholic University. Nevertheless, the curriculum and goals of Trinity demonstrated that the difference between liberals and conservatives was more a matter of degree than substance. To equip students for society the college provided courses equal to those of the best women's institutions such as Bryn Mawr, Wellesley, and Vassar. At the same time, however, courses such as domestic economy would be offered to prepare the girls for their proper role as guardian of the home and educator of their children. Intellects were to be developed, but students were to remain feminine, gentle, sweet, fearful of the Lord, offsetting the new woman, who violates Christ's canons.[35]

Other women's colleges established at this time reflected the same dichotomy: strong liberal arts to prepare women of the world and, on the other hand, requirements to preserve the faith and foster spirituality, gentility, and the traditional role of housewife. The College of New Rochelle even offered a course in laundry work, a "good, practical course in the washing and ironing of plain and standard pieces; the doing of fine lace; the removal of stains."[36] The confusion of goals was typified in St. Theresa's College (Minnesota), whose object was to prepare students as homemakers but to ensure they were "thoroughly trained in every department of secular learning, militants to uphold the ideals of Christianity in society today."[37]

Like nineteenth-century academies, colleges, no matter what traditional values they espoused, developed the intellect and prepared women for an active life. An early European visitor to Trinity observed that their graduates were free to marry only men who pleased them, for they were fully capable of earning their own living.[38] Equally as surprising, the Catholic Student Association of America began to support equal suffrage before World War I, a reform most conservatives and even some liberal clergy found even more dangerous to traditional roles than higher education.[39]

Nowhere was the educational revolution of Catholic women more manifest than in mushrooming summer schools, evening schools, and reading circles. Bolstered by the Pastoral Letter of the Third Plenary Council of Baltimore, calling for popular education, literary societies spread rapidly. They were at first confined to men. However, after the establishment of the first female society and with the encouragement of the *Catholic World*, women's groups multiplied throughout the nation. Designed to advance their participants morally and spiritually, they included Fénelon's *Spiritual Letters* on their reading list and at a discount price.[40]

Reading circles led to the founding of the summer school at Cliff Haven, New York, in 1892, a type of Catholic Chautauqua that drew as many as ten thousand students a year. So successful was this experiment that it was imitated in Wisconsin, Louisiana, Maryland, and Connecticut. Designed to stimulate the intellectual and religious growth of young Catholics, the curriculum centered on contemporary problems and developments in art, science, philosophy, and history. Its program of lectures, concerts, and formal courses attracted primarily educators at first. Although open to both men and women, female enrollment dominated by about a three-to-one ratio. There were special components with women lecturers on topics of special interest to females. The third vice-president at Cliff Haven was a woman, the ubiquitous Toomy. Included among the prominent lecturers were Katherine Conway, editor of the *Boston Pilot*, Mary Elizabeth Blake, essayist and poet, and Eliza Allen Starr, art critic. Indicative of changing values were courses on women in history and women and the law.[41]

Women students developed close bonds with one another, a sense of fellowship, and at the same time a strong attachment to the schools and their purpose. An auxiliary of graduates kept Cliff Haven in touch with progressive women and raised money for faculty salaries and the building of a dining hall, auditorium, chapel, and athletic facilities.[42] Even more significant for the new Catholic woman than the educational and bonding experience was the fact that reading circles and summer schools encouraged wives to attend in order to maintain their individuality and be in a position to influence society.[43]

One of the alternatives allowing middle-class educated ladies to escape the confinement of home was the settlement house, wherein the innately nurturing skills of females could be applied to the problems of immigrants. Catholics rapidly established a tradition of caring for the victims of an urban and industrialized society. As early as 1817 the Roman Catholic Orphan Asylum was incorporated in New York, with similar institutions and foundling homes spreading throughout the nation soon afterward. By 1874 suffragists were claiming that the management of these facilities by females clearly demonstrated women's qualifications to vote.[44] The Sisters of Mercy, who came to the United States in 1857, even had a special apostolate of social work.[45] Nuns from several communities dared to redeem fallen women: they taught them skills, found them employment, and broke their dependency on drugs. Despite changes in canon law precluding nuns from maternity nursing and infant care, they continued to provide these services.[46]

Considerable attention was also given to the newest of victims — female immigrants. As early as the 1850s a Women's Protective Emigration Society was founded to safeguard Irish girls, and in 1886 Father Pietro Bandini organized the San Raphael Society in New York to provide temporary lodging and an employment service to female Italian immigrants.[47] In Buffalo these exiles were also aided by Elizabeth A. Cronyn, an opera singer.[48] With the help of Archbishop Ireland, Charlotte Grace O'Brien, who lived in New York tenements while investigating the conditions of immigrants, persuaded the Irish Catholic Colonization Society to establish a depot at Castle Gardens (the forerunner of Ellis Island) to care for Irish immigrant girls. The newcomers were provided with a temporary home, a chapel, employment, and counseling service. The undertaking was so successful that it soon spread to other ports.[49]

One of the most effective agents in rendering assistance to these refugees was a naturalized citizen, Mother Francesca Cabrini (1850–1917). In 1889 she began founding mission houses, orphanages, schools, and hospitals in Europe and Latin America and in urban and rural United States to care for Italian immigrants. Her spirited stance when establishing her order, the Missionaries of the Sacred Heart, was typical of the confidence of Catholic female reformers. When told by a Roman prelate that missionaries had always been men, the saint replied, "If the mission of announcing the Lord's resurrection to his apostles had been entrusted to Mary Magdalen, it

would seem a very good thing to confide to other women an evange-
lizing mission." Cabrini even clashed with Bishop Corrigan, who in
time yielded to her judgment. So contrary to stereotypes was Cabrini
that sometimes contemporaries resorted to male terms in describing
her, calling her "a great man," a "statesman."[50]

Although not directly concerned with immigrant women as such,
the Sisters of the Reparation of the Congregation of Mary served
many of them by caring for the homeless and friendless. Irish-born
Ellen O'Keefe (1844–1917), believing that God had called her to help
the unfortunate, nursed in city hospitals and jails and cared for prisoners while living the life of a religious. With the encouragement
of Corrigan she established the congregation to aid and administer
homes for forlorn women.[51]

Despite a tradition of caring, Catholics were slow to accept the
idea of settlements — residences established by middle-class laity in
poor neighborhoods to improve the quality of life. Traditionally the
church had reached the poor through parish structures that were not
concerned with social reform, and the notion of lay vocations was
slow to take hold.[52] Social problems were viewed by conservatives,
not as a failure of community, but as a failure of individuals to conform to moral precepts. The sanctification of the individual soul was
more important than the curing of social ills.[53] Thus quite typically
the St. Vincent de Paul Society, organized in the United States in 1845
to minister to the poor, had as its first premise, not the performance
of good works, but the sanctification of its members.[54] Furthermore,
to some the involvement of women in settlement work was unnatural,
for if residents really loved children, they would marry and raise a
family of their own. Reverend James Carey, a New York priest, won
the approval of a large Chicago audience of bishops, laity, and representatives of Catholic organizations when he castigated settlement
residents. To the applause and laughter of the first American Catholic Missionary Congress (1919), he ridiculed the personal appearance
of settlement workers, referring to them as he or she, claiming one
could not tell the difference, as the women were more masculine than
the men. He accused them of proselytizing and asserted they should
toil among the rich, teaching them the sacredness of marriage. Moreover, he asserted, there were three types of settlement workers: "a real
missionary, an out an out kidnapper"; the milder parlor-trained type
who wiggles her way into the hearts of children; and a third type, the
socialist who holds the red flag dear.[55]

Other voices, however, urged Catholics to emulate their Protestant brethren in this endeavor. As early as 1897 the *Catholic World*

exhorted well-to-do leisured ladies to follow the example of their London sisters and engage in social work to uplift the poor.[56] A. A. McGinley, in the same journal in 1900, appealed to convent school graduates to reside in settlements for a few years before marriage, vows, or a career.[57] According to the historian Robert D. Cross, Mary Theresa Elder, sister of the archbishop of Cincinnati, preached a liberal Catholic version of the "gospel of wealth." She asserted that wealth was good and that there should be more rich Catholics who could develop their virtue by motivating the destitute to overcome idleness and rise from the disgrace of poverty. On the other hand, Elder urged Catholic women to establish settlements and municipal clubs and thereby purify politics and reform the economic system.[58] But it was not until sectarian settlements were perceived as a threat to the faith of immigrants, especially to Italians, whom the Irish viewed as backsliding Catholics, that clerical attitudes changed and religious began to advocate the establishment of Catholic settlements.[59]

As one might expect, then, the earliest settlements were in Italian neighborhoods.[60] The first was founded in 1897 by Sister Blandina at the request of Archbishop Elder of Cincinnati, who had requested nuns to work among Italians. From basement origins there evolved the Santa Maria Educational and Industrial Home, including a nursery, kindergarten, residence hall, and in 1926 even its own Italian language magazine. Blandina was appointed a probation officer and, like lay residents, soon found herself far removed from traditional feminine roles. As she lobbied for white-slave legislation, she became deeply involved in political activity.[61]

The second Catholic settlement also directed its efforts primarily toward the Italian community. In 1896 a recent convert and Wellesley graduate, Marion F. Gurney, established and was the first resident at St. Rose's, a mission of the Dominican parish in New York City. There with her parents she taught reading and writing to immigrants at night. Gurney entered religious life and, as Mother Marianne of Jesus, in 1908 founded the Sisters of Our Lady of Christian Doctrine to promote settlement work, especially in New York's East Side. In 1910 at the request of New York's Cardinal John M. Farley (1842–1918) she founded Madonna House, the first diocesan settlement in the city.[62]

Catholic women organized many other settlements, and by 1915 there was one in every major diocese. Mary J. Workman started Brownson House in Los Angeles in 1911 to aid Mexicans in their "civic, social, and religious betterment through personal service and mutual helpfulness."[63] In Greenwich Village a self-supporting laundry and a music room were included in the settlement opened for Italians. Its founder, Annie Leary, envisioned it as a future Italian-American university.[64] Grace O'Brien established settlements in Brooklyn, outgrowths of parish sewing classes.[65] A bedridden invalid, Mary V. Merrick in 1891 founded the Christ Child Society in Washington, D.C., to bring joy to the poor at Christmas and succor year round. In time her efforts resulted in a national organization, with settlement houses providing summer camps, clubrooms, showers, and classes in handicraft and sewing and also recruiting volunteers to aid in parishes. In 1913 a "colored auxiliary" was begun, and by the time of Merrick's death in 1955 there were branches in thirty-six cities.[66]

Many Catholic settlements were organized by women's groups in cities such as Brooklyn, Pittsburgh, St. Paul, and Detroit. In Chicago the most successful of the women's leagues resulting from the Columbian Congress began cultural and educational work among the poor and undertook the protection of young girls. Within three months, "in a concerted effort to duplicate the work of humanitarians at Hull House," the league had established three settlements with a nursery, kindergarten, employment service, and sewing, library, and mother's clubs. Poor girls were met at railroad stations, and homes were provided for transients.[67]

The most prominent Chicago Catholic settlement was Madonna House (1904), an outgrowth of the Holy Guardian Angel Parish Mission. The pastor, Father Edmond Dunne, feared that nearby Hull House was succeeding in its goal to "draw our children from the Church."[68] Sarah Amberg, its founder, was also concerned about preserving the faith of the parish's Italian immigrants, some of whom she thought "unwittingly sold their Roman Catholic birthright for a mess of proselytizers' and humanists' pottage." The wife of a prosperous merchant and a graduate of Sacred Heart Academy, Amberg had visited Toynbee Hall, London, the first university settlement. One of the new Catholic women, she was convinced that "we cannot as Catholics be blind to any social implication in our Catholic doctrine and our faith. For the Kingdom of Heaven is seen through our works upon earth." Encouraged by Dunne, who believed settlements would promote better marriages, she established a parish Sunday school for immigrants. Soon she added a night school, undertook charity work, and became a resident as the mission evolved into a full-fledged settlement.[69]

The establishment of Madonna House did not end Catholic fears of nearby secular institutions. The Chicago diocesan paper, the *New World*, repeatedly assailed Hull House, Jane Addams, and settlement residents, whom on various occasions it described as long-haired sociologists, anarchists, socialists, amazons, and meddling fanatics. At one time it depicted the workers as "feminine busybodies who neglect their own homes in order to indulge in a little sentiment or gain notoriety by attempting to pauperize whole neighborhoods." These "hysterically emotional, childless female slummers" were an insult to real fathers and mothers, who had a sacred trust from the Creator. Special invective was saved for an "arrogant" Addams, the "patron saint of bigotry," who tolerated materialism and free love while fostering anticlericalism from her morally bankrupt Hull House.[70]

Ironically enough, Addams was criticized by older members of her residence for failing to provide religious direction and, on the other hand, was praised by liberal Catholics for her humanitarianism.[71] The head worker at Madonna House described Addams as a valued friend whose cooperation with the settlement was of major importance. Moreover, although the Hull House initiator found little value in organized religion, according to Amberg, Addams was a Christian, more Christian than "Catholic formalists." Even though Amberg believed it necessary to undermine Addams's advocacy of birth control, she appreciated the reformer's motive: family limitation to increase economic well-being.[72]

A handful of other Catholics also publicly praised Addams. The educator Thomas E. Shields was convinced that if she were a Catholic, she would be a nun; Father Félix Klein, a European visitor, thought her efforts worthy of emulation; and Alice Toomy, who admired her endeavors for moral and social elevation, had special praise for the Jane Club, established by Addams as a residence for working women.[73]

As a matter of fact, Hull House was so far from being a bastion of anti-Catholicism that its clientele influenced the conversion of two of its most prominent workers, one of whom was Frances Crane Lillie, a former medical student and mother of seven (three of whom were adopted). The daughter of a millionaire manufacturer, Lillie supported the organized labor movement and founded a residence for the widows of her father's employees. As a result of volunteer work among the poor, she became a close friend of Ellen Gates Starr, the cofounder of Hull House. Both became attracted to Catholicism through the faith of Italian and Polish immigrants and in time became converts. Typical of her commitment to working classes (which her daughter claimed was upside-down snobbery) was Lillie's reply to questions about her Catholicism, "I want to go to church with my cook and make a face at Mrs. Ritzbilt down the street."[74]

Her friend Starr had attended Rockford Seminary, where she became close friends with Jane Addams, a fellow student. About ten
years later, while traveling in Europe, they decided to establish a settlement in the United States. Starr's decision to become a settlement
worker was part of her search for a meaningful faith that led her
into the Socialist party, leadership in the National Women's Trade
Union League (resulting at one point in her arrest for picketing), and
into the Episcopal, Anglican, and finally the Catholic church. Her
decision to become a Catholic was influenced in part by her aunt,
Eliza Allen Starr, herself a prominent convert, and also by studying
religious tomes with her friend Lillie.[75] Starr's actual entrance into
the church was delayed because she hesitated to become part of a
religion so deeply opposed to socialism and so little interested in political and social progress. Not until the Bishops' Program of Social
Reconstruction was promulgated in 1919 was this final obstacle to
her conversion removed.[76]

The settlement movement provided independence and career alternatives as salaried female volunteers evolved into trained social
workers. This career led to women's performing other unfeminine
duties, such as those of probation officers, labor organizers, and observers at police stations and juvenile courts. The first step toward
professionalism for Catholics was taken with the establishment of
a school of sociology at Chicago's Loyola University in 1914. Even
more important, the following year Father Peter E. Dietz founded
the American Academy of Christian Democracy for women at Hot
Springs, North Carolina. There pupils studied nursing, social science,
and parliamentary law to prepare for a career in social work. Not
long after the establishment of the School of Social Work at Catholic University in 1921, Dietz's academy closed, but not before it had
prepared hundreds of young women for social service careers.[77]

Although social service workers were often spiritually motivated,
they nevertheless asserted considerable independence from the formalities of organized religion. Large numbers of Los Angeles women
resigned from Catholic settlements and volunteered at nonsectarian
houses when Bishop John J. Cantwell (1874–1947) of Los Angeles
removed autonomy from the houses by centralizing them under his
control.[78] Josephine Brownson shattered one of the largest taboos by
writing on theology. However, she often published under the male
name J. Van Dyke Brownson or took a priest as collaborator.[79] For
the most part, though, Catholic settlement workers, no matter how far
removed from traditional roles, were able to reconcile their life-style
with religion and frequently intertwined both commitments. Two of

the best examples were Kate Barnard (1881–1930) and Caroline Gleason (1886–1962).

Barnard, who was educated in a convent school, was advised by her confessor to abandon plans for a public-service career and continue teaching so she could keep house for her father. However, with the support of the Businessman's and Ministerial Alliance, she undertook charitable work in Oklahoma Territory and then studied at Graham Taylor's Chicago School of Civics and Philanthropy. On her return, Barnard crusaded for child-labor laws, compulsory school-attendance measures, and higher wages, and she established the Oklahoma's Women's International Union Label League. Barnard also became an enthusiastic supporter of the American Federation of Labor, organizing unemployed men into a Federal Labor Union. With labor's support she soon was a powerful political force, drawing audiences of over three thousand to her reform rallies.

She stumped the territory for the adoption of the state constitution, which incorporated many reforms recommended by her because of the unremitting pressure she applied at the constitutional convention. Barnard was the first woman elected to statewide office in Oklahoma, beginning two four-year terms as commissioner of charities in 1908, ten years before women were enfranchised in that state. The powers of her office and the support of women's clubs and religious groups were used by her to unseat a reactionary speaker and to enact liberal legislation establishing juvenile courts and prison reform. Barnard urged social workers to follow her example and form political alliances with labor unions to legislate needed changes.

Despite her political success, like many Catholic women Barnard was a traditionalist when it came to suffrage. According to her, such a change was unnecessary, and agitation on its behalf would detract from more serious issues. "I am more interested in saving the poor, destitute, blind, deaf, and insane than in securing votes for women." After all, she bragged, "her boys" always did what she wanted, thus there was no need for the ballot.[80]

Caroline Gleason, a University of Minnesota graduate, taught at St. Mary's College and Academy, Portland, Oregon, from 1904 to 1910. Like Barnard, she left her position to study at Taylor's school and lived at Chicago Commons Settlement while there. On her return to Oregon she headed the Catholic Women's League to aid self-supporting females by surveying working conditions and conducting a night school and employment bureau. At the request of the Consumers' League of Oregon, she investigated living and working conditions of wage-earning women in 1912 and 1913, clandestinely taking employment in several factories to obtain data. Her report and her lobbying were instrumental in the passage of a state minimum-wage law in 1913 and led to her appointment as head of the State Industrial Welfare Commission to enforce the statute. In 1916, convinced that only the tenets of Christianity could remedy the evils of industrial life, Gleason resigned and entered the Sisters of the Holy Name of Jesus and Mary under the name of Sister Miriam Theresa. She returned to school, receiving a master's degree from the University of Oregon and, from Catholic University, the first doctorate in sociology awarded to a nun. She continued her efforts for social justice, heading the sociology department at Maryhurst, lecturing throughout the state, and preparing a book on the history of labor reform (only partially completed at the time of her death). In 1959 the state's leading paper, the *Oregonian*, named her one of Oregon's leading citizens.[81]

In addition to providing an impetus for the establishment of settlement houses, the concept of redemption and social service resulted in other new undertakings by Catholic women. By 1905 most urban areas had women's leagues, clubs, or guilds to promote human welfare.[82] In every large city females organized missions for immigrants, with English classes, employment bureaus, food and clothing, day nurseries, and volunteers teaching the faith. Additionally in many cities women established institutions for the working poor, including homes for homeless girls, boardinghouses for children, and employment centers. At railroad stations they provided representatives to meet young rural women coming to the city in search of employment.[83] By the end of the century there were many formal auxiliaries to the St. Vincent de Paul Society caring for orphans and homeless women, running day nurseries and observing at police courts.[84] Although in 1895 the Knights of Columbus rejected the supreme knight's recommendation that women be made eligible for membership, many councils had ladies' auxiliaries. These groups aided in the social and charitable mission of the knights, and in time two of them achieved national status: the Daughters of Isabella and the Catholic Daughters of America. The Daughters united women for religious and social needs, for the defense of the faith, and to spread patriotism and raise money for charity.[85] There also seemed to be a new concern for the ill; Catholic women's organizations established homes for consumptives and hospitals for incurable cancer patients and continued to provide for unwed mothers and their babies.[86]

In 1908 many of these charitable organizations began holding a national conference at the same time and place as the St. Vincent de Paul Society, where they discussed common problems and social needs. These gatherings soon evolved into an umbrella organization, St. Elizabeth's Union, which was really the foundation of the National Conference of Catholic Charities. Founded in 1910, this annual conference of men and women's groups had a special section devoted to needs of women.[87]

Two of the female activists of this period, Josephine Brownson (1880–1942) and Mary Boyle O'Reilly (1873–1939), came from prominent Catholic families. Brownson, the granddaughter of Orestes, in her endeavors to reach Catholic children in public schools, foreshadowed the Confraternity of Christian Doctrine programs. A graduate of the University of Michigan and a public-school teacher, Brownson established programs to train catechism teachers, wrote texts for these courses, and lectured throughout the country urging other dioceses to follow Detroit's example. In order to reach the children more effectively and to provide wholesome recreation, Brownson's program included classes on boxing, swimming, and organized games and play.[88]

O'Reilly whose father, John, was an essayist, poet, and reform editor of the *Boston Pilot*, was committed to philanthropic endeavors. She claimed to have had the reputation of being the worst girl in the convent where she was educated. Nevertheless, O'Reilly did much for charities, founded a settlement house, and was a director of the Women's Educational and Industrial Union. Despite her advocacy of traditional roles for women, she lived an unusually exciting life. In 1910, disguised as a mill worker, she gathered data to expose "baby farms" in New Hampshire, where infants, supposedly receiving adequate care, were neglected. She wrote editorials for the *Boston Pilot*, nursed wounded in Belgium in 1914, and reported for the *Boston Globe* during World War I. After that conflict she remained in Europe doing relief work and upon her return to Boston founded St. Elizabeth's Settlement House in the South End. However, she refused to join the Massachusetts Anti-Suffrage Association only because the possibility of suffrage seemed so remote, while such a step would needlessly antagonize those that desired the ballot. Moreover she sought advice on social issues from Cardinal William H. O'Connell of Boston (1859–1944) and led a campaign against sex education in the public schools, charging it would undermine Christian morality.[89]

The notions of physical or moral redemption of the world through the sacrifice of females was not original with the new Catholic woman — it had always existed among the religious. The Spanish-American War provided another opportunity for this view to be put to

the test by nuns. As the conflict progressed, the danger of disease became as great as the threat from bullets. On behalf of the government
the Daughters of the American Revolution volunteered to examine,
engage, and transport nurses to care for the sick and wounded. A former vice-president of the daughters, the Catholic novelist Ella Loraine
Dorsey (1853–1935), worked primarily among her coreligionists on
this task, writing to various religious congregations for volunteers.[90]

Answering her appeal were 282 nuns from half a dozen religious
communities, 5 of whom gave their lives for the cause. The volunteers
served in Cuba and Puerto Rico, sailed with the sick on transports,
and nursed in southern and coastal hospitals.[91] Although the dedication of the nuns was praised by military authorities, it was obvious
even to sympathetic observers that, unlike their Civil War predecessors, they were not as well qualified as the laity.

Even before the war as nursing became more professional, inadequate training of nuns had been noted. Community rules and
traditions had impeded formal scientific education for sisters. Even
in those instances where nuns attended nursing schools, they were
barred from certain classes. As a result critics noted that if the army
established a permanent nurse corps, nuns probably would be excluded. If they were to regain their position of respect in the medical
field, it was apparent there would have to be a new nun.[92]

One of the areas influenced by the new Catholic woman was the
Catholic temperance movement. The first Catholic abstinence societies were founded in the late 1840s after a visit to the United States
by the Irish "apostle of temperance," Father Theobald Mathew. The
societies, local in character, often met in state conventions. In 1872,
then, 210 of them at a national convention established the National
Catholic Total Abstinence Union. (Women's groups were excluded
from membership. Ironically at that time the convention resolved it
inexpedient to take part in political or legislative agitation; instead,
it would rely upon moral suasion.[93]) In 1878, however, the union
decided to admit ladies as honorary members and two years later
recommended the formation of women's groups to be affiliated with
the union but represented at conventions by their spiritual directors.
Finally in 1887 the union allowed women's societies to select their
own delegates to annual meetings.[94]

Despite the protests of conservatives such as Bishop John J. Glen-
non (1862–1946) of St. Louis, who was opposed to women reformers
and disapproved of their role in the temperance movement, the numbers of women in Catholic abstinence organizations mushroomed.[95]
In 1890 Sally Moore addressed the union and was chosen third vice-

president, and the following year Sadie McNeele warned the delegates that the union could not succeed without its women members.[96] By 1902 there were 167 female societies with over ten thousand members affiliated with the union (16 percent of its membership), and one member, Leonora Barry Lake, was reputed to be leader of the entire Catholic temperance movement.[97]

Lake, who had established a ladies' association in St. Louis, where there was no male organization, had become a mainstay of the reform, lecturing throughout the country on behalf of abstinence. Often she gave over 150 talks a year and traveled over twenty thousand miles.[98] She defended herself from charges that she was violating the order of nature by abandoning the home (the same charges made against her when she was a union organizer) by claiming an attack on the evils of drink was a defense of the sanctity of the family. Furthermore, she asserted, women had a right to strive for temperance. If the movement was to grow and succeed, women, the foundation of the church, must be brought into the societies; after all, they were the ones who got men to attend Mass.[99]

About the time women began to enter the movement in large numbers, the union began to turn toward legislation to obtain its goal.[100] (This increased political involvement may have been one of the reasons more conservative churches opposed female membership.) As early as 1885 the *Catholic Examiner* of Baltimore advocated female suffrage as a means of legislating abstinence, a position also advocated by a Father Montgomery before a San Francisco women's Catholic abstinence society. In Brooklyn and in Boston the issue was also discussed before women's temperance groups.[101] Massachusetts's most prominent Catholic abstinence champion, Father Thomas Scully, repeatedly urged the ballot for women, whom he claimed by their very nature were finer than men. It was "unjust to allow men who are inferior to women in all moral, educational, and social matters to vote, and deny that right to women." Scully, who praised females for distributing "no license" circulars at the polls, asserted their enfranchisement would curb the liquor interests and thus implored the legislature to extend the ballot to them.[102]

Writing in the *Catholic World*, Mary A. Dowd not only advocated female suffrage as a means of fighting intemperance and thereby preserving the home but carried her argument to its logical conclusion by asserting that women could legislate and hold elective office.[103] Even the German Roman Catholic Central Verein, a federation of German men's societies to promote Catholic interests and social change, was driven by its reform orientation to women's concerns. The Verein encouraged Catholic women to pursue careers in social work and nursing and at its 1911 session upheld their moral superiority. "How great is your worth, O Catholic women! It depends on you whether or not the world will remain Catholic." However, four years later it too had reluctantly accepted female suffrage as a means of promoting social transformation while preserving womanly dignity and the family.[104] In 1916 it established the National Catholic Women's Union, which endorsed traditional family values, such as encouraging marriage, criticizing divorce and the employment of women, but nevertheless supporting female suffrage.

Often Catholic female activists, although following a life-style that was nonconventional and resembled their non-Catholic counterparts, imposed on themselves ideological limits restricting their feminism. Typical was Margaret Buchanan Sullivan (1847–1903), who emphasized femininity, subservience to men, and sanctity of the family but personified self-reliance in following a career that led to accolades as the most brilliant journalist in America.[105]

The Power of American woman reformers lies in the fact that they have always personally deserved public esteem; not one of them has dipped into eccentricities of base quality, such as advocating free love, or making a parade of dangerous socialist theories. Even from the earliest date, those who put themselves forward... are, without exception, irreproachable from the view of morals.... Whenever it shall please women to claim complete political rights, the men of their family and their circle will not resist; they are restrained by their own wisdom.[106]

As an infant Sullivan was brought from Ireland to Michigan, where she was educated at a Sacred Heart Convent and Detroit High School. After graduation she taught for a couple of years and then became a reporter and editorial writer for the *Chicago Post*. According to the *Woman's Journal*, "Men not knowing it, have gone to the ballot box and cast the talisman precisely as she bid them." While writing for Chicago papers, she lived in a Sacred Heart Convent where, she wrote, "I am surrounded by a greater number of cultivated, pure and intellectual women than I could possibly find elsewhere. In this convent women's right to her own soul and body is realized and fulfilled."[107]

In 1874 Buchanan married the lawyer and Irish-American patriot Alexander Sullivan. Nevertheless she continued to write for New York and Chicago newspapers, as well as for leading magazines such as the *North American Review* and the *Catholic World*. Her contributions were quite diverse, for she dealt with politics, law, religion, medicine, and education. She was especially successful in informing her readers about difficulties in Ireland, and with her friend Mary Blake wrote a book on little-known Mexico. Among the special events she covered were the Republican Convention of 1884, the opening of the Gladstone Parliament in 1886, and the Great Paris Exposition of 1889. Moreover she still found time to promote a school for the deaf in Chicago and to originate that city's Catholic Reading Circle.

Seldom did Sullivan write in support of feminism, although she did observe that "the dressmaker is the natural foe of progressive womanhood. It is not prophesy to say that while the dressmaker dominates, woman will not vote."[108] As a matter of fact, despite her independence, self-reliance, and renown, she remained on the surface a dutiful wife who was frequently praised for her femininity.[109] To one of her closest friends and admirers, Sullivan was "the very incarnation of wifely devotion...she did her best to obliterate the eminent writer in the loving wife....Her joy was in her household, with the beloved of her heart."[110]

Although the Catholicism of the new woman often imposed limitations on her feminism, clergymen frequently found it necessary to reemphasize traditional moral values. Conservative ecclesiastics feared that new approaches jeopardized old virtues, while liberals desired to protect the modern woman from the assaults of reactionary critics. In 1876 Cardinal Gibbons joined the National Vigilance Committee, established at the home of Grace Dodge, a philanthropist and organizer of the Association of Working Girls Societies. The committee's task was to monitor national morals and to influence legislation to uphold them.[111] At the National Purity Congress of 1893, Archbishop Ireland assailed birth control and easy divorce and called for legislation to raise the age of consent.[112] Easy divorce was also the bête noire of the American Federation of Catholic Societies (which, to the praise of the *New York Times*, called for legislation granting separation and limited divorce).[113] Leading works of pastoral theology, of course, glorified motherhood and condemned birth control, abortion, and the thoughtlessness that led to miscarriages.[114]

The *Catholic Girl's Guide* (1906) ignored changing concepts completely. About one-quarter of the book extolled chastity and virginity as the major virtues, and the remainder repeated the shibboleths that females were by nature pious and loving and found their true vocations in the home. Furthermore, the guide claimed that a true housewife was docile and patient before her lord and master husband and was prepared for this role by a Catholic education.[115] The

Jesuit Nicholas Walsh also fostered these notions, asserting that the unselfish wife and mother must act against her natural inclinations, and even "when tired and taxed, unfairly perhaps by others, she must either keep a *sweet* silence or say the right word . . . and conceal as best she can the interior impatience or pain which she cannot help feeling." Walsh, however, did quote St. Chrysostom to demonstrate the power of wives to form and shape their husbands.[116]

Equally as conservative was Archbishop McQuaid, whose views were old-fashioned but whose practices could have misled a superficial observer. Contrary to many other bishops, who believed the proximity of women was suggestive of evil, McQuaid had a domestic staff of nuns assigned to his seminary. As he proclaimed publicly: "Only women can do a woman's work. They attend to making up the rooms, the cleaning of the house, the kitchen, the laundry, they are waitresses in the serving and dining rooms. . . . It must be remembered that the moment a young man is ordained, the ordinary domestic service of his house will be rendered by women. If in the seminary the presence of a woman is suggestive of evil, it will be so after he leaves the seminary. Such a young man should avoid the priesthood." His traditionalism was expressed more succinctly when he warned his fellow ideologue Archbishop Corrigan that if women were not allowed to care for the New York Diocesan Seminary (Dunwoodie), "in about four years the Seminary will be overcome with vermin. . . . Men cannot keep a clean house."[117]

Adherence to convention by Corrigan and McQuaid did not preclude them from using a woman for political purposes when it fit their needs. An 1852 convert from an old New England family, Ella B. Edes (1832–1916) became a permanent resident of Rome about 1866. There she did secretarial work for the Congregation of Propaganda and reported on Vatican affairs for several American newspapers. By 1880, because of her extraordinary access to propaganda, she had become the agent of conservative American bishops with a special relationship to Corrigan and McQuaid. Edes reported on Roman intrigues, leaked material on Archbishop Ireland to his enemies, traduced the liberal hierarchy, and influenced the condemnation of Father McGlynn and the ideas of Henry George. She inveighed against the Knights of Labor and the establishment of Catholic University, placing critical articles on these issues in the Vatican newspaper *L'Osservatore Romano*. Moreover she was influential in the adoption of the directive on education in the Third Plenary Council.[118]

Her relationship with the conservatives was such that when John Boyle O'Reilly published uncomplimentary remarks in the *Boston*

Pilot about her reporting, McQuaid informed O'Reilly of his displeasure, and for the rest of their lives the relationship between the two men was strained.[119] Edes had been an ideal spokesperson for the status quo, for as she commented late in life, "The older I grow, the more utterly I hate modern ideas, progress, evolution, and especially and above all the modern woman."[120] Like many other traditionalists, however, she never recognized the contradiction between her life and her philosophy.

Edes was not the only Catholic woman who attempted to influence the Roman hierarchy on church matters. Maria Longworth Storer, convert and wife of former congressman and diplomat Bellamy Storer, was a prominent Republican whose circle of friends included Theodore Roosevelt. (Her nephew married Roosevelt's daughter Alice in 1906 during the controversy between the president and Maria Storer.) She was also a devoted friend of Archbishop Ireland. Her correspondence with the prelate on a variety of issues, including politics, revealed such self-assurance that he described her as "having an identity which no husband can claim as his own."[121] Storer was convinced that Ireland needed a red hat to offset the negative influences of ecclesiastics in the United States and Europe who were hampering his liberal endeavors. Consequently she intervened with the pope and other Vatican officials on his behalf, asserting that Ireland's promotion would be pleasing to President Roosevelt. When it appeared as if he might be elevated to the cardinalate, Ireland gratefully attributed the expected promotion to her "ceaseless planning and working."[122]

Nevertheless the consistory of 1905 passed him over. Undaunted, Storer continued her efforts on Ireland's behalf. When she defied the president's request to stop her maneuvering and released some of his earlier private letters and minutes of conversations, Roosevelt dismissed her husband as ambassador to Austria-Hungary. As the quarrel between Storer and the president became public, a distressed Ireland suggested his friend withdraw from the fray, but instead she broke off their relationship. Her ambition and zeal had embarrassed a president and an archbishop and had ended her husband's promising career.[123]

Even women deeply committed to traditional roles found themselves acting with nonladylike aggressiveness to achieve their ends. Eliza O. Lummis founded the Daughters of Faith, an organization of socially elite women to influence American values. Her book *Daughters of the Faith: Serious Thoughts for Catholic Women* revealed her strategy. Arguing from the moral superiority of women, Loomis called on Catholic females to restore the world to true values by their sweet, gracious, and Christian influence. Unlike the new women, however, their influence would be brought to bear not through politics but through the family. Under the direction of the Catholic woman, the home would be a place of comfort and peace for the husband, "the king of creation," whom she would endeavor to please. However, because of her goodness, "his sceptre would be swayed by her hand"; after all, "his soul has in a special manner been confided to her by Almighty God."[124]

Apparently matriarchy was not a sufficient means to thwart turn-of-the-century evils, for Loomis herself moved out of the traditional woman's orbit. Under the aegis of Cardinal Farley she founded the Catholic Theatre Movement to strengthen the soul against impurity by raising standards of dramatists and theater audiences. The movement encouraged the production of moral plays in which divine assistance was the means of resolving social problems. Moreover, lists of acceptable productions that adhered to a strict interpretation of the Sixth Commandment were distributed by Loomis's organization.[125] Conservatives like Loomis and liberals like Toomy demonstrated the truth of Mary Dowd's observation in 1894 in *Donahoe's Magazine* that women working out their own destiny was one of the greatest reform movements of the age.[126]

Chapter 8

WAGE-EARNING WOMEN AND ETHNIC CHURCHES: A ROAD TO AUTONOMY

It had always been necessary for large numbers of Catholic women to work. The church, albeit reluctantly, thus accepted the necessity of wage earning by unmarried daughters of poor families. However, as the nineteenth century drew to a close, clerical opposition to the employment of other classes of females began to wane. After all, women were better educated than ever before, new opportunities were available in the workplace, and society emphasized their role in service and redemption. Although manual labor was still to be avoided as unladylike, other forms of wage earning were perceived as permissible, as long as virtue was not endangered. Moreover, as not all women would opt for marriage, some churchmen even contended that girls should revise their aspirations and prepare for a career by developing their natural gifts.[1]

Unskilled work was usually the lot of female immigrants, the most common occupation being that of domestic servant. Since there was a surplus of Irish females because of disproportionate immigration in relation to men and because of the early death of many Irish-American males, there was a shortage of husbands for these women. Thus English-speaking Celts frequently began their employment as live-in servants. The labor historian David Montgomery has asserted that almost every Irish female, at some time or other, worked as a domestic.[2] Nevertheless, house servants escaped from that situation as soon as possible, for this type of employment restricted their freedom. Some even turned to industrial work and, despite lower pay, looked down on domestics. As one jute mill worker stated, "I hate the word 'service.' We came to this country to better ourselves, and it's not bettering to have anybody ordering you around."[3] Many of those engaged in factory work developed a trade union consciousness, moving away from purely ethnic and religious loyalties.[4]

More fortunate Irish women entered middle-class occupations such as sales and office work or, better still, teaching and nursing.[5] Suffering from discriminatory pay scales and exploitation, they too defied the church's ideal of submission and demanded improved working conditions. Even those who ceased employment with marriage often bore a relationship to their husband unlike that of the American ideal of the idle lady. About 15 percent of Irish-American women continued as income producers after marriage by taking in boarders, and thereby creating a relationship with their spouse that was less subservient than that glorified by the church.[6]

Other immigrant groups shared the experience and changing attitudes of the Irish. Large numbers of Germans and Poles also were employed as live-in servants. Because of language barriers, a shortage of single females, and differing religious and cultural traditions, Italians were seldom employed as domestics. As a matter of fact, ethnic mores inhibited any type of employment for these women. Nevertheless, circumstances often forced an abandonment of that ideal as wages of the male head of the family needed to be supplemented. In such cases it was considered more desirable that the daughter enter the work force than the mother, for neglect of formal education was not a problem. Schooling was not necessary to prepare girls for their lifetime role as mother and wife. (This lack of education may be one of the reasons that Italian women were slow to enter the professions.) As Virginia Yans-McLaughlin has observed, "Girls, even more than boys, sacrificed their own goals and accomplishments for the family interests." Nevertheless, wage earning in a factory was a step toward Americanization and independence. Working daughters were more likely to rebel, choose their own husbands, and marry outside village or family origins.[7]

Many young Italian-American women entered the needle trades. After marriage a large number did piecework at home, and some wives even continued to toil in factories and sweatshops. The percentage of Italian women working in 1910 was double the national average, while Italian wives were as likely to work as their German or Irish counterparts. In New York City 72 percent of female garment workers were Italian. This nationality also composed the largest percentage of married women in the needle trades.[8] Moreover, other wives ran boardinghouses.[9] More fluent in English than their mothers, the second generation obtained more desirable positions such as saleswomen in department stores, telephone operators, and office clerks.[10] By 1915 only 56 percent of family income was produced by men.[11] The necessity of relying upon home work or wages of wives and daughters undermined the dominant role of man and priest. Moreover, it engendered a sense of self-confidence and independence among the women who worked.[12]

These characteristics were further developed in the trade union movement. Working women gradually accepted the notion that marriage — although an escape from low pay, long hours, and dangerous conditions — was not a remedy. Even the most sheltered of immigrant women turned, although slowly, to unions. During the bitter New York shirtwaist strike of 1909, Italian "girls" were reluctant to join the demonstrators. As a result the Women's Trade Union League (WTUL) began a campaign to educate them to the union cause by hiring an Italian-speaking organizer, to attract them to the movement by establishing an Italian Mutual Benefit Association, and to appeal to their national pride by founding an Italian Girls' International League. The following year during the cloak-makers strike there was a newfound solidarity with male pickets, and by 1913 thousands of Italian women, described as militants, had been organized into an American Federation of Labor (AFL) affiliate. Traditional authority patterns had been further eroded.[13]

This new independence of wage-earning women was hailed by Mary B. O'Sullivan, even though she railed against feminism. A prominent turn-of-the-century writer, teacher, businesswoman, and editor of *Donahoe's Magazine*, O'Sullivan championed woman's right to work. "The time has gone by," she proclaimed, "when a girl was born to no higher duty than humiliating dependence on father and brother, or a sordid-loveless marriage." The author of many articles, including studies of famous Catholic females, O'Sullivan described as heroes those underpaid Catholic women whose faith saved them from prostitution. The raising of women's wages was a mission for America, "a nobler cause than clamoring for rights that do not belong to them, for positions they can never fill, even if men be so foolish as to let them try."[14]

Unlike O'Sullivan, most women dedicated to improving working conditions for females turned to the ballot, even if reluctantly, as a means of doing so. The first prominent Catholic labor leader, Augusta Lewis (c. 1840–1920), born in New York and educated at the Sacred Heart Convent School, was a convert. A reporter and social reformer as well as typesetter, she probably was fired for union activities from Susan B. Anthony's radical women's newspaper, the *Revolution*. President of Women's Typographical Union No. 1, organized under her initiative in 1868, she was the first female elected to national office in the International Typographical Union, which she served as corresponding secretary from 1870 to 1871. In 1874 she married George Troup, publisher of the *New Haven Union*. Although a bustling mother of seven children, she continued her efforts to improve social conditions. Troup raised money for charitable causes, advocated equal pay for equal work, aided Italian immigrants, and championed women suffrage as a means of alleviating the oppression of working women.[15]

The leadership in organizing women's unions was for the most part assumed by Irish-Catholics, as they were the first to enter nondomestic employment in large numbers, knew the English language, often were single, and possessed confidence and self-assurance even as they left the Emerald Isle. In 1878 a former Socialist, Elizabeth Flynn Rodgers (1847–1939), founded the first woman's union in Chicago and three years later was elected a Knights of Labor delegate. In 1886 she was chosen as master workman, head of all assemblies in Chicago, except for the stockyards. Despite her husband's entreaties and the responsibilities of twelve children, she persisted in reform, determined to prove that women could accomplish important things. In addition to promoting unions, she was active in the Irish Ladies Land League and the temperance and suffrage movements and established the Women's Catholic Order of Foresters, an insurance society.[16]

The earliest major effort to organize women was undertaken by Leonora Barry (1849–1930) on behalf of the knights. A thirty-seven-year-old mill worker and a widowed mother of two, she was engaged as a salaried, full-time general investigator in 1886. Placing one son in a convent school and the other with a sister-in-law, Barry traveled fifty weeks a year organizing women, raising money for female strikers, and preaching the gospel of equal pay and improved working conditions. Nevertheless, she found many women indifferent to her message because of religious scruples. Barry herself exemplified the dilemma of the Catholic woman worker, for she believed men should be the breadwinners, and only when necessary should women abandon their divinely instituted role as homemaker. Although the task of unions was to create favorable working conditions for mothers-to-be, the union was to be run by men, and women were only to assist "as God intended." In keeping with her convictions, when she married Obadiah Lake in 1890, Barry immediately resigned and concentrated on interests more typically feminine. Nevertheless, she continued to promote suffrage as a means of improving working conditions and protecting the home and campaigned for the ballot in Colorado in the 1890s. A wife, she asserted, is a wiser partner if she understands the political, economic, and social conditions of life.[17]

Mary Kenney (1864–1943) did not share the same qualms about women working as did Lake. A devout Catholic, Kenney organized women workers in Chicago while supporting herself and her widowed mother as a bookbinder. She was hired by Samuel Gompers, president of the AFL, as the federation's first female organizer. While campaigning for the union in Boston, she met and married Jack O'Sullivan. To enable his wife to continue her activities, he shared in the housework, caring for their four children and his mother-in-law. Mary O'Sullivan was active in the Woman's Educational and Industrial Union, founded a federal labor union, and volunteered for settlement duties. Convinced that women needed a special labor organization, she conceived the idea of and was instrumental in establishing the Women's Trade Union League in 1903, a year after her husband's death. Its purpose was to organize women workers and to press for protective legislation. O'Sullivan continued to push for working women's rights until her death, by advocating equal pay, administering relief during the Lawrence Strike of 1912, serving on the Women's International League for Peace and Freedom, functioning as a factory inspector in the 1920s and 1930s, and, most important, championing woman suffrage as a means of work reform. Not only did she write articles supporting enfranchisement, but she testified for it before state and federal legislative committees.[18]

Many other Catholic women played significant roles in the WTUL, including Elizabeth Maloney (fl. 1903–13), Margaret Hinchey (fl. 1913–26), Sarah Conboy (d. 1928), Maud O'Farrell Swartz (1879–1937), Eva MacDonald Valesh (1874–1952), Agnes Nestor (1880–1948), and Julia O'Connor (1890–1972). In their dedication to trade unions each of these women not only exemplified nontraditional lifestyles but, by advocating the right to earn wages and urging the extension of suffrage as a means of protecting women workers, undercut the conservative restraints imposed on the ideal lady.

Maloney, an executive board member of the league, organized a waitresses' union in 1902, wherein she united the goals of unionization with a version of feminine piety based on her Catholicism. She kept a print of the Madonna in union headquarters to inspire waitresses and insisted that these women be treated as ladies and that employers refrain from offensive language in their presence. These traditional views, however, did not prevent her from challenging accepted mores by lobbying legislators for woman suffrage.

After being jailed and blacklisted for her part in a 1912 strike, Irish-born Hinchey, a young laundry worker, joined the league to do whatever she could to improve conditions for women. Representing the league and the state Woman Suffrage party, she toured New York on behalf of the ballot. She directed her efforts toward Irish-Catholics and immigrant workers, promoting enfranchisement as a means of bettering working conditions. Hinchey was so successful in moving her audiences that the press dubbed her the Irish Vote Getter and the Billy Sunday of Suffragists.

Sarah Conboy began work at eleven when her father died and years later reentered the work force after the death of her husband. Her leadership of 680 striking female carpet workers in 1909 led to her appointment as a general organizer to the United Textile Workers of America, which she also served as secretary-treasurer from 1916 to her death in 1928. Conboy, who was also the first woman bank director in the United States, raised money to help support the activities of the labor priest Peter E. Dietz. Like most trade unionists she was a vigorous advocate of suffrage but an outspoken opponent of the equal rights amendment, which she feared would invalidate legislation protecting working women.[19]

Maud O'Farrell Swartz, a printer who was educated in a European convent school, was recruited by the league as a result of her campaigning in the Italian language for woman suffrage in 1912. From 1922 to 1926 she was president of the WTUL and served as secretary to the New York State Department of Labor from 1931 until her death. Like O'Sullivan, she was also a resounding advocate of world peace and internationalism.[20]

Described as "a feminine comet across the political sky" and called a vicious little pest by Ignatius Donnelly, founder of the Populist party, Eva MacDonald Valesh had been inspired as a child by Dominican nuns. She raised the concerns of "homeless, voiceless women, helpless to cope" in her lectures throughout the Midwest for the Knights of Labor, Farmers Alliance, and Populist party. As a newspaperwoman she continued to battle for justice by advocating enfranchisement and exposing employer exploitation. She was hired by the AFL as an organizer and writer for its paper the *Federationist* but quit when Gompers refused to put her name on the masthead. She continued to write pieces on reform and support social work and unionization. As a result of her disappointment at the hands of Gompers, she no longer emphasized unions as the major means of improving working conditions for women wage earners but stressed, instead, the importance of suffrage. This stance was in keeping with her nomination in 1888 for the Minneapolis school board, allegedly the first time a woman was so honored by a major party.[21]

Also influenced by Dominican nuns was Agnes Nestor, who helped found the International Glove Workers Union, which she served in a national capacity from 1903 until her death in 1948. Nestor, who was quite devout, was also a member of the executive board of the WTUL and chaired the Committee on Women in Industry of the National Council of Catholic Women. Like other union leaders, she lobbied for protective legislation, supported settlements, and championed suffrage as a means of promoting justice for women workers.

Another parochial-school product was Julia O'Connor Parker, who went to work for the telephone company at age eighteen. A graduate of the WTUL's school for organizers, she was president of the Boston League from 1915 to 1918 and on the national executive board from 1917 to 1926. More important, she led a series of successful strikes as head of the operators department (which she had helped form) of the International Brotherhood of Electrical Workers. Although married in 1925 and the mother of two daughters, Parker not only continued serving in the labor movement organizing for the AFL but was active in the presidential campaigns of 1932, 1936, and 1940, serving in the labor division of the Democratic National Committee.[22]

To assist working women the Ladies Catholic Benevolent Association was founded in Titusville, Pennsylvania, in 1890, the world's first exclusively female fraternal insurance organization. Presided over by Elizabeth B. McGowan of Buffalo, New York, from its birth to 1910 and then by Kate Maloney of Troy, it grew rapidly. By 1911 it had over 121,000 members and 1,100 branches and had paid $9 million in death benefits with another $2 million in reserve. This huge enterprise, including the position of "supreme medical examiner," was controlled entirely by women and was democratically organized with triennial conventions. As one might expect, it publicly endorsed woman suffrage.[23]

Nonprofessionals were not the only type of Catholic women to defy clerical admonitions by forming unions and promoting suffrage. Those who flooded the teaching vocation also turned to unions and the ballot as a means of obtaining equal pay and professional status.

In Chicago Margaret Haley (1861–1939) and her friend Catherine Goggin (1855–1916), both Catholic, founded the Chicago Teachers' Federation in 1897. They demanded equal pay for women and pushed for tax reform to finance the salary increase that would result. To realize these objectives the federation entered politics, and Haley became an outspoken advocate of suffrage, campaigning for the ballot in California, New York, and Illinois. She claimed the vote was a means of establishing "fundamental justice to all." Her commitment to democratic principles even led her to challenge a church lobbyist who opposed her efforts to introduce referendum procedures in Illinois; she asserted that if Catholicism and social change were not compatible, she would have left the church.

Haley's success encouraged other teachers to organize, especially those in New York, where the Interborough Association of Women Teachers was founded in 1906. Headed by a convert and former social worker, Grace Strachan Forsythe (1863–1922), the association struggled for equal pay and the right of married women to retain their position. To strengthen the organization's political power Forsythe rallied teachers to the suffrage movement and then lobbied for various pieces of progressive legislation. Believing herself the victim of religious prejudice when she was defeated for president of the National Education Association, she became a champion of civil liberties. She courageously opposed the repressive Lusk legislation of 1920, which required loyalty oaths from teachers, outlawed the Socialist party, and created a New York State Loyalty Bureau.[24]

As wage-earning women became increasingly free from traditional restrictions, immigrant housewives were also becoming less subservient to husband and church. They developed interests outside the family, while dominating relations in it. Observers believed Irish Catholic society to have been matriarchal, as values, fears, guilt, and strivings were passed on by mothers to their sons. Male children feared and sought approval from their mother, a source of power. Wives, on the other hand, manipulated their husbands and, according to one scholar, prevented them and their sons from developing as men. Allegedly the legendary drinking of Irish men was really a means of asserting masculinity.[25]

Although male dominance is frequently described as characteristic of the Italian family, Italian wives, like Irish wives, frequently maneuvered their husbands, telling them what to do, how to do it, and what to say. Usually they had the last word on important decisions, exercised real power through control of the purse, and wielded considerable authority outside the home on family affairs such as school matters.[26] Female dominance in this area was so strong that Italian women even challenged churchmen. In 1916, when the new Irish-American pastor of the Italian church in Trenton, New Jersey, planned to reduce the parish debt by replacing the Religious Teachers Filippini and renting the school to the city, women parishioners armed with clubs and sticks staged a sit-in at the school auditorium. They barred exits and refused to leave until the pastor relented and promised to keep the Italian order of nuns. The triumphant women then reported their success to the one hundred male members of the Holy Name Society who had been waiting outside.[27] As one scholar has stated, Italian women were feminists without the label.[28]

Despite such self-assertiveness these women apparently complied with the church's admonitions on sexual practices. Their fertility rate was considerably higher than that of other Catholic groups, and they devoted much time and imagination trying to protect their daughters from the advances of young men. Coeducation and employment, however, tended to dissolve this protective mantle, and American mores helped shape family size. The fertility rate for second-generation Italian women fell below that of the average Catholic. Furthermore, with each passing generation domestic skills were considered of less importance.[29]

Women of all classes participated in festivals and church organizations in Italian parishes. Many working women formed mutual-benefit societies, sometimes under church auspices, with dues, insurance coverage, and death benefits. As these activities weakened family ties, they were at times opposed by males. However, there was little opposition, if any, to wives of business and professional men forming female auxiliaries to the Sons of Italy. These chapters preserved Italian culture among immigrants and encouraged moral and cultural progress to help make newcomers better citizens.[30]

Ethnic churches, designed to strengthen the religious loyalty of immigrants, also fostered a knowledge of traditional language and culture and by their very nature stimulated political interest. Church participation then broadened the sphere of woman's concerns by promoting nationalism and sometimes providing benefits such as insurance that were not available elsewhere. Religious duties became patriotic duties as the national church preserved and transmitted the identity and culture of the motherland. As late as 1921 one priest in addressing one of the most nationalistic of immigrant groups proclaimed, "The Lord God created you Polish men and women, therefore do not seek, as they say foreign gods, but register and belong to a Polish parish." National parishes became a major force in weakening female domesticity by providing acceptable tasks outside the home, undertakings that increased one's self-worth. This was especially true among women whose native lands suffered from foreign oppression;

for them, chauvinism, piety, and women's liberation became intertwined.

The homeland of Polish-Americans was incorporated into the Russian Empire in 1830 after a brief period of nominal independence during which the czar of Russia was the king of Poland. The Russians then attempted to suppress Catholicism in Poland and Lithuania, thereby intensifying the relationship between religion and nationalism. To practice the faith was to defy Russian domination, an attitude that immigrants from the Baltic brought with them to the United States.[31]

Polish immigrants, about 92 percent of them Catholic, built up a community life characterized by their own church, press, and society. By the end of the nineteenth century, there were national orphanages, retirement homes, and even a seminary, and in 1906 Felician Sisters arrived from Poland to preserve the language and culture in their schools.[32] Nationalism fostered by such religious communities quickly spilled over to organizations that were primarily political and patriotic. As early as 1866 Gmina Polska, a Catholic group for a free and independent homeland, was established in Chicago.[33]

In 1898 the Polish Women's Alliance, consisting mainly of Chicago middle-class women, was started to promote Polish patriotism through a study of history and the preservation of national culture. Designed also to protect the welfare of immigrants, the alliance offered insurance, maintained an employment agency, dispensed aid, and taught working skills. By 1910 it was publishing its own weekly and was holding national conventions. To ensure that leadership positions would be available for women, the alliance did not affiliate with male organizations. Nationalistic oppression became related to women's liberation, for as the alliance promoted the rights of females and enlisted young girls in the cause of patriotism, it raised their consciousness as women.[34] Its newspaper was unabashedly feminist. "In the area of rights," the editors wrote, "everything must be taken and one must never wait to be given [them] for they will never be given. And so with woman when she struggles for a right she must win it and take it." Sections on the accomplishments of famous Polish women, articles on controversial issues such as suffrage and education, and attacks on the double standard of morality were among the fare offered its readers. Moreover, the paper even criticized the church for its conservative stance on women's issues.[35]

Women's interests were reflected in other patriotic organizations. As a result of female pressure separate departments with feminist overtones were fashioned in male organizations such as the Polish

National Alliance and the Polish Roman Catholic Union.[36] Active in this union was Mary Olszewski Kryszak (1875–1945), who had been assistant manager and bookkeeper of a Polish language daily from 1908 to 1922, founder and president of a local lodge of the Polish Women's Alliance from 1912 to 1945, and chairperson of the Ladies Auxiliary of the Polish Relief Committee in 1939. Kryszak, who was also involved in church affairs, was elected in 1928 to the Wisconsin House of Representatives. Except for 1938 she served there until her death, usually the only woman in an otherwise all-male assembly.[37]

During World War I the Polish Women's Alliance encouraged enlistments in the American army and joined with other national organizations in forming the Polish Central Committee to coordinate efforts for a free Poland at war's end. At the Woman's Peace Conference at the Hague in 1915, delegates from the alliance insisted that the restoration of Poland be an objective of the international peace movement. They railed against peace at any price as a crime against humanity and "raise[d] our mighty voice of mothers, daughters, sisters, and wives suffering beyond all measure, calling to all nations."[38] At the 1918 convention in Detroit in support of a Polish republic and independence, over 100 of the 946 delegates were women, and Marcella K. Sembrich (1858–1935), Metropolitan opera singer, came out of retirement to organize the American Polish Relief Committee and raise funds for the land of her birth.[39]

Devotion to one's native land involved women in untypical and "unfeminine" activities. The only nonconforming actions on the part of one of the most noted actresses in the country, the Polish-born Helena Modjeska (1849–1909) had been signing a dress-reform petition in 1893 and defending the legitimacy of her profession for women. Modjeska, however, performed at benefits to raise money for Polish causes and, more daringly, publicly assailed her nation's Russian masters. In her address "Women on the Stage" at the Chicago World's Fair of 1893, she denounced the Russian government for its treatment of Poles. Her speech so aroused the ire of the czar that she was prohibited from entering Russia and from being buried in her beloved Poland.[40]

In addition to the nationalistic pull that undermined traditional values and family relationships, wage earning contributed to assertiveness in Polish women, as it did in the case of Italians and Irish.[41] Greater participation in decision making must have resulted when many women supplemented their husband's income by taking in boarders or by toiling with their mates in fields and stores or by working as domestics or laborers. (In 1912 it was estimated that 37.7

percent of Polish families took in paying boarders.) The Polish Catholic settlement house in Chicago maintained a nursery for working mothers. By 1912 the Immigration Commission Report concluded that for Polish women "marriage is not suffered to be a bar to work," and still the numbers of wage-earning women increased even further in the 1920s and 1930s.[42] With their mother's example before them and a sense of independence resulting from their own employment, Polish daughters developed "flexibility in their attitude toward life and toward their part in it" and increasingly resented parental rulings.[43]

Once Lithuanian-American women rejected Polish clerical leadership in the 1890s, their national traditions and religious faith intertwined as it did for American Poles. Catholicism became a means of preserving their political heritage and a means of escaping confinement at home. According to one scholar, Lithuanian women participated more fully in community affairs than did their American counterparts.[44] In 1906 the Lithuanian Roman Catholic Federation was founded by 120 delegates from national organizations, four of whom were women. Its object was to advance the physical, spiritual, and cultural welfare of Lithuanians in the United States and promote freedom for those in Europe. (In 1569 Lithuania united with Poland to protect itself from Russian advances. In the last part of the eighteenth century, when Poland was partitioned between Austria, Prussia and Russia, Lithuania became part of Russia.) Catholic women were dissatisfied with the federation and desired an organization of their own. Fearing that a female society would substitute suffrage demands for nationalistic goals, the men withheld their assistance.

Nevertheless, in 1914 the American Lithuanian Roman Catholic Women's Alliance was begun. It grew rapidly: in only two years it acquired 1,039 members and began its own magazine. In addition to preserving Lithuanian culture and language, the alliance fulfilled a fraternal function by providing sick and death benefits. Its relationship to faith and freedom was reflected in its motto, "Serve Church and Country." (As late as 1925 Chicago Lithuanians protesting the use of English in church services as a violation of their natural rights distributed handbills urging parishioners to "uprise for the Lithuanian nationalism in our church.")[45] During World War I alliance members pushed for a free Lithuania and raised money for their destitute European brothers and sisters. Although English pages had to be added to the alliance's magazine in 1945 and a campaign initiated to recruit American-born members, Lithuanian women continued to demand freedom for their homeland. In 1949 a women's council moved from

Germany to New York to agitate for liberation, while the members of the alliance continued to demonstrate and demand freedom from Russian domination.[46]

Nationalistic goals of the alliance led its members directly, but cautiously, into governmental affairs. One of its founders distinguished between political activities, which were unacceptable for "ladies," and Lithuanian activities, which were permissible, even if political. More forthright was Mrs. Ursulla Daukantas, the first national president, who used her office to interest women in politics and to educate members in voting.[47] The trepidation of Lithuanian men had been realized — patriotism in the alliance was eroding traditional roles of women.

According to one scholar Irish-Americans perceived themselves not as ambitious emigrants but as "involuntary, nonresponsible exiles" compelled to leave their native land by the tyranny of the British and landlords. Probably more than other females, Irish women were deeply involved in national movements establishing a readily recognizable identity and a life outside church, kitchen, and work. Long before the Civil War they established auxiliaries to male organizations formed to assist the oppressed in their homeland.[48] Not satisfied with promoting Irish culture and history or raising relief funds or even writing on behalf of the cause, many women became directly involved in Ireland's quest for freedom and in so doing sometimes directly defied church authority.

The Fenian Brotherhood, organized in 1859, emphasized force and military methods as the means of establishing an Irish republic and thus confined its membership to men. Although the association was often condemned by the clergy for its adherence to violence, a Fenian Sisterhood was instituted almost immediately. This was one of the first large-scale organizations of women in the United States for political purposes. Females raised money for the brotherhood, exalted male militarism, lectured on Fenian goals, and, on at least one occasion, sought political support from a congressman. These activities led the Irish-born James Duggan (1825–99), bishop of Chicago, to denounce them from the altar as "bad women."[49] It was probably because of the sisterhood's unflinching loyalty that Irish men, as traditional as any, shattered precedent and at the National Irish Republican Convention in Washington in 1869 endorsed woman suffrage.[50]

As a result of ill-conceived military operations against Canada resulting in the imprisonment of several leaders and further condemnation by the church, the Fenians faded from existence. Many members, however, joined a secret society designed to create an Irish republic — the Clan na Gael, described as the most important nationalist organization in Irish-American history.[51] Again women were excluded, but once more they collected funds and assisted their men. Margaret Sullivan (Mrs. Alexander) probably served as a clan envoy to Irish nationalist leader Charles Parnell in 1886, warning him that if he did not strive for complete independence, rather than home rule, support for the National League would be withheld.[52]

Another radical, Margaret O'Donovan-Rossa, came to the United States when her husband, Jeremiah, received a life sentence for revolutionary activities in Ireland. She was a devout Catholic who attended daily Mass, recited a daily rosary, and tended an altar in her home. Yet she was a zealot in the cause of Irish freedom, working to strengthen the clan and mediate between its divergent wings. A mass of contradictions, she believed only males should direct nationalistic endeavors, yet she advocated woman's suffrage and so influenced her husband (whose sentence was reduced to banishment) that he referred to her as "the person who bosses the boss."[53]

This type of female maneuverability also existed in the Irish-American political scene. The wife of Chicago alderman and ward boss John J. Coughlin was so much in the background that many of his closest political associates were unaware that he was married. Yet Mary Kiley Coughlin instructed her husband in grammar and manners, insisting that "if you're going to be an alderman, you must talk and act like one."[54]

Of major concern to many Irish-American women was land reform, and over sixty Ladies' Land Leagues were established in the United States by Fanny Parnell, Charles's favorite sister. His mother, one of the league's earliest presidents, believed that women were more influential than men in the Land League, whose function was to ensure that the ownership of land rested with those who cultivated it.[55] To ease the fears of conservative males that feminism might become a corollary of the organization, many chapters publicly repudiated women's rights and emphasized that its role was the traditional female one of providing relief to the needy. Nevertheless, when Cleveland leaguers planned a fund-raising picnic, Bishop Gilmour chastised them, admonishing the women to reject the "undecorous role of noisy agitators" and to refrain from political activity. He reminded them, especially the unmarried, that home was their God-designed sphere and warned that if they violated their modesty or "forgot their womanhood" by continuing in the organization, they would be excommunicated. The following week, in order that "female modesty must be maintained, let the cost be what it may," he imposed the punishment. President Mary Roland defiantly thundered back, "We have organized a society to aid Ireland. If that be heresy, then we are heretics.... Our conduct, our pure high motives would be worthy of imitation by any lady." Despite Gilmour, or maybe because of him, the chapter added five new members at its next meeting and was defended by league presidents in other cities and by some of the Catholic press. It continued its activities and two months later even had as guest speaker Edward McGlynn, the New York reform priest. Ladies' Land Leagues did not disappear until the whole American movement collapsed following Parnell's change of policy in Ireland and the dissolution of the league there.[56]

Equally as daring as Roland's defiance was the female response to the excommunication of Father McGlynn and the banning of the Anti-Poverty Society of New York, an organization closely allied with Land Leaguers. The priest, an ardent champion of the league, had defied the Cleveland chancery by addressing the ladies' chapter. A few years later in 1886 he campaigned for Henry George, the radical candidate for mayor of New York who advocated the elimination of poverty by a single tax on unearned income obtained through rising land values. When founding the Anti-Poverty Society in 1887, an organization based on George's teachings, McGlynn appealed for female members, as they were "more moral, more religious, and more capable [than men] of ending anguish."[57] Four months later, New York's conservative bishop, Corrigan, excommunicated McGlynn and proclaimed membership in the society a reserved sin. Nevertheless, a large number of women continued to support the priest by attending his rallies, denouncing his removal, objecting to the bishop's policy, and even meeting in the basement of McGlynn's church, whose new pastor was forced to have the police eject them.[58] McGlynn urged his followers not to abandon Catholicism, informing them that according to canon law it was not necessary to confess membership in the society and that it was still permissible to receive the sacraments. Of course this pressure had little effect on the bishop. When forty-eight-year-old, Irish-born Theresa Kelly died, Corrigan refused to allow her to be buried in consecrated ground, for although she was a Sunday school teacher and, according to her pastor, a practicing Catholic, she was a society member.[59] Large numbers of Irish-American women continued to support McGlynn right up until 1892, when he was readmitted to the church by the pope's American representative after an investigation by the faculty of Catholic University.

One of McGlynn's defenders had been Sister Francis Clare (Margaret T. Cusack), a Dublin-born convert who had been active in the Land League in Ireland. Cusack, with the permission of the pope, had established the Sisters of Peace of St. Joseph to care for homeless and friendless girls. From her convent in New Jersey she continued to speak out for the peasants of Ireland. Deeply committed to "truth and peace," she rallied to McGlynn's side, publicly criticizing the harshness of ecclesiastical authorities and praising the priest's love and care for the poor. Her pro forma apology to Corrigan, delivered at her ordinary's instruction, so infuriated the bishop of Newark that he refused to allow any more women into the congregation and denied permission for novices to take vows. Cusack withdrew from her religious order and in time left the church.[60] Despite her daring in the cause of Irish nationalism and of justice, Cusack was really very traditional. Her book *Advice to Irish Girls in America* assumed the natural role of woman was that of wife, subservient to and ready to sacrifice all for her husband. If one must be a wage earner, Cusack recommended employment as a domestic, for Jesus was a servant. Young girls could then serve Jesus too and in so doing set an example for Protestant masters, who might very well convert to Catholicism.

Activities of Irish-American women nationalists increased dramatically with the outbreak of the First World War in Europe. To marshal mass support the Clan na Gael organized the First Irish Race Convention early in 1916, a two-day meeting of two thousand Irish-American men and women who established the Friends of Irish Freedom. The friends tried to keep the United States from entering the war on the side of England; failing that, it pushed for the application of Wilsonian ideals of self-determination to Ireland.

To publicize their cause the friends held huge rallies, sometimes in defiance of police authority. During the summer of 1917, ten thousand marched down New York's Broadway. Several women were arrested, including Margaret Curley, the niece of Boston's mayor. Curley "fanned the feeling of the crowd to a frenzy" as she kissed the flag of Irish revolution and harangued the mob in Gaelic before being carried away by the police.[61] Female partisans not only defied law-enforcement officers but even challenged the hierarchy as they publicly criticized Cardinal Farley of New York for prohibiting priests from presiding at meetings of the friends.[62]

In 1919 the friends, along with Mary McWhorter, the Irish-born president of the Ladies Auxiliary of the Ancient Order of Hibernians (AOH, a Catholic nationalist organization), called another Irish

Race Convention. Over fifty thousand attendees demanded that the Paris Peace Conference deal with Irish concerns. When the conference ignored these issues, the friends attacked the settlement and allied themselves with the Republican party to defeat the Treaty of Versailles in the American Senate.[63]

Also attempting to obtain justice for Ireland was the Irish Progressive League, an organization established in 1917 by male patriots and by Margaret E. Hickey and Dr. Gertrude Kelly. Hickey led a delegation of thirty-four men and women to the White House, where a petition for Irish independence was presented to the president's Irish-Catholic secretary, Joseph P. Tumulty. The league, dominated by women, was not in the least intimidated by repressive wartime legislation. In an effort to ensure that their views would be represented at the peace conference, Hickey, Kelly, and Mrs. Peter Golden opened a propaganda bureau in Washington, D.C. Unlike Irish-American males they were not afraid to visit Jeremiah O'Leary, whose anti-British stance had been criticized by President Wilson during the 1916 campaign and who was imprisoned for violating the sedition laws.[64]

Women Hibernians also set an example for their male counterparts. The men avoided controversial issues during the war. The women, led by the indefatigable McWhorter (who has been described as a gallant lady), petitioned Wilson, sold Irish nationalist papers at church doors, raised money for the Irish republic, and enthusiastically supported other nationalist organizations.[65] In 1918 on behalf of seventy-five thousand American women of Irish descent, the majority of whom she claimed had sons in the war, McWhorter testified before the House Committee on Foreign Relations in support of a measure requiring Irish representation at the Peace Conference. She was joined by Hughes of the Irish Women's Council; Ellen Jolly, also of the AOH; and Mrs. Adelia Christie of the United Irish Societies of Northern Ohio.[66] A year later McWhorter testified before the same committee for the appropriation of funds to pay "salaries of a minister and consuls to the Republic of Ireland," a de facto recognition of independence if the measure passed.[67]

Frustrated in their endeavors to obtain freedom for their native land, Irish-American women demonstrated before the British embassy in 1920, badgered the ambassador and his visitors, and for seventy-four nights picketed the White House. Like the militant suffragists, some were arrested and demanded to be treated as political prisoners.[68]

Political activities of ethnic women had moved them far from the pale of domesticity as preached by church and society. The need to earn wages and the necessity of improving conditions of employment had also led working-class women away from traditional stereotypes. The order of events pushed these women in the direction of suffrage, a reform opposed by most churchmen right up to its enactment. However, energies from all types of Catholic women were beginning to coalesce behind the movement and sweep aside what remained of clerical opposition.

Chapter 9

SUFFRAGE AND WAR: AN ERA OF CHANGE

Like her working-class sisters, the new Catholic woman also gravitated toward suffrage, a reform whose appeal to twentieth-century women often blurred class distinctions. Suffrage, like wage earning, challenged traditional values and thereby provoked clerical opposition. Its most prominent critic was Cardinal Gibbons, who feared that with the ballot women would cross into the domain of men and in so doing would lose reverence and dignity, endanger the home, and risk divorce. During World War I, at the request of a delegation of Catholic women, the cardinal reconsidered his views, admitted the inevitability of suffrage, and with almost a note of sadness confessed that maybe his ideas were based on old-fashioned notions. Nevertheless, when the Nineteenth Amendment was ratified, he expressed regret that "women had taken the plunge into the deep."[1]

This note of regret was missing from other Catholic critics, whose fears often made Gibbons's apprehensions appear trivial. It was alleged that suffrage was inspired by an anti-Christian spirit, linked to the birth control movement, and was a pagan step toward a socialist state. According to Bishop Sebastian J. Messmer (1847–1930) of Milwaukee, it was the panacea for those who refused to accept the "essential inequality of men and women." The American Federation of Catholic Societies coupled it with socialism as a major threat to the home and family.[2] Some spokesmen were not content to warn of the dangers inherent in women voting but urged females to become actively engaged in antisuffrage work — a rather bizarre recommendation, since these critics contended the ballot was dangerous because it would lure women from the home. Nevertheless, that was the conclusion of the article "Women" in the *Catholic Encyclopedia*, which also asserted that the female soul was inferior to that of the male.[3]

Many prominent Catholic women also continued to oppose suffrage and, like their nineteenth-century counterparts, were often social activists. To rally political opposition to enfranchisement one had to be relatively free of family responsibilities and possess middle-class contacts, education, and leisure. Consequently the striking anomaly of women's using political means to prevent political responsibilities from being thrust upon them became a characteristic of the opposition.

One of the most outspoken and prominent of these adversaries was Katherine E. Conway (1853–1927).[4] The underlying theme of her writings, especially apparent in her nonfiction, was a reenforcement of the traditional role of women. Three of her publications, *Bettering Ourselves, A Lady and Her Letters*, and *Questions of Honor in the Christian Life* (submitted to a Jesuit at Boston College for approval before publication), urged educated women not to defer marriage, for the first fruit of a liberal education was homemaking.[5] Although she exalted marriage as the normal state for women, her values for men were different. "The Place That Was Kept" was a short story of a young man who left the seminary to care for his family. Despite the attraction of an alluring female, he remained single and at the conclusion of his responsibilities returned to the seminary to find true happiness.[6]

Her most popular novel, *Lalor's Maples*, partially autobiographical, reflected the conflict between social and religious conservatism and independence in Catholic women. *Maples* is the saga of a wealthy Irish-American family whose daughter must go to work when the father encounters financial reverses after having mortgaged their beautiful home. The heroine resists her mother's blandishments to marry the holder of the mortgage because he insists on a Protestant ceremony; instead, in time, she finds happiness married to the man she loved. Although this appears to be a tale of liberation, it is not, since true satisfaction for women was found only in traditional roles. Furthermore, it is really the father who saves the homestead. A sympathetic figure who is ashamed of his inability to "shield and give [his family] shelter from the rough winds of the world," he rescues the mortgage holder, who in gratitude deeds Lalor's Maples to the daughter and returns to the church from which he had apostatized.[7]

Conway's opposition to the ballot was expressed more forcefully while managing the *Boston Pilot* (1905–8). Her editorials, despite her affection for the suffragists, berated them for injecting pride of sex into the voting controversy. Furthermore, she charged, the ballot diverted wives from their divinely ordained role, wherein they proudly surrendered their own names in order to merge their identities with that of their husbands. Sweetness, generosity, privacy, and virtue would be exchanged for a public burden. To prevent this disaster Conway became an active member of the Massachusetts Association Opposed to the Further Extension of Suffrage to Women.[8]

There were many other inconsistencies on women's issues in her life. In 1893 she campaigned against a woman's day at the Catholic Columbian Congress in Chicago, for it would "have a tendency to bring forward whatever we have in the way of cranks and publishers." However, while a delegate to the World's Columbian Congress, she presented two papers, "Women Has No Vocation to Public Life" and another encouraging the formation of reading circles and summer schools by colleges.[9] Despite her support of women's education, Conway's traditionalism led her to urge that reading circles and literary clubs be separated by gender. Such a grouping would avoid embarrassing women with the presence of men in class and would prevent clever and pretty students from attracting male escorts from the student body, a situation that would interfere with free discussions. However, such clubs should be under the "strong society of men," who would relate to female students as "protectors, fosterers, [and] teachers."[10]

Conway did not need any men to perform these duties for her. For many years she was president of the New England Women's Press Association, a trustee of the Boston Public Library, and a member of the Board of Massachusetts Prison Commissioners. She pioneered in and lectured before Catholic reading circles and summer schools, held the *Boston Pilot* together by working without salary and financing it with her own funds, championed equal pay for equal work, and from 1911 to 1915 taught at St. Mary's, Indiana, where she was a formative influence on one of the century's greatest Catholic educators, Sister Madeleva.[11]

Like Conway, Caroline Corbin (b. 1835), a convert, was a public opponent of political rights for women. The author of novels and essays dealing with women's issues, a social worker and member of the Society for the Promotion of Social Purity, Corbin was also the longtime president of the Illinois Association Opposed to Woman Suffrage. Her many pamphlets on the subject and the data she presented to Congress inextricably linked suffrage with socialism. The ballot would result in the abolition of private property, which would, she claimed, loosen the marriage bond and destroy the home. According to her the World's Anti-Slave Convention of 1840 proved that the idea of political rights for women stemmed directly "from Socialist or Communistic sources." Suffrage, an attempt to obliterate all differences between the sexes, would displace the ideal of the Blessed Virgin Mary and force women to share men's civic burden in a socialistic society.[12]

Another vigorous opponent who related suffrage and socialism was Martha Moore Avery (1851–1929). She and her lifelong friend David Goldstein, both former socialists and converts to Catholicism, became street preachers warning numerous gatherings of the evils of socialism and the virtues of Catholicism. In rallies and writings they associated the extension of suffrage with the perils of the "Red menace." Avery also debated enfranchisement with the president of the National American Woman's Suffrage Association, Dr. Anna H. Shaw, at Faneuil Hall and denounced it at the legislative hearings of 1908, 1910, 1914, and 1915.[13]

Although many Catholic women continued to oppose suffrage publicly (and many more privately), an increasing number of their coreligionists became outspoken advocates of the reform. Like non-Catholic suffragists, they often were from the middle class and agreed the ballot would enable women to protect the very values that opponents claimed it would destroy. Sometimes they contended that the vote was directly related to the role of women, that it would enable them to clean up politics, to protect their family by legislating prohibition, or to apply their housekeeping skills to municipal responsibilities such as street cleaning and trash collection.

Among the earliest Catholic suffragists was Jane Campbell (1845–1928), writer, editor, historian, poet, and teacher. She founded and for twenty years presided over the Philadelphia County Woman Suffrage Association.[14] Under her leadership the organization sponsored debates, provided speakers, distributed literature, and appealed to the legislature for the ballot. Campbell, a member of the executive committee of the National American Woman Suffrage Association, frequently addressed that organization's conventions, testified before state legislative committees, and promoted the reform at outdoor rallies.

Like most Catholics, Campbell was no starry-eyed feminist. She began every meeting with a prayer, and much of her case for enfranchisement was based on the assertion that it would lead political parties to nominate good men and would procure justice for women. Moreover, the vote was not detrimental to family life, she averred; women would not seek office, for instinctively they preferred home life to a public career.[15] Campbell's monthly, *Women's Progress in Literature, Science, Art, Education, and Politics*, illustrated the limitations of the Catholic feminist. On one hand, the journal emphasized new opportunities for women, advocated suffrage, and featured inspirational biographies. On the other hand, it included many pieces on the importance of woman's role as homemaker and in every issue included a mother's page, including such topics as recipes, fashions, and child care.[16]

Equally conservative in her endorsement of the vote was Mary McGrath Blake (1840–1907), who related suffrage to housekeeping: females would be ideal in teaching city fathers order and cleanliness (Blake herself advocated state legislation requiring the watering of streets) and in supervising public works.[17] This mother of eleven also promoted new opportunities for women, equal education with men, and dress reform. Yet in her voluminous writings Blake stressed gentleness and domesticity, characteristics that apparently inhibited her own commitment to women's rights and religious liberty. In 1890 as a member of the Public School Association, an organization dedicated to overcoming the religious animosities crippling the Boston educational system, she ran for school committee, emphasizing her qualifications as a mother. But in 1888 she apparently had heeded the archbishop's injunction warning Catholic women not to get involved in the factious school committee contest pitting Catholic against Protestant. She did not vote that year. Nor did she cast a ballot in 1889, during her husband's bid for reelection to the school committee, or on the statewide woman-suffrage referendum of 1895.[18]

Even more typical in reflecting the constraints that faith imposed on suffrage was the policy of Sara McPike (d. 1943), mainstay of St. Catherine's Welfare Association of New York. Founded by McPike, an executive secretary in General Electric, and by Winifred Sullivan, an attorney, St. Catherine's was an organization of Catholic women pledged to social and economic reform for the betterment of women and children. It promoted equal pay for equal work, prohibition of child labor, and enactment of an eight-hour work day law and vigorously supported suffrage as a means to these ends, but not as a right in itself. St. Catherine's worked closely with Carrie Chapman Catt, president of the National American Woman Suffrage Association (NAWSA), sponsoring suffrage rallies throughout New York State and devoting much of its efforts toward Catholics: converting priests to the cause, influencing sodalities, and chairing meetings in church halls and schools. McPike joined with Campbell and Janet Richards of Washington, D.C., in a futile effort to persuade Cardinal Gibbons to drop his opposition to enfranchisement. To offset clerical critics McPike and the association insisted their stance was perfectly ortho-dox, emphasized St. Paul's message that there was neither male nor female in Christ Jesus, and affirmed that suffrage would not endanger the home. After the vote was extended in New York State, McPike and her companions urged Catholic women to go to the polls to offset the ballots of feminists and Bolshevists.[19]

Other prominent Catholic women also publicly reconciled tradi-tional perceptions with their advocacy of the ballot. Helen P. Mc-Cormick (1889–1937) retained her family name upon marriage and served as the first female assistant district attorney in Brooklyn. Nevertheless, she advocated suffrage not as a matter of justice but because women would vote for social reform. Society was but an extension of the home, she claimed, and "women's interest in so-cial and democratic movements is a response to the urge of mother love that is experienced by every normal woman, whether married or unmarried."[20] Janet E. Richards (d. 1948), a suffrage worker in the Washington-Baltimore area, revealed a fairly common perception of woman as temptress when in 1922 she warned that boys must be pro-tected from vamps who were given over to heavy petting. Standards of behavior must be raised, she claimed, and only boys could do it.[21] Rosa Marie Levis (1878–1959), a social service volunteer, claimed to be the first Italian-American suffragette. Although many of her rallies were conducted in front of churches, her children were ostracized as a result of their mother's outspoken views. Furthermore, men would "jibe" her and wives feared her, for their husbands "didn't take too kindly" to her views.[22]

Among other prominent Catholic advocates of enfranchisement were Sarah Irwin Mattingly (1857–1934), an educator in Washing-ton, D.C.; the Detroit resident and author Mary Catherine Crowley (1857–1921); Eleanor O'Donnell McCormack (1867–1931), educa-tor, musician, and president of the Tennessee Federation of Women's Clubs; Adelaide Delaney (b. 1875), a settlement house worker, editor, and exposer of child-labor abuses; and Hortense Ward (1872–1944), the first Texas woman admitted to the bar and the first woman to prac-tice before the Supreme Court of the United States. One of the leading Catholic intellectuals of the era, Louise Imogen Guiney (1862–1920), poet, essayist, and ambassador to the Boston Brahmins, may well have become a leader in the suffrage movement if she had not taken up permanent residence in England in 1901, for in 1895 she had signed a petition for municipal suffrage.[23] It is possible, based on her name, that the business manager of the *Woman's Journal* was Catholic. Agnes E. Ryan, after earning her way through Boston University by housekeeping and waitressing, worked for a publishing house and a Boston daily before joining the *Journal* in 1910. Ryan's many poems frequently dealt with traditional womanly themes: the glories of motherhood and married love, mourning for unrequited love, and the joy one realizes when entering church.[24]

Some suffragists were not content merely to write and petition but instead adopted tactics resembling those of English radicals. Mary O'Toole (b. 1874), lawyer, clubwoman, and president of the District of Columbia Equal Suffrage Association, not only organized and addressed street-corner rallies but for two weeks toured the East in her "yellow flyer," declaiming for suffrage.[25]

Even more audacious was Teresa O'Leary Crowley (1874–1930), the mother of three children. Bored with domestic life, she resumed legal studies with the encouragement of her husband. After graduating from Boston University Law School, she passed the bar in 1899 and began a practice specializing in real-estate law. Convinced that the most important public cause was woman suffrage, she devoted a great deal of time and energy to that reform and participated in open-air rallies as early as 1908. An outstanding debater, Crowley addressed national suffrage conventions, testified before legislative committees, and chaired the Good Government Board of the Boston Equal Suffrage Association and the Legislative Committee of the Massachusetts Woman Suffrage Association. Many of her activities, however, exceeded the norms of acceptable Catholic female behavior. Crowley led a march of 1,500 suffragettes through the streets of Boston and canvassed thousands of men to vote for the suffrage amendment to the state constitution in 1915. (When Governor David I. Walsh signed the bill putting the amendment on the ballot, he presented the pen to Crowley.) More outrageous to the hierarchy was her direct intervention in the political process; she led a campaign that was instrumental in defeating eight state senators who were up for reelection, including the president of the senate. A few years later she was an active participant in a special nonpartisan committee that was successful in defeating one of the state's United States senators and replacing him with the first Catholic to represent Massachusetts in that body, the suffragist supporting Walsh. Two years later, after the ratification of the Nineteenth Amendment, Crowley retired from public life to devote her talents to her law practice and her family.

Even more contentious was Margaret Foley (1875–1957), a onetime officer in the Hat Trimmers Union and the Boston branch of the Women's Trade Union League, who was hired by the Massachusetts Woman Suffrage Association in 1906 as an organizer. In 1911, although renowned for her aggressive campaigning, including the distribution of suffrage literature from a balloon, Foley studied more radical methods in England. On her return she adopted even bolder approaches, heckling opponents, haranguing crowds, and discombobulating rallies of antisuffrage candidates, including an incumbent lieutenant governor. So successful were her tactics that she traversed the nation on behalf of suffrage, frequently concentrating her efforts on working-class coreligionists. In 1918 she was appointed chair of the Organizing and Industrial Committee of the Margaret Brent Suffrage Guild, an organization of Catholic suffragists. On behalf of that group she testified before the legislature and organized local branches throughout the state, frequently meeting in parish churches, often with nuns and priests.[26]

If radicalism is measured by the number of days jailed for a cause, Lucy Burns (1879–1966), whom her confessor once called "as gentle a woman as I have ever met," was the most radical of all suffragists. While studying in England, she was arrested for demonstrating with the militant wing of the suffrage movement. With Alice Paul, an American with whom she had been incarcerated in England, Burns, on her return to the United States, broke from the NAWSA to establish the National Woman's party to make militancy relevant to the suffrage struggle. She edited the party's paper, crisscrossed the county on its behalf, and picketed the White House. Following her arrest for this demonstration, she was force-fed when she engaged in a hunger strike to protest her treatment as a criminal rather than as a political prisoner. Refusing to put suffrage aside during the war effort, she continued her campaign, denouncing "Kaiser Wilson," picketing public places, and engendering massive publicity for the cause. Her militant methods, however, so shocked moderates that even some suffragists questioned her motives. In 1914 Burns had written to her friend Paul, "I am rumored in New York to be an agent of the Jesuits, leading the movement to militancy, and thus destroying it from inside."[27]

Catholic suffragists may have appeared single minded in their dedication to the reform, but an Irish sense of humor still surfaced. In an *Atlantic Monthly* article in 1910, the novelist Margaret Deland criticized the new woman for demanding the vote for the qualified and unqualified without distinction. "We have suffered many things at the hands of Patrick," she wrote; "the New Woman would add Bridget also." Every St. Patrick's Day until 1919 Deland received a postcard with the message: "Margaret Deland: You don't want me and Bridget to vote. It would be better, my dear, if you were as honest as Patrick and as chaste as Bridget. (Signed) Patrick and Bridget."[28]

As an increasing number of Catholic women turned to suffrage, churchmen were obliged to clarify their opposition to enfranchisement and make it clear that their stance was a personal one, that there was no official Catholic position.[29] Even more encouraging than those pronouncements was the support that began to develop among Catholic publications, priests, and some of the hierarchy (Bishops John L. Spalding, Bernard McQuaid, Austin Dowling, John S. Foley, and Michael J. Gallagher). Enheartened by such benediction, many Catholic women, even if it meant challenging their local ordinary, organized suffrage societies and led church-affiliated female organizations in endorsing the ballot.[30]

These new partisans frequently explained their conversion by citing the need for protective legislation because of an increase in the number of wage-earning women. More often, though, they justified suffrage by the special ladylike qualities of women. Morally superior females would clean up politics and prevent corruption, and motherly virtues applied to the political arena would protect the home and cherished values. As the *Los Angeles Tidings* proclaimed, in the hands of women the ballot was a sacred trust, a power for good.[31] As suffragists clamored for moral reform, an article in *Ave Maria* directly linked the ballot to Catholic teachings. "What is fallaciously called 'Feminism' is in reality a powerful impulse toward Catholic ideals — a Catholic code of morality."[32]

Once the ballot was extended, suffrage opponents seized upon the concept of ennoblement to exhort women to vote and offset the influence of Protestants and radical feminists. As early as 1889, when school-committee voting was the only suffrage available to most women, some Catholic spokesmen, despite their qualms, urged women to exercise the franchise to protect their children's right to an education free of Protestant indoctrination.[33] When state constitutions were amended, clerical critics often became priestly proponents. Among those whose stance shifted were Archbishop Patrick W. Riordan (1841–1914) of San Francisco, Bishop Paul Rhode (1871–1945) of Chicago, Joseph J. Rice (1871–1938) of Vermont, and most important, Cardinal Gibbons, who advised even nuns to vote. In their 1919 pastoral American bishops displayed some reservations about enfranchisement as they proclaimed, "To reach the hearts of men and take away their bitterness... this is woman's vocation in respect of public affairs and the service which she by nature is best fitted to render." Nevertheless, the document asserted that the ballot could prove an advantage, as women might purify and elevate political life. More optimistic was the presiding officer at the 1920 National Conference of Catholic Charities, who advocated that women join political parties and, "in response to the urge of mother love that is experienced by every normal woman," become involved with issues affecting the home, such as inflation, schools, and child labor.[34]

Catholic periodicals and lay opponents such as Avery also reassessed their position and pleaded with females to vote. *The Catholic World* implored women, "For God and country [outvote] the Socialist, the feminist, the pacifist and the radical."[35] The same sentiments were expressed at the first meeting of the National Council of Catholic Women, whose members were instructed to register and save the country from those who would destroy it. A year later, in 1922, delegates approved a resolution calling on Catholic women to defend the "principles sacred to Christian civilization" by voting. As late as 1931 appeals to exercise the franchise still were couched in terms of risking one's femininity for a higher principle, the protection of Catholic values.[36]

One of the factors that led many males to change their minds and support enfranchisement was the female record of accomplishment during World War I. Women entered industry in record numbers, served in the navy as yeomenettes, drove streetcars, and tended crops in the Woman's Land Army. Practically no traditional male activity was left untouched. Catholic women participated in all of these endeavors; church-sponsored undertakings, however, as with the Catholic attitude toward suffrage, was engulfed in traditionalism.

Under the initiative of Father John J. Burke, editor of the *Catholic World*, the National Catholic War Council (NCWC) was organized in 1917 "to promote the spiritual and material welfare of the United States troops at home and abroad and to study, coordinate, and put into operation all Catholic activities incidental to the war." At that time there was no organization to act for the church as a whole, thus there was administrative chaos, overlapping responsibility, and confusion. The government was at a loss as to where to turn for the official voice of the American church. The council overcame this disorder with an executive board drawn from a national committee comprising representatives from diocesan committees, which in turn consisted of delegates from lay societies, the Catholic press, and appointees of each bishop.[37]

One of the council's specific functions, according to Cardinal Gibbons, was to be "a means of combating immorality near camps; the safeguarding of Catholic young men and girls." In his keynote address at the group's very first meeting, its episcopal director, Burke, restated this goal with special emphasis on the grave problem of safeguarding young women living in towns where soldiers were billeted. According to him, since modern women resented chaperons, there was "a greater need of watchfulness" and an insistence on conduct that avoided temptation.[38]

Despite these fears Burke believed that women must share in the war effort, that their role, although different from that of men, was not secondary. In some ways, he contended, their burden was heavier, for they were the ones left desolate with tears and aching hearts. Maybe this view led him to believe that women were more serious and dedicated than men and to recruit many of them to serve the council. According to Mary Hawks, one of his chief assistants, Burke was never condescending to women and, believing in their mental and spiritual equality with men, entrusted them with serious responsibilities.[39] Nevertheless, it was apparent in many ways that the council had not come to terms with the new Catholic woman.

There were seven subcommittees of the NCWC, including one on women's activities — headed by a male with a male executive secretary. At one time this position was held by Father John Cooper, an anthropologist, who believed women were incapable of running their own organization.[40]

The women's committee, in which no woman held a leadership position, immediately took a census of 4,470 women's societies in order to coordinate and stimulate wartime involvement and inform the groups of national needs. Local chapters of the Red Cross and Chaplain's Aid (also founded by Burke) were begun by the committee. Before long, houses were opened at training camps and embarkation points where, under proper supervision, young women could visit soldiers. (These centers welcomed 1,400,000 guests and served 572,600 meals.) Community houses with an average attendance of 1,638 a month were established in twenty-one large cities. Here special attention was given to young women who arrived in the city searching for war work. The dwellings, a cross between settlement and boarding houses, provided cafeterias, restrooms, recreation facilities, employment bureaus, and education classes. After the war they evolved into Catholic settlement houses.[41]

One of the committee's most enduring projects was the establishment of the National School of Social Service on the campus of Catholic University to prepare young women for social work at home and abroad. The courses were taught in a religiously charged atmosphere. At graduation students signed a contract renouncing liquor, cigarettes, paint, and powder and agreed to dress in the uniform of the War Council. Before going overseas, they attended Mass and, in an "Act of Consecration for Social Workers," pledged themselves to the service of Jesus Christ and the National Catholic War Council. In Belgium, Italy, Poland, and France 127 volunteers maintained twenty-four establishments for nurses, Red Cross workers, civilian refugees, orphans, and visitors.[42]

Local organizations performed a variety of functions. The Catholic Women's Service League of Albany raised $130,000, conducted classes in first aid and home care for the sick, provided five thousand articles to the Red Cross, cared for the dependents of servicemen, and helped educate refugees. The League of Catholic Women for Civic and Social Reform sponsored a huge patriotic rally in New York's Shubert Theatre in 1917 to register female volunteers to aid the war effort. Other women supported the activities of the Knights of Columbus by hostessing in their serviceman's clubs, giving concerts, and raising money. (The knights, however, were more conservative than the War Council, allowing women to serve overseas only in a clerical capacity, for "scrupulous regard for the comfort of young women would [not] warrant placing them to work in surroundings which plainly demanded men workers.") The Ohio Catholic Women's Association even won the avid support of Archbishop Henry Moeller (1849–1925), one of the most traditional members of the hierarchy. Few possibilities were overlooked; the Women's Committee of the War Council established Victory Boys and Victory Girls divisions.[43]

There were also noteworthy contributions by several individuals. Alice O'Brien (1891–1962), a staunch suffragist who introduced the visiting radical English suffragette Emmeline Pankhurst, nursed the wounded in the front lines of France for seven months.[44] One of the most distinguished artists of the American colony in Paris, Elizabeth Nourse (d. 1938), was decorated for her wartime service to wounded allied soldiers and refugees.[45] Mrs. Euphemia Haynes headed the Committee for the Advancement of Colored Catholics to train black Catholics as social workers in military camps and to eliminate discrimination in the church. In time the committee evolved into the Catholic Interracial Council.[46]

The National Catholic War Council was so effective that Gibbons asked Roman approval for a similar peacetime organization to represent the hierarchy. Despite reservations from some ordinaries who feared such activity would usurp their power, the National Catholic Welfare Conference was established in 1919. (The conference was nearly suppressed because of the opposition of several bishops, but in 1922 it received a decree of approval from the Consistorial Congregation after having been first sanctioned by Benedict XV in 1919.) Under its direction the National Council of Catholic Women (NCCW) was instituted to guide national woman's organizations and shape legislation to reconstruct society on Catholic lines.

Among the NCCW's early undertakings was an immigration bureau in New York and campaigns against impure movies, birth control, and the Sheppard-Towner Bill, which established public health programs with infant and maternity care centers.[47] The council's most significant contribution in its early years was the establishment of the National Catholic Service School, a graduate program for social workers at Catholic University. This two-year program was a direct outgrowth of the National School of Social Service, whose debt was liquidated by the NCCW. The woman's organization also purchased a site, buildings, and furnishings as well as providing scholarships and the majority of the trustees for the new institution. (In 1947 the school merged with the School of Social Work of Catholic University, which had been founded in 1934.) Like its predecessor, the National School was pervaded with religiosity. Only single or widowed Catholics were admitted, daily Mass was an unwritten law, and free time was regulated with set hours for rising and retiring (11:00 P.M.) and permission required for absences.[48]

One of the most arresting women in the undertaking was Agnes Regan (1869–1943), without whom there would have been no school. The executive secretary of the NCCW, she also served the school as an instructor and assistant director or director from 1922 to 1943. After having taught or administered schools for thirty years in California, she had been selected by her archbishop to represent San Francisco at the organizational meeting of the NCCW. Shortly thereafter she was appointed executive secretary, a post she held for twenty years, and moved to Washington, D.C. In her new office she developed programs to provide housing for working women, promoted social legislation, and testified before congressional committees on a wide variety of proposals. Under the aegis of the NCCW she championed world peace, modesty in dress and on the stage, and railed against birth control and the equal rights amendment.[49] At the time of her death she was hailed for demonstrating that there were more than two vocations for women — marriage and religious life.[50]

Despite the prominent role allocated to Regan, increasing Catholic support for suffrage and the myriad of women's wartime activities, hierarchical and clerical views of females had changed but little. During the war church spokesmen seemed almost as concerned to ensure that women did not transgress their sphere by performing men's work as they were concerned with an Allied victory. One spokesman was distressed because long after the war, society would still be plagued by evils resulting from unmarried women earning their own income and being "under no one's control."[51] The Jesuit editor of *America* feared the war would result in the "perversion of a woman's finest instinct," blurring the distinction between a Christian lady and a mere woman, between a good mother and a mannish female.[52] The Bishops' Pastoral of 1919 ignored new wage-earning opportunities by emphasizing that woman's role was to rule the home and, through her gentleness and dignity, reach the hearts of men. The program of Social Reconstruction of the American Bishops went even further in its acceptance of prewar thinking. It insisted that the number of women in industry be kept at a minimum and encouraged employers to hire men rather than women who demanded equal pay for equal work. Furthermore, it suggested that women be eased into domestic occupations, where they would receive a wage adequate only for decent individual support as contrasted with their appeal in justice to pay "all adult males" a family wage.[53] To monitor progress in achieving these goals and assist in implementing them, the hierarchy now had an effective tool, the NCCW, chaired by Bishop Joseph Schrembs of Toledo (1866–1945). The council's task was to safeguard from feminist assaults, which flouted Christian morality, "marriage, home, parenthood, family life, the education and protection of the young, the foundation stones of national structure."[54] However, in the implementation of these objectives the council provided new opportunities for women outside the home, for leadership roles, and for the exercise of administrative skills. Even for conservatives it was no longer a man's world.

Chapter 10

"LADY" NOVELISTS: TWENTIETH-CENTURY ICONOCLASTS

Changes in attitudes toward their assigned roles were reflected in the writings of Catholic women novelists and essayists of the twentieth century. Heroines of these authors often defied conventions, unlike the characters of nineteenth-century novelists, who, although strong and assertive, adhered to traditional shibboleths. Sometimes, too, modern authors by their life-style directly challenged clerical and societal norms. Serving as sort of transitional figures to these novelists were Mary McKee Waggaman (1846–1931) and Anna T. Sadlier (1859–1932).

Waggaman, the daughter of an Irish immigrant, was raised in a convent as a result of her mother's untimely death. When she was fourteen, her father, a southern sympathizer, took her to England during the Civil War. On her return to the United States she began to write and continued to do so after marriage while her young husband established his medical practice. She concentrated on children's fiction when the oldest of her eleven children reached the age for first communion. Her earlier adult romances usually told of a Catholic, often a woman, who clung to the faith under adverse circumstances. Unlike the characters in many other nineteenth-century Catholic novels, Waggaman's heroes earned a reward here on earth by achieving the happiness that accompanied middle-class life.

More typical of the new woman was Waggaman herself. According to her daughter, she was "ashamed of making money" on her stories. Nevertheless, earning an income and helping support the family gave her a "sense of power," made her feel "as if she had wings," and provided a role model for her children. Waggaman's daughter, an author of some note, had no qualms about writing for money, for she had seen her mother do it all her life — it was perfectly natural.[1]

Anna Sadlier, the Canadian-born and Catholic-educated daughter of Mary A. Sadlier, asserted that by proclaiming a spiritual equality with men, Christianity was the major factor in emancipating women. Moreover, according to her, the Virgin Mary inspired males to reverence females, and ladies to behave in such a fashion as to merit adoration.[2] This theme was often reflected in her choice of subjects and in her plots. One of her early works, *Women of Catholicity* (New York, 1885), was an account of historical Catholic women whose lives demonstrated the efficacy of church teachings in ennobling, purifying, and forming their characters. Even when her stories dealt with more typical females, it was love for women that moved and inspired men. In "Mistress Rosamond Trevor" the heroine's father believed serious issues were beyond the ken of females, detracting from their wifely duties. Nevertheless, Rosamond was prepared to die for the faith, engaged in serious discussions with her fiancé, and still enjoyed a happy marriage.[3]

The more popular of the twentieth-century writers — Agnes Repplier (1855–1950), Elizabeth Jordan (1867–1947), Lucille Papin Borden (1873–1963), Kathleen Thompson Norris (1880–1966), Margaret Culkin Banning (1891–1982), and Katherine Kurz Burton (1890–1969) — were as different from each other as from their nineteenth-century predecessors. Yet each in her own way further challenged the stereotype of demure, obedient, domestic, pious women and in so doing contributed to the ideal of a new woman.

Agnes Repplier, a widely published and respected essayist, whose friends included the most brilliant writers of the day, manifested her independence and unconventionality at an early age. According to Repplier her major achievement at a Sacred Heart convent school was learning to smoke. (She later became a chain smoker and when in one of her "mannish moods" liked to light up a small black cigar.) At school she exhausted the nuns' patience and was dismissed for insubordination. In time, she also was expelled from the school of Agnes Irwin, a fellow Philadelphian who later became the first dean of Radcliffe and Repplier's friend.[4] As a young girl Repplier was deeply influenced by her mother, who introduced her to the world of books and was "the first woman I knew who used her mind." On the other hand, her father believed that cardplaying was the only achievement appropriate for a young lady.

Convinced that women were equal to men and had equal societal responsibilities, Repplier urged humanistic education to develop female understanding and ideals. "It would be better to go back to the good old-fashioned Eastern custom of drowning superfluous female infants than let them grow up and fight the world without a fair chance," she wrote.[5] Furthermore, Repplier accused advocates of "practical subjects" as being fearful of educated women and assailed those critics who patronized single females. Celibacy, she asserted, was often freely chosen in order to devote more time and energy to a career than wives were able to do. Repplier had little patience with those nuns who saw marriage and consecrated virginity as the only alternatives for young women.[6] So committed to women's equality was Repplier that she derided the notion of chivalry, the idealization of women, and the hypocrisy of male reverence, for these attitudes protected females from the consequences of their own action.[7]

Despite her advocacy of equality Repplier was not a supporter of woman suffrage; to her it was irrelevant, for women could achieve equality without it. Moreover, as a strong proponent of the Allied cause in World War I, she claimed feminists were more concerned with the relatively minor issue of the ballot than with an Allied victory. "The only agreeable thing to be recorded in connection with Europe's sudden and disastrous war," she wrote, "is the fact that people have stopped talking about women, and began to talk about men." She deplored the use by suffragists of arguments based on the moral superiority of women or on the particular nature of their sex rather than demands for enfranchisement as a matter of justice. Justification of this type she dismissed as a form of emotional rather than intellectual feminism.[8]

As an exponent of equality Repplier demanded her writings be evaluated on their own merit, not as the product of a female essayist. "The right to be judged as men are judged is perhaps the only form of equality which feminists fail to demand."[9] Nor did she want to be classified as a Catholic writer. "I have found my creed to be a matter of supreme indifference to the rest of the world as it is a matter of supreme importance to me.... It is impossible for me to believe that anybody cares what catechism I studied when I was a child, or what church I go to now."[10] However, she never concealed her faith in her writings, something she believed she could not do even if she tried. Moreover, she was convinced that religious sentiment should not be excluded from fiction, for its omission would rob the piece of inspiration; on the other hand, religion in literature must be dealt with judiciously. Repplier denigrated Catholic novelists who, lacking delicacy of taste (this she attributed to parochial schools), wrote flavorless stories permeated with Catholicism and culminating in the conversion of the Protestant characters, who usually were introduced in the first chapter.[11]

Although she was a champion of women's causes, Repplier was not willing to abandon tradition. She claimed that the new woman could never exist as a type, for "nature, who has her own uses for women, will always see to that." As a matter of fact, in 1897 she denied there was any such thing as the new woman, for arguments on behalf of progressive feminism were really very old, merely a reflection of great-grandmother's contempt of men and an account of female achievers of the past. The new woman who is vilified today will, she predicted, be revered in the future as a great-grandmother.[12] It was probably this type of traditionalism that led her to support gentility between the sexes, even as she assailed chivalry. Her denunciation of the "militant" Woman's party and Christabel Pankhurst, the English suffragette, was really an arraignment of the decline of female reticence, which she believed had led to a distasteful frankness of speech, obsession with sex, and the introduction of sex education in schools. To her the last-mentioned item was particularly abhorrent, for evil understood was not evil conquered.[13] Even Jane Addams was an object of her scorn. Repplier assailed wealthy women like Addams as misplaced idealists. Their sympathy with prostitutes as social victims and their support of New York's shirtwaist strikers who resorted to violence in attacking scabs she found repugnant. The community should feel no guilt over exploited factory workers, for after all, Repplier contended, they could get jobs as domestics.[14]

Nearly contemporary with Repplier was Elizabeth Jordan, who was also convent trained (Notre Dame, Milwaukee) and who drew upon this experience for many of her stories.[15] Her well-educated, non-Catholic mother objected to Jordan's desire to become a nun. To keep peace in the family the daughter agreed to postpone a decision on religious life for four years. During that time she moved to New York and supported herself by writing (she had sold her first story at age fourteen). At the end of the probationary period, Jordan continued her career, becoming the support of her parents when her wealthy father suffered financial reverses during the depression of 1893. Jordan wrote thirty novels and numerous short stories and reported and served as assistant editor for the *New York World* (her accounts of Lizzie Borden's murder trial were the sensation of the day). She edited *Harper's Bazaar* (1900–1913) and was literary adviser for *Harper's*, editorial director of Goldwyn Pictures, and drama critic of *America* (1922–45), where she proudly exposed "the dirt of communism."[16] The young midwesterner on her own in the huge city found the winks, stares, and passes of young men horribly degrading. In a rather typical Catholic perspective on the sinfulness of women, Jordan believed that maybe she was responsible for this behavior, that something in her elicited it.[17]

Despite her fascinating career and interesting friendships with such people as Henry James, Mark Twain, and Sinclair Lewis, Jordan's writings treated traditional Catholic themes. A series of short stories reflecting her continuing interest in convent life were republished under the title *Tales of the Cloister*. These writings humanized nuns by removing the veil of austerity and seriousness and presenting them and Catholic teachings in a lighthearted and appealing fashion. Her religious were happy in both their divine love and their love for pupils, whom they continued to influence long after graduation. Equally significant, the students themselves lived full and rich lives after leaving the convent and found fulfillment in social causes and human love.

One of the characters in *Tales of the Cloister*, May Iverson, based on Jordan herself, became the central figure in a series of stories and books tracing her life from age fourteen to twenty-three. Iverson was a free-spirited, prosuffrage young woman, with a deep-seated social conscience, torn between a career and family. She never seriously contemplated reconciling both choices, for she believed a married woman's place was at home. Thus she opted for marriage, abandoning her future as a writer, a profession for which she had been well prepared by the nuns. Jordan, despite this conventional ending, was denounced by some Catholics for describing ultramodern situations and for suggesting Catholics were capable of divorce and sin.[18]

Maybe the criticism was because, unlike Iverson, Jordan chose a career and had no regrets for so doing. She had many companions, including males, maintained her convent friendships, and adopted and raised an infant daughter whom she sent to Smith College.[19] Her advice to young women, "Work, love, and pray," seemed to be characteristic of her life. Nevertheless, despite these manifestations of traditionalism Jordan was a vigorous supporter of social reform and woman suffrage. In addition to touring, speaking, and writing on its behalf, she ghostwrote the memoirs of her friend Anna Howard Shaw, president of the National American Woman Suffrage Association (1904–15) and donated her royalties to the cause.[20]

Catholicism permeated the writings of Lucille Papin Borden even more thoroughly than the works of Repplier or Jordan. Furthermore, she was more old fashioned in her personal life than they, yet she dealt with subjects seldom treated by previous authors. Descended from an aristocratic, St. Louis Catholic family, she graduated from Sacred Heart Convent, Maryville, and at age twenty-five married a wealthy New Yorker. Henceforth, she divided her time between various parts of the United States and Europe, even managing a club in Paris for American servicemen during World War I. The Bordens were very devout and maintained a chapel in their summer home for visiting clergy. He was decorated by Pope Pius X, and she wrote in order to get readers to think along moral lines and draw them to the church and God. According to her, a novelist must "bring to his work a will conformed to God's." Consequently her plots were all quite similar: the protagonist was forced to choose between the attraction of divorce or immorality justified by a materialist philosophy or select the hard path of virtue and family.[21]

The Gates of Olivet (1922), a novel of conflict between earthly and spiritual love, strangely enough was dedicated to her husband. When the heroine realized her destiny was to serve God and enter religious life, she revealed her decision to David her lover. He replied, " 'Sweet little sister, you've slipped away from me to the Love that is greatest. Not the love of any man is great enough to fill that loving heart of yours. Only God, the love of God, can do that. I gave you a man's biggest love...but even what I gave you could never fill your life. Isn't that it?' Her face was radiant. 'Oh, you *do* understand!' "

Her book *The Candlestick Makers*, the story of an unhappy marriage because a wife was too modern to have children, dealt with birth control, one of her favorite targets and one that she associated with the woman's rights movement. Those who limited their families were depicted as hard and bitter, except for warmhearted Protestants who abandoned the practice and became converts. In a melodramatic chapter entitled "March of the Unborn," a selfish modern wife lay dying as a parade of souls to whom she denied existence passed before her eyes, moving her to contrition and to request baptism. Borden defended censorship, including that of the mails, as a desirable method of preventing the dissemination of birth control information. In her novel *The Shining Tree*, she implied that World War II was a punishment for sin and that the ravishing of France by Germany was a just retribution for French acceptance of birth control. Her other writings also emphasized Catholic themes: divorce is attacked and Catholicism acclaimed in *Starforth; King's Highway* hails Jesuits for civilizing and Christianizing American Indians; and in *Silver Trumpet Calling* Borden describes an attempt (which she predicted would succeed) to redeem the Soviet Union through the power of religion. She also produced biographies of Jesus, St. Francis, and others while proclaiming the glories of Catholicism. However, like her nineteenth-century counterparts, Borden often overstated her cause; as one critic wrote, "Fiction, in any case, has no room for stark propaganda, and one doubts, greatly, whether religion needs it."[22]

The writings and personal life of Katherine Thompson Norris, one of the most popular Catholic novelists of the first half of the century, contrasted dramatically with that of Borden. Norris was the oldest daughter of a middle-class Irish-American family from San Francisco. At age nineteen, when her parents died, she and her brother went to work to hold the family of six together. As a youngster she had dedicated herself to the Virgin Mary and dressed in blue. Nevertheless she married — Charles Norris, the brother of the muckraker Frank Norris. It was her ambition to be a distinctly Catholic author. Protests from readers and advice from her publisher, however, led her to de-emphasize Catholicism in her writings, a decision for which she was sometimes criticized.[23] On the other hand, she believed novels should show the influence of religion even as they avoided monkishness and sentimentality. "If our faith is the most important influence in our lives, it should have its place in our books. And conversely, if our books are to be true, they cannot live without it."[24] As a result the general theme in her eighty-one novels was the triumph of ideals and virtue, with subtle references to the Catholic faith as decent girls faced such issues of the modern world as family, marriage, and divorce.

Her only really Catholic novel, *Little Ships*, was autobiographical, the story of a large Irish-Catholic family in San Francisco whose doting mother guides "the little ships" into a safe harbor. The underlying message was that children were all that was needed for happiness. Norris's first novel, *Mother* (1911), which appeared serially in both *American Magazine* and *Ladies Home Journal*, developed the same theme as it praised motherhood, attacked "race suicide," and lauded Theodore Roosevelt for defending large families. One admirer praised this novel as "probably the most smashing single blow ever delivered by the press to the creeping cult of birth control since that hydra began to air itself publicly."[25] Norris herself, despite many years of crippling arthritis, ill health, and seven operations, had three children (two of whom died in infancy), adopted another, and raised three children of her dead sister.

Although she was a champion of motherhood, Norris rejected the conservative views of her own mother, who not only viewed "strong-mindedness" in women with horror but castigated short-haired suf-

fragists and asserted that "nice people" were not concerned with social and economic issues. Instead, influenced by her businessman father, Norris defied convention and her husband to champion a whole
series of reforms and unpopular causes. In so doing, she manifested
at times a type of female superiority, on one occasion comparing men
to mischievous boys who must be made to behave by women.[26] As a
zealous reformer she attacked the evils of child labor in one of her first
stories (1909), campaigned for woman suffrage, promoted the equal
rights amendment, and lectured on behalf of prohibition and in opposition to capital punishment.[27] For thirty years she championed
disarmament and pacifism and during the Cold War was a strong
critic of nuclear testing. Furthermore, Norris lectured on behalf of
the Woman's International League for Peace and Freedom, was president of the Mothers of America (a pacifist group), and was one of
the founders of the isolationist America First. As a result of these
stands she was accused in the 1950s of being a Communist, a rather
bizarre accusation, for in the late 1930s she had been charged with
being pro-Nazi; moreover, she had been a vigorous critic of the "left-
ist New Deal" and a dedicated campaigner for the 1940 Republican
presidential nominee, Wendell Willkie.[28]

Although she prided herself on being a Catholic writer and was
also of Irish descent, Margaret Culkin Banning was as different from
Norris as Norris was from Anna Sadlier. The author of over forty
books and hundreds of short stories and commentator on her own
weekly National Broadcasting Company program (1940–41), Banning
was a 1912 graduate of Vassar, where she was given over, in her words,
to "passionate socialism." Two years after graduation she married and
eventually bore four children, whom she raised alone, for in 1934 she
divorced her husband from whom she had separated years earlier. In
1944 she remarried but continued to write under the name of her first
husband, Banning, who had died in 1937.[29]

Trained as a social worker at the Chicago School of Civics and Philanthropy, Banning participated in many activities promoting social
betterment and civic progress. She was employed for a year as a social
worker, served on several national boards and committees, including
the navy's Civilian Advisory Committee (1946), was one of the organizers of the Committee of Catholics to Fight Anti-Semitism (1939),
and was decorated by the Treasury Department for her participation
in bond drives during the Second World War. While her husband
was in the Netherlands during World War I, she worked for the Red
Cross in Belgium and England.[30] This trip abroad, her first, was followed by many others: in 1921 to England and again to that country in

1942 as a correspondent of the North American Newspaper Alliance, where she observed the role of women in industry; in 1936 to Spain with two of her children, where she was caught up in the civil war; in 1941 to six Latin American nations to study woman's views (resulting in the book *Salud: A South American Travel Journey*); and in 1948 and 1951 to study European postwar conditions. There were also journeys to Russia, Mexico, and the South Pacific.[31] Unlike Norris she was a staunch internationalist, but like her contemporary she was an active Republican. Her attraction to that party was rooted in her belief that it stood for decentralized government and the profit system. Convinced that Franklin D. Roosevelt's policies would destroy democracy, she campaigned for his opponents in 1932, 1936, 1940, and 1944. In 1948 she publicly supported Thomas E. Dewey, and in 1952 and 1956 enthusiastically championed Dwight Eisenhower.

As one might expect, Banning was a strong proponent of woman's rights in her writing, speeches, and life-style. She once described herself as an "arrogant, hard-shelled, old-style feminist" and urged women "to get over being afraid of being seen without men." She was disappointed in the languor of American women and implored them to become active politically, excel in all undertakings, maintain their independence, and stop wasting their power and energy in women's clubs. Moreover, she berated overprivileged women who dodged responsibility and political activism.[32]

Naturally Banning championed the right of women, including that of wives, to work. During the depression, when it was commonly assumed working females selfishly displaced male heads of families, she urged women to fight legislative efforts to curtail their employment. During World War II, unlike most Catholics, she insisted that mothers be hired as defense workers and claimed such a policy would not endanger the family. "The finest women are those who take care of their children and their home and do other jobs outside the homes as well, from factory to battle line. There is no single or generic place for women any longer." According to Banning a woman's first task was to see that life was created; however, she had the right to demand that her life not be wasted and to achieve fulfillment by wage earning. To harness women power Banning even called for national registration during the war and a program of retraining women workers with federally supported child care. Unlike many others she was convinced that newly employed women would want to continue to work after the conclusion of hostilities.[33]

To get females to sustain the war effort she wrote the highly acclaimed *Women for Defense*.[34] This study charged that Nazism, whose philosophy threatened woman's rights, could not be defeated without the efforts of women: on the farm, in the factory, in civilian defense, and in the military. While researching portions of this book in England, she wrote another in the form of letters to her daughter. This work, *Letters from England*, also emphasized the Nazi threat to woman's rights, hailed the disappearance of women of leisure in England, and concluded by Banning encouraging her daughter to join the military.

In addition to her unusual approach to the subject of working women, Banning's forthright discussion of sex and sexual relationships was also rare for a Catholic woman. In 1937 she authored *The Case for Chastity*, intended primarily for women and girls for whom religion was not an adequate inducement to modest behavior. Banning warned of the ineffectiveness of contraceptives, alerted her readers to the 700,000 annual abortions, and condemned petting as unfitting a girl for marriage and ruining normal sexual relations by making intercourse anticlimactic. When it came to marriage, men preferred virgins, she asserted; furthermore, "unchastity checks and stints the development of love. It breeds lonely women and selfish men." Banning made a clear distinction between romantic caresses and experiments in sexual sensation. Like New England Puritans, she believed that one of the ways of preserving chastity was to encourage early marriage. This would be done, she claimed, by making it easier for young men to find employment and by providing financial assistance to graduate students.[35]

That a satisfactory sex life was one of the goals of marriage (although certainly not emphasized by the church) was further promulgated in Banning's article "Sex Life after Middle Age." Here she advocated that couples build a new life in their middle years as sex became wiser, less selfish, more informed. "There is no time limit on sex," she wrote as she sought to reassure older men that their insecurities were irrational.[36] Even more daring than this discussion was her character in *The Vine and the Olive* who enjoyed an orgasm.

Equally surprising from a Catholic writer was her sympathetic treatment of birth control and her sensitivity toward mixed marriages. The latter was probably based on her own experience. She believed one of the purposes of a novel was to tell a story thoroughly understood by the writer wherein the character grapples with religion but without the author's proselytizing the reader. Her novel *Mixed Marriage* (1930), written anonymously but readily identified as hers, was the account of a well-educated, wealthy, Catholic woman married to a freethinking non-Catholic. Despite her ill health, she refused to practice contraception and instead abstained from sexual relations, thereby weakening her marriage bond. In her confusion the wife fled to Paris, had an affair, and then realized her Catholic lover saw her only as a sex object. After drifting away from religion, she returned to her husband, strengthened in her adherence to the church's teachings, not merely as an act of obedience but as an act of faith. As a result her husband loved her more, with a fervor that was greater than mere passion. Thus they came to realize that abstinence can strengthen and temper one. Banning's approach would have scandalized earlier Catholic authors, especially her contention, "My heroines could be unchaste, but not for long."[37]

Nearly thirty-five years later, during the Vatican II era, Banning wrote *The Vine and the Olive*, a novel even more sympathetic with family planning. Concerned with overpopulation, the well-being of mothers, and unwanted babies, the most admirable characters advocate limiting the number of children. Critics of the practice are an overzealous, intolerant priest and the wealthy wife of a baby-food manufacturer. The book, which was praised by John Rock, the Catholic physician who developed the birth control pill, quotes Cardinal Richard Cushing (1895–1970) of Boston on the new appreciation of the truths of the faith and suggests that the only difference between Catholics and Protestants on birth control was means. Furthermore, Banning expressed the hope that there soon would be a "foolproof system" that was in keeping with the natural (church) law. After citing the scriptural passage that "the wife should be as a fruitful vine," the novel concludes with a priest writing a book on married life in which he observes, "The vine must be fruitful if possible. For good fruit is needed. But the husbandman must take great care in its cultivation lest the vine wither. Nor should he seed his olive plants so closely that they are in danger of not attaining full growth."

Banning's female characters were strong, independent, and intelligent like their creator and, like her, faced issues of divorce, birth control, and mixed marriage complicated by an adherence to Catholicism. Two novels based on her own experiences are prose versions of Francis Thompson's "Hound of Heaven," reflecting Banning's unsuccessful attempt to flee from the church. *Fallen Away* (1951) is the account of a Catholic who divorces her irresponsible non-Catholic husband. Despite her failure to obtain an annulment, she married for a second time, convinced that such a step was no sin. Although attempting to adhere to Catholic practices as much as possible, she suffers spiritual turmoil and drifts so far from the church that when she is free at least to marry in a Catholic ceremony, because of her first husband's death, she is unable to do so. Years later, aided by the counsel of a sympathetic bishop and her experience in defending the religious beliefs of Catholic refugees in war-torn Austria, she finally makes her peace and reenters the church. As in *The Vine and the Olive*, the only reprehensible character in the book is a self-righteous, intolerant, misogynistic priest.

The identical problem of divorce and remarriage for a Catholic is developed in *Magda Townsend*, a largely autobiographical novel. (The major difference is that Banning's first husband, from whom she was divorced, died, leaving her free to marry a second time.) Following the death of her second husband, Townsend, with the help of a sympathetic bishop, is reconciled to the church and prepares a will hoping to leave her grandchildren "the belief in God and religion that has held me in its grasp, even when I tried to break away."

In practically all of Banning's novels women manage to reconcile wage earning with family responsibilities while maintaining an interest in politics. *Spellbinder* (1922), directed toward newly enfranchised females, was the account of women who organized politically without jeopardizing their home or family or disquieting their husbands. In this as in other novels that touched on politics, Banning advocated conservative, Republican tax policies while criticizing Democrats for high taxes, especially on the business community.[38]

Banning had no difficulty in reconciling her advocacy of financial and psychological independence for married women with a commitment to the family. She led antipornography campaigns as a means of protecting the family, lectured on the threats wartime disruption posed for it, and called for international cooperation to defend its integrity. In 1963 she received a citation from the Merrill Palmer Institute of Detroit for "constructive understanding of the family and the needs and problems of young mothers" and for devoting a large part of her talents "to the interpretation of family life."[39]

Banning also reconciled her feminism with gentility, traditionalism, and ladylikeness, asserting that equal rights advocates must maintain values and moral principles and add to human accomplishment.[40] In *Letters to Susan* (1936), written to her daughter while away at college, Banning stressed the need of developing proper manners while learning to make a living. But professional skills were to be kept in perspective, for as she advised Susan, "I want you to marry. I think that marriage is the best material out of which any woman can make a beautiful and becoming life."[41] Banning went on to advocate conventional family views, asserting that a wife should make marriage her main job and work only if necessary or if her skills are of exceptional value to society. A husband's interests come first, she asserted, for a wife can return to her career when the children are older. With her daughter, Banning wrote a book on manners, maintaining that formalities between ladies and gentlemen, such as women preceding men and males holding the doors open for females, keeps the satisfaction of sex from being limited to physical intercourse. Young girls should be taught to expect such attention, for women must help men preserve these courtesies, "a kind of constant repayment for what women alone can do for the race." Almost incidentally Banning mentioned that her son was in the navy, where he was learning such skills as sewing buttons and making beds, talents that would make him a better husband, for he would know that housework does not demean men.[42]

Katherine Kurz Burton was a strong feminist and, like Banning, advocated that men share in household tasks. The daughter of German Lutheran parents, she worked in a factory while attending Western Reserve and then taught school. In 1912 she married Henry Burton, who became editor of *McCall's Magazine*, which she served as assistant editor from 1928 to 1930. Her husband's ill health and their subsequent estrangement forced her to reassess the role of women. In 1930 she converted to Catholicism, was associate editor of *Redbook* from 1930 to 1933, and then became a free-lance writer, authoring twenty-five books (often biographies of Catholic women), and for twenty years produced a column, "Woman to Woman," the most popular feature in the *Sign* magazine.[43]

The passage of time intensified Burton's commitment to women in politics, which had been revealed early in her life when she vigorously supported enfranchisement. Repeatedly she appealed to her sex to participate in politics and government, but unlike Repplier, she argued from the unique nature of women and their special concerns. The state and the nation, although threatened by geopolitical problems, were merely extensions of the home, she claimed. Every woman had a duty to protect her home, to use her broom and sweep the world clean — including ridding school libraries of books by dangerous Communists such as Howard Fast and Paul Robeson.[44] If women entered government, their special quality of love would be the saving grace of the world, enabling them to keep the country free and end wars. Furthermore, Burton claimed, with skills superior to those of men, women, the "loaf givers," would have been able to solve the Great Depression without plowing under crops in the midst of hunger. In the same way that Eleanor Roosevelt, Frances Perkins, and Lorine Pruette did, other women could use lessons from the home in making

a decent world for children.[45] As a devout Catholic, Burton readily
endorsed the teachings of Pope Pius XII that her sex's greatest responsibility was in the home; she defined a real woman, however, as
one who sees all problems of human life from the perspective of the
family and enters political and social service to save it.[46]

Burton was somewhat ill-at-ease with the church's disparaging attitude toward females. As a result outstanding Catholic women were
frequently the subjects of her biographies, one of which, *According
to Pattern*, was the account of the efforts of Dr. Agnes McLaren and
Anna Dengel to get the Vatican to drop its opposition to nun physicians and to establish a sisterhood of doctors and nurses to serve in
missionary lands. Burton reveled when St. Teresa of Avila and Catherine of Siena were recognized as doctors of the church, a step, she
claimed, that acknowledged the unique and necessary role of women
in salvation.[47]

Many other Catholic writers were active in the first half of the
twentieth century, but their works were not as popular as those mentioned or were not written for Catholic audiences with Catholic
themes. Among them were Mary E. Mannix (1846–1938), who wrote
of the joys of marriage and the rewarding lives of converts; Susan L.
Emery (1846–1912), a convert who was on the staff of the *Sacred
Heart Review* from 1891 to her death; and Edith O'Shaughnessy
(1876–1939), a novelist who objected to the expression "Catholic
writer" and believed books of piety devoid of true adventure. However, O'Shaughnessy was convinced that one's faith was revealed
in her character's attitudes toward fundamentals — love, marriage,
divorce, and suffering as a way to God.[48] Nevertheless, she was criticized for depicting Catholics as capable of divorce and for writing of
sex, which she believed was a legitimate subject for literature if dealt
with in an inspiring manner, full of glory and dreams.[49]

Anne O'Hare McCormick (1880–1954), the first woman to serve
on the *New York Times* editorial board and the first woman to win
a Pulitzer Prize, had a mind so keen, factual, and logical that many
men, revealing stereotypical attitudes, marveled she could still retain her femininity.[50] Her columns indicated a deep belief in the
unchanging moral order and a concern that rising materialism was
undermining spiritual life and values.[51] She was convinced these qualities were the special province of women, who had an obligation to
fight for moral standards and a belief in God.[52] An indication of her
gentleness and traditionalism was her pretense that it was necessary
for her to rely on her husband, even after he had suffered a stroke.
On her success as a female in a male profession, she wrote, "We tried

hard not to act like ladies or to talk like ladies are supposed to talk —
meaning too much — but just to sneak toward the city desk and the
cable desk, and the editorial sanctum and even the publisher's office
with masculine sang-froid."[53]

Blanche M. Kelly (1881–1966), for over forty years a professor
of English at Mt. St. Vincent College, wrote poetry and verse. Her
analysis of literature emphasized that Catholicism "infused into English literature a quality which accounts for most of what it has of
greatness."[54] Frances Parkinson Keyes (1885–1970), a wealthy convert, was raised in the belief that a lady's name appeared in print
only when she was born, married, or died. Despite this conviction,
severe illness and near helplessness forced her to write, and she produced over forty-one books and numerous articles. Deeply involved
in politics as the wife of a governor and senator, she wrote of political matters, but she also authored romantic novels where young,
beautiful heroines ennobled older, experienced men by their love.[55]
Helen Constance White (1896–1967), the only female full professor
of the College of Letters and Science of the University of Wisconsin, specialized in Renaissance and Medieval literature. Yet she was
a strong feminist who believed women should be subject to the draft
and was a member of St. Joan's Alliance, a Catholic organization
promoting the equality of women. She also demonstrated her belief in women's responsibilities to society by serving as president of
the American Association of University Women (1941–47) and the
American Association of University Professors (1956–58) and on the
national committee of UNESCO.[56] The notion of a new woman even
inspired Eleanor Donnelly. As early as 1905 she edited a handbook
designed to enlighten and reform men's judgments about the valor of
women and to inspire females by revealing triumphs of their sex.[57]

The most widely acclaimed of this country's Catholic novelists
was Flannery O'Connor (1925–64), a Georgian who suffered long
from lupus. Her plots were often bizarre tragedies with, as one critic
claimed, three levels of meaning: natural, symbolic, and analogical.[58]
Although she was deeply religious, O'Connor did not use Catholic
settings or characters in her writings, emphasizing instead a personal
loyalty to the presence of Christ in human nature. According to her
a Catholic novel was grounded in the truths of fall, redemption, and
judgment and represented reality in a world of things and human relationships — but not necessarily a Catholic world. If a novelist tries
to see with the eyes of the church, the result, O'Connor claimed, was
pious trash.

Most of the Catholic authors mentioned in this chapter would

have difficulty recognizing O'Connor's works as Catholic. Her favorite story, "The Artificial Nigger," had as its theme redemption
through suffering. Referring to her two novels (*Wise Blood*, "a book
about a kind of Protestant saint that reduced Protestantism to its
twin ultimate absurdities," and *The Violent Bear It Away*, an account
of a fourteen-year-old prophet and fugitive from Christ who bap-
tizes his idiot cousin as he drowns him), O'Connor wrote, "I have
found...that my subject in fiction is the action of grace in territory
held largely by the devil. I have also found that what I write is read
by an audience that puts little stock in either grace or the devil."[59]

There was no hint of feminism in her writings or her life. For the
most part, O'Connor's female characters could just as well have been
male, while she herself hailed the papal pronouncements against birth
control and believed that the church, more than any other force, had
contributed to the liberation of women.[60]

By her writings and her life the Catholic novelist of the twentieth century, like her sister of the nineteenth century, contributed
substantially, even if unintentionally, to the growing independence of
Catholic women and to a restlessness with the constraints imposed by
society and church. Without her the radicalism of the 1960s would
have been stillborn.

Chapter 11

BETWEEN THE WARS: CONTINUING TENSIONS

In the period between the wars churchmen and church organizations increasingly railed against feminism, which allegedly had reached a dangerous level in the United States. A large number of bishops informed Pope Pius XI, "The granting of the franchise to women has made many of them aggressive and their new power has excited many and led them to adopt the most radical ideas."[1] Cardinal O'Connell attributed this belligerence to the weakness of men, who by unnaturally abdicating their power thus become effeminate, with disastrous results to the moral and spiritual order.[2] The "new woman" was accused of abandoning her natural selflessness for selfishness by adopting a man-made philosophy that increased vulgarity, lust, crudity, and superstition while decreasing virtue, purity, modesty, romance, and patriotism.[3] An officer of the NCCW, after linking feminism with "Bolshevism, Fascism, Socialism, [and] Communism," described its consequences as "free love, easy divorce, motherhood regarded as a public function, and the complete independence of married women." She concluded by appealing to members of the council to accept male leadership even within the organization itself.[4]

To preclude these deplorable occurrences Catholic women were reminded of their God-destined role. "No man ever looked upon a woman as his equal; he looks either up to her or down upon her." Wives must follow the example of Mary by being subject to their husband. She "no doubt was superior to Joseph in regard to wisdom and spirituality," but he led the Holy Family.[5] Repeated appeals to follow and promulgate Mary's example were coupled with praise of motherhood and family. Admonitions that the degradation of woman

161

was the devil's objective were followed by warnings of dire consequences to those who would abandon the charm of womanhood and
the inheritance of Jesus for a false philosophy.[6]

Renewed emphasis was placed on the obligation of women not
to lure men into sin. Because it was commonly believed that women
were not as sexually impulsive as men, churchmen taught it was the
duty of females to resist male aggression, to guard morals, and to raise
sexual ethics. It was precisely because women were so obligated that
feminism was so dangerous. This false philosophy, it was asserted,
encouraged woman to abandon God, to ignore her task of civilizing
man, and instead of leading him to heaven, to plunge him into hell.[7]

To offset these dangers the church stressed the values of purity.
Repeatedly women were warned of the dangers of bobbed hair, close
dancing, cosmetics, divorce, sex education, and especially immoral
clothing. Improper dress was defined in 1928 by the Sacred Congregation of Religious as a garment "cut deeper than two fingers'
breadth under the pit of the throat, which does not cover the arms at
least to the elbows and scarce reaches below the knee." Flesh- colored
stockings were also forbidden by the edict. So serious did churchmen
view clothing offenses that Bishop George A. Guertin (1869–1932) of
Manchester, New Hampshire, held them responsible for much of the
turmoil in the world. The bishop in Bellevue, Illinois, Henry Althoff
(1873–1947), refused communion to violators. The Sacred Congregation even recommended a special committee of vigilance in each
diocese to watch over women's styles.[8]

Aiding in the effort to preserve the virtue of purity were Catholic women's organizations, which frequently passed resolutions on
dress, theater, sexual behavior, and sexual mores. The Motion Picture Committee of the International Federation of Catholic Alumnae
was the official reviewing agency for the Legion of Decency, later
known as the National Catholic Office of Motion Pictures. Chaired
for thirty-five years by Mary H. (Mrs. James) Looram (1899–1969),
the committee was described by Will H. Hays, who headed the self-
regulating instrument of the Motion Picture Association, as the "most
severe of all groups in ... approval of pictures." Looram, who edited
a weekly movie broadcast over twenty-three stations from 1923 to
1935, exposed and attacked "the insidious Communist propaganda"
that was infiltrating films and especially assailed movies featuring the
burlesque star Gypsy Rose Lee. In 1948 Looram received an honorary degree from Fordham University in recognition of her service
to the legion.[9]

Morality in the legitimate theater was the concern of one of America's leading actresses, the Canadian-born convert Margaret Anglin (1877–1958). She helped inaugurate the weekly "Convert's Hour" on radio, using that means, lectures, and the press to advocate clean, wholesome plays, while at the same time emphasizing that theatrical dullness was not the same as purity. Anglin's hope was to create a young audience who would demand good but not decadent drama.[10]

Despite clerical emphasis on purity and century-old traditions against birth control, temptations to limit family size were greater than ever because of assaults on Comstockery, the opening of family clinics, and changes in sexual mores. Although religious handbooks had warned against birth control for many decades, there was no extensive exposition on the subject until 1916. In that year the sociologist and moral theologian John A. Ryan published a full discourse on the issue in a clerical journal, the *Ecclesiastical Review*. Three years later, under the influence of Ryan's piece, the bishops promulgated a pastoral condemning the practice and citing the description of it in Genesis as a "detestable thing." A special statement condemning family limitation as an "affront to all genuine Christians," a position commonly repeated in press and pulpit, was issued by the administrative committee of the National Catholic Welfare Conference (NCWC) in 1922.[11] One ecclesiastic asserted, "Wedlock has no other independent justification than a family."[12]

Many churchmen even condemned the rhythm method as a means of birth control. In her *Sign* magazine column the Catholic novelist Katherine Burton referred to a menstrual chart that could be used in implementing rhythm. She received hundreds of inquiries asking where the chart could be obtained and a letter of praise from a priest mentioning that he and a nurse ran a rhythm clinic to compete with the Planned Parenthood League. Suddenly, according to Burton, discussion of the practice was banned in the diocese of New York City. A book approving rhythm, with an imprimatur by Bishop John F. Noll (1875–1956), Fort Wayne, and a Nihil Obstat by Cardinal Patrick J. Hayes (1867–1938), New York, was recalled, publication of the chart was halted and she was unable to contact her priest correspondent. She believed these steps were taken by Cardinal Francis J. Spellman (1899–1967). Finally Burton was told by a reporter friend that all discourse on the subject in New York had to be in Latin, that a cloak of silence had fallen over the issue.[13] The type of reasoning that led to censorship was exemplified in *Babies Not Bullets*. In this compilation of articles from the *Catholic World*, rhythm was assailed because of its consequences and was described as a nonheroic "compliance...with the spirit of birth control.... It may get a man into heaven but with

his rump scorched." Furthermore, it asserted, the practice of rhythm
would not fill the world with Catholics.

One of the reasons for this type of diatribe was that the Catholics
were ignoring strictures against birth control. As early as 1918 Ryan
deplored the fact that a substantial number of his coreligionists engaged in it but believed they did not realize its sinfulness and would
desist when so informed.[14] An Augustinian in the same year found little difference between Protestants and Catholics on the issue and, like
Ryan, believed Catholics thought it a matter of little importance.[15]
A crusade against contraception was demanded by another theologian in 1929, who bemoaned its "distressing growth" even among
unmarried Catholics.[16] Two years later another moralist was even
more despondent. As he observed the widespread practice of birth
control, he noted, "Even our Catholic people are no longer accepting
these truths."[17] Catholics continued to ignore pronouncements from
the pulpit, the press, and Rome. Despite the flood of warnings, over
43 percent of 509 Catholic women surveyed in 1940 used methods
of contraception condemned by the church. By 1952 only 51 percent
of Catholics thought birth control sinful, and family planning was
fairly common among even Italian and Irish believers. By 1955, some
30 percent of Catholic parents practiced contraception, and only ten
years later the figure had soared to 53 percent.[18]

One of the ways that churchmen attempted to preserve traditional sexual values was in the teaching given in the Catholic college
for women, which often continued to exalt motherhood as woman's
natural sphere and to proffer the Virgin Mary as the exemplar for
young ladies.[19] In what Rosemary Radford Ruether has described
as a kind of Catholic anti-intellectualism, administrators of woman's
colleges criticized institutions that trained females for careers outside the home and taught subjects that were unrelated to that end.
Instead many Catholic schools emphasized special training in virtue
and the management of the home, for their object was to produce an
ideal woman, not an ideal student. One educator even advocated a
semester course in the senior year on "house practice," where four
to six students would live on a budget, prepare food, do the laundry
and cleaning, decorate, plan the furnishing, and keep the house.[20]
Churchmen missed few opportunities to promote Catholic education
for women. When John F. Fitzgerald, the mayor of Boston, was about
to send his daughter Rose (the mother of President John F. Kennedy)
to Wellesley, the college she desired to attend, Cardinal O'Connell intervened. The prelate convinced the mayor to send his daughter to
a Catholic institution.[21]

Those who believed that woman's destiny was motherhood decried coeducation as absurd. Repeatedly they attacked it as irreconcilable with the goals of female education and asserted, furthermore, that mixed classes provided a temptation for men, a position supported by Rome. In his encyclical on the Christian Education of Youth (1929), Pius XI condemned coeducation for mistaking "a leveling promiscuity and equality for the legitimate association of the sexes," and as late as 1951 the Sacred Congregation of Religious asserted that no Catholic could defend the practice on principle.[22]

Although never abandoning the goal of preparing "ladies," Catholic educators, like social reformers, increasingly emphasized vocational training, which had the effect of undermining their objective. When Marymount College opened in 1918 in Tarrytown, New York, the aim of its founder, Mother Marie Joseph Butler (1860–1940) of the Congregation of the Sacred Heart of Mary, was to provide an education equal to that of the best secular institutions. In recognition of women's changing status students were introduced to political science and law, with social service training also available.[23] In 1928 Mary Molloy, the dean of St. Theresa's in Winona, Minnesota, described the end of undergraduate education as a career in public service, a life of scholarship or graduate school, and college teaching. Years earlier at a conference on women's colleges, Molloy had asserted the need for Catholic women to be intellectually fit and trained to assume the leadership in professions and in every movement in which their sex was paramount. To achieve these goals she urged Catholic institutions to de-emphasize music, home economics, and languages, whose emphasis had made them little more than finishing schools. Even more extreme was her call for the elimination of many small, struggling colleges so resources could be applied to the development of a "few great institutions."[24] This same radical suggestion was made by the dean of St. Margaret's College to her local bishop in the hope that her recommendation would be taken up by the NCWC.[25]

Emphasis on higher standards and vocational preparation, however, did not mean a complete break with the ideological concepts confining women to proper spheres. The male president of Mt. Mary College, in Milwaukee, Wisconsin, although defining the school's objective as preparing "gentlewomen" for economic work, indicated little had changed when he listed as examples teaching, nursing, business secretary, and social work.[26] Even Sister Madeleva Wolff (1887–1964), who inaugurated "revolutionary" opportunities for the theological education of women, was quite traditional. The daughter of German immigrants, Wolff transferred from the University of Wisconsin to St. Mary's, graduating in 1909. She entered the Congregation of Holy Cross and obtained a master's degree, and then a Ph.D. from UCLA. After additional graduate work at Oxford she began a career in education, culminating in the presidency of St. Mary's (1934–61). According to the 1934–35 catalog, because large numbers of women engaged in gainful occupations, the college would prepare students for careers; their proper place was in the home, however, and the school would develop a more refined and perfect womanhood. "Out of order and zeal of all things Catholic will come effective feminism." Wolff closely supervised the institution, raised academic standards, and in 1942 introduced, for the first time in the United States, graduate programs in theology for women at a Catholic college. A traditionalist had proffered a real challenge to the clerical perceptions of women.[27]

Increasingly women's colleges assumed a dual mission: preparation for marriage and motherhood and preparation for a career. To many the bridge between the two was a liberal arts education. Such a program would allow for female uniqueness while developing an aesthetic taste, part of her refining qualities. At the same time she would be prepared for participation in government and society, where she would apply these qualities in an effort to change the world.[28] Even so, some critics began to claim that there was too much emphasis on vocational training and that Catholic schools were no longer preparing young women to be mothers. As late as 1959 a teaching nun demanded the restoration of the old-fashioned goal of education for the home.[29]

Not only were the "new women" graduates of Catholic colleges pursuing careers, but an ever-increasing number of Catholic women were entering the nonprofessional work force. One scholar at the time explained such behavior as a new manifestation of the old notion of joint responsibility for the home. A century earlier females had contributed economically to the family by spinning and weaving; now, because of inadequate male income, they were once again earning wages to sustain the family.[30] However, the reservations of many Catholics, lay and clerical, remained and, like those of non-Catholics, intensified with the Great Depression. Not only did they assert that by working, women took jobs from men, but they claimed that educating girls to support themselves fostered an unnatural desire to seek equality at a time when young women should be taught there was no higher calling than that of wife and mother — unless it was religious life. One critic even contended that the greatest evils of the day — divorce, birth control, and juvenile delinquency — were attributable to the employment of women. Another advocated a state subsidy to encourage females to assume their natural responsibility as mothers.[31]

An increasing number of Catholic organizations designed to assist women provided additional opportunities for their members to exercise leadership and assertiveness and to pursue interests outside the home. Among these new groups were the Women's National Federation of Catholic Charities and the Catholic Professional Women's Club, established in Boston in the 1930s.[32] The membership of the League of Catholic Women of Boston, founded in 1910, soared to over 400,000 in less than a decade. Designed to promote "moral, religious, and cultural interests" under the direction of Cardinal O'Connell, it ran a placement service, performed social work among Italians, established a society similar to Traveler's Aid to protect young girls, and cooperated with juvenile courts on probation for girls. During World War I it cooperated with the War Service Council and also purchased an ambulance for use overseas. However, it was careful not to cater to the "Protestant Service mentality" and devoted some of its energies to its own members. For their betterment it sponsored lectures and maintained a clubhouse with sleeping and dining facilities and a library.[33]

During the Great Depression Catholic women again rallied to the plight of the needy and in so doing exercised leadership and organizational talents that exceeded by far the stereotypical characteristics of subservient, helpless women.

Genevieve Brady (1884–1938), former president of the Social Services Relief Board of New York City, along with her financier husband established a reputation early in life for charitable work. Upon his death in 1930 she used much of his bequest of $12 million to continue such endeavors. The National Woman's Committee on Welfare and Relief Mobilization was organized in 1932 by her, when she recruited one thousand prominent female members. Convinced that her sex must provide hope and neighborliness, she called on all women to assist those wracked by the depression. Brady set the example by raising funds and coordinating local relief drives while working in tandem with Catholic Charities and the National Council of Catholic Women. One of her favorite charities was the Girl Scouts. She urged every young woman to join that organization, which she served as national treasurer, executive committee member, and informal liaison to Catholic clergy. Brady was decorated by the French and Belgium governments for relief work for those orphaned in World War I, was knighted by the pope in 1937 for her charities, and received the first honorary degree granted to a woman by Georgetown University.[34]

A more nontraditional philanthropist during those years was Alice O'Brien (1891–1962), who, after learning Swahili and exploring the Congo for five months in 1928, spent the next fifteen years in charitable and civic endeavors. The poor were treated free of charge at the children's hospital in St. Paul that she helped establish. She also founded the Women's City Club for charitable work and for the social and intellectual betterment of its members and sponsored cultural activities such as the St. Paul Community Theatre and local opera and ballet.[35]

One of the most important of the depression organizations, the Catholic Worker was founded in 1932 by a woman, Dorothy Day (1897–1980), and her social philosopher, friend, and mentor Peter Maurin.[36] After quitting the University of Illinois at the conclusion of her sophomore year, Day reported for the *New York Call*, whose Socialist orientation she shared. She also flirted with the Industrial Workers of the World and the Communist party and was arrested and jailed for picketing the White House with "radical" suffragists. (Her cellmate, Lucy Burns, many years later sent Day a contribution when the worker movement was strapped for funds.) Day became a convert in 1927 after the birth of her daughter from a common-law marriage and then spent the next few years studying Catholicism.

Her organization, the Catholic Worker, was founded to serve the poor and needy in "a radical personalist action" and to join "with the worker in his struggle for recognition as a man and not as a chattel."[37] To achieve these ends Day formed lecture groups, opened houses of hospitality, and founded a newspaper, selling for one cent a copy, the *Catholic Worker*.

The circulation of the *Worker*, for which Day chose the news, wrote the copy, and composed the editorials, soared to 200,000 in a few years. Committed to racial equality, it had a masthead depicting a black worker and a white worker and it featured articles attacking lynching and denouncing racism. As part of its commitment to social justice, the *Worker*, although anti-Communist, commiserated with Communist dedication to social and working-class objectives. Day lived worker ideals. She participated in the civil rights movement, picketed the German embassy in the 1930s to protest Nazi treatment of Jews, helped establish the "Committee of Catholics to Fight Anti-Semitism," denounced the Jew-baiting of the Reverend Charles E. Coughlin, and protested as unjust the arrest and trial of American Communists under the Smith Act.

The *Worker* sympathetically reported all of the major labor disputes of the 1930s, beseeching its readers to exercise moral responsibility by supporting strikers and boycotting products of oppressive management. As early as 1938, under Day's leadership, the paper began championing the plight of migratory workers, a cause for which she was jailed for eleven days in 1973 at age seventy-three. The *Worker*, nevertheless, hoped to bring an end to labor bitterness and class war by its proposal that employees "share in the ownership, management, and profits of industry and business."[38]

In addition to demanding justice for the poor, the movement provided many services, chief of which was hospitality houses, where the unemployed were provided free room and board. Volunteers, many of them women, lived in poverty at the houses applying Christian principles to the social problems around them. (By 1939 forty of these houses scattered throughout the nation's city slums were sheltering as many as 150 poor at a time.) In addition to providing refuge for the unemployed and rallying dispirited workers, the houses provided food and shelter for strikers, often setting up kitchens on picket lines. Catholic workers, including Day herself, organized laborers in many industries, participated in sit-down strikes, and even censured Cardinal Spellman for his reactionary stand on striking cemetery workers.

Even more controversial than her approach to working-class issues was Day's commitment to pacifism. Believing that the Sermon on the Mount mandated nonviolence, Day, unlike most Catholics who supported the fascist revolutionary Francisco Franco, favored total neutrality in the Spanish Civil War. Furthermore, she objected to the preparedness movement in the United States, criticized the lifting of the arms embargo in 1939 as a step toward war, and even after the attack on Pearl Harbor called for Americans to turn the other cheek and love their enemy. Members were urged not to manufacture munitions or to purchase defense bonds, and funds were raised by Day to support Catholic conscientious objectors. Day continued to preach pacifism during the Cold War and denounced the policy of nuclear deterrence as morally bankrupt. She was arrested five times and jailed on four occasions for defying civil-defense drills and with others in 1962 founded Pax, an organization of Catholic pacifists, which to her delight in 1972 became known as Pax Christi.[39]

Despite her seemingly radical approach to social issues, Day remained a conservative, traditional Catholic, somewhat uncomfortable with the changes of Vatican II. She was adamantly opposed to birth control, teaching instead the "passion and purity of sex." She also indicted the sexual revolution of contraception, abortion, and free love that even had influenced some of her followers. Although incarcerated for picketing with suffragists, she was not a proponent of suffrage or of equal rights and claimed that woman's liberation was a lure to capture a man. In the ideal society, she claimed, men would be paid enough so that women would be relieved of the burden of wage earning, leaving them free for duties and functions that differed from those of men. Most surprisingly for a woman who was such an activist was Day's observation that "men who are the revolutionaries...do not dally on the side as women do, complicating the issue by an emphasis on the personal."[40]

When Day established the Committee of Catholics to Fight Anti-Semitism," in 1939, she was aided by Baroness Catherine de Hueck (1900–1985), who was already renowned for her dedication to social justice and minority rights. Like Day and many other Catholic women, who enjoyed lives of fulfillment in partnership with the church, de Hueck was not a proponent of feminism. Also like Day, she believed women had achieved opportunity and status equal to men because of the efforts of the church.[41] Born into a wealthy Russian family and married to a baron at age fifteen, de Hueck, nevertheless, was decorated after serving as a nurse's aid at the front during World War I.

As a result of the Bolshevist purge, she and her husband fled to Canada, but after regrouping their fortunes, they separated from one another. De Hueck then resolved to devote herself to the lay apostolate and to live among the poor. She established Friendship House, an interracial residence for the destitute of Toronto. A few years later, at the request of New York clergy, a similar settlement was opened in Harlem in 1937. There nine staff workers and thirty to forty volunteers lived in poverty with her, "show[ing] the face of God to Negroes." While atoning for the treatment of blacks by her coreligionists, de Hueck hoped to produce a number of Negro Catholic lay leaders. She also saw this second Friendship House as a means of offsetting Communist influence among blacks. Communists, she wrote, "are made by hypocritical Christians, Catholics included, who render to Christ lip service only."[42]

Success in Harlem spurred the opening of Friendship Houses in Chicago, Washington, D.C., Portland, and Shreveport. Like the worker movement, such efforts led to the establishment of spiritually centered farms in several states. During World War II de Hueck labored as a factory hand and as a waitress in order to study social trends. She concluded that the church could undercut the appeal of "godless Communism" and win back lost workers by reaching out on a one-to-one basis. This redemption would include prostitutes, whom de Hueck believed had been forced into their life-style by deplorable working conditions. As a result she appealed to the hierarchy to become more actively involved in obtaining justice for labor.[43]

Thousands of recruits, many of whom were women, were attracted to de Hueck's program of "holy poverty." One of the most famous was Thomas Merton, a volunteer at Harlem House before entering the Trappists.[44] When Eddie Doherty, a reporter, was assigned to write a series on Harlem, he met de Hueck, volunteered for Friendship House, and married her in 1943 after getting the approval of de Hueck's friend Bishop Bernard J. Shiel (1886–1969) of Chicago. Four years later they took up residence in Toronto, where they established Madonna House, a rural community where laity and priests could share life and prayers as they prepared for the lay apostolate.[45]

Among the more interesting groups of the 1930s was the Catholic Association for International Peace, founded in 1927 to promulgate the Catholic view on international affairs. As its philosophy was rooted in the just-war theory, it soon advocated an internationalist viewpoint on foreign affairs, with a marked tendency (which continued through the Cold War) to endorse American foreign policy.

Women played the major role in the association, even though membership was open to both sexes. According to one scholar, the influence of Elizabeth Sweeney, its longtime executive secretary and mainstay during World War II, cannot be overestimated. In the period from 1928 to 1933 alone, she directed the publication of twenty-four pamphlets. Other key members of the association included Marie Carroll, librarian of the World Peace Federation, and Sister Vincent Ferrer, O.P., of Rosary College.[46]

One of the prominent Catholic pacifists of this period was Marie (Mrs. William) Meloney (1878–1943), who contributed an essay to the anthology *Why War Must Cease* (1934). One of her friends was killed in World War I, her husband served in France during that conflict, and she was decorated by the Belgium and French governments for her contributions to rebuilding devastated areas. Hailed as a pioneering newspaperwoman, Meloney began her career at eighteen as the Washington correspondent for the *Denver Post*. Later she was editor of the *This Week*, the Sunday supplement of the *Herald Tribune*, associate editor of *Everybody's*, and editor of *Delineator*. She was honored by the Polish government for bringing the Polish-born Marie Curie to the United States and helping her to obtain radium for her research.[47]

Catholic organizations dedicated to peace and social change were criticized frequently, even by other Catholic groups, as the xenophobia of the 1920s was followed by the conservatism of the 1930s. The

League of Catholic Women undertook an Americanization campaign directed at immigrants and supported the reactionary *Woman Patriot* in its fight against Bolshevism, hailing its opposition to legislation on child labor, maternity care, and education. The league's goal had changed from charitable and cultural purposes to a defense of true Christian ideas "against attacks now so persistently launched by the neo-pagan influence of our day.... [The new woman] is not a real woman at all but rather the gospel of the unsexed."[48] Even changes during World War II affecting the status of women had little influence on the league's perceptions. In May 1943 members passed a resolution deploring any program that lost sight of the "basic or divinely ordained distinction between the sexes."[49]

Equally as conservative was the National Council of Catholic Women; nevertheless, it provided acceptable outlets for the talents of traditionalists. One observer wrote in reference to the ratification of the Nineteenth Amendment and the establishment of the NCCW that "Catholic women might well have been rendered a trifle giddy in the quaffing of such heady draughts in the brief space of four months."[50] Its members assailed immodest dress, divorce, birth control, feminism, and the equal rights amendment. Although they condemned the government for interfering with the rights of parents, they called for government action to curb salacious books and movies.[51] On the other hand, council members also pushed for changes promoting social justice and helping the handicapped; among these causes were minimum wages, unions for women, and assistance to those who fled Nazi persecution.[52]

Churchmen attempted to prevent the notion of the new woman from influencing nuns by drafting additional regulations for communities. In 1917 changes in canon law further restricted the lives of these women by detailing cloister rules, declaring nursing and maternity cases unsuitable for nuns, and requiring superiors to make reports to Rome every five years. One scholar has described the result as pushing the nuns behind walls.[53] It was now easier for the local bishop to exercise greater authority. In Boston, for example, Cardinal O'Connell used the charge of incompetence to obtain tighter control over communities, added his own projects to their undertakings, and intervened in elections.[54]

Sisterhoods nevertheless preserved their own identities and often engaged in political activity for religious ends. Nuns lobbied for legislation, met with governors and legislators, petitioned representatives, and encouraged social-action organizations in their colleges in the 1920s and 1930s.[55] On occasion they even challenged the hierarchy.

Despite Cardinal O'Connell's threat to withhold charitable donations, the Sisters of Charity of St. Vincent de Paul refused to accede to his demand that he be made president and treasurer of the hospital they administered.[56]

There were dramatic undertakings by old and new communities during these two decades. Mary Rogers (1882–1955), inspired by Protestant mission societies while a student at Smith College, founded a foreign Catholic women's mission society in 1925. The new order, Maryknoll, soon sent nuns to the Far East and, beginning in 1942, to Central and South America.[57] Six sisters of Notre Dame, defying anti-Americanism bought about by the exclusion bill, established a school in Kobe, Japan, in 1924.[58] Mother Alice, O.S.F. (Catherine Henry, 1879–1960), an Irish immigrant, nurse, and first nun pharmacist in Massachusetts, assumed control of a failing hospital in Miami in 1927, saved it, and then opened two others in Florida. Her reputation as a hospital administrator was such that in 1934 she was sent to New York to establish St. Clare's Hospital to care for the poor in Manhattan's Hell's Kitchen.[59]

Many Catholics, however, were at best uncomfortable with women in the health professions. A 1920 book of ethics warned Catholic nurses of the temptations stemming from too much familiarity with physicians and from attending male patients — especially when alone. To decrease these dangers Catholic nurses were urged to pray and receive the sacraments frequently.[60] Canon law prohibited women religious with public vows from practicing medicine. Moved by the pressing need for women physicians in the missions, Dr. Agnes McLaren (1837–1937), a Scottish convert and member of St. Joan's Alliance, a Catholic feminist organization, pushed for change. She was supported by her protégée Austrian-born Anna Dengel (1892–1980), a physician missionary in India. With the able assistance of a former missionary bishop, Cardinal Dennis Dougherty of Philadelphia (1865–1951), who made two trips to confer with Pius XI on the issue, Rome finally revised its regulations and encouraged religious to undertake health care. The Medical Missionaries of Mary was founded in 1936 under Dengel's leadership, with its motherhouse in Philadelphia.[61] For some time Dougherty had shown an interest in the problems of women and minorities. He was a strong supporter of black rights, chairing the Negro and Indian Missions. Under his auspices in 1929 a clinic opened in Philadelphia, run by women for women with psychological and gynecological problems and offering post- and prenatal care for the married and unmarried.[62]

About the same time as the Vatican revision, a female doctor wrote in the *Catholic World*, appealing for members of her sex to become physicians, especially in the fields of gynecology and obstetrics. The author, who claimed these specialties were inappropriate for men, asserted that females tended to turn to women physicians and that in order to reduce the evils of birth control and therapeutic abortions, more and more Catholic women physicians were needed.[63] However, apparently there was no substantial increase in the profession. The 1911 *Catholic Who's Who* listed eleven women physicians, some of whom were married and all of whom were active in charitable, political, or professional organizations; the 1950–51 edition had only nine.

During the interwar years Catholic women also entered the field of politics but, despite clerical reservations on suffrage, encountered little criticism from churchmen for so doing. Significant numbers of women served as assistant district attorneys, judges, commissioners of various types, state legislators, and United States congresswomen. The first Catholic female to serve in Congress was Mae Hunt Nolan (1886–1973), the daughter of Irish immigrants, who upon her husband's death was appointed to his seat and then elected to a term in her own right. A liberal Republican, Nolan served on the labor committee, which her husband had chaired, and was the first woman appointed to chair a house committee — that of Expenditures in the Post Office. Nolan, however, found political life incompatible with her role as a woman; she refused to run for reelection, returning to her ten-year-old daughter and California home. "Politics," she stated, "is entirely too masculine to have any attraction for feminine responsibilities."[64]

Mary Hopkins Norton (1875–1959), a New Jersey Democrat, had a completely different perception. According to Norton, women had a finer moral sense than men and therefore should be in politics, where they could advance the interests of their sex and families in addition to applying Christian values to social problems. Furthermore, Norton believed it was the responsibility of every woman to prove that females were "neither brainless nor useless." When a congressional colleague agreed to yield to "the lady," she retorted, "I'm no lady; I'm a member of Congress, and I'll proceed on that basis."[65] Nevertheless, Norton, according to Congressman Francis Walter of Pennsylvania, liked to be thought of primarily as a wife and mother.[66]

Following the death of her only child, Norton had turned to charitable work and then to politics, organizing and registering women voters for the Democratic party and successfully running for county office and in 1924 for Congress.[67] During the 1920s Norton fought to

repeal the Eighteenth Amendment, advocated tariff reduction, arguing that such a policy would decrease the cost of goods to housewives
and working women, and vigorously supported Al Smith in 1928. As a
liberal Democrat she championed Franklin D. Roosevelt's New Deal
and seconded his nomination for president at the 1936 convention.
For ten years Norton chaired the House Labor Committee, where she
pushed wages and hour legislation, anti-poll-tax measures, and a permanent Fair Employment Practice Commission and authored much
of the labor legislation of that decade.

Congresswoman Edith Nourse Rogers (1881–1960) asserted that
"the cause of women never had a finer friend than [Norton]. She
believed in their having their place in the sun.... She was a very religious woman, a power in her church and her county."[68] Norton had
identified herself with a whole variety of women's issues: federal legislation for equal pay, a woman's rights law (she opposed the equal
rights amendment because she believed it would remove legal pro-
tections from working women), legislation for soldier's families, the
right of married women to work, and the opportunity for wartime
women workers to retain their jobs at the conclusion of World War II.
According to Norton, nevertheless, women's right to employment
was not absolute, for it should not be exercised at the expense of
"defeminized womanhood" and unemployment for men. Moreover,
woman's spiritual influence was of paramount importance in protecting society from the impersonal, materialistic forces of life.[69] Norton
received an award from Archbishop Cushing as the outstanding Catholic woman of 1947 and was the recipient of an honorary degree from
the College of St. Elizabeth (New Jersey) for the political and social achievement of this "true type of valiant woman in this modern
day."[70]

Although Norton and many Catholics had reconciled the new
Catholic woman with the church, neither that institution nor society
itself were ready for fundamental changes in the perception of the duties and role of women as demonstrated during the World War II era.

Chapter 12

THE ENDING OF AN ERA

The labor shortage accompanying World War II forced many Americans to reconsider their perceptions of women as housebound wives and mothers whose fulfillment was to be found in raising a family. Not only did society advocate startling new functions for women, but wartime realities even gave additional impetus to legislative efforts to provide for the constitutional equality of women. Numbers of churchmen, however, attempted to protect society from these changes, which they believed endangered religious values.

As American involvement in the conflict drew closer, the voices promoting the traditional roles of women grew shriller. One of the more interesting examples was a commencement address at the College of Notre Dame (Maryland), where a Jesuit orator described women as the most "reverent thing on the face of the earth," other than religion. He called for a reintroduction of the sense of reverence of which they were the divinely ordained custodians and for the reestablishment of the God-given domesticity that was threatened by feminism. Furthermore, he urged a proper evaluation of suffering, a "mortification and purification of flesh that spirit may be liberated to attain summits of Christian perfection," a quality that particularly benefits women.[1]

Many religious journals continued to glorify conventional femininity. Most noteworthy for clinging to old values in the face of dramatic change was the highly praised program at the College of New Rochelle (New York). Introduced in 1941 for "the express purpose of training for motherhood," the courses were designed so that "day after day college women [would] have their minds turned from a career in industry or science or the arts to their all-out career of Catholic wife and mother." It was suggested that other Catholic women's colleges follow the New Rochelle example.[2]

In 1942 the American government announced that the war emergency necessitated hiring unprecedented numbers of women for industry. Catholic spokesman were so troubled over the possibility of working mothers that many tacitly accepted the employment of single girls and childless wives. Bishops and writers repeatedly called for enlisting mothers only in the last analysis and then advocated employment limitation on hours and working conditions. Minorities and single women should be hired first. If forced to hire wives, a situation that could well lead to planned parenthood, mothers should devote quality time to their children and ensure that their offspring received proper day care. To many churchmen this need meant private ministration for government child centers — a Russian idea, according to the *Boston Pilot*, that would destroy the "American Way."[3]

Some critics assailed the employment of any women, emphasizing the moral dangers in such a happenstance: a coursening process, an occasion of sin, and "convivial equality" that was plunging females into paganism. Bishop Noll, chairman of the Department of Lay Organizations of the NCWC, described full employment as a moral issue contributing to a lack of modesty and to cursing and surreptitious lovemaking.[4] Other observers feared that it would be difficult to ease women out of their jobs when the war was over and censured those who saw employment as a step toward equal rights rather than the destruction of women's special dignity.[5] Bishop John A. Duffy (1884–1944) of Buffalo seemed to represent the vast majority of institutional churchmen when he asked what the United States was fighting for — if the nation lost the home, where women belonged, it lost the war.[6]

A handful of Catholics, cognizant that women had always worked or believing that females had a right to be wage earners, vigorously championed equal treatment and equal pay. One woman in *America* wrote, "The belief that all women can remain in the security and leisure of a protected home environment is a genteel middle-class assumption which has never applied to the masses of women."[7] Although mindful that most female jobs were dirty, dull, and marginal, an author in the *Catholic World* asserted women must be allowed to work if they desired to do so. Society must provide an outlet for those who choose to remain single, for the "ability to work is a protection against the tyranny of man." However, the employment of wives, she asserted, although compatible with family life, endangered marital happiness and robbed husbands of their responsibility. Therefore, it was suggested that measures be taken to make it advantageous to have children, while reducing the need for a two-income family.[8] Less equivocal was the presidential address of Helen White at a conference of the American Association of University Women. This Catholic educator asserted that the gainful employment of females, including military service, was "the logical counterpart of the increased privileges of citizenship" and that the association should ensure that women play a part in relieving the manpower shortage while maintaining the country's cultural traditions.[9]

A more pressing problem for churchmen than employment was the role of women in the military. Daring achievements of nuns during the Civil War made it impossible to argue that tradition precluded the participation of women. Wartime nursing, clearly a woman's province, was readily acceptable to most Catholics. Even the hierarchy encouraged enlistment for these purposes.[10] But further military involvement was another matter.

As early as May 1941, legislation, advocated by Congresswoman Norton, was introduced to create a Women's Auxiliary Army Corps (WAAC, later changed to WAC). By January it had become obvious that the manpower shortage necessitated the use of female service personnel, as machine operators, cooks, drivers, and aircraft warning operators.[11] Clergy who expressed an opinion on the legislation were opposed. The most outspoken and the most influential was Bishop John J. O'Hara (1888–1960), delegate to the military vicar of the armed forces. While the measure was being debated in Congress, O'Hara in a widely quoted address condemned it as another threat to the inviolability of the family. Ignoring the duties that women were slated to perform, he declared to an audience of policemen, "I'm sure, however, that for the sanctity of the home you'd prefer to peel potatoes and darn your own socks rather than have women in the army."[12] Bishop Bartholomew J. Eustace (1887–1956) of Camden, New Jersey, and Chicago's Archbishop Samuel A. Stritch (1887–1958) were also critical of a women's army corps; however, their opposition was not as well known as O'Hara's. Eustace requested that the NCCW condemn the proposal, but before that organization could act, its parent body, the Administrative Board of the NCWC, debated the issue.[13] After discussing the deleterious effect female military would have on the family, the board, despite the stand of these three bishops, took no position, leaving it to individual members of the hierarchy to do as they pleased.[14]

Bishop James Cassidy (1869–1951) of Fall River, Massachusetts, seized the opportunity and, in a highly publicized statement a few days after Congress enacted legislation creating the WAAC, de-

nounced the corps from his cathedral. He claimed the WAAC violated
the principles and teachings of the church and was a danger to the
morals of women. This tirade concluded with the hope that Catholic
women would refuse to enlist.[15]

There were assaults from many other quarters such as the Catholic Central Verein of America, the National Catholic Women's Union,
and the *Catholic World*. The *Boston Pilot* indicted the corps as a German rather than an American idea; *America* arraigned the bill as "neo
pagan"; and the *Brooklyn Tablet* asserted the WAAC would "degrade
[woman] by bringing back the pagan, female goddess of de-sexed,
lustful sterility."[16]

Some Catholic publications, as a last resort, reluctantly accepted
the notion of women in the military. Usually, however, such a stand
was accompanied by the following caveats: service must be voluntary,
family obligations must be preserved, and a nucleus of women must
remain at home.[17]

The corps did everything possible to counter religious objections
to its existence. Many of its personnel were engaged in public relations, emphasizing the compatibility of femininity and military
service. A National Civilian Advisory Committee consisting of representatives of different faiths was established to assist in recruiting
and in disseminating news about the WAAC. As early as June 1942
Anne S. Hooley, director of the Women's Division of the National
Catholic Community Service, was appointed to a committee to select officer candidates.[18] Captain Louise E. Goeden, a former English
teacher and one of the first WAAC officers, was assigned to public
relations. This Wisconsin native wrote several articles on the corps
for Catholic magazines and spoke before Catholic groups such as the
Catholic Rural Life Conference and Catholic Big Sisters. After tracing
the traditional relationship between Catholicism and love of country,
Goeden discussed the corps' encouragement of religious practices. She
asserted that the devotion of enlistees increased and claimed, moreover, that because of their training recruits would be better prepared
to raise families. She even compared enlistees with nuns, underscoring uniforms, community life, regimentation, goal orientation, and
service to God in schools, hospitals, and battlefields. According to
Goeden, WAACs were the first American women permitted to use
their education "to work directly in this way to preserve American
standards of honor and decency"; despite disparate backgrounds, all
had a common motive in entering the corps — to pay a debt to their
country.[19]

Immediate action was taken to refute slanderous charges of im-

morality that had culminated in assertions by a syndicated columnist
that contraceptives and prophylactics were distributed to WAACs.
Heated denials were issued by Eleanor Roosevelt, Secretary of War
Henry L. Stimson, and WAAC director Oveta Culp Hobby. More important, a delegation of clergy was taken on a tour of training centers
to inspect hospitals, clubs, and barracks and to interview trainees,
chaplains, and officers. Included in the contingent was Monsignor
Michael J. Ready of the NCWC, who not only announced that he
was proud that "the USA has the WAAC" but joined with others
in signing a statement reassuring parents of the moral and spiritual
health of their daughters and asserting that life in the WAAC would
strengthen their "womanly character."[20]

The corps also invited a select group of newspaperwomen, including a staff member of the NCWC News Service, to spend five days
observing a training center. These witnesses were impressed with programs designed to foster the religious values of recruits. In a release
sent to all Catholic papers, the NCWC representative cited the remarks of a Catholic chaplain pertaining to the alleged issuance of
condoms as an "insult to womanhood...a gigantic nationwide plot
instigated by Axis agents." The chaplain was especially indignant, for
he knew "the government is safeguarding the dignity of American
womanhood."[21]

By 1943 much of Catholic opposition had disappeared; the Pas-
sionist magazine *Sign* published an article attacking charges of immorality as a "terrible injustice" and pointing out that the behavior
of a woman in the army would be the same as if she had remained in
civilian life.[22] Catholic publications began to hail WACs and WAVES
and featured photos at chapel, choir, and Mass, with articles on chaplains and Catholic enlistees. A physical education teacher at Alber-
tus Magnus College (New Haven, Connecticut) wrote to the Navy
Department for the WAVES' physical training program to prepare
large numbers of interested students for enlistment in the WAVES or
WACs.[23]

America, which had assailed the formation of the corps, now featured an editorial asserting that if it was made clear that enlistments
were freeing men to fight, American women would give up their high-
paying jobs and flock to the banner.[24] After inspecting WAC facilities,
the Advisory Council of Women, whose members included the presidents of the National Council of Catholic Women and the National
Catholic Community Service, asserted that the corps not only was
a "tremendous contribution to the war effort but a lasting contribution to women's place in our national life."[25] Only a year after

the women's military had been authorized, even Bishop O'Hara was moved to write, "The WAAC system seems to be working out well."[26]

One WAC scholar believes the shift in Catholic position is attributable to the large number of Catholic enlistees, about 25 percent of the total.[27] Two of these Catholic women were destined for prominent careers in the army: Mary A. Hallaren (b. 1907) and Elizabeth P. Hoisington (b. 1918). Hallaren, a former teacher, graduated with the first officer candidate class in July 1942. By June 1946 she was deputy director and one year later headed the corps. A regular churchgoer who probably would have enlisted even if she knew of clerical opposition, Hallaren repeatedly stressed the femininity and ladylike qualities of the WAC and adjudged it an excellent career for those not called to marriage. (She did point out, however, that the army provided a banner opportunity to find a husband.) On the other hand, Hallaren led the fight to obtain regular status for the corps and, when selective service was resumed in 1948, advocated the drafting of women. Her ability to reconcile the apparent anomaly of femininity with women soldiers was manifest in 1951, two years before her retirement, when she described WACs as "women who are opposing with all the force of their feminine nature that communism which would destroy the Christian dignity of womankind. They are women who, without families of their own, are doing their mightiest to achieve that restoration of the family for which Pius XII pleads."[28]

Hoisington, the daughter of a career army officer, was the seventh director of the corps (1966–71) and the first female brigadier general in the nation's history. Like Hallaren, she had little patience with feminists, dismissing them as "a bunch of dumb bunnies." She too emphasized the femininity of the corps, stressing that its members had responsibilities as ladies. Consequently she restricted the use of the fatigue uniform and prohibited slacks, chewing gum, and riding of motorcycles when on post or in uniform. Despite changing mores and the legalization of abortion in several states, she held to stringent policies: discharge for illegitimacy or abortion. Little wonder that her sobriquet among the troops was "the Lady."[29]

By the end of World War II and the beginning of the Cold War, females in the military seemed to be accepted by nearly all. WACs, WAVES, and women marines became part of the regular establishment in 1948 with the Women's Armed Forces Integration Act. With only males subject to the draft, Hallaren relied on clergymen to help recruiting. The military vicar, Cardinal Spellman, praised the WACs in a Tokyo address as having earned the gratitude of the nation.[30] Any residue of opposition from mainstream Catholics must have been

overcome in 1949, when Pius XII concluded an audience with Hallaren and Captain Joy Hancock, director of the WAVES, with the
admonition, "Never forget the great responsibility which you carry; I
desire to bless your work and to bless all the families of the women
under your guidance."[31]

One other way Catholic women could contribute to the war effort was to defend American values, and no one was more dedicated
to this struggle than Frances Sweeney (1908–44). From her saloon-
keeper father she learned at an early age the duty of defending minorities. When informed such endeavors would shorten her life, already
endangered because of a weak heart, Sweeney retorted, "Well, then,
I'll die fighting for what I believe, won't I?" and continued her "one-
woman crusade against the anti-Semites, the Christian Fronters [a
quasi-military anti-Communist body with anti-Semitic proclivities,
organized at the behest of Father Charles E. Coughlin], and fanatical
isolationists." Sweeney organized the American-Irish Defense Association to support an internationalist foreign policy, but at its first
meeting, Pearl Harbor Sunday, December 7, 1941, she shifted its objective to a war on racial prejudice. Sweeney was determined to prove
that anti-Semitism was not a by-product of Irish Catholicism.[32]

While continuing her employment in a Boston advertising agency,
Sweeney began to edit the *Boston City Reporter*, which proclaimed
"The News about Bigots, Racism, and Work Accomplished against
Them That Is Not Printed Elsewhere." She attacked and exposed
"respectable" anti-Semitism, employment discrimination, and castigated Boston's clergy and politicians for not assuming leadership roles
against anti-Semites. Moreover, she championed legislation to protect
the rights of Jews and blacks. Sweeney attracted a large number of
volunteers, many of whom were Jewish boys who did investigative
research for her. One of them, the author Nat Hentoff, states that
Sweeney changed his biased perceptions of women and Catholics. She
was the "single most powerful model for me at sixteen;... [I wanted]
to match her courage, integrity, independence, and joy in stubbornly
prevailing against odds."[33]

A devout Catholic, Sweeney was angered by clerical acceptance
of intolerance and Fascism. She wrote, "It is very bewildering for a
small 'd' democrat like me to see a Roman Catholic priest, with diocesan permission, arouse his audience 'to wild applause, whistling and
stomping' as he attacked our allies. ... It is very difficult to discount
him as a lone clerical dissenter when he is pictured with... other
priests. It is a strange paradox to see a priest who has called our government 'Communistic' go unchallenged when Notre Dame lay pro-

fessor Francis McMahon was discharged for calling a foreign dictator, Francisco Franco, a Fascist."[34] These repeated attacks on Catholic clergy apparently resulted in her being summoned to appear before Cardinal O'Connell, who threatened her with excommunication.[35]

One of Sweeney's clerical targets was Father Edward Lodge Curran, described by one scholar as "one of the most outspoken isolationists, Coughlinites, and anti-Semites in America." A friend of Coughlin and founder of the reactionary Catholic Truth Society, Curran was invited by one of the city's leading hatemongers to speak at the St. Patrick's Day celebration of 1942. As the city had appropriated funds for the observance (known officially as Evacuation Day to mark the withdrawal of British troops from Boston in 1776), Sweeney appeared at city hall to protest Curran's appearance and to get the invitation withdrawn. Politicians and the cardinal avoided the controversy, and Sweeney was dismissed as a troublemaker. She then was bodily ejected from the lecture by two large ushers. Curran proceeded to assail his critics as bigots, while the arrangements chairman castigated Sweeney as an "alleged" Irish-American, a Communist who feels completely at home with Earl Broader, head of the American Communist Party. This was neither the first nor the last time Sweeney was the victim of baseless charges.[36]

Not all of Sweeney's efforts ended in failure. She pressured the Boston police chief to order the Christian Front to disband, she founded a rumor clinic to uncover and refute anti-Semitic, anti-black, and anti-Allied tales, she got the New York newspaper *P.M.* to publish the story of gang attacks on young Jews and police brutality toward the victims, she prevailed upon the governor to appoint a committee on Racial and Religious Understanding, and she was herself vice-chair of the Massachusetts Citizen's Committee for Racial Unity.[37]

Sweeney's ideals lived on after her. In recognition of her commitment to social justice and of her war against prejudice and injustice, Sweeney was awarded posthumously the Pope Leo XIII Medal by the Bishop Sheil School of Social Service.[38] For about six years after her death, the Frances Sweeney Committee, consisting of her disciples, pushed for legislation creating the Massachusetts Commission against Discrimination, attacked McCarthyism, and encouraged the improvement of the Boston Public School system.[39]

As women flocked to factories and the military, societal attitudes began to change. As a result of the new wartime spirit, it soon appeared as if a measure long championed by feminists might be adopted. An equal rights amendment (ERA) to the Constitution had been first introduced in Congress in 1923, but for nearly two decades it was not even reported out of committee favorably. However, in 1940 a major party, the Republicans, for the first time in history, incorporated it into their platform, and during the war years the amendment began receiving favorable reports from congressional committees. Some observers believed it was only a matter of time before the ERA would be part of the Constitution.

In 1943 Winifred C. Stanley (b. 1909), congresswoman at large from New York, became the second woman in the House of Representatives and the first Catholic congresswoman to endorse the amendment. An attorney and the first female prosecutor in Erie County, Stanley during her two years in the legislature battled for several progressive measures, including an equal pay bill and a proposal to eliminate the poll tax. Although she campaigned for reform nationally, fought the New Deal, and urged women to plunge into politics, at a meeting of the Women's National Press Club she declared along with Congresswoman Luce, that homemaking was woman's greatest career.[40]

The preponderance of Catholic opinion, however, was opposed to the ERA.[41] The NCWC and especially the NCCW railed against it, asserting that it was a violation of natural law, and that it would weaken the family, increase divorce, encourage birth control, drag women down to the level of men, and invalidate protective legislation, thereby endangering future mothers. Agnes Regan of the NCCW became a familiar figure on Capitol Hill testifying against the proposal. Catholic groups passed resolutions criticizing it, and religious periodicals condemned it.

For years the major force behind the ERA was the National Woman's Party (NWP). Although it did not at first recognize the strength of Catholic opposition, the party did publicize its Catholic supporters. Among them was Maggie Hinchey, who in 1919 broke with the Women's Trade Union League for embracing regulatory legislation for transit workers, a measure that led to the dismissal of 1,500 female employees. Anxious to find an organization that would support a woman's right to work when and where she pleased, Hinchey became an officer in the party and a lobbyist for the ERA all during the 1920s.

Mary Murray (1868–1952), mother of five children, also became an enthusiastic supporter of the Woman's Party and the ERA, when protective legislation banned night work for women in New York State. For twenty years she lobbied legislatures and toured the country protesting such laws, claiming that they were a male scheme to reduce the number of women in industry and thereby lessen competition. She even publicly criticized Father John Ryan of the NCWC for advocating protective laws and decrying the amendment.

The NWP also hailed and trumpeted the views of St. Joan's Alliance, an English feminist organization, the successor to the Catholic Woman Suffrage Society. Dedicated to securing political, social, and economic equality for women, the society disparaged protective legislation as a handicap for women, and its bulletin, the *Catholic Citizen*, sympathetically reported the Woman's Party campaign for an ERA.

On the other hand, Catholic opposition was so strong it overshadowed the amendment's proponents such as Margaret Culkin Banning and Mary Merrick. As wartime support grew, Catholic objections became more strident. The NCCW, state councils of Catholic women, and lobbyists threatened to retaliate at the polls against legislators who voted for the proposal. Emma Guffey Miller, a member of the Democratic National Committee, attributed the 1943 adverse report of the House Judiciary Committee to the effectiveness of Catholic pressure and urged the Woman's Party to challenge the church and to get Catholic groups to support the measure. Bishop Edmond J. Fitzmaurice (1881–1942) of Delaware, who sympathized with NWP goals, suggested the organization seek an endorsement from his mentor Cardinal Denis Dougherty (1865–1951) of Philadelphia. He further recommended, like Miller, that they organize Catholic partisans.

Although Dougherty was approached within a week of Fitzmaurice's suggestions, it was three and one half years before he publicly approved the amendment. An organization was established with only slightly less difficulty. By the spring of 1943 Dorothy Shipley Granger (b. 1899), an NWP activist, had tried unsuccessfully on two different occasions to form Catholic women into a vehicle to support the ERA.

A direct descendant of Adam Shipley, who came to Maryland in 1668, Granger was a devout Catholic, a career woman, who chose to ignore her husband's injunction to be cautious in this endeavor. In August 1943, drawing upon lists of Catholic NWP members provided by state officers, she formed an association named for St. Joan of Arc and dedicated to securing equality of women before the law. Immediately it endorsed the ERA and began to lobby, petition, and object when amendment critics implied they spoke for the church. The society was also instrumental in getting Democrats to include an ERA plank in their 1944 presidential platform. However, activities of St. Joan's appalled many Catholics. The Administrative Board of the NCWC dismissed the society's claim to represent Catholic women and alleged it confused the issue by creating misunderstanding and adversely influencing judiciary committee recommendations. To offset St. Joan's effectiveness the board contemplated asking bishops to disapprove the organization. A nationally circulated column, "Father Quiz," flouted it as an organization of alleged Catholics deceptively created by the NWP; the International Federation of Catholic Alumnae and the NCCW warned that St. Joan's did not have episcopal approval. Granger, herself, described a meeting on the ERA with NCCW officers as "beautifully refined torture," during which "the boys who made the Inquisition rolled in their graves in envy."

Meanwhile representatives of the NWP and St. Joan's, including Granger, began writing and visiting Dougherty fairly regularly. They were pleasantly received but obtained little satisfaction. After further pressure by nuns from the convent where he vacationed and by Ethel E. Murrell, a Florida lawyer who had helped that religious community, the cardinal finally revealed he was in full accord with the ERA. However, he refused permission to publicize his views, as "it might seem to the public that I was rebuking certain of my coreligionists, some perhaps, of high ecclesiastical rank."[42] In the fall of 1945 he at long last made his position public by providing NWP officers with a letter of unqualified support for the ERA. The document was described by the press as sensational.

Although the Administrative Board of the NCWC again voted against the amendment, Dougherty's approbation made it easier for women to reconcile faith and feminism. In no uncertain terms he had made it clear that there was no Catholic position on the matter and that a woman would not jeopardize her orthodoxy by supporting the amendment. But Dougherty's endorsement had little effect on either the passage of the bill or the quantity of Catholic opposition. For the rest of the decade the NCCW, the Catholic press, fraternal organizations such as the Catholic Daughters and Daughters of Isabella, and various councils of Catholic women repeated their charges that the amendment would weaken the family and invalidate protective legislation. With the new conservatism of the 1950s, the opponents of the ERA grew in strength and numbers so that its proponents were practically overwhelmed. St. Joan's faded from existence.[43]

The institutional church did provide an acceptable outlet for the participation of "ladies" in the war effort. In the spring of 1941 the administrative board of the NCWC established the National Catholic Community Service (NCCS) to provide for the spiritual, material, and educational needs of men and women in the armed forces and defense industries. A special women's division was created to assist in military camps and industrial centers. With the support of many Catholic women's organizations, the service established a headquarters in Washington, D.C., with regional divisions. The NCCS and five other private welfare groups were incorporated into the United Service Organization (USO) for purposes of planning, coordinating, raising money, and obtaining governmental assistance. Immediately the NCCS began recruiting volunteers and established a training center for leaders at the National Catholic School of Social Service, where for two weeks pupils studied organization, recruitment, Catholic social principles, and how to encourage homemaking among women.[44] Under community auspices clubs and houses were opened throughout the nation for educational and recreational purposes and to relieve congestion around defense plants. (By war's end there were 137 clubs and 490 houses here and abroad.) Furthermore, local units participated in scrap-metal drives, selling war bonds, and distributing religious objects. The NCCW cooperated fully with the service by recruiting volunteers and training hostesses. Moreover, it collected garments, diapers, layettes, and sewing needs for refugees. These Catholic women had accepted the traditional role of healing the wounds of war, a catastrophe they attributed to the breakdown of family life, which in turn was ascribed mostly to the employment of mothers. Thus they advocated the strengthening of home, school, and church to avoid future wars.[45]

This view was enthusiastically approved by Anne S. Hooley (b. 1894), president of the NCCW in 1934–35 and executive director of the Women's Division NCCS. A native of Kansas City and founder and director of secretarial schools there, she was a social worker before her election in 1928 to the Board of Directors of the council. She chaired its committee on youth, broadcast nationally on juvenile matters every week, hosted conventions, and developed programs and activities for locals. Youthful leisure, according to her injunctions, should be filled with creative play, thought, and prayer. As head of Community Service, she defined her task "to provide recreation in the true sense of the word to re-create the body, mind and spirit and to acquaint these girls with their new community." Moreover, volunteers were reminded by her always to keep in mind threats to the family. As a result of her injunction much of NCCS resources were devoted to playgrounds for children and houses for women.[46]

Other Catholic authorities warned that if peace was to last, women must return to motherhood, their divinely ordained mission, and willingly accept the number of children sent by God. A commission to study postwar conditions, sponsored by the NCWC in 1943, repeated the warning of Pius XI that "Communism is particularly characterized by the rejection of any link that binds women to the family and

~~~ home, and her emancipation is proclaimed as a basic principle."
~~~ 1945 Pius XII reenforced this teaching when he proclaimed that
every woman is called to be a mother in a physical or more exalted
spiritual sense. Consequently, the pontiff asserted, women should not
be employed outside the home.[47]

These views intensified in the 1950s as Catholic churchmen, theologians, and publications were in the vanguard of the American
attempt to restore the ideal prewar "lady" and to glorify motherhood. It was emphasized that men and women had different spiritual
and emotional qualities as well as physical ones and that the female
intellect often was inferior to that of the male. Men must reassert
their influence in society, while women would find happiness by being submissive in the home. The wife, it was alleged, had a moral
duty to obey her husband, while he was obliged to guide her and help
her to develop new vitality, beauty, and happiness through mother-
ing a large family. Repeatedly Mary was hailed as the ideal Catholic
woman, one who devoted herself to "washing dishes, sweeping the
house, preparing meals, washing and mending clothes, caring for her
child, and performing a hundred other duties as the wife and mother
of today." If the traditional home was restored, Catholics were told,
women would lead us all to "the Eternal Spouse now and forever."
Two Catholic psychiatrists blandly asserted that "the basic function of
the married woman is pregnancy" and blamed the breakdown of marriage on the "emancipation of woman," wherein she renounced her
dependence on man and even wanted "equality of salary." Their ideal
of "true womanhood" was an Italian mother of twenty-two children
who "continually contribute to her happiness and her joy."[48]

To encourage further this restoration of women's sphere, the Christian Family Movement, primarily a female organization, was established in 1947 as a means of confronting divorce and sanctifying the
home. The National Catholic Woman's Union of the Catholic Central Verein issued a series of pamphlets promoting fathers as head
of the family and objecting to the employment of women. Cardinal
O'Hara formed the Committee for Christian Home and Family to
assist mothers in realizing the spirituality of their vocation. Cardinal
Cushing was the most forthright: he asserted bluntly that for women
to work after marriage was not Catholic.[49]

Motherhood was so exalted that sometimes maidenhood was denigrated, unless of course it was raised to supernatural status as a bride
of Christ. It was charged that career girls defy nature and that the popular appellation "old maid," even if cruel, was somewhat accurate.[50]

This conservative revival raised once again the issue of women and politics. One theologian asserted that a wife was morally forced to vote as her husband, another questioned the value of extending the ballot to women, while a third implicitly attributed the increase in sex crimes and the coming of World War II to the enfranchisement of women. An offspring of Protestantism, feminism had destroyed piety, chastity, generosity, humility, gentility, prudence, and selflessness. But most important, woman's capacity for suffering, a means of redeeming the world, had been demolished.[51]

To restore these Christian values the Grail Movement was brought to the United States from Holland in 1940. Designed to offset the "ultra masculine" nature of Western society, it sought to train young women to accept the challenge of Christianity and the modern world by cultivating feminine virtues such as spiritual receptivity and compassion — the womanly potential of Jesus. The Jesuit founder believed that if the church did not recover its lost sense of the feminine, contemporary women would engage in a woman's movement outside the church. The Grail spread rapidly in the United States. By 1943 it had attracted to its training courses recruits from all over the country. A few years later there was a full-time residence for workers and centers in many cities, and by 1953 over six thousand women had participated in its programs, and lay missionaries were being trained for work abroad. Convinced that rural life helped physical and spiritual development and heightened motherly qualities, the movement included a special rural apostolate encouraging a return to the land and a women's agricultural school at Loveland, Ohio.[52]

Although the leaders and administrators of the Grail were women, they promoted very traditional views. They attributed the evils of birth control, divorce, and juvenile delinquency to the increased numbers of working women. In ignoring their role as mothers, these females were failing to achieve happiness and fulfillment, the Grail alleged. Lydwine Van Kersbergen, who established the American Grail, repeatedly attacked feminism for destroying the difference between the sexes, secularizing culture, and denigrating large families. Although she exalted motherhood, Van Kersbergen glorified virginity. Therein, she claimed, one shared the supernatural by becoming a bride of Christ, liberating her spirit and obtaining freedom to work directly in building a Christian society. As in the writings of many theologians and nineteenth-century women, there was a strong manifestation of female supremacy in Van Kersbergen's teachings. She described the redeeming nature of women as a type of superiority that by loving surrender inspires others to God. "In the Divine plan,

Eve, the lover and helpmate, is destined to safeguard the Godward direction of men."[53]

As in the post–World War I period, many Catholics believed reform of the schools was necessary to promote the traditional views of women. The director of the Downtown Division of Denver's Regis College criticized feminists for advocating identical education for boys and girls, schooling which by its very nature failed to emphasize preparation for motherhood, the proper attitude toward home, and appropriate relations with men.[54] In 1952 at the National Catholic Educational Association convention, Bishop Edwin V. O'Hara (1881–1956) of Kansas City defended coeducation in Catholic schools — providing that boys and girls were educated separately. Provisions must be made for subjects such as manual training for males and domestic science for females. "We strive to make manly men and womanly women," the prelate proclaimed, with no attempt of "raising the woman's fallen divinity upon an equal pedestal with man."[55] As late as 1959 a teaching nun asserted that the obligation of all teachers was to prepare students for the career of marriage and the profession of motherhood, positions on which the fate of the world depended.[56]

These beliefs were implemented in a widely praised course "The Eternal Woman" at Brescia, a coeducational Ursuline college in Kentucky. Taught in the school's "pink room" and designed to develop a Christian, feminine woman, the course accentuated her mission as a helpmate to man, a "submission...[that] is an expression of all creation to its Creator." Included in the course of instruction were lectures on politeness and classes in the development of personal outer beauty. The latter was justified on the grounds that a woman's body was the temple of the Holy Ghost. "In figure, face, hair, posture, voice, vocabulary, styles, grooming, the whole woman is taken apart and put together again."[57]

The course at Brescia was an extreme manifestation of a widely accepted philosophy. Presidents of 109 accredited four-year colleges that admitted women agreed in 1961 that the sexes differed emotionally and psychologically and that females had a specific social role that was complementary to that of males. As a result over 90 percent of those administrators believed females should have an education different from that of men. The overwhelming majority holding this view were convinced that the curriculum should focus on preparation for their fundamental duty — marriage and motherhood. Less math and science and more home economics, then "she will not be disillusioned by the monotony of daily chores because such tasks have assumed deeper meaning in the broader context of human existence." Happiness and adjustment, it was claimed, would follow such a preparation. The educator who undertook the survey concluded, "Surely we do not want education to be the great leveler of the sexes. If this comes to pass, neither would excel in the particular gifts with which nature has endowed it."[58]

A corollary to the renewed attention on family and femininity was the renewed emphasis on purity and modesty. Females were reminded of their duty to set society's ideal for purity. It was asserted that modesty was the chief means of winning the love and respect of both God and men. Pamphlets attacking birth control and advocating restraint in dress and behavior were common.[59]

Church services sanctified these norms. Often the 7:00 A.M. Mass on Sunday was the woman's Mass, timed so wives could return home, complete the housework, and start dinner. But more meaningful, parish missions were divided into those for males and those for females (from which even the ushers were excluded) and further subdivided into services for single and married women. The avoidance of sexual sins in marriage was often the homily for wives. Sermons on purity and resisting male advances were common for single women, often part of a congregation consisting primarily of teenagers. At closing ceremonies females of all ages would consecrate themselves to Mary.[60] Men as well as women were taught to practice holiness in the exercise of sexual functions. A spirit of self-denial and voluntary abstinence was encouraged to show love of God. To ignore this sacrifice was to be guilty of hedonism.[61]

Although the church encouraged large families and tolerated the rhythm method of birth control only for grave reasons, there apparently was a wide gap between these injunctions and Catholic practice. According to eight national surveys between 1943 and 1961, "lay Catholics are generally farther from sharing their church's views concerning family size than they are from sharing that of non-Catholics."[62] Efforts to limit the number of children either by rhythm or contraceptives were fairly common. By 1955 over four-fifths of Catholic wives capable of conception used some means of birth control, with over one-half of the respondents practicing a method considered immoral by churchmen.[63]

There were many other indications that the return to normalcy was not entirely successful or even entirely welcome. An article in the *Catholic World* called for less pink tea and bridge on women's campuses. Society needed the minds of women to help restore order, the author claimed. Furthermore, she deplored the mores that encouraged females to obscure their intellectual abilities in order not to deflate male ego. Such tactics robbed women of self-confidence and courage while fostering duplicity.[64] Although Catholic schools may have been encouraging feminine subservience, nuns provided role models that undercut this message, and in women's colleges females assumed positions of leadership in student government and extracurricular activities. Furthermore, to enable students to fulfill their future roles as educators of their children, faculty encouraged critical thinking. Minds once awakened to inquiry often turned to careers and challenges unanticipated by the school. Of women of that generation entering politics, a disproportionate number were the products of small, Catholic women's colleges.[65]

Meantime, many Catholic women of achievement, even if ideologically traditional, were providing examples of careers outside the home. Kathryn E. Granahan (1906–1979), a Democrat long active in women's affairs, was elected to Congress in 1956 and served until 1963. The first woman to represent Philadelphia in the Capitol, she chaired the House post office subcommittee. She must have pleased churchmen willing to tolerate women in politics in the hope they would champion family and moral values. Granahan used her office to conduct a campaign against smut, pushing legislation to regulate the use of the mails for obscene publications and urging the formation of private groups to crusade against filthy literature, photos, and movies. In 1962 she was named treasurer of the United States by John F. Kennedy, holding that office until 1966.[66]

The most prominent Catholic female politician was Clare Boothe Luce (1903–87), playwright, editor, author, and war correspondent. She served in the House from 1943 to 1949 and was the keynote speaker at the Republican National Convention of 1944. One of the famous converts of Bishop Fulton J. Sheen (1895–1979), director of the Society for the Propagation of the Faith, she became a Catholic in February 1946 and a few years later retired from politics because "I just wanted to be home." Luce asserted that wives' first duties were to their husbands and that their most important and challenging task was raising children. Consequently they should not be employed outside the home. Additionally, in that sanctuary they had freedom, for there they could be their own boss. Nevertheless, she claimed not all women were called upon to be wives and function in the home. Millions of women, not just nuns, could bestow benediction on a life without marriage by performing effective duties in offices, schools, and hospitals.[67]

But Luce herself did not stay home long. She became a renowned anti-Communist, raised money for the church, and unsuccessfully sought a last minute Senate nomination in 1952 after having labored zealously for the Republican presidential nomination of Dwight Eisenhower. A grateful president offered her the post of secretary of labor, which she rejected. Together they then agreed on her appointment as ambassador to Italy (1953–57). Her confirmation was a little stormy, for it was feared, as the first Catholic ambassador to that nation, that she might violate the American tradition of separation of church and state by seeking a formal audience with the pope. To avoid criticism she remained in Rome over a year before visiting Pope Pius XII. In order to reconcile her public responsibilities with her duties as a wife, Luce and her husband agreed that he would reside in Rome six months every year and that she would spend a three-month vacation in the United States.[68]

Jane Hoey (1892–1968), who declared that her faith was the source of her strength, never held elective office but for most of her adult life was involved in public service and on the fringes of politics. Under the influence of William J. Kerby, "founder of scientific social work among Catholics," and John A. Ryan, chair of the Social Action Department of the NCWC, priests whose examples inspired her throughout her life, she completed graduate studies and began a career in social work. Hoey was an assistant to Harry Hopkins on the New York City Board of Child Welfare and during World War I was director of field service of the Atlantic Division of the Red Cross. Through her brother, a state legislator, she became friends with Al Smith and Robert Wagner and often stayed overnight at the governor's mansion with Franklin and Eleanor Roosevelt. In 1926 she was the only female appointed by Smith to an eleven-member commission to examine crime; the following year she began a decade as a member of the State Commission of Corrections. During the depression Hoey appealed to Catholic women to take their place in the world, not by speaking, but by acting like Catholics and caring for the needy.[69]

With the New Deal, Hoey went to Washington and helped set up the Temporary Emergency Relief Administration. In 1936 she was appointed the first director of the Bureau of Public Assistance under the Social Security Board, a position she held for eighteen years until Eisenhower replaced her. During her incumbency she championed the extension of medical care under Social Security, fought state discrimination against blacks and Indians in the social security program, argued for a guaranteed annual income, and during World War II criticized the handling of Japanese evacuees from the West Coast. Hoey was president of the National Council of Social Workers (1940–

41) and vice-president of the National Catholic Welfare conference (1953), represented the United States before the social commission of the United Nations Economic and Social Council, and after leaving government service became director of social research for the National Tuberculosis Association.[70]

Along with her achievements, in many ways Hoey exemplified traditional Catholicism. It was natural, she claimed, for women to undertake social work, for females were innately concerned with the welfare and rights of other people. The feminine qualities of humility and faith helped condition them for the such a career especially, since many of its basic principles stem from a belief in the divine origins of man.[71]

Other Catholic women were making their mark in business. In January 1930 Patricia Murphy (b. 1911) opened a tearoom in Brooklyn only a year after arriving in the United States with but sixty dollars. Surmounting the hardships of female entrepreneurship, she established many other eateries from London to Florida. Known as "one of the nation's top restauranteurs," Murphy saw her Long Island place gross $1.5 million its first year.[72] Lillian Westropp (1885–1968) and her sister Clara E. Westropp (1886–1965) founded the Women's Savings and Loan Company of Cleveland in 1922. Convinced that a woman would much rather bank with a member of her own sex than with males, the company was run by women for women, without a single man in the business. The sisters had to overcome male opposition to their idea and in the beginning trekked from store to store and factory to factory to get savings accounts. So successful were they that by 1953 the bank was the third largest in the county with assets of over $38 million. In 1965 at the time of Clara's death it had $137 million in assets.[73]

Both women, who had been active in the suffrage movement, also had abiding interests in philanthropy, social problems, and religion. Lillian, who was president of the bank, had abandoned the stage because of her mother's charge that acting was irreligious. Instead she attended Cleveland Law School, graduating first in her class in 1915. After a number of years in private practice, she served as assistant county prosecutor from 1929 to 1931, and from 1931 until 1959 as municipal court judge in Cleveland, assuming the leadership in bail-bond reform and in obtaining a psychiatric clinic for the court. Clara, who was a music teacher before becoming executive secretary and treasurer of the bank, was elected president of the Cuyahoga County Savings and Loan League in 1952. In 1965 she was honored as Catholic woman of the year for her devotion to the missions: she had chaired the diocesan mission program, raised money for missionaries in India, and founded St. Francis Xavier Mission Association, wherein 464 individual circles each supported one missionary. Clara was also active in the NCCW and established the Holy Family Cancer Home.

The extent to which the sisters' faith permeated the bank was remarkable. Each day a rosary was offered for world peace by its officers and employees. Sodality and mission groups met in the bank, which contained a prayer room where weekly Mass was celebrated. Religious statues were displayed on the main floor, and bank officers even urged patrons to pray more frequently.[74]

Other women, relatively well known for religious activities during this period, included Catherine C. McParlan (1856–1958), Sister Ignatia, O.A.A., and Mary Ellen Kelly (1903–61). After the death of her husband and five-year-old daughter in 1896, McParlan joined the House of Calvary, an association of Catholic widows to care for the cancerous. A few years later she was instrumental in founding a hospital for cancer patients and at age ninety-seven was still its full-time administrator.[75] The efforts of Ignatia, who established the Rosary Hill Solarium in Cleveland for alcoholics, led to the creation of Alcoholics Anonymous. This shy, retiring nun was presented a Siena Medal in 1960 for her contributions to Catholic life. Kelly, confined to bed with paralysis from age fifteen, established the League of the Shut-In Sodalists to unite the sick, aged, and disabled. The league attempted to make serious illness more tolerable by stressing the values and merits of suffering. She wrote books and religious articles and edited *Action Now*, the league's magazine. In 1954, the year in which Kelly received a Christopher Award for using her talents in a constructive way, she appeared on the national TV program "Strike It Rich" to raise money for her organization. Kelly's patient suffering, high spirits, and worldwide travel on her mobile bed offered inspiration and hope to thousands of Catholics and non-Catholics alike.[76]

One of the most famous Catholics of this period asserted that the chief moral influence all during her life was that of the mistress of boarders at the Notre Dame Academy she attended. Academy Award winner and "undisputed First Lady of the American theater," Ethel Barrymore (1879–1959) was a spearhead of the Actors Equity Strike of 1919, starred in outlawed benefit performances, and signed the agreement with management for the union. She was an active member and fund-raiser for the Catholic Actors' Guild. In addition to demonstrating a commitment to her fellow performers, Barrymore was faithful to her church. For several years at Eastertime she read the Passion from St. Matthew for Father Peyton's family theater and after eleven years of trying to save her marriage obtained the permission of New York's Cardinal Hayes to divorce her husband, a civil action for professional purposes; as she stated, "My divorce is merely legal. ... [It] is recognized legally but not by the church nor by me. And I've never thought of marrying again — never given it a thought."[77]

With many prominent women opting for careers, the right to be single was defended more and more frequently. Even some traditionalists approved of unmarried women seeking careers if spiritual motherhood was a part of the profession such as a doctor, nurse, teacher, and even politician.[78] Furthermore, some critics demanded that the church do more to make single women welcome and comfortable. This was the objective of the Bethany Conference movement, a regularly scheduled gathering of unmarried women patterned on the Cana Conference.[79] Even the League of Catholic Women seemed to acknowledge changing mores by establishing a Young Business Girls' branch. Here women from age seventeen to twenty-eight met in discussion groups, studied leadership and psychology, and met career-minded females with similar interests.[80] One of the more surprising indications that women were resisting unrealistic injunctions from the clergy to be homemakers was a sympathetic account of Betty Friedan's *Feminine Mystique* in *Commonweal*. The reviewer claimed that Friedan's analysis was applicable to Catholic women, who were conditioned to attribute discontent with domesticity to their sinful nature. All these beleaguered women really want, she asserted, is an opportunity to put their training and ability to work.[81]

One of the ways in which women continued to assert themselves without directly challenging the repression of the 1950s was by assuming further leadership in the world of religion.[82] In addition to providing examples like Day and de Hueck, females moved directly into areas hitherto closed. Women were either editors or staffers of a large number of Catholic magazines, including *Jubilee*, *Cross Currents*, and *Commonweal*. Dorothy Dohen (1923–84) assumed the leadership of *Integrity*, which taught women to be more than complementary to men. They should be "present in society," she contended, participating in the civil rights movement and political reform.[83] The Grail, which had encouraged feminine participation in social actions such as co-ops and credit unions, began to put greater emphasis on graduate studies and increased involvement with world issues such as the peace and civil rights movements. A more serious challenge to orthodoxy was the Grail's development of a theology of women that rejected the male experience of God and advocated a nonsexist worship.[84]

Changing relationships were also recognized by *Ave Maria* in 1964 with a ten-week series "The New Catholic Women and the Parish." The articles called upon church men to stop subjugating women and to recognize their problems, concerns, insights, and spiritual gifts — to see them as persons, not wives and mothers. The author concluded by stating that, with no disrespect to St. Paul, it was a shame if women did not speak about and in the church.[85]

American nuns, too, were changing in the 1950s as they realized the need for further adaptation and renewal. Community modifications and the renovation of life such as the horarium (the daily order of religious exercises from rising to bedtime) and habit were begun. Furthermore, many communities required greater professionalization of nuns and sought increased cooperation and collaboration among various sisterhoods. In 1954 the quarterly *SF Bulletin*, the first journal by and for sisters, was begun. Dedicated to formation topics and the role and nature of congregations, it became a vehicle for change and for the implementation of Pius XI's charge to religious women to be aware of problems in the contemporary world.[86]

The postwar years had indeed set the stage for dramatic events.

EPILOGUE

The decade of the 1960s was a turning point in the history of Catholic women, as it was for American women in general. On the secular side in 1961 President John F. Kennedy appointed a commission on the status of women; equal-pay legislation was enacted in 1963, the year the National Organization for Women was established, and Title VII of the Civil Rights Act of 1964 prohibited discrimination in the employment of women. Equally as important for Catholics were Pope John XXIII's encyclical *Pacem in Terris* and the documents of Vatican II. The encyclical reflected and encouraged new perceptions by observing that "since women are becoming even more conscious of their human dignity, they will not tolerate being treated as mere material objects, but demand rights befitting a human person in domestic and public life."

Council documents condemned every type of discrimination (including that of sex) with respect to the fundamental rights of a person. Furthermore, they proclaimed women's right "to embrace a state of life or to acquire an education or cultural benefits equal to those recognized for men." Equally as important, they asserted that females must be allowed to participate in the church's apostolate. Communities of nuns were called on by the "Fathers" to adjust to the times and culture where they lived and worked and to take into account the prevailing manners of contemporary life. Many American Catholic women ignored the qualifications in these pronouncements and seized upon the statements as hierarchical approbation to accelerate two centuries of evolution toward equality with men in both church and state. The movement was marked by new liturgies, demands for ordination, increasing reliance on individual conscience at the expense of hierarchical authority, and greater latitude for nuns, especially in facing the challenges of society.[1]

As one group of women capitalized upon changes in church and state to create a late twentieth-century Catholic feminism, itself a form of renewal, another group found the action not only unnecessary but dangerous. Structural modifications, liturgical reform, collegiality, questioning of authority, and the new woman so shattered tradition, they believed, that the church's salvational mission was compromised. In short, to some Vatican II had not gone far enough; to others it had gone too far.

The same church that brought forth St. Joan's Alliance (a United States chapter was founded in 1965), with female ordination an integral part of its goal of equality in church and state, and the Women's Ordination Conference (1976), which while advocating a female priesthood, questioned the clerical and institutional structure of the church, also produced the Catholic Charismatic movement (about 1966). This later band, allied with Protestant evangelicals, emphasized a personal relationship with Jesus and the Holy Spirit so intimate that it de-emphasized the role of priest and church. Other Catholic women began to question Mary as a role model, for the simultaneous exaltation of virginity and motherhood seemed at best incongruous; yet membership in the Legion of Mary has increased, and the United Catholic Women of America, boasting forty thousand members, was founded in 1984 to restore Marian values. In her campaign to defeat the ERA and promote the family, Phyllis S. Schlafly (b. 1924) extols Mary. So too does Marlene Elwell, who helped organize the National Right to Life Committee to fight for the repeal of abortion laws and presently leads a campaign to foster established family values.[2] Yet Eleanor Smeal (b. 1939), the former president of the National Organization for Women (1977–82, 1985–87) and a vigorous exponent of a woman's right to an abortion, states, "There is no other religion than Catholic. And I intend to be buried with the rites of the Church."[3]

The activities of women religious also became controversial as these women assumed what appeared to be unprecedented authority and responsibilities. The Conference of Major Superiors of Women (1956), despite Vatican trepidations, became the Leadership Conference of Women Religious (1971), emphasizing social justice and the "empowerment of women." Its spokesperson, Theresa Kane, in greeting the pope in 1979, urged the pontiff to hear the appeal of women who believed all ministries should be open to their sex. Among other new organizations founded by nuns was Network, a national Catholic social justice lobby started in 1971 and based in Washington, D.C. However, many believers view associations such as these as an abandonment of the historical calling of sisters and contend that such irregular activities are symbolized by the substitution of modern dress for traditional garb. To them, the ideal nun is in a convent or parochial school or, if serving the world, is doing so in a fashion marked by humility and subservience.[4]

Promoting these changes are Catholic feminist theologians such as Elisabeth Schüssler Fiorenza (b. 1938), Rosemary Radford Ruether (b. 1936), and Anne Carr (b. 1939). Traditionalists, however, have assailed the very premises of these scholars.[5]

Division among Catholic women came to the front most dramatically while clergy were researching the draft of the American bishops' pastoral *Partners in the Mystery of Redemption: A Pastoral Response to Women's Concerns for Church and Society.* "Listening" sessions at one hundred dioceses, sixty colleges, and forty-five military bases revealed the contrast between those who advocate change and those who are wedded to preservation. Despite an unprecedented attempt to understand feminist issues, the hierarchy of the country allied itself with the status quo. The document states that some biblical, anthropological, and theological scholars "do not find all the arguments put forth in *Inter Insignores* [the 1976 statement of the Congregation for the Doctrine of the Faith, arguing that the priesthood must be confined to males] to be convincing or persuasive" and that the tradition justifying such a stance frequently "arose from prejudicial attitudes toward women." Nevertheless, the bishops proclaim this practice "normative" and not subject to change. Even inquiry into the teaching is circumscribed, for study of the issue is encouraged only "to place in the proper light the church's consistent practice."[6] Furthermore, despite frequent advocacy of opportunity and justice for female wage-earners, the familial role of wife and mother is repeatedly emphasized and implicitly glorified.[7]

The document also recognizes that "many women experience official teaching on family planning not as liberating but as oppressive," with the result that there is a wide gap between church teaching and actual practice. However, the bishops dismiss the problem with an endorsement of *Humanae Vitae* (Paul VI's encyclical banning artificial contraception), a plea for compassion for those that reject this teaching, and an appeal for a dialogue between these women and those who find the natural regulation of births enriching their marriage.[8] The pastoral concludes by offering Mary as a model for all Christians, men and women: as the mother of Christ and the church, however, she is a special "symbol" for women.[9]

For feminists these pronouncements offer little hope. As Monsignor William H. Shannon points out, the method of the pastoral is "seriously flawed," for the ecclesiastics examined what "heritage" revealed about the issues raised by women, when it was the heritage itself that "hurt and alienated" so many of them. To the hierarchy, heritage was the solution; to many women, it was the problem.[10] Thus when the bishops wrote that "each day more barriers to the full recognition of [women's] equality before God fall, more stereotypes crumble, more doors open," they were hailing changes that according to Catholic feminists, are merely cosmetic. Yet if the bishops had been more amenable to feminist concerns, traditionalists would be further alienated. Nevertheless, it appears as if heritage should be modified by historical circumstances. The American experience indicates that diversity has always been a characteristic of Catholic women. This diversity itself has been a sign of vitality and growth; without prophets raising issues, challenging shibboleths, and living lives of sacrifice, the church becomes moribund. The history of American Catholic women, however, indicates there is little chance of such stultifying tranquillity in the future.

NOTES

Chapter 1 — Tenuous Traditions: Women and the Church in British and Revolutionary America

1. Mary P. Carthy, *English Influences on Early American Catholicism* (Washington, D.C., 1959), 12–17.

2. Florent Ancourt, *The Lady's Preceptor; or, A Letter to a Young Lady of Distinction* (Philadelphia, 1759), 21, 43.

3. Richard J. Challoner, *The Catholic Christian Instructed in the Sacraments, Sacrifice, Ceremonies, and Observances of the Church* (Philadelphia, 1786), 193–95. This was the earliest edition available to me.

4. Richard J. Challoner, *The Garden of the Soul* (Philadelphia, 1792), 226–28, 294; and idem, *A Manual of Catholic Prayers* (Philadelphia, 1774), 102.

5. *The Catechism of the Council of Trent, Published by Command of Pope Pius the Fifth* (New York, 1829; reprint, New York, 1905), 229.

6. The first Lord Baltimore, George Calvert, died before the actual settlement; his son, Cecilius, was the proprietor, and his brother, Leonard, the governor (John J. Shea, *The Catholic Church in Colonial Days, 1521–1763* [New York, 1886], 32).

7. Clayton C. Hall, *Narratives of Early Maryland, 1633–1684* (New York, 1910), 123–24.

8. Edwin W. Beitzell, *The Jesuit Missions of St. Mary's County, Maryland* (N.p., 1959), 38–40; H. S. Spalding, *Catholic Colonial Maryland: A Sketch* (Milwaukee, 1931), 88–89.

9. If this interpretation is correct, Brent was one of the earliest beneficiaries of "pedestal fallout," whereby male perceptions of what is ladylike enabled women to act more effectively in nontraditional roles. See Lois G. Carr, "Margaret Brent," in *Notable American Women, 1607–1950: A Biographical Dictionary* (henceforth *NAW*), ed. Edward T. James, Janet Wilson James, and Paul S. Boyer (Cambridge, Mass., 1971), 1:23; Eudora R. Richardson, "Margaret Brent — Gentleman," *Thought* 7 (March 1933): 533–47; Spalding, *Catholic Colonial Maryland*, 85–87; Julia C. Spruill, *Women's Life and Work in the Southern Colonies* (Chapel Hill, N.C., 1938), 231–41.

10. Jay P. Dolan, *The American Catholic Experience: A History from Colonial Times to the Present* (Garden City, N.Y., 1985), 83, 93–94.

11. James Hennesey, *American Catholics: A History of the Roman Catholic Community in the United States* (New York, 1981), 49.

12. Beitzell, *Jesuit Missions*, 65.

13. Hall, *Narratives*, 115–16.

14. Edwin H. Burton, *The Life and Times of Bishop Challoner, 1691–1781* (London, 1909), 2:125. At various times there had been Catholics in other colonies. Hundreds of Arcadian exiles had been scattered in English settlements. New York even had an Irish-Catholic governor, Thomas Dongan (1682–1688), and Cotton Mather revealed, apparently with great satisfaction, that one of the first witches executed in New England was a Roman Catholic who spoke only Irish ("Memorable Providences Relating to Witchcraft and Possessions," in *Narrative of Witchcraft Cases, 1648–1706*, ed. George L. Burr [New York, 1914; reprint, New York, 1970], 103, 105).

15. Arthur J. Riley, *Catholicism in New England to 1788* (Washington, D.C., 1936), 263–69; Carthy, *English Influences*, 24.

16. Elizabeth Ellet, *The Women of the American Revolution*, 4th ed. (New York, 1850; reprint, New York, 1969), 3:240–68.

17. Mary Lee was the mother of ten children. See M. C. Lee, "A Revolutionary Governor and His Family," *Catholic World* 50 (March 1890): 776–78; Laurita Gibson, *Some Anglo-American Converts to Catholicism prior to 1829* (Washington, D.C., 1943), 88; Washington to Mrs. Mary Lee, October 11, 1780, in *The Writings of George Washington from Original Manuscript Sources, 1745–1799*, ed. John C. Fitzpatrick (Washington, D.C., 1931–44), 20:168.

18. James A. Farrell, "Thomas FitzSimons: Catholic Signer of the Constitution," *Records of the American Catholic Historical Society of Philadelphia* 39 (September 1928): 175–224.

19. George W. Corner, ed., *The Autobiography of Benjamin Rush: "His Travels through Life"* (Princeton, N.J., 1948; reprint, Westport, Conn., 1970), 201–2.

20. J. J. O'Connell, *Catholicity in the Carolinas and Georgia: Leaves of Its History* (New York, 1879; reprint, Spartanburg, S.C., 1972), 414–19.

21. Peter A. Guilday, *The Life and Times of John England: First Bishop of Charleston, 1786–1842* (New York, 1927), 1:124; 2:153; Alice E. Mathews, "The Religious Experience of Southern Women," in *Women and Religion in America: A Documentary History*, ed. Rosemary Radford Ruether and Rosemary S. Keller (San Francisco, 1981–86), 2:193–204; J. Herman Schauinger, *William Gaston: Carolinian* (Milwaukee, 1979), 3–8; Ellet, *Women of the Revolution*, 2:136–41; Clyde Pitts, ed., *Guide to the Microfilm Edition of William Gaston Papers* (Chapel Hill, N.C., 1966), 8–9.

22. John Carroll to Charles Plowden, February 28, 1779, in *John Carroll Papers*, ed. Thomas O. Hanley (Notre Dame, Ind., 1976), 1:43. On September 15, 1788, he wrote to John Hock, the bishop of Mainz, that freedom of religion was such that Catholics participated everywhere in government. The greatest obstacle to their advancement was poverty (p. 329).

23. Annabelle M. Melville, *John Carroll of Baltimore: Founder of the American Hierarchy* (New York, 1955), 170–71. It has been asserted that Carroll invited these nuns to come "to pray for the American mission." There is no such indication, however, in the Carroll correspondence. See Peter Guilday, *The Life and Times of John Carroll* (New York, 1922; reprint, Westminster, Md., 1954), 488.

24. Rose L. Martin, "The First Nun Professed in the Original United States," in *Catholics in America*, ed. Robert Trisco (Washington, D.C., 1976), 39–41; Beitzell, *Jesuit Missions*, 144. Carberry was not the first nun from the American colonies. Lydia Longley (1674–1758) from Groton, Massachusetts, was captured by Indians in 1694, ransomed in New France, and became a convert and, in time, superior of the Congregation of Notre Dame at Isle de Orleans. Mary Ann Davis of Salem, Massachusetts, who was captured by Indians in 1686, was converted by a missionary, educated by Ursulines, and entered their novitiate in Quebec a year after Longley was received into the Congregation of Notre Dame. For these and similar captive converts, see Gibson, *Anglo-American Converts*.

25. Philip Gleason, ed., *Documentary Reports on Early American Catholicism* (New York, 1978), 2–4; Lambert Schrott, *Pioneer German Catholics in the American Colonies* (New York, 1933), 12, 94–95; Claude C. Robin, *New Travels through North America, in a Series of Letters*, trans. Philip Freneau (Philadelphia, 1783), 46; David N. Doyle, *Ireland, Irishmen, and Revolutionary America, 1760–1820* (Dublin, 1981), 69; Dolan, *Catholic Experience*, 114–15.

26. Robert H. Lord, John E. Sexton, and Edward T. Harrington, *History of the Archdiocese of Boston in Various Stages of Its Development, 1604–1943* (New York, 1944), 1:354, 435–36.

27. Richard Shaw, *John Dubois: Founding Father* (New York, 1983), 52–53; Gibson, *Anglo-American Converts*, 171–89, 195–219.

28. Annabelle M. Melville, "Elizabeth Bayley Seton," in *NAW*, 3:263–65.

29. Beitzell, *Jesuit Missions*, 81; Mary R. Mattingly, *The Catholic Church on the Kentucky Frontier, 1785–1812* (Washington, D.C., 1936), 131–32.

30. Charles Nerinckx, "A Look at the Present State of the Roman Catholic Religion in North America," ed. and trans. Joseph A. Agonito and Magdeleine Wellner, *Records of the American Catholic Historical Society of Philadelphia* 83 (March 1972): 3–36; J. Herman Schauinger, "Mary Rhodes," in *NAW*, 3:140–41.

31. J. Herman Schauinger, "Catherine Spalding," in *NAW*, 3:328–30.

32. M. Benedict Murphy, "Pioneer Roman Catholic Girls' Academies: Their Growth, Character, and Contributions to American Education; a Study of Roman Catholic Education for Girls from Colonial Times to the First Plenary Council of 1852" (Ph.D. diss., Columbia University, 1958), 168.

33. Dolan, *Catholic Experience*, 120.

34. John Mullanphy to Reverend Stephen Badin, October 29, 1804, in Alice L. Cochran, *The Saga of an Irish Immigrant Family: The Descendants of*

John Mullanphy (New York, 1978), 48–49; W. J. Howlett, *Life of Charles Ner-inckx: Pioneer Missionary of Kentucky and Founder of the Sisters of Loretto at the Foot of the Cross*, 2d ed. (Techny, Ill., 1940), 139, 141, 164.

35. "Journal of the Seminary of St. Thomas," quoted in Mattingly, *Church on the Kentucky Frontier*, 216. As late as 1897 Catholics were reminded that it was difficult to attend a dance without serious sin and were asked, "How would you like, dear Christian, to meet death in the ballroom?" (Ferreol Girardey, *Mission Book for the Married* [New York, 1897], 127).

36. John Carroll, "Report to Leonardo Antonelli," March 1, 1785, in Hanley, *John Carroll Papers*, 1:180.

37. John Carroll to Charles Plowden, February 12, 1803, in Hanley, *John Carroll Papers*, 2:408; Carroll to Leonardo Antonelli, March 1, 1875, in ibid., 1:181–82. Of course sometimes it was the Protestant who changed religion. When Ellen O'Brien married Samuel Abell, the Protestant sheriff of St. Mary's County, Maryland, they agreed she would raise the girls as Catholics, and he the boys as Protestants. To the chagrin of his father, however, the son, inspired by his mother's devotion, became a Catholic. The father also became a convert on his deathbed (Edward J. McDermott, "Some Roman Catholics in Kentucky," in *Catholic Builders of the Nation: A Symposium on the Catholic Contribution to the United States*, ed. C. E. McGuire [Boston, 1923], 1:313).

38. John Carroll to his sister, Elizabeth, August 18, 1809, in Hanley, *John Carroll Papers*, 3:42.

39. John Carroll to Leonardo Antonelli, April 23, 1792, June 17, 1793, in Hanley, *John Carroll Papers*, 2:32, 94–95; to Bernadine Matthews, March 1, 1793, February 20, 1795, pp. 84, 136–37; to John Thayer, May 9, 1793, p. 88; to Jean Hubert, January 15, 1794, pp. 109–10; to Charles Plowden, September 3, 1800, December 15, 1800, pp. 319, 330.

40. Dolan, *Catholic Experience*, 121; Hennesey, *American Catholics*, 92.

41. Edmund Goebel, *A Study of Catholic Secondary Education during the Colonial Period up to the First Plenary Council of Baltimore, 1852* (Washington, D.C., 1936), 49, 102.

42. Charles Carroll to Mary Caton, January 28, 1798, August 6, 1804, docs. 993, 1101; to Elizabeth Caton, May 22, 1817, doc. 1403, in *The Charles Carroll Papers*, 3 microfilm rolls, ed. Thomas O. Hanley (Wilmington, Del., 1972).

43. Ellen H. Smith, *Charles Carroll of Carrollton* (Cambridge, Mass., 1942), 112, 131, 162.

44. Elizabeth Seton to Mrs. George Gottesberger, August 23, 1817, quoted in Marie de Lourdes Walsh, *The Sisters of Charity of New York, 1804–1959* (New York, 1960), 1:45–46.

45. François Fénelon, *A Treatise on the Education of Daughters, Translated from the French and Adapted to English Readers by the Rev. T. F. Dibdin* (Boston, 1806; reprint, Boston, 1821), 15–18, 159, 171.

46. René Houdet, *A Treatise on Morality, Chiefly Designed for the Instruction of Youth* (Philadelphia, 1796), 83–89, 99–101.

47. John Carroll to Charles Plowden, May 26, 1788, in Hanley, *John Carroll Papers*, 1:312.

48. John Carroll to Clare Joseph Dickinson, September 23, 1804, in Hanley, *John Carroll Papers*, 2:453.

49. John Carroll to Robert Molyneux, June 19, 1808, in Hanley, *John Carroll Papers*, 3:65.

50. Elizabeth Seton to Simon Bruté, quoted in Shaw, *John Dubois*, 89.

51. Shaw, *John Dubois*, 50–56, 75, 89–90; Annabelle M. Melville, *Elizabeth Bayley Seton, 1774–1821* (New York, 1951), 167–83; Mother Seton to John Carroll, May 13, 1811, January 25, 1810, in Melville, *John Carroll*, 370–71, 266–67.

Chapter 2 — The Catholic Lady: A Concept Further Refined

1. Mary Beth Norton, *Liberty's Daughters: The Revolutionary Experience of American Women, 1750–1800* (Boston, 1980); Linda K. Kerber, *Women of the Republic: Intellect and Ideology in Revolutionary America* (Chapel Hill, N.C., 1980); Joan Hoff Wilson, "The Illusion of Change: Women and the American Revolution," in *The American Revolution: Explorations in the History of American Radicalism*, ed. Alfred F. Young (De Kalb, Ill., 1976), 383–445; Gerda Lerner, "The Lady and the Mill Girl: Changes in the Status of Women in the Age of Jackson," *Mid-Continental American Studies Journal* 10 (Spring 1969): 5–15.

2. Barbara Welter, "The Cult of True Womanhood, 1820–1860," *American Quarterly* 18 (Summer 1966): 151–74.

3. Robert Walsh, *Didactics: Social, Literary, and Political* (Philadelphia, 1836; reprint, New York, 1972); Mary F. Lochemes, *Robert Walsh: His Story* (New York, 1971), 161, 230; idem, "Robert Walsh," *Catholic Encyclopedia* (New York, 1967), 14:783–84.

4. Walsh, *Didactics*, 1:18, 119, 123; 2:25, 38–39.

5. Ibid., 1:71; 2:91.

6. Girardey, *Mission Book*, 30.

7. Walsh, *Didactics*, 1:24, 29, 123; 2:19, 127.

8. Jean F. Landriot, *The Valiant Woman: A Series of Discourses Intended for the Use of Women Living in the World*, trans. Helen Lyons (Boston, 1872), 19, 30–31, 51, 88, 108, 141, 175–78, 244–45, 260.

9. Bernard O'Reilly, *The Mirror of True Womanhood; and True Men As We Need Them* (New York, 1881 [two works printed together]), *True Men*, 38.

10. O' Reilly, *True Womanhood*, 29, 33, 57–61, 64, 104.

11. Girardey, *Mission Book*, 31.

12. Edward Heston, trans., *Circular Letters of Very Rev. Basil Anthony*

Mary Moreau, Founder of the Religious of Holy Cross (Notre Dame, Ind., 1943), 1:61.

13. Mary Ewens, *The Role of the Nun in Nineteenth Century America: Variations on the International Theme* (New York, 1978), 104, 217; Walsh, *Sisters of Charity*, 1:160; Barbara Misner, "A Comparative Social Study of the Members and Apostolates of the First Eight Permanent Communities of Women Religious within the Original Boundaries of the United States, 1790–1850" (Ph.D. diss., Catholic University, 1981), 51; Eleanore M. Brosnahan, *On the King's Highway: A History of the Sisters of the Holy Cross of St. Mary of the Immaculate Conception* (New York, 1931), 157; Patricia Byrne, "Sisters of St. Joseph: The Americanization of a French Tradition," *U.S. Catholic Historian* 5 (Summer/Fall 1986) 262. For the relationship between the "cult of true womanhood" and nuns, see Joseph G. Mannard, "Maternity... of the Spirit: Nuns and Domesticity in Antebellum America," *U.S. Catholic Historian* 5 (Summer/Fall 1986) 305–24.

14. Conrad Sickinger, *A Sure Way to a Happy Marriage: A Book of Instruction for Those Betrothed and for the Married*, trans. Edward Taylor (New York, 1881), 234–36. In his encyclical on Christian marriage, *Arcanum* (1880), Pope Leo XIII also emphasized a wife's subjection to her husband; see especially par. 11.

15. Katherine E. Conway, ed., *Watchwords from John Boyle O'Reilly* (Boston, 1891), 24.

16. *Catechism of the Council of Trent*, 229, 234; *The Mission Book: A Manual of Instruction and Prayers Adapted to Preserve the Fruits of the Mission* (New York, 1853), 330, 349, 372; Girardey, *Mission Book*, 28, 39.

17. Hugh J. Nolan, ed., Pastoral Letters of the American Hierarchy, 1792–1970 (Huntington, Ind., 1971), 158; Sickinger, *Sure Way*.

18. John Ireland, "Social Purity: Address Delivered to the World's Congress on Social Purity," frame 58, *John Ireland Papers*, microfilmed by the Minnesota Historical Society (St. Paul, 1984).

19. Ewens, *Nun in Nineteenth Century*, 104.

20. Pastoral of May 19, 1830, in Hugh J. Nolan, *The Most Reverend Francis Patrick Kenrick, Third Bishop of Philadelphia, 1830–1851* (Philadelphia, 1948), 446–47.

21. *Catechism of the Council of Trent*, 291.

22. George Deshon, *Guide for Catholic Young Women, Especially for Those Who Earn Their Own Living*, 31st ed. (New York, 1897; first published, 1868), 242; *Mission Book*, 400; Hugh J. Nolan, "Francis Patrick Kenrick: First Coadjutor Bishop, Diocese of Philadelphia," in *The History of the Diocese of Philadelphia*, ed. James F. Connelly (Philadelphia, 1978), 446–47.

23. Guilday, *John England*, 2:138, 470; Paul J. Foik, *Pioneer Catholic Journals* (New York, 1930; reprint, Westport, Conn., 1969), 91; Ignatius Reynolds, ed., *The Works of John England, First Bishop of Charleston* (Baltimore, 1849), 1:13.

24. John England, "Constitution of the Diocess [sic] of Charleston," in

Reynolds, *Works of John England*, 5:101; Peter Clarke, *A Free Church in a Free Society: The Ecclesiology of John England, Bishop of Charleston, 1820–1842, a Nineteenth Century Missionary Bishop in the Southern United States* (Hartsville, S.C., 1982), 258–59.

25. Quoted in Richard C. Madden, *Catholics in South Carolina: A Record* (Lantham, Md., 1985), 60.

26. Orestes Brownson, *The Convert; or, Leaves from My Experience* (New York, 1877), 85–91, 100–101.

27. Hugh Marshall, *Orestes Brownson and the American Republic: A Historical Perspective* (Washington, D.C., 1971), 82–83.

28. See all of the following by Orestes Brownson: "Modern French Literature," *Brownson's Quarterly Review* (henceforth *BQ;* April 1842), in *The Works of Orestes A. Brownson*, ed. Henry F. Brownson (henceforth *Works;* Detroit, 1882–85), 19:56, 62; "Literature, Love, and Marriage," *BQ* (July 1864), in *Works*, 19:496–97; "Cooper's Ways of the Hour," *BQ* (July 1851), in *Works*, 16:345–46; "Religious Orders," *Ave Maria* (1871), in *Works*, 8:244; "The Family, Christian and Pagan," *BQ* (October 1875), in *Works*, 13:542; "The Worship of Mary," *BQ* (January 1853), in *Works*, 8:83. Also see Walter G. Sharrow, "Northern Catholic Intellectuals and the Coming of the Civil War," *New York Historical Quarterly* 57 (January 1974): 48–49.

29. Orestes Brownson, "The Woman Question — Article 2," *BQ* (October 1873), in *Works*, 18:407; idem, "The Woman Question," *Catholic World* 59 (May 1869): 147, 150, 157, quoted in "Religious Liberty," *Catholic World* (1870), in *Works*, 13:239–40.

30. James J. Kenneally, "Eve, Mary, and the Historians: American Catholicism and Women," *Horizons* 3 (Fall 1976): 191; Sickinger, *Sure Way*, 363.

31. Murphy, "Pioneer Catholic Girls' Academies," 208, 233; Margaret Marie Doyle, *The Curriculum of the Catholic Woman's College* (Berrien Springs, Mich., 1931), 27.

32. *The Ursuline Manual; or, A Collection of Prayers, Spiritual Exercises... Necessary for Forming Youth to the Practice of Social Piety, Originally Arranged for Young Ladies at the Ursuline Convent, Cork* (New York, 1840), 9, 12–15.

33. Girardey, *Mission Book*, 49–50.

34. Mannard, "Maternity of the Spirit," 321.

35. Louise Callan, *The Society of the Sacred Heart in North America* (New York, 1937), 727–28.

36. Sarah J. Hale, "The Ursuline Convent," *American Ladies Magazine* 7 (September 1834): 418–19, 425–26; Eleanor W. Thompson, *Education for Ladies, 1830–1860: Ideas on Education in Magazines for Women* (New York, 1947), 369; Virginia Penny, *Think and Act: A Series of Articles Pertaining to Men and Women, Work and Wages* (Philadelphia, 1839; reprint, New York, 1971), 227.

37. The view that "ladies" should not be gainfully employed was not

unique to Catholicism. On a visit to the United States, Michel Chevalier reported that one of the most striking features of American life was the interpretation of male superiority to mean a masculine monopoly on toil (*Society, Manners, and Politics in the United States: Letters on North America*, ed. John William Ward [Ithaca, N.Y., 1961], 331).

38. Deshon, *Guide*, 163, 236–37; O'Reilly, *True Womanhood*, 414–17.

39. "Woman," *Catholic World* 4 (December 1867): 419–20; Deshon, *Guide*, 15, 17, 24, 26, 152, 163, 167, 178, 186, 208.

40. See the following essays by Mathew Carey in *Miscellaneous Pamphlets* (Philadelphia, 1831): "Essays on the Public Charities of Philadelphia" (Philadelphia, 1830), "To the Ladies Who Have Undertaken to Establish a House of Industry in New York" (N.p., n.d.), and "Wages of Female Labour" (N.p., n.d.). Also see "Female Wages and Female Oppression," nos. 1–3 (Philadelphia, 1835); "Female Wages and Female Oppression, Addressed to Ladies of the United States" (Philadelphia, 1835).

41. Thomas M. Schwerter, "Eleanor Donnelly: The Singer of Pure Religion," *Catholic World* 105 (June 1917): 355; Raymond H. Schmandt, "Catholic Intellectual Life in the Archdiocese of Philadelphia: An Essay," in Connelly, *Diocese of Philadelphia*, 619–20.

42. Eleanor C. Donnelly, "Wife and Mother" and "Women in Literature," both in *Girlhood's Hand-Book of Woman: A Compendium of the Views on Woman's Work — Woman's Sphere — Woman's Influence and Responsibilities*, ed. Eleanor C. Donnelly, 2d ed. (St. Louis, 1905), 371, 15–16.

43. Eleanor C. Donnelly to Ignatius Donnelly, March 17, 1856, reel 2, frame 212–13, Ignatius Donnelly Papers, microfilm copy of originals at Minnesota Historical Society. Her brother served as lieutenant governor of that state and as representative in Congress and helped form the Populist party; see Martin Ridge, *Ignatius Donnelly: The Portrait of a Politician* (Chicago, 1962). It is quite likely that Eleanor's mother attempted to find a husband for her daughter and failed; see Gretchen Kreuter, "Kate Donnelly versus the Cult of True Womanhood," in *Women of Minnesota: Selected Biographical Essays*, ed. Barbara Stuhler and Gretchen Kreuter (St. Paul, 1977), 23.

44. John T. Dwyer, *Condemned to the Mines: The Life of Eugene O'Connell, 1815–1891: Pioneer Bishop of Northern California and Nevada* (New York, 1976), 248–49; Dennis Clark, *Proud Past: Catholic Lay People of Philadelphia* (Philadelphia, 1976), 227.

45. Eleanor C. Donnelly, Introduction to Jane Campbell, "Women and the Ballot," in Donnelly, *Girlhood's Hand-Book*, 190–91; Donnelly, "Women in Literature," in ibid., 16–17.

46. Quoted in Honor Walsh, "Eleanor C. Donnelly," *Records of the American Catholic Historical Society* 28 (September 1917): 281.

Chapter 3 — "Lady" Novelists: Unwitting Innovators
of the Nineteenth Century

1. "The American Novel — with Samples," *Catholic World* 28 (December 1878): 326. Although a large number of Catholic female novelists stressed the same theme of domesticity as did their Protestant sisters, they have been frequently ignored in general studies of women writers. Neither Nina Baym, *Women's Fiction: A Guide to Novels by and about Women in America, 1820–1870* (Ithaca, N.Y., 1978), nor Mary Kelley, *Private Woman, Public Stage: Literary Domesticity in Nineteenth Century America* (New York, 1984), deals with Catholics.

2. For the Irish immigrant, see Colleen McDannell, *The Christian Home in Victorian America, 1840–1900* (Bloomington, Ind., 1986), 169; Sister Mary Francis Clare to *London Tablet*, n.d., Archives, Sisters of St. Joseph of Peace, Jersey City, N.J.

3. "American Novel," 326–27; Brownson, "Literature, Love, and Marriage," 493–516; Paul R. Messbarger, *Fiction with a Parochial Purpose: Social Uses of American Catholic Literature* (Boston, 1971), 11–20. For a general assessment of these novels, see David S. Reynolds, *Faith in Fiction: The Emergence of Religious Literature in America* (Cambridge, Mass., 1981); James A. White, *The Era of Good Intentions: A Survey of American Catholic Writing between the Years 1880–1915* (New York, 1978); and Willard Thorp, *Catholic Novelists in Defense of Their Faith, 1829–1865* (Worcester, Mass., 1968; reprint, New York, 1978).

4. Katherine E. Conway, *Lalor's Maples* (Boston, 1901), 15.

5. Katherine E. Conway, "The Literature of Moral Loveliness," *Catholic Reading Circle Review* (1892), reprinted in *Immortelles of Catholic Columbian Literature*, ed. M. Seraphine Leonard (Chicago, 1897), 204–5.

6. Anna H. Dorsey, *The Oriental Pearl; or, The Catholic Emigrants* (Baltimore, 1843), 7.

7. Little is known of Meaney. See Maureen Murphy, "Mary L. Meaney," in *American Women Writers: A Critical Reference Guide from Colonial Times to the Present*, ed. Lina Mainiero (New York, 1979), 3:152–53.

8. Lelia H. Bugg, *Orchids: A Novel* (St. Louis, 1894), n.p.; Madeline V. Dahlgren, *Divorced: A Novel* (Chicago, 1887), 5.

9. Maurice F. Egan, *Confessions of a Book Lover* (New York, 1922), 28.

10. This tactic was not as farfetched as it appears at first blush. In an 1849 edition of the *Evangelist*, the Reverend John Todd suggested that employers force their domestics to eat meat on Fridays; see Charles E. Rosenberg, *The Cholera Years: The United States in 1832, 1849, and 1866* (Chicago, 1947), 138.

11. Mary Sadlier, "Iban Dempsey's Story," in *A Round Table of the Representative American Catholic Novelists*, ed. Eleanor C. Donnelly (New York, 1896), 241–71.

12. Eleanor C. Donnelly, "A Lost Prima Donna," in Donnelly, *Round Table*, 9–50.

13. Madeline V. Dahlgren, "Liberties of Our Daughters," *Ladies Home Journal* 7 (November 1890): 2.

14. Lelia H. Bugg, *The Prodigal's Daughter and Other Tales* (New York, 1898).

15. Anna H. Dorsey, "The Mad Penitent of Today," in Donnelly, *Round Table*, 53–95.

16. See the following by Molly Elliot Seawell: *The Ladies' Battle* (New York, 1911), 17–48, 107–10; "The Creative Faculty in Women," *Critic* 19 (November 1891): 292–94; "The Ladies' Battle," *Atlantic Monthly* 106 (September 1910): 290–94, 301; see also *New York Times*, May 14, 1911, and April 20, 1913.

17. White, *Era of Good Intentions*, 47.

18. I have been unable to obtain *Bessy Conway*, but see Thorp, *Catholic Novelists*, 106.

19. For her life, see Donnelly, *Round Table*, 51–52; Agnes B. McGuire, "Catholic Women Writers," in McGuire, *Catholic Builders*, 4:191–93; Leonard, *Immortelles*, 30–31; Suzanne Allen, "Anna Hanson McKenney Dorsey," in Mainiero, *American Women Writers*, 1:531–32; James J. Daly, "Catholic Contributions to American Prose," in McGuire, *Catholic Builders*, 4:127.

20. Thomas F. Meehan, "The House of Sadlier," *America* 47 (June 4, 1932): 214–15; Leonard, *Immortelles*, 19–22; Thomas N. Brown, "Mary Anne Madden Sadlier," in *NAW*, 3:219–20; McGuire, "Catholic Women Writers," 187–91; *Revolution*, September 8, 1890; *Woman's Journal*, October 1, 1890.

21. See chapter 6 for further details about Dahlgren's life.

22. Stephen Bell, *Rebel, Priest, and Prophet: A Biography of Dr. Edward McGlynn* (New York, 1937), 71; obituary, *New York Times*, May 25, 1918.

23. Lelia H. Bugg, *The Correct Thing for Catholics*, 12th ed. (New York, 1891), 105; idem, *The People of Our Parish: Being the Chronicle and Comment of Katherine Fitzgerald, Pew holder in the Church of St. Paul the Apostle* (Boston, 1901), 104–14.

24. The best account of her life and religion is Per Seyersted, *Kate Chopin: A Critical Biography* (Baton Rouge, La., 1969). Also see Daniel S. Rankin, *Kate Chopin and Her Creole Stories* (Philadelphia, 1932), and Cynthia Wolff, "Kate Chopin," in *American Writers: A Collection of Literary Biographies*, ed. Leonard Unger (New York, 1979), supp. 1, part 1, 200–226. These studies and Messbarger, *Fiction with a Parochial Purpose*, claim she left the church. However, Emma K. Temple, "Our Catholic Short Story Writers," in McGuire, *Catholic Builders*, 4:160, and Stephen Nissenbaum, "Kate O'Flaherty Chopin," in *NAW*, 1:333–35, both describe her as Catholic, the latter claiming she was ardent in her faith all during her life.

25. See the following stories in *The Complete Works of Kate Chopin*, ed. Per Seyersted (henceforth *Complete Works*; Baton Rouge, La., 1969): "Love on the Bon-Dieu," 153–63; "Désirée's Baby," 240–45; "A Dresden Lady in Dixie," 345–51.

26. "Wiser than a God," in *Complete Works*, 39–47.
27. *At Fault*, reprinted in *Complete Works*, 739–877.
28. "Madame Célestin's Divorce," in *Complete Works*, 276–79.
29. "The Story of an Hour," in *Complete Works*, 352–54.
30. "Charlie," in *Complete Works*, 638–70.
31. Anne G. Jones, *Tomorrow Is Another Day: The Woman Writer in the South, 1859–1936* (Baton Rouge, La., 1981), 144, 158. For an excellent introduction to *The Awakening*, see the edition edited by Sandra Gilbert (New York, 1983). Chopin's most daring story, one that by no account could be reconciled with traditional Catholicism, was not published until 1969: "The Storm," in *Complete Works*, 592–96. In the story an adulterous afternoon led to happiness even for the spouses of the offenders; sex without marriage was enjoyed without guilt.
32. For her life, see Annette S. Driscoll, *Literary Convert Women* (Manchester, N.H., 1928), 48–51; Daly, "Catholic Contributions," 125; Messbarger, *Fiction with a Parochial Purpose*, 124–30.
33. Orestes Brownson to Isaac Hecker, December 19, 1871, in *The Brownson-Hecker Correspondence*, ed. Joseph F. Gower and Richard M. Leliaert (Notre Dame, Ind., 1979), 321.
34. Orestes Brownson, "Women's Novels," *BQ* (July 1845), in *Works*, 19:601–2; "Review," *Catholic World*, 19 (September 1874): 858.
35. Mary A. Tincker, *Grapes and Thorns; or, A Priest's Sacrifice* (New York, 1872), 118.
36. Ibid., 174.
37. Ibid., 139.

Chapter 4 — "Ladylike" Nuns: Nineteenth-Century Activists

1. Mary Oates, " 'The Good Sisters': The Work and Position of Catholic Churchwomen in Boston, 1870–1940," in *Catholic Boston: Studies in Religion and Community, 1870–1970*, ed. Robert Sullivan and James M. O'Toole (Boston, 1985), 180.
2. Felix M. Kirsch, *The Spiritual Direction of Sisters: A Manual for Priests and Superiors* (New York, 1931), 97–98. Until 1983 the terms "nuns" and "sisters" had precise and distinct meanings based primarily on the solemnity of the vows and rules governing enclosure. However, I will use the terms interchangeably.
3. The best studies of the nineteenth-century nun are those by Ewens; see especially, *Nun in Nineteenth Century*. Also see John T. Smith, "The Catholic Sisterhoods in the United States," in *Our Church and Country: The Catholic Pages of American History* (New York, 1905), 2:359–72; Amanda E. Porterfield, *Feminine Spirituality in America from Sarah Edwards to Martha Graham* (Philadelphia, 1980), 110–19, 123. The family priest and counselor of the prominent Catholic family the Gillespies advised the mother, "Eliza

should never marry; I do not know a man who is her intellectual superior." Eliza became a nun, Mother Angela Gillespie, American founder of the Congregation of Holy Cross (Anna S. McAllister, *Flame in the Wilderness: Life and Letters of Mother Angela Gillespie, C.S.C., 1824–1887, American Foundress of the Sisters of Holy Cross* [Paterson, N.J., 1944], 60). For a general survey of the history of American nuns, see Ewens, "Women in the Convent," *American Catholic Women: A Historical Exploration*, ed. Karen Kennelly (New York, 1989): 12–47.

4. Mother T. Guérin to Superior General, February 18, 1852, in *Journals and Letters of Mother Theodore Guérin, Foundress of the Sisters of Providence of Saint-Mary-of-the-Woods, Indiana,* ed. Mary T. Mug (Saint-Mary-of-the-Woods, 1937), 324; Ewens, *Nun in Nineteenth Century,* 175–76; Harold E. Hammond, ed., *Diary of a Union Lady, 1861–1865* (New York, 1962), 165; Penny, *Think and Act,* 220–21.

5. Mary Ewens, "Removing the Veil: The Liberated American Nun," in *Women of Spirit: Female Leadership in the Jewish and Christian Traditions,* ed. Rosemary Ruether and Eleanor McLaughlin (New York, 1979), 266–67; idem, "Political Activity of American Sisters before 1970," in *Between God and Caesar: Priests, Sisters, and Political Office in the United States,* ed. Madonna Kolbenschlag (New York, 1985), 42.

6. Mary Ewens, "The Double Standard of the American Sister," in *An American Church: Essays in the Americanization of the Catholic Church,* ed. David Alvarez (Moraga, Calif., 1979), 26–27; Howlett, *Nerinckx,* 249; Nerinckx, "Look at the Present State," 5; Misner, "First Eight Permanent Communities," 63–67; Florence Wolff, *From Generation to Generation: The Sisters of Loretto. Their Constitutions and Devotions, 1812–Vatican II* (Louisville, Ky., 1982), 7.

7. For revisions of community rules, in Ewens, *Nun in Nineteenth Century* see Charity of Nazareth, 56–57; Kentucky Dominicans, 59–60, 86; Visitandines, 39–40; Charity of Emmitsburg, 48; see also Joseph B. Code, *Great American Foundresses* (New York, 1929; reprint, Freeport, N.Y., 1968), 90–101.

8. Ewens, "Double Standard," 32; idem, "Political Activity," 43; idem, *Nun in Nineteenth Century,* 202; Frances J. Woods, "Congregations of Religious Women in the Old South," in *Catholics in the Old South: Essays on Church and Culture,* ed. Randall M. Miller (Macon, Ga., 1983), 106.

9. Ewens, *Nun in Nineteenth Century,* 134; Walsh, *Sisters of Charity,* 3:20.

10. Peter Guilday, *A History of the Councils of Baltimore, 1791–1884* (Baltimore, 1932; reprint, New York, 1969), 179–80, 238–39.

11. Oates, "Good Sisters," 177–78.

12. Misner, "First Eight Permanent Communities," 255; Gerald P. Fogarty, *The Vatican and the American Hierarchy* (Stuttgart, 1982), 103–32, 285.

13. Misner, "First Eight Permanent Communities," 50.

14. Byrne, "Sisters of St. Joseph," 259.

15. Lucille P. Borden, *Francesca Cabrini: Without Staff or Script* (New York, 1946), 102–3; Ewens, *Nun in Nineteenth Century*, 257.

16. Borden, *Cabrini*, 102–3; Margaret S. Thompson, "Discovering Foremothers: Sisters, Society, and the American Catholic Experience," *U.S. Catholic Historian* 5 (Summer/Fall): 288.

17. Columba Fox, *The Life of the Right Reverend John Baptist Mary David (1761–1841): Bishop of Bardstown and Founder of the Sisters of Charity of Nazareth* (New York, 1925), 29–30.

18. In time the nuns were separated from New York and became the Sisters of Charity of Halifax under the bishop there. See George P. Jacoby, *Catholic Child Care in the Nineteenth Century* (Washington, D.C., 1941; reprint, New York, 1974), 97; Walsh, *Sisters of Charity*, 1:127–37, 148–49, 158; John R. G. Hassard, *Life of John Hughes: First Archbishop of New York* (New York, 1866; reprint, New York, 1969), 290–302; Richard Shaw, *Dagger John: The Unquiet Life and Times of Archbishop John Hughes of New York* (New York, 1977), 209–12.

19. Shaw, *Dagger John*, 318; Walsh, *Sisters of Charity*, 3:21.

20. The quotations are found in Clyde F. Crews, "American Catholic Authoritarianism: The Episcopacy of William George McCloskey, 1868–1909," *Catholic Historical Review* 70 (October 1984): 567, 568.

21. Wolff, *Generation to Generation*, 30–31, 46, 53.

22. Mary Eulalia Herron, *The Sisters of Mercy in the United States* (New York, 1929), 17–18; Kathleen Healy, *Frances Warde: American Founder of the Sisters of Mercy* (New York, 1973), 204–6, 214–18, 288–89; "The Sisters of Mercy: Chicago's Pioneer Nurses and Teachers, 1846–1921," *Illinois Catholic Historical Review* 3 (April 1921): 350, 355, 362.

23. Mary E. Evans, *The Spirit Is Mercy: The Story of the Sisters of Mercy in the Archdiocese of Cincinnati, 1858–1958* (Westminster, Md., 1959), 149–55.

24. Healy, *Frances Warde*, 399–404, 432, 451–52.

25. Ibid., 230–44; Code, *American Foundresses*, 358–77; *Leaves from the Annals of the Sisters of Mercy, by a Member of the Order of Mercy* (New York, 1889), 395–406.

26. Ewens, "Women in the Convent," 27–32.

27. Mug, *Journals and Letters of Guérin*, 217.

28. *Life and Work of Mother Theodore Guérin: Foundress of the Sisters of Providence of Saint-Mary-of-the-Woods, Vigo County, Indiana, by a Member of the Congregation*, 4th ed. (New York, 1904), 285 and 285–350. Also see Code, *American Foundresses*, 292–316; Mug, *Journals and Letters of Guérin*, 186, 201–5.

29. Code, *American Foundresses*, 230–52; Woods, "Congregations of Religious Women," 110–11.

30. M. Grace McDonald, *With Lamps Burning* (St. Joseph, Minn., 1957), 65–190; M. Incarnata Girgen, *Behind the Beginnings: Benedictine Women in America* (St. Joseph, Mo., 1981), 13–26; Dwyer, *Condemned to the Mines*, 190–91, 222–23; Ruether and Keller, *Women and Religion*, 1:131.

31. Brosnahan, *On the King's Highway*, 302–3; McAllister, *Flame in the Wilderness*, 208, 230–36, 244–54; Catherine McPartlin, "The Work of the Teaching Sisterhoods," in McGuire, *Catholic Builders*, 5:381.

32. Misner, "First Eight Permanent Communities," 158–66.

33. Anna B. McGill, *The Sisters of Charity of Nazareth, Kentucky* (New York, 1917), 58–69; Schauinger, "Catherine Spaulding," 328–29; Fox, *Life at David*, 180–85.

34. Misner, "First Eight Permanent Communities," 40–41.

35. Robert F. Trisco, *The Holy See and the Nascent Church in the Middle Western United States, 1826–1850* (Rome, 1962), 297–343; Edmond Pendergast, ed. and trans., *Diary and Visitation Record of the Rt. Rev. Francis Patrick Kenrick, Administrator and Bishop of Philadelphia, 1830–1851* (Lancaster, Pa., 1916), 111, 117, 142, 177; "Statement by a Lawyer on Ejection of Poor Clares," in *United States Documents in the Propaganda File Archives*, 19th ser., ed. Finbar Kenneally (Washington, D.C., 1966–77), vol. 1, doc. 1675.

36. S. M. Hester Valentine, ed., *The North American Foundations: Letters of Mother M. Theresa Gerhardinger* (Winona, Minn., 1977), 115–16.

37. M. Carmeline Koller, *Walk in Love: Mother Mary Frances Streitle, Foundress at the Sisters of the Sorrowful Mother* (Chicago, 1981), 170–71.

38. Louise Callan, *Philippine Duchesne: Frontier Missionary of the Sacred Heart, 1769–1852* (Westminster, Md., 1957), 298, 314, 318–19, 421, 452; idem, *Society of the Sacred Heart*, 461–62.

39. Byrne, "Sisters of St. Joseph," 257–58; Mary E. Mannix, *Memoirs of Sister Louise: Superior of the Sisters of Notre Dame* (Boston, 1907), 50, 86, 113.

40. P. M. Abbelen, *Venerable Mother M. Caroline Friess: First Commissary General of the School Sisters of Notre Dame in America* (St. Louis, 1893), 263.

41. Valentine, *North American Foundations*, 34–40.

42. Callan, *Duchesne*, 332; for snakes in Mississippi, see James J. Pillar, *The Catholic Church in Mississippi, 1837–65* (New Orleans, 1944), 71–75.

43. Giovanni Schiavo, *Italian American History: The Italian Contribution to the Catholic Church in America* (New York, 1949; reprint, New York, 1975), 506.

44. Ewens, "Political Activity," 265–66; idem., *Nun in Nineteenth Century*, 121–22, 152; Mug, *Journals and Letters of Guérin*, 90; Herron, *Sisters of Mercy*, 195, 154; Mary Garvey, *Mary Aloysia Hardey: Religious of the Sacred Heart, 1809–1886* (New York, 1925), 102; Valentine, *North American Foundations*, 74; Abbelen, *Caroline Friess*, 183–97; Sister M. Gonzaga, "The 'Native American' Riots of 1844," *American Catholic Historical Researches* 8 (April 1891): 89–90; Lord, Sexton, and Harrington, *History of Archdiocese of Boston*, 2:330. For indication that the burning of the Ursuline convent may have been the result of the failure of nuns to behave in typical nineteenth-century ladylike fashion, see James J. Kenneally, "The Burning of the Ursuline Convent:

A Different View," *Records of the American Catholic Historical Society of Philadelphia* 90 (1979): 15–21.

45. Ewens, *Nun in Nineteenth Century*, 102–3.

46. John Hughes, "Reminiscences," in *U.S. Documents in Propaganda Fides* (microfilm, University of Notre Dame), 2; no. 1417, fols. 490RV, 523–24; Pendergast, *Diary and Visitation Record of Kenrick*, 76–78; Rosenberg, *Cholera Years*, 45, 64, 68, 95, 119, 121, 139–40; Misner, "First Eight Permanent Communities," 234; M. J. Spalding, *Sketches of the Life, Times, and Character of the Rt. Rev. Benedict Joseph Flaget, First Bishop of Louisville* (Louisville, Ky., 1852; reprint, New York, 1969), 276–77; Timothy Walch, "Catholic Social Institutions and Urban Development: The View from Nineteenth Century Chicago and Milwaukee," *Catholic Historical Review* 64 (January 1978): 30; *Revolution*, March 9, 16, 1871; *Woman's Journal,* September 28, 1878. For manifestations of the same kind of courage during the Civil War, see chapter 6.

47. Code, *American Foundresses*, 406–36.

48. Ibid., 254–91.

49. L. V. Jacks, *Mother Marianne of Molokai* (New York, 1935); Mary L. Hanley, "Mother Marianne of Molokai," in Trisco, *Catholics in America*, 170–73.

50. Code, *American Foundresses*, 437–47; McPartlin, "Work of the Teaching Sisterhoods," 381.

51. Valerie Mathes, "American Indian Women and the Catholic Church," *North Dakota History* 37 (Fall 1980): 20–25.

52. Lord, Sexton, and Harrington, *History of Archdiocese of Boston*, 3:412–13; Leonard, *Immortelles*, 440.

53. Rose H. Lathrop, "Women and Mammon," in Donnelly, *Girlhood's Hand-Book*, 161, 164, 168.

54. Maria M. Lannon, *Mother Mary Elizabeth Lange* (Washington, D.C., 1976); Grace H. Sherwood, *The Oblates' Hundred and One Years* (New York, 1931); Misner, "First Eight Permanent Communities, 46–49, 119–20; John T. Gillard, *The Catholic Church and the American Negro* (Baltimore, 1929), 16, 27; Miriam T. Murphy, "Catholic Missionary Work among the Colored People of the United States, 1776–1866," *Records of the American Catholic Historical Society* 35 (March 1924): 120; C. G. Woodson, *The Education of the Negro prior to 1861: A History of the Education of Colored People of the United States from the Beginning of Slavery to the Civil War* (Washington, D.C., 1919; reprint, New York, 1969), 139–40; Michael F. Rouse, *A Study of the Development of Negro Education under Catholic Auspices in Maryland and the District of Columbia* (Baltimore, 1935), 30–31, 40–42; M. B. Goodwin, "Schools and Education of the Colored Population in the District," in *Special Report, Department of Education* (Washington, D.C., 1870), 204–6; Murphy, "Pioneer Catholic Girls' Academies," 171–72; M. Reginald Gerdes, "To Educate and Evangelize: Black Catholic Schools of the Oblate Sisters of

Providence (1828–1880), *U.S. Catholic Historian* 6 (Spring/Summer 1988): 183–200.

55. John T. Gillard, *Colored Catholics in the United States* (Baltimore, 1941), 119–20; idem, *Church and the American Negro*, 30, 140–41; William Osborne, *The Segregated Covenant: Race Relations and American Catholics* (New York, 1967), 30.

56. Gillard, *Church and the American Negro*, 197; idem, *Colored Catholics*, 135–36.

57. Woods, "Congregations of Religious Women," 122.

58. Misner, "First Eight Catholic Communities," 51, 205; Gillard, *Church and the American Negro*, 25–26, 136; Stephen L. Theobold, "Catholic Missionary Work among the Colored People of the United States, 1776–1866," *Records of the American Catholic Historical Society* 35 (March 1924): 330–31.

59. Rouse, *Negro Education under Catholic Auspices*, 83; Ewens, *Nuns in Nineteenth Century*, 153; Byrne, "Sisters of St. Joseph," 254.

60. Byrne, "Sisters of St. Joseph," 260.

61. *The Catholic Guide* (New York, 1920), 271–73.

62. Gillard, *Church and the American Negro*, 260.

63. Nancy Hewitt, "Mother Mary Katherine Drexel," in *NAW, the Modern Period: A Biographical Dictionary*, (henceforth *NAW Modern*), ed. Barbara Sicherman et al. (Cambridge, Mass., 1980), 206–8; Consuela Marie Duffy, *Katherine Drexel: A Biography* (Philadelphia, 1966), especially 360.

64. Nolan, *Pastoral Letters*, 19, 56, 83, 94–95; Ewens, *Nun in Nineteenth Century*, 260–62; Mary M. Bowler, *History of Catholic Colleges for Women in the United States of America* (Washington, D.C., 1933), 10; Hennesey, *American Catholics*, 106.

65. Code, *American Foundresses*, 129; O'Reilly, *True Womanhood*, 359, 397; Valentine, *North American Foundations*, 184; "Instructions of the Congregation de Propaganda Fides concerning Children Attending American Public Schools, November 24, 1875," in *Documents of American Catholic History*, ed., John T. Ellis (Milwaukee, 1962), 402.

66. Quoted in Goebel, *Catholic Secondary Education*, 197. Also see M. Benedicta Riepp to Ludwig-Missionverein, December 15, 1853, quoted in Girgen, *Behind the Beginnings*, 36; Garvey, *Mary Hardey*, 248–50; Edward J. Power, *A History of Catholic Higher Education in the United States* (Milwaukee, 1958), 178–84; Valentine, *North American Foundations*, 44.

67. Mary Christina, "Early Convent Schools," *Catholic Educational Review* 39 (January 1941): 30–34.

68. Guilday, *John England*, 2:145.

69. Lyle Saxon, *Old Louisiana* (New York, 1929), 182, 233, 241.

70. Alexander Mackey, "The Western World," extracted in *Through Other Eyes. Some Impressions of American Catholics by Foreign Visitors from 1775 to Present*, ed. Dan Herr and Joel Wells (Westminster, Md., 1965), 55; Girgen, *Behind the Beginnings*, 36; Catherine Clinton, *The Plantation Mistress: Woman's World in the Old South* (New York, 1982), 128.

71. Sarah J. Hale, "Convents are Increasing," *American Ladies Magazine* 7 (December 1834): 560–64; idem, "How to Prevent the Increase of Convents," ibid. (September 1834): 519–21; C. E. Beecher, *The Evils Suffered by American Women and American Children: The Causes and the Remedy and an Address to the Protestant Clergy of the United States* (New York, 1846), 7, 18–19.

72. Quoted in Misner "First Eight Permanent Communities," 185.

73. Guérin to Superior General, February 18, 1852, quoted in Mug, *Journals and Letters of Guérin*, 329.

74. M. Mother Williams, *Second Sewing: The Life of Mary Aloysia Hardey* (New York, 1942), 440.

75. McAllister, *Flame in the Wilderness*, 318.

76. Power, *History of Catholic Higher Education*, 185; Murphy, "Pioneer Catholic Girls' Academies," 52–53, 176; Harold A. Buetow, *Of Singular Benefit: The Story of Catholic Education in the United States* (New York, 1976), 60, 129; Ewens, *Nun in Nineteenth Century*, 99–100.

77. Orestes Brownson, "The Democratic Principle," *BQ* (April 1873), in *Works*, 18:244–45; idem, "Conversations of Our Club," *BQ* (1858–59), in *Works*, 11:421–22; Mary F. Clarke, "Woman's Place in the Economy of Creation," *Boston Pilot*, March 7, 1874; Mary Onahan Gallery, *Life of William J. Onahan* (Chicago, 1929), 45–46. For an excellent study that interprets the rule of nuns and academies as more inhibiting than I do, see Eileen Mary Brewer, *Nuns and the Education of American Catholic Women, 1860–1920* (Chicago, 1987).

78. Callan, *Society of the Sacred Heart*, 734.

79. Aaron I. Abell, *American Catholicism and Social Action: A Search for Social Justice* (New York, 1966), 20–21; Williams, *Second Sewing*, 278; Buetow, *Of Singular Benefit*, 64.

80. Walsh, *Sisters of Charity*, 1:203, 3:40–42.

81. Evans, *The Spirit is Mercy*, 61–76; John Tracy Ellis, "Mother Mary Baptist Russell," in *NAW*, 3:213–14. Also see Eileen Mary Brewer, "Beyond Utility: The Role of the Nun in the Education of American Girls, 1860–1920" (Ph.D. diss., University of Chicago, 1984), 53–54, 76–77. These nuns exemplified how motherly tasks outside the home drew women further and further away from a "ladylike" sheltered existence. This change was also true for nuns who opened foundling homes to reduce infanticide and was especially true at the end of the century for social workers. See Walsh, *Sisters of Charity*, 1:210.

82. Smith, "Catholic Sisterhoods," 360, 367; Mary Ewens, "The Leadership of Nuns in Immigrant Catholicism," in Ruether and Keller, *Women and Religion*, 1:101–3; Dolan, *Catholic Experience*, 289.

Chapter 5 — Conformity and Refractoriness among
Nineteenth-Century "Ladies"

1. "Diurnal of Right Rev. John England," *Records of the American Catholic Historical Society of Philadelphia* 6 (January 1985): 37.

2. Thomas A. Emmet, *Incidents of My Life: Professional — Literary —
Social, with Service in the Cause of Ireland* (New York, 1911), 197, 334–38.

3. John O'Grady, *Catholic Charities in the United States: History and
Problems* (Washington, D.C., 1930), 318–20, 322; Florence D. Cohalan, *A
Popular History of the Archdiocese of New York* (New York, 1963), 34; Hughes,
Reminiscences, 510; Daniel T. McColgan, *A Century of Charity: The First
One Hundred Years of the Society of St. Vincent de Paul in the United States*
(Milwaukee, 1951) 2:224.

4. Augustus J. Thébaud, *Forty Years in the United States of America,
1839–1885*, ed. Charles G. Hermann (New York, 1904), 128, 157–58.

5. Margaret Quinn, "Sylvia, Adèle, and Rosine Parmentier: Nineteenth
Century Catholic Women of Brooklyn," *U.S. Catholic Historian* 5 (Summer/Fall 1986): 345–54; Cecyle S. Neidle, *America's Immigrant Women*
(Boston, 1975), 75–6; Thomas F. Meehan, "Andrew Parmentier, Horticulturalist, and His Daughter, Madame Bayer," *Historical Records and Studies,
United States Catholic Historical Society* 3 (December 1904): 446–56; Ben H.
McClary, "Adèle Parmentier Bayer," *NAW*, 1:115–16.

6. Hugh Francis Blunt, *Great Wives and Mothers* (New York, 1927), 371.

7. M. Catherine Joseph Haughery, "A Candle Lighted: A Capsule Biography of Margaret Gaffney Haughery, 1813–1887," *Records of the American
Catholic Historical Society* 114 (June 1953): 113–20; Robert Tallant, *The
Romantic New Orleanians* (New York, 1950), 282–83; Roger Baudier, *The
Catholic Church in Louisiana* (New Orleans, 1939), 395–96; Grace King, *New
Orleans: The Place and the People* (New York, 1895; reprint, New York, 1968),
374–79; Katherine E. Conway, "Individual Catholic Women," in McGuire,
Catholic Builders, 2:405–6.

8. *Woman's Journal*, April 11, 1903.

9. Don C. Seitz, *The James Gordon Bennetts: Father and Son Proprietors
of the New York Herald* (Indianapolis, 1928), 78, 110, 147–48; Isaac C. Pray,
Memoirs of James Gordon Bennett and His Times by a Journalist (New York,
1855), 280.

10. Albro Martin, *James J. Hill and the Opening of the Northwest* (New
York, 1976), 61–64, 86, 417, 420–21, 453.

11. Katherine Burton, *In No Strange Land: Some American Catholic Converts* (New York, 1942), 35–42.

12. Margaret R. King, *Memoirs of the Life of Mrs. Sarah Peter* (Cincinnati,
1889), 1:238; 2:313.

13. Ibid., 1:223; 2:353–56, 430, 435–36, 503; Anna S. McAllister, *In Winter We Flourish: Life and Letters of Sarah Worthington King Peter, 1800–1887*
(New York, 1939), 290, 302–3, 322; Conway, "Individual Catholic Women,"
407–10; John A. H. Keith, "Sarah Worthington Peter," in *Notable Women*

of Pennsylvania, ed. Gertrude B. Biddle and Sarah D. Lowrie (Philadelphia, 1942), 133–34.

14. Joseph J. Cascino to author, November 8, 1982; Mary F. Lovell and Mrs. John H. Easly, "Caroline Earle White," in Biddle and Lowrie, *Notable Women of Pennsylvania,* 186–87.

15. Emma F. Carey to Cardinal O'Connell, October 27, 1911, May 20, November 21, 1912, no. 9/d, file 3:9, O'Connell Papers, Archives of the Archdiocese of Boston.

16. Catholic Club Minutes, 1901–12, Catholic Club Papers, Radcliffe College Archives, Cambridge, Massachusetts.

17. Driscoll, *Literary Convert Women,* 56–57; Lord, Sexton, and Harrington, *History of Archdiocese of Boston,* 3:723–24.

18. John B. Blake, "Mary Sargeant Neal Gove Nichols," in *NAW,* 2:627–29.

19. Henry Conwell, *Sundry Documents Addressed to St. Mary's Congregation* (Philadelphia, 1821).

20. *The Trial of the Rev. William Hogan, Pastor of St. Mary's Church, for an Assault and Battery on Mary Connell, Tried April 1822* (Philadelphia, 1822). For general accounts, see Francis E. Tourscher, *The Hogan Schism and Trustee Troubles in St. Mary's Church, Philadelphia, 1820–1829* (Philadelphia, 1830); and Arthur J. Ennis, "The New Diocese of Philadelphia," in Connelly, *Diocese of Philadelphia,* 84–104.

21. In time McGlynn was reinstated, but in 1895 the Sacred Congregation ordered her religious community "to efface all traces of Miss Cusack. See James J. Kenneally, "Sexism, the Church, Irish Women," *Eire-Ireland* 21 (Fall 1986): 11–16.

22. Crews, "American Catholic Authoritarianism," 571–72.

23. Harriet Thompson to Pius IX, October 29, 1853, *U.S. Documents in Propaganda Fides,* fols. 2, 770–75.

24. Abell, *Catholicism and Social Action,* 11–12.

25. Ellen M. Biddle, "The American Catholic Irish Family," in *Ethnic Families in America,* ed. Charles H. Mindel and Robert W. Habenstein (New York, 1976), 96. Also see Robert E. Kennedy, Jr., *The Irish: Emigration, Marriage, and Fertility* (Berkeley, Calif., 1973), 50–167 passim; and J.J. Lee, "Women and the Church since the Famine: Women in Irish Society," in *Women in Irish Society: The Historical Dimension,* ed. Margaret MacCurtain and Donncha Ó. Corráin (Westport, Conn., 1979), 37–39.

26. Faye Dudden, *Serving Women: Household Service in Nineteenth Century America* (Middleton, Conn., 1983), 59–60, 70, 202–3; Dennis P. Ryan, *Beyond the Ballot Box: A Social History of the Boston Irish, 1845–1917* (Madison, N.J., 1983), 43–46; Carol Groneman, "Working-Class Immigrant Women in Mid-Nineteenth Century New York: The Irish Woman's Perspective," *Journal of Urban History* 4 (May 1978): 258–59; George Potter, *To the Golden Door: The Story of the Irish in Ireland and America* (Boston, 1966), 515.

27. Robert Ernst, *Immigrant Life in New York City, 1825-1863* (New York, 1979), 66-69.

28. Groneman, "Working-Class Immigrant Women," 262; idem, " 'She Earns as a Child; She Pays as a Man': Women Workers in a Mid-Nineteenth Century New York Community," in *Class, Sex, and the Woman Worker*, ed. Milton Cantor and Bruce Laurie (Westport, Conn., 1977), 84-89; Biddle, "American Catholic Irish Family," 95-107.

29. Potter, *To the Golden Door*, 509; Biddle, "American Catholic Irish Family," 101.

30. Deshon, *Guide*, 12, 15, 24, 26, 152, 163, 167, 178, 186, 208, 236-37; "Woman," *Catholic World* 4 (December 1867): 418-23; Walsh, *Sisters of Charity*, 3:32.

31. Mrs. S. C. Hall, "An Irish Servant Girl," *Catholic Expositor* 3 (March 1893): 360-64.

32. Laurence Glasco, "The Life Cycles and Household Structure of American Ethnic Groups: Irish, Germans, and Native-Born Whites in Buffalo, New York, 1855," *Journal of Urban History* 1 (May 1975): 354-60. The fertility rate declined even further with second-generation women (Michael R. Haines, "Fertility and Marriage in a Nineteenth Century Industrial City: Philadelphia 1850-1880," *Journal of Economic History* 40 [March 1989]: 150). For the efforts of one Catholic woman in the 1890s to limit the number of births, see Mary Kincaid's letters to Mamie Goodwater in Elizabeth Hampsten, comp., *To All Inquiring Friends: Letters, Diaries, and Essays in North Dakota, 1880-1910* 2d ed. (Grand Forks, N.D., 1980), 18-20.

33. John T. Noonan, Jr., *Contraception: A History of Its Treatment by the Catholic Theologians and Canonists* (Cambridge, Mass., 1956), 394, 400, 422; William W. Sanger, *The History of Prostitution: Its Extent, Causes and Effects throughout the World* (New York, 1859; reprint, New York, 1972), 460, 545; Groneman, "Working-Class Immigrant Women," 20; Dennis Clark, *The Irish in Philadelphia: Ten Generations of Urban Experience* (Philadelphia, 1973), 102; Thomas N. Brown, *The Irish Layman* (Dublin, 1970), 217 n. 60.

34. Jacoby, *Catholic Child Care*, 205-8; Jay P. Dolan, *The Immigrant Church: New York's Irish and German Catholics, 1815-1865* (Baltimore, 1975), 133; Clark, *Irish in Philadelphia*, 102; O'Grady, *Catholic Charities*, 166-80.

35. Cardinal James Gibbons, "The Needs of Humanity Supplied by the Catholic Religion," in *The World's Parliament of Religions*, ed. John H. Barrows (Chicago, 1893), 2:491; Anne M. Butler, *Daughters of Joy, Sisters of Mercy: Prostitutes in the American West, 1865-1900* (Urbana, Ill., 1985), 63-67.

36. Nelson J. Callahan, ed., *The Diary of Richard L. Burtsell, Priest of New York: The Early Years, 1865-1868* (New York, 1978), 386.

37. Dolan, *Immigrant Church*, 133, 193; Jacoby, *Catholic Child Care*, 144; Walsh, *Sisters of Charity*, 3:40-42; Walch, "Catholic Social Institutions," 23; Lord, Sexton, and Harrington, *History of Archdiocese of Boston*, 3:171.

38. See chapter 7 for further discussion of Social Purity.

39. James C. Mohr, *Abortion in America: The Origins and Evolution of National Policy, 1800–1900* (New York, 1978), 182–83, 187, 243; Gibbons, "Needs of Humanity," 488; Ryan, *Beyond the Ballot Box*, 54; Arthur Mitchell, "A View of the Irish in America, 1887," *Eire-Ireland* 4 (Spring 1969): 10.

40. Andrew Klarmann, *The Crux of Pastoral Medicine: The Perils of Embryonic Man: Abortion, Craneotomy and the Caesarian Sections, Myra and the Porro Sections* (New York, 1905), 38, 61.

41. John F. Richmond, *New York and Its Institutions, 1609–1871: A Library of Information* (New York, 1871), 354–56; Cohalan, *Popular History*, 92; Walsh, *Sisters of Charity*, 3:64–73.

42. Quoted in Marian J. Morton, "Go and Sin No More: Maternity Homes in Cleveland, 1869–1936," *Ohio History* 93 (Summer/Autumn 1984): 125.

43. In 1933, when Bishop Joseph Schrembs (1866–1945) celebrated the sixtieth anniversary of the hospital, he stated that the unwed mother was "more sinned against than sinner," for she would rather bear the shame of her illicit pregnancy than "stain her hands with the blood of her unborn child" (ibid., 128).

44. Ryan, *Beyond the Ballot Box*, 26–27.

45. McColgan, *Century of Charity*, 1:230–31; O'Grady, *Catholic Charities*, 130–43.

46. O'Grady, *Catholic Charities*, 73, 75, 78–82, 85, 87, 101, 107, 111; Thomas O. Wood, "The Catholic Attitude toward the Settlement Movement, 1866–1914" (M.A. thesis, University of Notre Dame, 1958), 13; Ryan, *Beyond the Ballot Box*, 24.

47. Elinore P. Stewart, *Letters of a Woman Homesteader* (Lincoln, Nebr., 1961), 226, 185, 214–16, 279–82.

48. N. Levering, "Recollections of the Past," *Iowa Historical Record* 2 (1886): 276.

49. John Mack Faragher, *Women and Men on the Overland Trail* (New Haven, Conn., 1979), 95–97; Johnny Faragher and Christine Stansell, "Women and Their Families on the Overland Trail to California and Oregon, 1842–1867," *Feminist Studies*, nos. 2/3, (1975): 151–61; Lucy J. Bledsoe, "Adventuresome Women on the Oregon Trail, 1840–1867," *Frontiers* 7 no. 3 (1984): 22–29; Lillian Schlissel, *Women's Diaries of the Westward Journey* (New York, 1982), 82–101.

50. Hubert H. Bancroft, *Chronicles of the Builders of the Commonwealth: Historical Character Study* (San Francisco, 1892–93), 1:17–55; Potter, *To the Golden Door*, 297; Hugh Quigley, *The Irish Race in California and on the Pacific Coast* (San Francisco, 1878), 177–206.

51. Virginia Reed Murphy, "Across the Plains in the Donner Party (1846): A Personal Narrative of the Overland Trip to California," *Century Magazine* 22 (July 1891): 409–26; Patrick Breen, "Diary," in *Overland in 1846: Diaries and Letters of the California-Oregon Trail*, ed. Dale Morgan (Georgetown,

Calif., 1963), 2:306-22; Quigley, *Irish Race in California*, 211-13; George R. Stewart, *Ordeal by Hunger: The Story of the Donner Party* (New York, 1936), 20, 78, 160, 172, 179, 214, 245, 282.

52. Mary E. Ackley, *Crossing the Plains and Early Days in California: Memoirs of Girlhood Days in California's Golden Age* (San Francisco, 1928), 8, 11, 14, 17, 21, 23, 33, 41.

53. John J. Hogan, *On the Mission in Missouri, 1857-1868* (Kansas City, Mo., 1892), 44-46.

54. Dwight G. McCarthy, *Stories of Pioneer Life on the Iowa Prairie* (Emmetsburg, Iowa, 1973), 7-8, 17, 93, 148.

55. Mrs. Kate Merritt, "Belle of the Sixties Recalls Dramatic Incidents," *Frontier Times* 5 (April 1928): 272-77, in *Women Tell the Story of the South West*, ed. Mattie L. Wooten (San Antonio, Tex., 1940), 7-9.

56. The marriage survived. Garesche was killed fighting for the Union during the Civil War (Louis Garesche, *Biography of Lieut. Col. Julius P. Garesche, Assistant Adjutant General, U.S. Army* [Philadelphia, 1887], 89, 105-8, 190, 220, 269).

57. Nancy Hamilton, "The Great Western," in *The Women Who Made the West: Western Writers of America* (New York, 1980), 186-97. It was a Catholic, Adina De Vavala (1861-1955), who led the campaign to preserve the Alamo as a shrine, at one time barricading herself in the building for three days to prevent it from being torn down (L. Robert Ables, "Adina De Vavala," *Keepers of the Past*, ed. Clifford Lord [Chapel Hill, N.C., 1965], 203-12).

58. Mary G. Boyer, *Arizona in Literature: A Collection of the Best Writings of Arizona Authors from Early Spanish Days to the Present Time* (Glendale, Calif., 1934), 366-79; Carolyn Niethammer, "The Lure of Gold," in *Women Who Made the West*, 71-85.

59. Mary E. Henthorne, *The Irish Catholic Colonization Association of the United States* (Champaign, Ill., 1932); James P. Shannon, *Catholic Colonization on the Western Frontier* (New Haven, Conn., 1957).

60. Mary Gilbert Kelly, *Catholic Colonization Projects in the United States, 1815-1860* (New York, 1939), 120-21.

61. Ibid., 248-53; Aquinata Martin, *The Catholic Church on the Nebraska Frontier, 1654-1885* (Washington, D.C., 1937), 29-30; Henry W. Casper, *The Catholic Church in Nebraska: The Church on the Northern Great Plains, 1838-1874* (Milwaukee, 1960), 74-77.

62. Patrick H. Ahern, ed., *Catholic Heritage in Minnesota, North and South Dakota* (St. Paul, 1964), 126-31.

63. Martin, *Church on Nebraska Frontier*, 148-50.

64. Carl Wittke, *The Irish in America* (Baton Rouge, La., 1956; reprint, New York, 1970), 73-74.

65. Phyllis Cancilla Martinelli, "Italian Immigrant Women in the Southwest," in *The Italian Immigrant Woman in North America*, ed. Betty Boyd Caroli, Robert F. Harney, and Lydio F. Tomasi (Toronto, 1978), 324-36. One

of the most interesting Italian immigrants to the West was a Neapolitan, Antonietta Pisanelli (b. 1869), who after the death of her husband and child left New York for San Francisco. There she established Italian theaters, including opera and variety shows that appealed to newer immigrants. She even defied an Irish priest by opening a variety show across from his church; see Maxine Seller, "Theater and Community: The Popular Italian Theater of San Francisco 1905–1925," in *The Urban Experience of Italian Americans,* ed. Patrick J. Gallo (Staten Island, N.Y., 1975), 54–60.

66. Some of the earliest Catholic schools on the frontier were founded by laywomen. In 1805 four females established the first parochial school in the Detroit area, a Miss Steele opened one of the earliest in Denver in 1863, and religious schools were begun by laywomen in Omaha and Nebraska City before 1863. See Sister M. I. H. M. Rosalita, "Four Women Lay Apostles of the Old Northwest," *Historical Records and Studies* 31 (1940): 119–36; W. J. Howlett, *Life of the Right Reverend Joseph P. Machebeuf D. D.: Pioneer Priest of Ohio, Pioneer Priest of New Mexico, Pioneer Priest of Colorado, Vicar Apostolic of Colorado and Utah, First Bishop of Denver* (Pueblo, Colo., 1890), 311; Martin, *Church on Nebraska Frontier,* 80–81.

67. Ignatius Donnelly, *In Memoriam: Mrs. Katherine Donnelly* (St. Paul, 1895). Donnelly's mother and sister opposed his marriage and for five years did not talk to his wife (Ridge, *Ignatius Donnelly,* 12–13).

68. Ignatius Donnelly, *The Golden Bottle; or, The Story of Ephraim Benezet of Kansas* (New York, 1892; reprint, Upper Saddle River, N.J., 1968).

69. Gretchen Kreuter, "Kate Donnelly versus True Womanhood," 33.

70. Dwyer, *Condemned to the Mines,* 28; Sytha Motto, *No Banners Waving* (New York, 1966), 50–54; Paul Horgan, *Lamy of Santa Fe: His Life and Times* (New York, 1975), 158–64, 198, 210–11; M. Lilliana Owens, "Our Lady of Light Academy, Santa Fe," *New Mexico Historical Review* 13 (April 1938): 129–45; "Diary of the Sisters of St. Joseph to Tucson, Arizona, 1870," *St. Louis Catholic Historical Review* 2 (April–July 1920): 101–13; Trudelle Thomas, "Planting the Cross in the Wilderness: A Tribute to the Brown County Ursulines," *Queen City Heritage* 43 (1985): 42–48; Marcella Holloway, "The Sisters of St. Joseph of Carondelet: 150 Years of Good Works in America," *Gateway Heritage* 7 (1986): 24–26.

71. Jean Baptiste Salpointe, *Soldiers of the Cross: Notes on the Ecclesiastical History of New Mexico, Arizona, and Colorado* (Banning, Calif., 1898), 203.

72. Owens, "Lady of Light Academy," 138–42; Blandina Segale, *At the End of the Santa Fe Trail* (Milwaukee, 1948), 89–92; Horgan, *Lamy of Santa Fe,* 315, 341–47, 396.

73. Goebel, *Catholic Secondary Education,* 35–37; Thomas J. Jenkins, *Six Seasons on Our Prairies and Six Weeks in Our Rockies* (Louisville, Ky., 1884), 60–62.

74. Callan, *Society of the Sacred Heart,* 275, 292–94, 306; Carol J. Berg, "Agents of Cultural Change: The Benedictines at White Earth," *Minnesota*

History 93 (Winter 1982): 158–70; Ahern, *Catholic Heritage*, 103–4. For a perceptive summary, see Mother M. Agatha, "Catholic Education and the Indian," in *Essays on Catholic Education in the United States*, ed. Roy J. Deferrari (Washington, D.C., 1942), 523–53.

75. Callan, *Society of the Sacred Heart*, 234.

76. Thomas Richter, ed., "Sister Catherine Mallon's Journal," *New Mexico Historical Review* 52 (1977): 141–47; Mary Xavier Holworthy, *Diamonds for the King* (Corpus Christi, Tex., 1945), 19, 21; Sytha Motto, "The Sisters of Charity and St. Vincent's Hospital: An Amplification of Sister Mallon's Journal," *New Mexico Historical Review* 102 (1977): 230.

77. See the following, all by Susan C. Peterson, "From Paradise to Prairie: The Presentation Sisters in Dakota, 1880–1896," *South Dakota History* 10 (Summer 1980): 211–22; "Religious Communities of Women in the West: The Presentation Sisters' Adaption in the Northern Plains Frontier," *Journal of the West* 21 (April 1982): 65–70; and "A Widening Horizon: Catholic Sisterhoods on the Northern Plains, 1874–1910," *Great Plains Quarterly* 5 (Spring 1985): 125–32. Also see Susan C. Peterson and Courtney Ann Vaughn-Roberson, *Women with Vision: The Presentation Sisters of South Dakota, 1880–1895* (Urbana, Ill., 1988), 63–71.

78. Kathryn Kish Sklar, *Catherine Beecher: A Study in American Domesticity* (New Haven, Conn., 1973), 171–74.

79. Richter, "Catherine Mallon's Journal," 239–40.

80. Motto, *No Banners Waving*, 79.

81. Lucille McDonald, "Mother Joseph," in *Women Who Made the West*, 120–24; Mary Jo Weaver, *New Catholic Women: A Contemporary Challenge to Traditional Religious Authority* (San Francisco, 1985), 219; Mary T. McCrosson, *The Bell and the River* (Palo Alto, Calif., 1957), 77, 237–38, 283.

82. Dudley G. Wooten, "A Noble Ursuline," *Catholic World* 111 (August 1920): 588–602.

83. Segale, *End of Santa Fe Trail*, 199, 250–51.

Chapter 6 — Civil War and Reconstruction: A Challenge to "Ladies"

1. John R. McKivigan, *The War against Proslavery Religion: Abolition and the Northern Churches, 1830–1865* (Ithaca, N.Y., 1984), 27–28, 38, 51, 164, 190.

2. Pillar, *Church in Mississippi*, 173, 269.

3. Madden, *Catholics in South Carolina*, 113.

4. Adele Cutts Douglas did play a minor role in the political struggle over slavery. Cutts, a Washington belle, became Stephen A. Douglas's second wife in 1856 after a whirlwind courtship. She then accompanied him on his campaign tours, meeting with Democratic women and supporting his idea of popular sovereignty. Douglas's children from his first marriage became Catholics because of her influence. See Marie Perpetua Hayes, "Adele Cutts,

Second Wife of Stephen A. Douglas," *Catholic Historical Review* 31 (July 1945): 180–91.

5. Michael Williams, *American Catholics in the War* (New York, 1921), 58; Ella Lonn, *Foreigners in the Union Army and Navy* (Baton Rouge, La., 1951), 117–20, 550; idem, *Foreigners in the Confederacy* (Chapel Hill, N.C., 1940), 376; Cornelius Buckley, trans., *A Frenchman, a Chaplain, a Rebel: The War Letters of Pere Louis-Hippolyte Gache, S.J.* (Chicago, 1981), 103; Miecislaus Haiman, *Polish Past in America, 1608–1865*, 2d ed. (Chicago, 1974), 144.

6. Beauregard to Julia Deslands, April 2, 1864, and to Augusta Evans, October 1866, quoted in T. Harry Williams, *P. G. T. Beauregard: Napoleon in Gray* (Baton Rouge, La., 1954), 204–5.

7. Lonn, *Foreigners in the Union*, 559; Bell I. Wiley, *The Life of Billy Yank: The Common Soldier of the Union* (New York, 1952), 339.

8. *Leaves from the Annals of the Sisters of Mercy*, 3:277–78, 281.

9. L. P. Brockett and Mrs. Mary C. Vaughan, *Woman's Work in the Civil War: A Record of Heroism, Patriotism, and Patience* (Philadelphia, 1867), 647–49; Frank Moore, *Women and the War: Their Heroism and Self-Sacrifice* (Hartford, Conn., 1886), 37–52.

10. Wiley, *Life of Billy Yank*, 337–38.

11. C. J. Worthington, ed., *The Woman in Battle: A Narrative of Exploits, Adventures, and Travels of Madame Loreta Janeta Velazquez, Otherwise Known as Lt. Harry T. Bufort* (Hartford, Conn., 1876), reprinted in Meníe M. Dowie, ed., *Woman Adventurers* (New York, 1893), 1–51.

12. Rose O. Greenhow, *My Imprisonment and the First Year of Abolition Rule in Washington* (London, 1863), 113–14; Mary Elizabeth Massey, *Bonnet Brigades* (New York, 1966), 90–93; Ishbel Ross, *Rebel Rose: Life of Rose O'Neal Greenhow, Confederate Spy* (New York, 1954), 56, 61, 259, 272; Woodward, *Mary Chestnut's Civil War*, 255.

13. Eliza A. Starr to Cousin Mary, July 9, 1863, in *The Life and Letters of Eliza Allen Starr*, ed. James J. McGovern (Chicago, 1905), 185; Michael J. O'Connor, *Archbishop Kenrick and His Work: A Lecture, January 18, 1863* (Philadelphia, 1867), 14–15.

14. Hammond, *Diary of a Union Lady*, 275–76; Eliza A. Starr to Cousin Mary, March 28, 1865, in McGovern, *Life and Letters of Starr*, 236–37; Anna S. McAllister, *Ellen Ewing: Wife of General Sherman* (New York, 1936), 295–97.

15. Moore, *Women and the War*, 37–52; Brockett, *Woman's Work in Civil War*, 647–49.

16. O'Grady, *Catholic Charities*, 310–11; Hammond, *Diary of a Union Lady*, 283–84; James J. Kenneally, *Women and American Trade Unions* (Montreal, 1981), 3.

17. Adrian Cook, *The Armies of the Streets: The New York Draft Riots of 1863* (Lexington, Ky., 1974), 126, 146–47, 164–65, 196, 256–75; Hammond, *Diary of a Union Lady*, 246, 249; J. T. Headley, *The Great Riots of New York,*

1712 to 1873, Including a Full and Complete Account of the Four Days' Draft Riot of 1863 (New York, 1873), 254–56.

18. Buckley, *A Frenchman, a Chaplain,* 159–66; Emory M. Thomas, *The Confederate State of Richmond: A Biography of the Capital* (Austin, Tex., 1971), 119–21.

19. Woodward, *Mary Chestnut's Civil War,* 718, 722–23, 740. Sherman, although married to one of the nation's most prominent Catholic women, Ellen Ewing, was not himself a Catholic.

20. Katherine M. Jones, *When Sherman Came: Southern Women and the Great March* (Indianapolis, 1964), 185–87, 203–5; Sarah A. Richardson, "Burning of the Ursuline Convent," in *South Carolina Women in the Confederacy,* United Daughters of the Confederacy (Columbia, S.C., 1903), 304.

21. Callan, *Society of the Sacred Heart,* 521–22.

22. Ann Douglas Wood, "The War within a War: Women Nurses in the Union Army," *Civil War History* 18 (September 1972): 128; Francis Butler Simkins and James Welch Patton, *The Women of the Confederacy* (Richmond, Va., 1936), 94–95; O'Grady, *Catholic Charities,* 193.

23. Ewens, "Removing the Veil," 270–71; Mary D. Maher, "'To Do with Honor': Roman Catholic Sister Nurses in the United States Civil War" (Ph.D. diss., Case Western Reserve University, 1988), 1, 2, 144; Hennesey, *American Catholics,* 155.

24. For general accounts, see George Barton, *Angels of the Battlefield: A History of the Labors of the Catholic Sisterhoods in the Late Civil War* (Philadelphia, 1898), and Ellen Ryan Jolly, *Nuns of the Battlefield* (Providence, R.I., 1927), both of which identify by name six nuns as victims of the war. However, that figure is probably too small, as many died back at their communities, where accurate records were seldom kept on wartime service. Furthermore, Maher indicates there were at least eight deaths. Also see Mary A. Livermore, *My Story of the War: A Woman's Narrative of Four Years' Personal Experience* (Hartford, Conn., 1888), 218–19; Madden, *Catholics in South Carolina,* 83–87; Maher, "To Do with Honor," 252–54; Woodward, *Mary Chestnut's Civil War,* 158, 171, 414.

25. O'Grady, *Catholic Charities,* 194–95.

26. Nina B. Smith, "The Women Who Went to the War: The Union Army Nurse in the Civil War" (Ph.D. diss., Northwestern University, 1981), 875–76; Walsh, *Sisters of Charity,* 4:171; Louisa May Alcott, *Hospital Sketches,* ed. Bessie Z. Jones (Cambridge, Mass., 1960), xxxi; Maher, "To Do with Honor," 195, 208, 223–24; William Q. Maxwell, *Lincoln's Fifth Wheel: The Political History of the United States Sanitary Commission* (New York, 1956), 8. Frequently cited is the observation of an officer to Mary Livermore that nuns never brought government investigators to the scene. Sisters' complaints, however, were responsible for government investigators dismissing the hospital administration at Shelby Springs, Mississippi, and Ursulines in Galveston,

Texas, were reprimanded for defying their male military superiors (Pillar, *Church in Mississippi*, 248; Maher, "To Do with Honor," 175, 340).

27. William E. Barbinger, "Mary Eugenia Jenkins Surratt," in *NAW*, 2: 410–11.

28. Nolan, *Pastoral Letters*, 157.

29. Jacqueline Jones, *Soldiers of Light and Love: Northern Teachers and Georgia Blacks, 1865–1873* (Chapel Hill, N.C., 1980), 25–26, 87–88, 129, 155.

30. Herron, *Sisters of Mercy*, 293; Jones, *Soldiers of Light and Love*, 155, 255 no. 9; Pillar, *Church in Mississippi*, 274; Williams, *Second Sewing*, 430; Goodwin, "Schools and Education," 234, 242, 262; Holworthy, *Diamonds for the King*, 47; Callan, *Society of the Sacred Heart*, 540–43; Madden, *Catholics in South Carolina*, 103. Also see chapter 4.

31. Orestes Brownson, "The Republic of the United States," *BQ* (April 1849), in *Works*, 16:92; idem, "Religious Liberty," *Catholic World* (1870), in *Works*, 13:231, 239–40; idem, "Woman Question — Article 2," 399–417.

32. *Woman's Journal*, March 24, October 13, 1877; Howlett, *Life of Machebeuf*, 413–14; Horgan, *Lamy of Santa Fe*, 373; Elizabeth C. Stanton et al., eds., *History of Woman Suffrage* (New York, 1891–1922; reprint, New York, 1969), 3:720–21.

33. James Gibbons, "Relative Condition of Women under Pagan and Christian Civilization," *American Catholic Quarterly Review* 11 (October 1886): 656.

34. "Review of Women's Suffrage: A Reform against Nature," *Catholic World* 10 (February 1870): 715–16.

35. *Woman's Journal*, October 4, 1879.

36. *Revolution*, April 15, 29, July 1, 1869, February 10, 1870; *Woman's Journal*, March 19, August 20, 1870, July 4, 1873.

37. *Revolution*, July 21, 1870, January 12, February 9, 1871; U.S. Congress, Senate Committee on Privileges and Elections, *Arguments in Behalf of a Sixteenth Amendment and Protest against Woman Suffrage* (Washington, D.C., 1878), 43–45; Stanton, *History of Woman Suffrage*, 2:69, 101, 103, 495; the following letters written in 1871 from Madeline V. Dahlgren to James Garfield are all in James Garfield Papers, Library of Congress: January 1, 19/10; January 3, 19/20; January 20, 19/149; February 1, 20/20, 20/22, 20/24, 20/29, and February n.d., 20/23. See also Madeline Dahlgren, *Protest against Woman Suffrage to Committee on Privileges and Elections of U.S. Senate on Sixteenth Amendment* (Washington, D.C., n.d.); "A Catholic Lady on Woman Suffrage," *Donahoe's* 19 (June 1888), 515–16, and all of the following in Madeline Dahlgren, *Thoughts on Female Suffrage and in Vindication of Woman's True Rights* (Washington, D.C., 1871): "Female Suffrage or Social Disintegration," "Children's Rights," "Suffrage Anti-Suffrage," "Female Suffrage — New Tactics," "Woman Suffrage," "Appeal for Women," and "Pro Aris et Focis."

38. James J. Kenneally, "A Question of Equality," in Kennelly, *American*

Catholic Women, 127. For Indian Missions, see *Manual of Catholic Indian Missionary Association* (Washington, D.C., 1875).

39. Dahlgren, "Pro Aris," 8–9; idem, "Appeal for Women," 5–7; Kenneally, "Question of Equality," 128–29.

Chapter 7 — Stereotypes Endangered: Middle-Class "Ladies" Become Reformers

1. Robert D. Cross, *The Emergence of Liberal Catholicism in America* (Cambridge, Mass., 1967), 50, 100–111.

2. Katherine F. Mullaney, "The Public Rights of Women: A Second Round Table Conference," *Catholic World* 109 (June 1894): 308–12.

3. John T. Murphy, "The Opportunities of Educated Catholic Women," *American Catholic Quarterly Review* 23 (July 1898): 611–17.

4. John L. Spalding, *Means and Ends of Education,* 5th ed. (Chicago, 1909), 106.

5. *Woman's Journal,* May 12, 1888, and July 5, 1890; John L. Spalding, *Education and the Higher Life,* 7th ed. (Chicago, 1902), 25, 280; idem, "Victory of Love," in *Religion, Agnosticism, and Education,* 3d ed. (Chicago, 1916), 25, 55.

6. James Gibbons, "On the Opening of Johns Hopkins Medical School to Women," *Century* 91 (February 1891): 633.

7. John Ireland, "Congress on Social Purity," "Sermon, St. Joseph's Academy," and "America on France," all in *The Church and Modern Society: Lectures and Addresses* (St. Paul, 1909), 2:333, 340, 300–301; 1:360–61.

8. William H. Hughes, ed., *Souvenir Volume of Three Great Events in the History of the Catholic Church in the United States,* 2d ed. (Detroit, 1890; reprint, New York, 1978), vii, xii, 28, 63, 66, 128–29.

9. *The World's Columbian Catholic Congresses and Educational Exhibit* (Chicago, 1893; reprint, New York, 1978), 13–15, 103. The only paper actually read by a woman dealt with the Virgin Mary and art and was presented by one of the most traditional females in attendance. Eliza Allen Starr, its author, was awarded a gold medal at that congress (*Boston Pilot,* October 7, 1893).

10. Rose H. Lathrop, "Women and Mammon," *World's Columbian Congresses,* 82–83.

11. Emma F. Cary, "The Elevation of Womanhood Brought About through the Veneration of the Blessed Virgin: A Paper Read at the World's Congress in Chicago 1893," in Leonard, *Immortelles,* 296–303.

12. Mary Maher, "The Catholic Woman as an Educator," in *The World's Congress of Representative Women,* ed. Mary W. Sewall (Chicago, 1894), 1:134–35.

13. Mary Josephine Onaham, "Catholic Women's Part in Philanthropy," in Sewall, *World's Congress,* 2:819–20; *World's Columbian Congresses,* 28–33.

14. Alice T. Toomy, "Effect of Modern Changes in Industrial and Social Life on Woman's Marriage Prospects," in Sewall, *World's Congress*, 2:598–99.

15. *World's Columbian Congresses*, 104.

16. Louise Girod, "The Catholic Women's Association," *Catholic World* 122 (January 1901): 497–510.

17. Abell, *Catholicism and Social Action*, 123; *Woman's Journal*, June 3, 1893; Catholic Women's League of Chicago, *Annual Announcements* (Chicago, 1911–17); Charles H. Shanabruch, "The Catholic Church's Role in the Americanization of Chicago's Immigrants, 1833–1928" (Ph.D. diss., University of Chicago, 1975), 365; idem, *Chicago's Catholics: The Evolution of an American Identity* (Notre Dame, Ind., 1981), 139.

18. F. M. Edselas [M. Catherine Chase], "Institute for Woman's Professions," *Catholic World* 57 (June 1895): 509–20.

19. F. C. Farinholt, "A Teacher's View," in "The Public Rights of Women: A Second Round Table Conference," *Catholic World* 57 (June 1894): 294–320.

20. Elizabeth A. Cronyn, "The Apostolate of the Convent Alumna," in Donnelly, *Girlhood's Hand-Book*, 186–88; Katherine Tynan, "The Higher Education for Catholic Girls," *Catholic World* 51 (August 1890): 616–21.

21. Thomas Ewing Sherman, "Higher Education of Catholic Women," *Catholic Educational Association Bulletin*, no. 3 (1906), reprinted in *Higher Education for Catholic Women: An Historical Anthology*, ed. Mary Oates (New York, 1987), 106–8.

22. O'Connell, *Catholicism in the Carolinas*, 67–68. Also see Landriot, *The Valiant Woman*, 46–47, 55, 66; Murphy, "Opportunities of Educated Catholic Women," 611.

23. Nicholas Walsh, *Woman*, 2d ed. (New York, 1904), 20, 65–66.

24. Janet E. Stuart, *The Education of Catholic Girls* (London, 1911), 87, 91, 225–26 (this book was written with an American audience in mind); A. L. O'Hara, "Woman in the Twentieth Century," *Catholic School and Home Magazine*, 3 (June 1894): 90–91.

25. Thomas E. Shields, *The Education of Our Girls* (New York, 1907), 187, 205, 211–12, 215; Kenneally, "Eve, Mary, and the Historian," 191.

26. At the turn of the century, journalists and pundits discovered a "new woman," who, although expecting to marry, defied convention by seeking a life beyond the home in the world of men. See Peter Filene, *Him/Her/Self: Sex Roles in Modern America*, 2d ed. (Baltimore, 1986), 18–19, 42–43.

27. Mary Consuela, "The Church of Philadelphia, 1884–1918," in Connelly, *Diocese of Philadelphia*, 304.

28. Introduction to Abbelen, *Caroline Friess*, 18.

29. Constance O'Hara, *Heaven Was Not Enough* (Philadelphia, 1955), 96–97.

30. Buetow, *Of Singular Benefit*, 192; Patricia C. Johnston, "Reflected Glory: The Story of Ellen Ireland," *Minnesota History* 48 (Spring 1982): 13–23; Leonard, *Immortelles*.

31. Mary A. Sadlier, *The Young Ladies Reader, Compiled and Arranged for Advanced Classes* (New York, 1875).

32. Frederick J. Zwierlein, *The Life and Letters of Bishop McQuaid* (Rochester, 1927), 3:396, 403–5; *Woman's Journal*, January 31, 1894.

33. "Address at Dedication of Holy Cross College 1899," quoted in David F. Sweeney, *The Life of John Lancaster Spalding, First Bishop of Peoria, 1840–1916* (New York, 1965), 264–65.

34. John L. Spalding, "Woman Is the God-Appointed Educator," *Donahoe's* 45 (February 1901): 176. Also see idem, *Women and Higher Education: Lecture before the Auxiliary Board of Trinity College, January 16, 1899* (Washington, D.C., 1899), 7–27; idem., Introduction to Abbelen, *Caroline Friess*, 18; idem, *Means and Ends*, 101–10; M. Rose Ethel Jendrus, "Bishop Spalding and His Position with Respect to the Higher Education of Women" (M.A. thesis, Notre Dame University, 1946), 37–40, 43, 46, 49, 59, 66, 84.

35. "Prospectus of Trinty College" in Oates, *Higher Education for Catholic Women*, 83–98; *Boston Pilot*, November 1, 1900; Power, *History of Catholic Higher Education*, 306; Sarah W. Howe, "Trinity College," *Donahoe's* 45 (February 1901): 39; William Seton, "The Higher Education of Women and Posterity," *Catholic World* 123 (May 1901): 61–63; Angela E. Keenan, *Three against the Wind: The Founding of Trinity College*, Washington, D.C. (Westminster, Md., 1973), 10–11, 21, 106, 109–12; *The American Foundations of the Sisters of Notre Dame de Namur, Compiled from the Annals of Their Convents by a Member of the Congregation* (Philadelphia, 1928), 551–52, 555.

36. Power, *History of Catholic Higher Education*, 191.

37. Karen Kennelly, "Mary Molloy: Women's College Founder," in Stuhler and Kreuter, *Women of Minnesota*, 125; Bowler, *Catholic Colleges for Women*, 85–88. By 1917 its president, Sister Mary Molloy, was demanding the right to prepare for professions those students who opted not to marry and have a family. See Barbara Miller Solomon, *In the Company of Educated Women: A History of Women and Higher Education in America* (New Haven, Conn., 1985), 154–55.

38. Félix Klein, *In the Land of Strenuous Life* (Chicago, 1905), 112.

39. Solomon, *Company of Educated Women*, 112.

40. "The Columbian Reading Union," *Catholic World* 122 (October 1900): 143–44.

41. James A. White, *The Founding of Cliff Haven: Early Years of the Catholic Summer School of America*, ed. John J. Meng (New York, 1950), 3–16, 47–58, 79–86; John J. Dolan, ed., *The Catholic Summer School of America, 1892–1916* (N.p., n.d.), 1–34; *Woman's Journal*, August 20, 1892; *Boston Pilot*, August 6, 1898.

42. Morgan M. Sheedy, "History of the Catholic Summer School of America," *Records of the American Catholic Historical Society* 27 (December 1916): 288–94; *Woman's Journal*, July 23, 1890.

43. Mary A. Spellissy, "Public Rights of Women: A Second Round Table Conference," *Catholic World* 59 (June 1894): 306.

44. *Woman's Journal*, March 7, 1874.

45. Mary E. Morgan, *Mercy, Generation to Generation: History of the First Century of the Sisters of Mercy, Diocese of Sacramento, California* (San Francisco, 1957), 19.

46. Ewens, *Nun in Nineteenth Century*, 104, 274; Katherine E. Conway, *In the Footsteps of the Good Shepherd, New York, 1857–1907* (New York, 1907), viii–ix, 23, 94; Richmond, *New York and Its Institutions*, 312, 339–41, 344–45; Abell, *Catholicism and Social Action*, 31–33.

47. Wittke, *Irish in America*, 19; Luciano J. Iorizzo and Salvatore Mondello, *The Italian Americans*, rev. ed. (Boston, 1980), 221.

48. Conway, "Individual Catholic Women," 403.

49. George G. Hoffman, "Catholic Immigrant Aid Societies in New York from 1880 to 1920" (Ph.D. diss., St. John's University, 1947), 28–32; Maureen Murphy, "Mission of Our Lady of the Rosary for the Protection of Irish Immigrant Girls," in *Irish-American Voluntary Organizations*, ed. Michael E. Funchion (Westport, Conn., 1983), 227–28; Richard M. Linkh, *American Catholicism and European Immigration (1900–1929)* (New York, 1975), 55, 58–59; Abell, *Catholicism and Social Action*, 51; Maureen Murphy, "A Mission Remembered," American Irish Historical Society, *Recorder* 43 (1982): 104–5.

50. Mary Louise Sullivan, "Mother Cabrini: Missionary to Italian Immigrants," *U.S. Catholic Historian* 6 (Fall 1987): especially 266–67. For brief accounts of her life, also see A Daughter of St. Paul, *Mother Cabrini* (Boston, 1977); Cecyle S. Neidle, *America's Immigrant Women* (Boston, 1975), 72–74; Annabelle M. Melville, "Saint Frances Xavier Cabrini," in *NAW*, 1:274–76.

51. Sisters of the Reparation of the Congregation of Mary, *Blessed Are the Merciful: The Life of Mother Mary Zita, Foundress* (New York, 1953).

52. Margaret M. McGuinness, "Response to Reform: An Historical Interpretation of the Catholic Settlement Movement, 1897–1915" (Ph.D. diss., Union Theological Seminary, 1985), 119–20.

53. Shanabruch, "Church's Role in Americanization," 365–66.

54. Also rather typically, women were not allowed to join the society, as they would "create confusion and sow dissatisfaction." See Ryan, *Beyond the Ballot Box*, 30; McColgan, *Century of Charity*, 2:392–94, 473.

55. James B. Curry, "Settlement Work," in *First American Catholic Missionary Congress*, ed. Francis B. Kelley (Chicago, 1909), 155–64.

56. "The Church and Social Work," *Catholic World* 66 (December 1897): 404.

57. A. A. McGinley, "A New Field for the Convent Graduate in the Social Settlement," *Catholic World* 121 (June 1900): 396–401.

58. Hennesey, *American Catholics*, 211; Wood, "Catholic Attitude toward Social Settlement," 61; Cross, *Emergence of Liberal Catholicism*, 164; M. T. Elder, "The Wrath of Mother Nature," *Catholic World* 55 (August 1892): 707–

15; idem, "Put Money in Thy Purse," *Catholic World* 50 (February 1890): 618–20; George Zurcher, *The Apple of Discord; or, Temporal Power in the Catholic Church, by a Roman Catholic* (Buffalo, N.Y., 1905), 492–93.

59. Robert A. Woods and Albert J. Kennedy, *The Settlement Horizon: A National Estimate* (New York, 1922), 372–73; McGuinness, "Response to Reform," 152–53; Wood, "Catholic Attitude toward Social Settlement," 57–60. For fear of the proselytization of Italians, see E. M. Dunne, "Memoirs of 'Zi Pre,'" *American Ecclesiastical Review* 49 (August 1913): 200–203; Henry J. Browne, "'The Italian Problem' in the Catholic Church of the United States," United States Catholic Historical Society, *Historical Records and Studies* 35 (1946): 90; Anna C. Minogue, *The Story of the Santa Maria Institute* (Cincinnati, 1922), i, 3, 50–51, 65, 98; Daisey A. Moseley, "The Catholic Social Worker in an Italian District," *Catholic World* 114 (February 1922): 626; Joseph McSorley, "The Church and the Italian Situation in New York," *American Ecclesiastical Review* 48 (March 1913): 268–82; Moseley, "Catholic Social Worker," 626; Maxine Seller, "Protestant Evangelicalism and Italian Immigrant Women," in Caroli, Harney, and Tomasi, *Italian Immigrant Woman*, 124–25, 127, 133; Richard N. Juliani, "The Settlement House and the Italian Family," in ibid., 115, 120.

60. The actual number of Catholic settlements is almost impossible to discover because of the varying definitions of a settlement. Linkh, *Catholicism and European Immigration*, 60–61, states that prior to World War I there were only about two dozen in the country but points out that other estimates range from 22 to 2,500.

61. Minogue, *Story of the Santa Maria Institute*, 6–130; idem, "Meeting the Italian Situation in Cincinnati," *National Catholic Welfare Conference Bulletin* 8 (September 1926): 21; O'Grady, *Catholic Charities*, 289.

62. O'Grady, *Catholic Charities*, 290–91; Laurence Franklin, "The Italian in America: What He Has Been, What He Shall Be," *Catholic World* 71 (April 1900): 70; Burton, *In No Strange Land*, 206–11; Abell, *Catholicism and Social Action*, 127–65; *New York Times*, February 11, 1957.

63. Mary J. Workman, "Brownson House, Los Angeles, Cal.: A Catholic Social Settlement," *St. Vincent de Paul Quarterly* 20 (August 1915): 175–76; O'Grady, *Catholic Charities*, 293.

64. Linkh, *Catholicism and European Immigration*, 55; "To Teach Italians," *New Century* 3 (April 28, 1906).

65. Grace O'Brien, "Catholic Settlement Work in Brooklyn," *Survey* 24 (May 7, 1910): 203–4; Allen F. Davis, *Spearheads for Reform: The Social Settlements and the Progressive Movement, 1890–1914* (New York, 1967), 15.

66. Henri J. Wiesel, "Miss Mary V. Merrick and Her Work for Children," *America* 57 (August 14, 1937): 439–40; "Christ Child Society," *Commonweal* 26 (April 30, 1937): 18; "Mary Merrick and the Christ Child Society," in Katherine Burton, *Woman to Woman* (New York, 1960), 21–22; O'Grady, *Catholic Charities*, 296, 325–26; "The Laetare Medal Awarded to

Miss Mary V. Merrick, Washington, D.C.," *St. Vincent de Paul Society* 20 (May 1915): 127–29; obituary, *New York Times*, January 12, 1955.

67. O'Grady, *Catholic Charities*, 327–30.

68. *The New World*, March 18, 1889, quoted in Shanabruch, "Church's Role in Americanization," 109.

69. Quoted in Mary Agnes Amberg, *Madonna Center: Pioneer Catholic Social Settlement* (Chicago, 1976), 207; Dunne, "Memoirs of 'Zi Pre,' " 203.

70. *The New World*, quoted in Shanabruch, "Church's Role in Americanization," 132–37; Rudolph Vecoli, "Prelates and Peasants: Italian Immigrants and the Catholic Church," *Journal of Social History* 2 (Spring 1969): 226; McGuinness, "Response to Reform," 163–65.

71. Jane Addams, *Twenty Years at Hull House, with Autobiographical Notes* (New York, 1910), 4.

72. Amberg, *Madonna Center*, 83, 134, 189–92.

73. Thomas E. Shields, *The Education of Our Girls* (New York, 1907), 180; Klein, *Land of Strenuous Life*, 147–50; Alice T. Toomy, "A Great Forward Movement," *Catholic World* 58 (January 1894): 483–88.

74. "Notes on Ellen Gates Starr by Miss Josephine Starr," 7–8, folder 27, Ellen Gates Starr Papers, Sophia Smith Archives, Smith College, Northampton, Massachusetts; Mary P. Barrows, *Frances Crane Lillie, 1869–1958: A Memoir* (Privately printed, 1969), 20, 69, 75, 84–85, Starr Papers. The quotation is from page 85.

75. Eliza Starr (1824–1901), who had studied art in Boston and Europe, was a daily communicant who believed her mission was to familiarize Catholics with Christian art. To inform her coreligionists of their great but little-known heritage, she lectured, wrote, and taught on the subject, even though she believed women belonged at home. In recognition of her efforts she was decorated by Leo XIII and received the Laetare Medal from the University of Notre Dame. See Eliza Starr, "Women in Art," in Donnelly, *Girlhood's Hand-Book*, 58–59; McGovern, *Life and Letters of Starr*, 19, 40, 44; Driscoll, *Literary Convert Women*, 39–45; *New York Times*, March 26, 1900.

76. Ellen Gates Starr, "A Bypath into the Great Roadway," *Catholic World* 119 (May 1924): 177–90; (June 1924): 358–73; Allen F. Davis, "Ellen Gates Starr," in *NAW Modern*, 58–90; Starr, "Notes on Ellen Gates Starr"; Barrows, "Frances Crane Lillie," 82.

77. Abell, *Catholicism and Social Action*, 181–82; Mary Harrita Fox, *Peter E. Dietz, Labor Priest* (Notre Dame, Ind., 1953), 146–92 passim.

78. McGuinness, "Response to Reform," 196–97.

79. Walter Romig, *Josephine Van Dyke Brownson* (Detroit, 1955), 68–69.

80. The quotation is from Helen C. Bennett, *American Women in Civic Work* (New York, 1915), 111. Also see A. J. McKelway, " 'Kate' the 'Good Angel' of Oklahoma," *American Magazine* 66 (October 1908) reprinted in *Lives to Remember*, ed. Leon Stein (New York, 1974), n.p.; Bennett, *Women in Civic Work*, 93–111; Keith L. Bryant, "Kate Barnard: Organized Labor and

Social Justice in Oklahoma during the Progressive Era," *Journal of Southern History* 35 (May 1969): 145–64; obituary *New York Times*, February 24, 1930.

81. Caroline J. Gleason, "For Working Women in Oregon," *Survey* 36 (September 9, 1916): 585–86; "Caroline Gleason," *Catholic Charities Review* 1 (January 1917): 23; Olga Freeman, "Sister Miriam Theresa and Women's Rights," *Today's Family Digest* 26 (January 1971): 66–70; see also data provided by Sister Caroline A. Gimpl, the archivist of Gleason's religious community. Her *Legislation for Women in Oregon* (Washington, D.C., 1929) was also published by the Women's Bureau in 1931.

82. Abell, *Catholicism and Social Action*, 166.

83. For example, see Mary V. Toomey, "The Queen's Daughters' Society," *Catholic Charities Review* 1 (January 1917): 43–46, for the story of Mary Hoxey and over sixty houses in the St. Louis area. Also see Marie Thérèse Blanc, *The Conditions of Women in the United States: A Traveler's Notes* (Boston, 1895; reprint, New York, 1972), 254–55; Mary Jane Burns, "The Protectorate of the Catholic Women's League of Chicago," *Catholic Charities Review* 1 (January 1917): 46–47; *Woman's Journal*, October 17, 1903; Mrs. John A. Logan, *The Part Taken by Women in American History* (Washington, D.C., 1912; reprint, New York, 1972), 617. For fifteen years Mrs. John J. Brown assisted Judge Benjamin Lindsey of Denver in rescuing young offenders who appeared before his juvenile court, the first in the nation. Brown was better known as the "unsinkable Molly Brown," one of the heroes of the *Titanic* disaster, whose leadership in a lifeboat saved the lives of several passengers. See *New York Times*, April 20, 1912, October 27, 1932; Dixon Wecter, *The Saga of American Society: A Record of Social Aspirations, 1607–1937* (New York, 1937), 248.

84. Auxiliaries had previously been allowed only on an informal basis. See McColgan, *Century of Charity*, 2:320–21, 326, 394, 399, 401.

85. Christopher J. Kauffman, *Faith and Fraternalism: The History of the Knights of Columbus* (New York, 1982), 125–26; P. K. Kerwin, "Catholic Daughters of America," in *Catholic Encyclopedia*, 3:217; J. F. Maguire, "Daughters of Isabella," in *Catholic Encyclopedia*, 4:653–54.

86. Lily A. Toomey, "Some Noble Work of Catholic Women," *Catholic World* 57 (May 1893): 234–43; Cohalan, *Popular History*, 309; Lord, Sexton, and Harrington, *History of Archdiocese of Boston*, 3:380; obituary of Catherine McParlan, *New York Times*, January 30, 1958.

87. McColgan, *Century of Charity*, 2:310; O'Grady, *Catholic Charities*, 265.

88. Romig, *Brownson*, 1–141 passim.

89. *Woman's Journal*, December 22 and 19, 1906; Executive Committee Meeting, January 24, 1908, Papers of the Massachusetts Association Opposed to the Further Extension of Suffrage, Massachusetts Historical Society. See O'Reilly to Cardinal O'Connell, March 17, September 29, 1910, O'Connell Papers, 8:9; obituaries in *New York Times* and *Boston Globe*, October 22, 1939. Her sister, Elizabeth Boyle O'Reilly, was a poet, author of books on

Europe, and a Red Cross nurse serving overseas during World War I. She too promoted conventional values until she suffered a nervous breakdown after returning from Europe. See Conway, "Individual Catholic Women," 397; obituary, *Boston Transcript*, September 13, 1922; Elizabeth Boyle O'Reilly, *My Candles and Other Poems* (Boston, 1903).

90. Dorsey, who was educated at a Visitandine convent in Washington, was a newspaper reporter for ten years before turning to the writing of short stories, primarily for children. Although emphasizing traditional roles, Dorsey recognized the contributions of women that heretofore had been frequently unacknowledged. Furthermore, she often depicted females as redeemer figures. See Donnelly, *Round Table*, 97–98; Suzanne Allen, "Ella Loraine Dorsey," in Mainiero, *American Women Writers*, 1:534; Ella Loraine Dorsey, "A Salem Witch," *Ave Maria*, reprinted in Leonard, *Immortelles*, 464–65; idem, "Speculum Justitiae," as in Donnelly, *Round Table*, 99–120.

91. Mary M. Wirmel, "Sisterhoods in the Spanish-American War," United States Catholic Historical Society, *Historical Records and Studies* 32 (1941): 1–67 passim; also Alice Worthington Winthrop, "The Work of the Sisters in the War with Spain," *Ave Maria* 49 (September 23, 1899): 385–88; (September 30): 426–30; George Barton, "A Story of Self-Sacrifice: Being a Record of the Labors of the Catholic Sisterhoods in the Spanish-American War," *Records of the American Catholic Historical Society* 38 (March 1926): 104–42; Gertrude Fenner, "The Daughters of Charity in the Spanish-American War," *Vincentian Heritage* 8 (1987): 141–64. There were about 120 lay nurses, 7 of whom died as a result of tending the sick (Winthrop, "Work of the Sisters," 428).

92. Winthrop, "Work of the Sisters," 420; Thomas Dwight, "The Training Schools for Nurses of the Sisters of Charity," *Catholic World* 61 (May 1895): 190–92; Ewens, *Nun in Nineteenth Century*, 246–50, 272–74; Peterson and Vaughn-Roberson, *Women with Vision*, 197–98.

93. P. J. O'Callaghan, "Catholics in the Temperance Movement," in McGuire, *Catholic Builders*, 2:260–71.

94. Joan Bland, *Hibernian Crusade: The Story of the Catholic Total Abstinence Union in America* (Washington, D.C., 1951), 97–101, 144; Joseph Gibbs, *History of the Catholic Total Abstinence Union of America* (Philadelphia, 1907), 43, 49, 58, 85. Although Catholic women began to join the CTAU, large numbers of them reacted to the antifeminism in that organization and enlisted instead in the Women's Christian Temperance Union and semi-Protestant organizations (Debra Campbell, "Reformers and Activists," in Kennelly, *American Catholic Women*, 164–65).

95. Bland, *Hibernian Crusade*, 233–34.

96. *Woman's Journal*, August 15, 1891; Gibbs, *Catholic Total Abstinence Union*, 95, 97.

97. Gibbs, *Catholic Total Abstinence Union*, 158; Zurcher, *Apple of Discord*, 492.

98. Bland, *Hibernian Crusade*, 214–58 passim.

99. Ibid., 208–9; Gibbs, *Catholic Total Abstinence Union*, 153.

100. Bland, *Hibernian Crusade*, 220.

101. *Woman's Journal*, August 1, 1885, September 5, 1891, April 18, 1893.

102. Ibid., December 25, 1886, January 25, 1896, August 13, 1898, September 20, 1902.

103. Mary A. Dowd, "The Public Rights of Women: A Second Round Table Conference," *Catholic World* 59 (June 1894): 314–39.

104. Mary L. Brophy, *The Social Thought of the German Roman Catholic Verein* (Washington, D.C., 1941), 18–20, 22–27; Philip Gleason, *The Conservative Reformers: German American Catholics and the Social Order* (Notre Dame, Ind., 1964), 23–24, 184.

105. *Woman's Journal*, January 9, 1904; Blanc, *Condition of Woman*, 89.

106. Blanc, *Condition of Woman*, 88–89.

107. The quotations are from the *Woman's Journal*, January 6, 1872. For surveys of Sullivan's life, see ibid., January 9, 1904; Conway, "Individual Catholic Women," 399–401; idem, "Margaret F. Sullivan, Journalist and Author," *Donahoe's* 51 (March 1904): 220–23; Leonard, *Immortelles*, 380; and obituaries in the *New York Times*, December 24, 1903, and *Boston Pilot*, January 2, 1904.

108. *Woman's Journal*, August 16, 1873.

109. Ibid., January 9, 1904; *Boston Pilot*, January 2, 1904; Katherine A. O'Mahoney, *Famous Irishmen* (Lawrence, Mass., 1907), 192.

110. Conway, "Margaret F. Sullivan," 221.

111. David Pivar, *Purity Crusade: Sexual Morality and Social Control* (Westport, Conn., 1973), 244.

112. Ireland, "Social Purity," frames 61–64.

113. *New York Times*, August 2, 3, 1906.

114. Klarmann, *Crux of Pastoral Medicine*, 27, 30, 32, 39.

115. Francis X. Lasance, *The Catholic Girl's Guide: Counsels and Devotions for Girls in the Ordinary Walks of Life* (New York, 1906).

116. Walsh, *Woman*, especially 17, 41.

117. Zwierlein, *Life and Letters of McQuaid*, 3:445; Cross, *Emergence of Liberal Catholicism*, 173–74.

118. There is no biography of Edes, but see R. F. McNamara, "Ella B. Edes," in *Catholic Encyclopedia*, 5:102, and the following works, which mention her several times: Robert E. Curran, *Michael Augustine Corrigan and the Shaping of Conservative Catholicism in America, 1878–1902* (New York, 1978); James H. Moynihan, *The Life of Archbishop Ireland* (New York, 1953); John Tracy Ellis, *The Life of James Cardinal Gibbons, Archbishop of Baltimore, 1834–1921* (Milwaukee, 1952); Thomas T. McAvoy, "Public Schools vs. Catholic Schools and James McMaster," *Review of Politics* 28 (January 1966): 19–46; Fogarty, *Vatican and American Hierarchy*; Colman J. Barry, *The Catholic Church and German Americans* (Milwaukee, 1953).

119. Francis G. McManamin, *The American Years of John Boyle O'Reilly* (New York, 1976), 139–40.

120. Curran, *Corrigan*, 488.

121. John Ireland to Maria Storer, September 11 and October 23, 1903, in Maria Longworth Storer, *In Memoriam: Bellamy Storer with Personal Remembrances of President McKinley, President Roosevelt, and John Ireland, Bishop of St. Paul* (Privately printed, 1923), 80, 84.

122. John Ireland to Maria Storer, April 24, 1904, ibid., 106–7.

123. For a summary see Henry F. Pringle, *Theodore Roosevelt: A Biography*, rev. ed., (New York, 1955), 320–22; Moynihan, *John Ireland*, 345–63; Alice Roosevelt Longworth, *Crowded Hours: Reminiscences* (New York, 1933), 125–26; Dorothy G. Wayman, ed., "Some Unpublished Correspondence between Bellamy Storer and Cardinal O'Connell, 1908–1929," *Catholic Historical Review* 40 (July 1954): 129–30, 140–42, 162–63; Marvin R. O'Connell, *John Ireland and the American Catholic Church* (St. Paul, 1988), 472–98; "The Case of Mrs. Bellamy Storer," *Outlook* 84 (December 15, 1906): 901–2. This incident did not end Storer's involvement in church politics. Years later, after she suggested that the entire American hierarchy appeal to President Wilson for representation at the Paris Peace Conference (1919), Cardinal Gibbons described her as "a mischief maker for years" who had caused much discomfort by meddling in ecclesiastical affairs (Ellis, *Gibbons*, 2:273–74).

124. Eliza O. Lummis, *Daughters of the Faith: Serious Thoughts for Catholic Women* (New York, 1905), 111.

125. John M. Berry and Frances Panchok, "Church and Theatre," *U.S. Catholic Historian* 6 (Spring/Summer 1987): 153, 176–78.

126. Dowd, "Public Rights of Women," 320.

Chapter 8 — Wage-Earning Women and Ethnic Churches: A Road to Autonomy

1. "Woman as Bread Winner," *Catholic World* 17 (May 1873): 223, 224; Edselas, "Institute for Woman's Professions," 509–20; Spellissy, "Public Rights of Women," 307–8.

2. David Montgomery, "The Irish and American Labor Movement," in *America and Ireland, 1776–1976: The American Identity and the Irish Connection*, ed. David N. Doyle and Owen Dudley Edwards (Westport, Conn., 1980), 208.

3. Helen Campbell, *Prisoners of Poverty. Women Wage-Earners, Their Trades, and Their Lives* (Boston, 1887; reprint, Westport, Conn., 1975), 224–27; David M. Katzman, *Seven Days a Week: Women and Domestic Service in Industrializing America* (New York, 1978), 60, 70, 163–64, 232, 271–72. The quotation is from page 71.

4. Montgomery, "Irish and American Labor," 274.

5. Clark, *Irish in Philadelphia*, 42; Dolan, *Catholic Experience*, 143.

6. For statistics on ethnic families taking in boarders, see Elizabeth Pleck, "Mother's Wages: Income Earning among Married Italian and Black

Women, 1896–1901," in *The American Family in Social-Historical Perspective*, ed. Michael A. Gordon, 2d ed. (New York, 1978), 496.

7. Virginia Yans-McLaughlin, *Family and Community: Italian Immigrants in Buffalo, 1880–1930* (Ithaca, N.Y., 1977), 172; Josephine Roche, "The Italian Girl," in *The Neglected Girl*, ed. Ruth S. True (New York, 1914), 110; Humbert S. Nelli, *From Immigrants to Ethnics: The Italian Americans* (New York, 1983), 144. In this study and in "Patterns of Work and Family Organization: Buffalo's Italians," *Journal of Interdisciplinary History* 2 (Autumn, 1971): 299–327, Yans-McLaughlin contends that in Buffalo, at least, tradition kept Italian women at home or working as "part of a family unit." Similar conclusions were recorded for Pittsburgh by Corinne A. Krause, "Urbanization without Breakdown: Italian, Jewish, and Slavic Women in Pittsburgh, 1910–1945," *Journal of Urban History* 4 (May 1978): 295. On the other hand, some studies indicate that poverty and job opportunity were the determining factors in the employment of Italian women outside the home and that their experience was not much different from that of other groups. Elizabeth Pleck in "Mother's Wages," 490–505, describes custom barriers to the employment of married Italian women as a low chain-link fence, not a high stone wall. Also see Louise C. Odencrantz, *Italian Women in Industry: A Study of Conditions in New York City* (New York, 1919), especially 179, 225; Joan Y. Dickinson, *The Role of the Immigrant Women in the U.S. Labor Force, 1890–1910* (New York, 1980), 145–46; Robert A. Orsi, *The Madonna of 115th Street: Faith and Community in Italian Harlem, 1880–1950* (New Haven, Conn., 1985), 98.

8. Miriam Cohen, "Italian-American Women in New York City, 1900–1950: Work and School," in Cantor and Laurie, *Class, Sex, and Woman Worker*, 124; Robert F. Foerster, *The Italian Emigration of Our Time*, (Cambridge, Mass., 1921; reprint, New York, 1967), 380–81.

9. Angelo M. Pellegrini, *Americans by Choice* (New York, 1956), 139–46, 200–203.

10. Judith E. Smith, *Family Connections: A History of Italian and Jewish Immigrant Lives in Providence, Rhode Island, 1900–1940* (Albany, N.Y., 1985), 66.

11. Ibid., 50–52, 63.

12. Leonard Covello, *The Social Background of the Italo-American School Child: A Study of the Southern Italian Family Mores and Their Effect on the Social Situation in Italy and America* (Leiden, 1967), 39; Dolores Liptak, *The Catholic Church in the United States: At the Crossroads* (Washington, D.C., 1983), 56.

13. Columbia M. Furio, "The Cultural Background of the Italian Immigrant Woman and Its Impact on Her Unionization in the New York City Garment Industry, 1880–1910," in *Pane e Lavoro: The Italian American Working Class*, ed. George E. Pozzetta, (Toronto, 1980), 91–96; Adriana Spadoni, "The Italian Working Women of New York," *Colliers*, March 3, 1912, reprinted in Wayne Moquin and Charles Van Doren, *A Documentary*

History of Italian Americans (New York, 1974), 127–30; Edwin Fenton, *Immigrants and Unions: A Case Study; Italians and American Labor, 1870–1920* (New York, 1975), 488–97, 523–27.

14. Mary B. O'Sullivan, "Are Girls a Burden?" *Donahoe's* 29 (March 1893): 359; idem, "Should Married Women Work? A Symposium," ibid. (May 1893): 633; Leonard, *Immortelles*, 213; and also two articles by O'Sullivan in *Immortelles:* "The Sacrifice of the Shop Girl," 224–32, and "Women Who Have Made History," 217–24.

15. George A. Stevens, *New York Typographical Union No. 6: Study of a Modern Trade Union and Its Predecessors* (Albany, N.Y., 1913), 432–38; Eleanor Flexner, "Augusta Lewis Troup," in *NAW* 3:478–79; obituary, *New Haven Journal Courier*, September 15, 1920. One of the few labor organizers to oppose suffrage was "Mother" Mary Harris Jones (1830–1930), who believed it would detract from substantial reform. Jones, who was born a Catholic and even taught in a parochial school, left the church until shortly before her death because it was too closely allied with the "plutocrats." See Kenneally, *Women and Trade Unions*, 92–118. Also see Mary H. Jones to Terrence V. Powderly, March 22, 1914, and "Speech to Pan American Organization of Labor," January 13, 1921, both in *Mother Jones Speaks: Collected Writings and Speeches*, ed. Philip Foner (New York, 1983), 602–3, 323–26 .

16. Kenneally, *Women and Trade Unions*, 12–13; Meredith Tax, *The Rise of the Women: Feminist Solidarity and Class Conflict, 1880–1917* (New York, 1980), 41–53; Susan Levine, *Labor's True Woman: Carpet Weavers, Industrialization, and Labor Reform in the Gilded Age* (Philadelphia, 1984), 136–38; *Knights of Labor*, March 5, 1887.

17. Kenneally, *Women and Trade Unions*, 13–16; Levine, *Labor's True Woman*, 138–41; *Woman's Journal*, July 22, 1888; Mrs. O. B. Lake, "Is Labor Dignified?" in *The Congress of Women Held in the Woman's Bloc, World's Columbian Exposition, Chicago, 1893*, ed. Mary K. Eagle (Chicago, 1895), 508–9.

18. Kenneally, *Women and Trade Unions*, 20–22, 42–44; idem, "Catholic and Feminist: A Biographical Approach," *U.S. Catholic Historian* 3 (Spring 1984): 239–45.

19. Obituary, *New York Times*, January 9, 1928; Mary H. Fox, *Peter Dietz, Labor Priest* (Notre Dame, Ind., 1953), 132, 207.

20. David Brody, "Maud O'Farrell Swartz," in *NAW*, 3:413–15; *New York Times*, April 7, 1919, October 21, 1923, November 13, 1928, and obituary, February 23, 1939.

21. Annie L. Diggs, "The Women in the Alliance Movement," *Arena* 6 (1892), reprinted in Stein, *Lives*, 172–73; Ignatius Donnelly to *Miner's Journal*, January 5, 1891, Donnelly Papers, reel 159, vol. 116, frame 145.

22. Maurine W. Greenwald, *Women, War, and Work: The Impact of World War I on Women Workers in the United States* (Westport, Conn., 1980), 200–205, 219–22; Stephen H. Norwood, "Julia Sarsfield O'Connor Parker," in *NAW Modern*, 525–26.

23. *Woman's Journal,* August 2, 1902, July 4, 1913, July 20, 1907, August 20, 1910; *Woman Citizen,* August 11, 1917; advertisements in the *Los Angeles Tidings* all during 1911.

24. Mrs. John A. Logan, *The Part Taken by Women in American History* (Wilmington, Del., 1912; reprint, New York, 1972), 617; *New York Times,* July 22, 1922. Obviously many working women, even professionals, clung to traditional perceptions. An excellent example is Alice J. Stevens (1860–1947), who edited the *Los Angeles Tidings,* a Catholic newspaper, from 1908 to 1913. "To promote the educational, literacy, news and businesss interests" of its members, in 1911 she helped establish the Catholic Press Association, in which she held office. However, Stevens refused to let her name appear on the masthead of the *Tidings* and in 1913 resigned these positions to accept "a woman's higher place in life" by marrying William Tipton (Francis J. Weber, *California Catholicity* [Los Angeles, 1979], 23–25).

25. John K. Pearce and Monica McGoldrick Orfanidis, "Family Therapy with Irish-Americans," in *Growing Up Irish: Mental Health in Cultural Context,* Working Papers in Irish Studies 83-1, (Boston: Northeastern University, 1983), 57–59; Andrew M. Greeley, *That Most Distressful Nation: The Taming of the American Irish* (Chicago, 1972), 101, 134–35, 251.

26. Nelli, *Immigrants to Ethnics,* 113; Orsi, *Madonna of 115th Street,* 131–34.

27. Margherita Marchione, "Religious Teachers Filippini in the United States," *U.S. Catholic Historian* 6 (Fall 1978): 356–57.

28. Linda B. Cateura, *Growing Up Italian* (New York, 1987), 112.

29. By 1965 Italians were the most likely of all Catholics to use contraceptives. See Ira Rosenwaike, "Two Generations of Italians in America: Their Fertility Experience," *International Migration Review* 7 (Fall 1983): 280. Also see Francis X. Femminellas and Jill S. Quadango, "The Italian-American Family," in Mindel and Habenstein, *Ethnic Families,* 215; for protection of daughters, Luigi O. Barzini, *America! When You and I Were Young* (New York, 1977), 121–32 and for domestic skills, Femminella, "Italian-American Family," 80, and Lydio F. Tomasi, *The Italian American Family* (New York, 1972), 26–27.

30. Smith, *Family Connections,* 142–43, 162.

31. James S. Olson, *Catholic Immigrants in America* (Chicago, 1986), 74–75.

32. Aloysius J. Wycislo, "The Polish Catholic Immigrant," in *Roman Catholicism and the American Way of Life,* ed. Thomas T. McAvoy (Notre Dame, Ind., 1960), 199, gives a figure of 92 percent; Helen S. Zand, "Polish Family Folkways in the United States," *Polish American Studies* 13 (July–December 1956): 81, estimates that 98 percent were Catholic. For Polish community life, see Joseph Swastek, *The Polish American Story* (Detroit, n.d.), especially 8–10; Anthony Kuzniewski, "Polish Catholics in America," in Trisco, *Catholics in America,* 90; Mary T. Doman, "Polish American Sisterhoods and Their Contribution to the Catholic Church in the United

States," in *The Contribution of the Poles to the Growth of Catholicism in the United States*, ed. F. Domanski (Rome, 1959), 371-606; Ellen Marie Kuznicki, "The Role of the Felician Sisters in Shaping American Polonia," paper given at the cultural exchange, current research, at Jagiellonian University, Krakow, July 13-20, 1986; idem, "An Ethnic School in American Education" (Ph.D. diss., Kansas State University, 1972); Robert A. Slayton, *Back of the Yards: The Making of a Local Democracy* (Chicago, 1986), 80-83.

33. Victor R. Greene, "For God and Country: The Origins of Slavic Self-Consciousness in America," *Church History* 35 (December 1966): 449.

34. Thaddeus C. Radzialowski, "Let Us Join Hands: The Polish Women's Alliance," *Review Journal of Philosophy and Social Science* 11, no. 2, reprinted in Maxine Seller, *Immigrant Women* (Philadelphia, 1981), 182-201; Kenneth D. Miller, *Peasant Pioneers: An Interpretation of the Slavic People in the United States* (New York, 1925), 96-97; Swastek, *Polish American Story*, 12; Maxine Seller, "The Education of the Immigrant Woman, 1900-1935," *Journal of American History* 4 (May 1978): 329; Mary O. Kryszak, "Polish Women's Alliance of America," in *Poles of Chicago, 1837-1937* (Chicago, 1937), 154-58.

35. John J. Bukowczyk, *And My Children Did Not Know Me: A History of the Polish-Americans* (Bloomington, Ind., 1987), 39.

36. Frank Renkiewicz, *For God, Country, and Polonia: One Hundred Years of the Orchard Lake Schools* (Detroit, 1985), 83; Bukowczyk, *And My Children*, 39.

37. Alfred J. Sokolnicki, "Mary Olszewski Kryszak," in *NAW*, 2:350-51.

38. "Protest of the Polish Women's Alliance against Peace at Any Price," in *The Poles in America, 1608-1972*, ed. Frank Renkiewicz (New York, 1973), 33; Joseph J. Parot, *Polish Catholics in Chicago, 1850-1920: A Religious History* (De Kalb, Ill., 1981), 165, 170, 225.

39. Stanley R. Puszka, "Polish American Community and Rebirth of Poland," *Polish American Studies* 26 (January-June 1969): 40-41, 47; obituary, *New York Times*, January 12, 1935.

40. The speech is in Sewall, *World's Congress*, 738-47; Helen Modjeska, *Memories and Impressions: An Autobiography* (New York, 1910), especially 512-18; *Woman's Journal*, February 6, 1886, April 15, 1893; obituary, *New York Times*, April 19, 1909; Mary J. Oates, "Catholic Women in the Labor Force," in Kennelly, *American Catholic Women*, 93.

41. Those who married and remained at home exercised considerable authority over the family, including the management of the husband's salary (Slayton, *Back of the Yards*, 75, and Ellen Marie Kuznicki to author, May 1, 1988). For an account of one particular family, see Paul Friggens, "Mama Krol and the Wonderful Report Cards," *Reader's Digest* 74 (February 1959): 128-32. Polish housewives were so intrepid that in 1935 over two hundred of them picketed local meat markets in a Detroit suburb demanding lower prices. Their leader, Mary Zuk, at that time a Catholic, was arrested and as

a result of her new notoriety was elected to the city council (Georg Schrode, "Mary Zuk and the Detroit Meat Strike of 1935," *Polish American Studies* 48 [Autumn 1986]: 5–39).

42. The Immigration Commission Report is quoted in Paul Fox, *The Poles in America* (New York, 1922; reprint, New York, 1970), 71; Winifred D. Bolin, "Past Ideals and Present Pleasures: Women, Work, and the Family, 1920–1940" (Ph.D. diss., University of Minnesota, 1976), 394; Slayton, *Back of the Yards*, 177.

43. Helena Z. Lopata, "The Polish American Family," in Mindel and Habenstein, *Ethnic Families*, 23–29; Fox, *Poles in America*, 71; Zand, "Polish Family Folkways," 78, 84–85; William I. Thomas and Florian Znaniecki, *The Polish Peasant in Europe and America* (New York, 1927), 2:1801–2; Helen Z. Lopata, *Polish Americans: Status Competition in an Ethnic Community* (Englewood Cliffs, N.J., 1976), 99.

44. William Wolkovich, "Lithuanian Catholics in America," in Trisco, *Catholics in America*, 100.

45. James W. Sanders, *The Education of an Urban Minority: Catholics in Chicago, 1833–1965* (New York, 1977), 53.

46. "American Lithuanian Roman Catholic Women's Alliance," in *Encyclopedia Lituanica* (Boston, 1970) 1:91–92; Antanas Kučas, *Lithuanians in America* (Boston, 1975), 105, 300–301; Donna Zilis, *American Lithuanian Roman Catholic Woman's Alliance, 1914–1964* (N.p., 1964), 67–75, 84; interview with Julia Mack, February 23, 1985. Lithuanian women were also dominant figures in the family, it was estimated that in Chester, Pennsylvania, 40 percent of the Lithuanian wives managed the families' financial affairs. See Peter P. Jonitas, "The Acculturation of the Lithuanians of Chester, Pennsylvania" (Ph.D. diss. University of Pennsylvania, 1951) reprinted in *Lithuanians in the United States: Selected Studies*, ed. Leo J. Alilunas (San Francisco, 1978), 96.

47. Oral histories of Mrs. Veronica Lutukus and Mrs. Ursulla Daukantas, Public Library, Worcester, Massachusetts.

48. Potter, *To the Golden Door*, 212–13. McDannell, *Christian Home*, especially xvi and 73, asserts that Protestant Victorian values and culture were accepted by the Irish as reflected in their literature. If so (and chapter 3 indicates this claim is probably in error), it was only a superficial acceptance, as the rest of this chapter will indicate.

49. Charles Callan Tansill, *America and the Fight for Irish Freedom: An Old Story Based on New Data* (New York, 1951), 27–36; James H. Hurst, "The Fenian Brotherhood," in Funchion, *Irish-American Voluntary Organizations*, 106–14; John Devoy, *Recollections of an Irish Rebel: A Personal Narrative* (New York, 1929), 113, 355; Fenian Brotherhood, *Proceedings of the First National Congress, 1863* (Philadelphia, 1863), 227–29; *The Irish People* (Dublin), February 6, March 5, 19, 26, 1864; John J. Patrick, "The Cleveland Fenians: A Study in Ethnic Leadership," *Old Northwest* 9 (Winter 1983–84): 312, 316, 321; Hammond, *Diary of a Union Lady*, 227–29;

William D'Arcy, *The Fenian Movement in the United States* (Washington, D.C., 1947), 376.

50. *Revolution*, April 1, 1869.

51. Michael F. Funchion, "Clan na Gael," in Funchion, *Irish-American Voluntary Organizations*, 88.

52. Ibid., 90.

53. Margaret O'Donovan-Rossa, *My Father and Mother Were Irish* (New York, 1939), 15–18, 47, 105, 185–86; William O'Brien and Desmond Ryan, *Devoy's Post Bag, 1871–1928* (Dublin, 1948), 1:401; 2:482–83.

54. Lloyd Wendt and Herman Kogan, *Bosses in Lusty Chicago: The Story of Bathhouse John and Hinky Dink* (Bloomington, Ind., 1974), 21–22, 32.

55. D'Arcy, *Fenian Movement*, 404; Maureen Murphy, "Ladies Land League," in Funchion, *Irish-American Voluntary Organizations*, 221; McManamin, *O'Reilly*, 87.

56. *Catholic Universe*, May 25, June 1, 1882; *Cleveland Leader*, June 6, 1882; *New York Times*, June 3, July 12, 1882; M. F. Boff to Bishop Corrigan, August 8, 1882, Archives of the Archdiocese of Cleveland; Michael J. Hynes, *History of the Diocese of Cleveland: Origins and Growth, 1847–1952* (Cleveland, 1953), 137–44; Paul J. Hallinan, "Richard Gilmour: Second Bishop of Cleveland 1872–1891" (Ph.D. diss., Case Western Reserve University, 1963); Kenneally, "Sexism and the Church," 4–11.

57. Sylvester Malone, *Dr. Edward McGlynn* (New York, 1918; reprint, New York, 1978), 20, 43, 79. For the relationship between the league and the society, see Eric Foner, "Class, Ethnicity, and Radicalism in the Gilded Age," *Marxist Perspective* 1 (Summer 1978), reprinted in idem, *Politics and Ideology in the Age of the Civil War* (New York, 1989), 150–200.

58. Curran, *Corrigan*, 192, 303; Bell, *Rebel, Priest, and Prophet*, 49, 51, 53.

59. *New York Times*, October 25, 27, November 15, 1882.

60. Kenneally, "Sexism and the Church," 13–16.

61. *New York Times*, August 30, September 2, 1917; Nelson M. Blake, "The United States and the Irish Revolution, 1914–1922" (Ph.D. diss., Clark University, 1936), 227–28.

62. Blake, "United States and Irish Revolution," 255.

63. Francis M. Carroll, "Friends of Irish Freedom," in Funchion, *Irish-American Voluntary Organizations*, 119–26; Devoy, *Recollections*, 499, 452.

64. Carroll, "Friends of Irish Freedom," 206–10; idem, *American Opinion and the Irish Question, 1910–1923* (New York, 1978), 155, 239, 251; Patrick McCartan, *With DeValera in America* (Dublin, 1932), 39–40; Alden Jamison, "Irish-Americans: The Irish Question and American Diplomacy, 1845–1921" (Ph.D. diss., Clark University, 1942), 616; Jeremiah A. O'Leary, *My Political Trial and Experiences* (New York, 1919), 185, 218.

65. Alan J. Ward, *Ireland and Anglo-American Relations, 1899–1921* (Toronto, 1969), 73; McCartan, *With DeValera*, 39–40, 46; Dorothy Macardle, *The Irish Republic: A Documented Chronicle of the Anglo-Irish Conflict*

and the Partitioning of Ireland, with a Detailed Account of the Period 1916–1923 (New York, 1965), 279.

66. U.S. Congress, House Committee on Foreign Affairs, *The Irish Question*, Hearings, 65th Cong. 3d sess., December 12–13, 1918 (Washington, D.C., 1919), 29, 64–77, 32–35.

67. U.S. Congress, House Committee on Foreign Affairs, *Hearings to Provide for the Salaries of a Minister and Consuls to the Republic of Ireland*, 66th Cong., 2d sess., December 12–13, 1919 (Washington, D.C., 1920), 151, 231–32, 275–76.

68. McCartan, *With DeValera*, 216–22.

Chapter 9 — Suffrage and War: An Era of Change

1. *Woman's Journal*, October 13, 1894, August 16, 1913; Cardinal Gibbons, "The Restless Woman," *Ladies Home Journal* 19 (January 1902): 6; *New York Times*, April 22, 1913, June 28, 1915, February 5, 1917, August 15, 1920; *Woman's Protest*, October 1912; Ellis, *Gibbons*, 2:539–41; Kenneally, "Question of Equality," 125–40. An indication of growing self-assertiveness on this issue was the comment of Mrs. Frank J. Mott when interviewed by a Denver newspaper on the prelate's opposition, "But it makes no difference who says those things that are ascribed to Cardinal Gibbons. We who live here know they are not true. We know that families are not broken up nor divorce sought on account of equal suffrage. In fact, I believe it is exactly the reverse" (*Woman's Journal*, November 17, 1900).

2. *New York Times*, May 14, 1913; Joseph W. McKee, "Shall Woman Vote?" *Catholic World* 102 (October 1915): 50, 53–54; *Woman's Journal*, August 9, 1913; C. J. Sullivan to Patrick J. Waters, February 10, 1914, file M 901, Archives of the Archdiocese of Boston; *San Francisco Monitor*, June 24, 1911; Alfred J. Ede, "The Lay Crusade for a Christian America: A Story of the American Federation of Catholic Societies" (Ph.D. diss., Graduate Theological Union, 1979), 237–40; James J. Kenneally, "Catholicism and Woman Suffrage in Massachusetts," *Catholic Historical Review* 53 (April 1967): 461.

3. Augustine Rössler, "Woman," in *Catholic Encyclopedia*, 15 (1912): 691–94; Antoinette Iadarola, "The American Catholic Bishops and Woman: From the Nineteenth Amendment to the ERA," in *Women, Religion, and Social Change*, ed. Yvonne Y. Haddad and Ellison B. Findly (Albany, N.Y., 1985), 461.

4. For her life, see Colleen M. McDannell, "Katherine Eleanor Conway," in Mainiero, *American Women Writers*, 1:393–94; Myra B. Lord, *History of the New England Women's Press Association, 1885–1930* (Newton, Mass., 1932); Paula M. Kane, "The Pulpit of the Hearthstone: Katherine Conway and Boston Catholic Women, 1900–1920," *U.S. Catholic Historian* 5 (Summer/Fall 1986): 355–70.

5. See *Bettering Ourselves*, especially 72–80. Except for this portion, the book received a favorable review from the suffragist *Woman's Journal*

because of Conway's advocacy of higher education and of increased opportunities for females (September 23, 1898).

6. Katherine E. Conway, *The Woman Who Never Did Wrong and Other Stories*, 2d ed. (Boston, 1909).

7. An indication of Conway's puritanical views on sex appears in the passage quoted above in chapter 3 (see no. 4).

8. Katherine E. Conway, "Present Aspect of Woman Suffrage," *Donahoe's* 35 (1896): 368-94; idem, 'Woman Has No Vocation to Public Life," in "The Woman Question among Catholics: A Round Table Conference," *Catholic World* 57 (August 1895): 681-89; idem, "Is It a Disadvantage to Be a Woman? Symposium," *Boston Globe*, January 19, 1908; idem, "Catholic Literary Societies," in *Summer School Essays* (Chicago, 1896), 1:203-15.

9. Kane, "Pulpit of the Hearthstone," 366; Dolan, *Catholic Summer School*.

10. Conway, "Catholic Literary Societies," 280.

11. For the *Pilot*, see Katherine Conway to Cardinal O'Connell, January 31, February 2, 1910, O'Connell Papers, 3:15; Sister M. Madeleva, *My First Seventy Years* (New York, 1959), 41.

12. See especially Caroline F. Corbin, *A Woman's Philosophy of Love* (Boston, 1893), 12-15; idem, *Socialism and Christianity, with Reference to the Woman Question* (Chicago, 1905), 9-10, 24-30; this work went through many editions, including two in German. Also see the following by Corbin: *His Marriage Vow* (Boston, 1891); *Rebecca; or, A Woman's Secret* (Chicago, 1868); *Letters from a Chimney Corner: A Plea for Pure Honor and Sincere Relations* (Boston, 1896); *One Woman's Experience* (Chicago, n.d.); *Position of Women in the Socialist Utopia* (Chicago, 1901).

13. Kenneally, "Catholicism and Woman Suffrage," 53.

14. For Campbell and other suffragists mentioned in this chapter, see Kenneally, "Question of Equality," 131-40.

15. Jane Campbell, "Women and the Ballot," in Donnelly, *Girlhood's Hand-Book*, 198, 200.

16. Campbell, *Women's Progress*, for the years 1893-95.

17. Kenneally, "Catholic and Feminist," 229-39.

18. For Archbishop Williams's warning, see *Boston Pilot*, September 29, 1888, and Katherine E. Conway and Mabel W. Cameron, *Charles Francis Donnelly: A Memoir* (New York, 1909), 30. Blake was never elected to the school committee. The first Catholic woman to serve in Boston was Julia Duff, a teacher, a Democrat, and, like Blake, the wife of a physician. Although described as a "home-loving woman," the press depicted her as militant because of her leadership in school reform. Her successful campaigns in 1900 and 1903 attracted large numbers of women to the polls and stimulated female interest in politics (Massachusetts women had been permitted to vote for school committee since 1879). See *Woman's Journal*, December 1, 1900, November 22, 29, 1902, December 5, 1903, and obituaries in the following Boston papers on November 2, 1932: *Transcript, Globe,* and *Post*.

NOTES TO PAGES 136–139

19. Annie Christich, "America's Catholic Women Suffragists," *Catholic Citizen* 8 (March 15, 1922): 17–18; Ida Husted Harper, *History of Woman Suffrage*, 6:487–88. McPike became one of the first female members of the Democratic State Committee, an outspoken opponent of prohibition, and secretary of the New York State Department of Labor; see obituary *New York Times*, February 27, 1943.

20. *New York Times*, November 18, 1917, September 30, 1920, and obituary, February 23, 1937.

21. *New York Times*, February 7, 1922, and obituary, April 15, 1948.

22. Introduction to Rosa Marie Levis Papers and clippings in files 11 and 18, Schlesinger Library, Radcliffe College.

23. *Woman's Journal*, November 9, 1895; S. M. Parrish, "Louise Imogen Guiney," in *NAW*, 2:101–2.

24. *Woman's Journal*, May 6, 1911, December 16, 1916. See Agnes Ryan, *A Whisper of Fire* (Boston, 1919), especially "Church," 93; "Hungry Hearted," 13; "Dead Faith," 58; "Elemental," 22; "Alone," 22; and "Married," 70.

25. In 1920 President Warren G. Harding appointed her a municipal court judge (Harper, *History of Woman Suffrage*, 6:109–10; *Woman Citizen*, 1919).

26. Kenneally, "Catholic and Feminist," 245–53.

27. Quoted in Sidney P. Bland, "Techniques of Persuasion: The National Woman's Party and Woman Suffrage" (Ph.D. diss., George Washington University, 1972), 79.

28. Margaret Deland, "The Change in the Feminine Ideal," *Atlantic Monthly* 105 (March 1910): 299; idem, *Golden Yesterdays* (New York, 1941), 289.

29. *San Francisco Monitor*, May 20, 1911; *Los Angeles Tidings*, September 15, 1911; *New York Times*, April 22, 1917; "Catholic View of Woman Suffrage," *Literary Digest* 44 (June 8, 1912): 1211–12; "An Archbishop on Woman Suffrage," *Ave Maria* 76 (April 1913): 468; Margaret H. Rorke, *Letters and Addresses on Woman Suffrage by Catholic Ecclesiastics* (New York, 1914), 2; Helen Haines, "Catholic Womanhood and the Suffrage," *Catholic World* 102 (October 1915): 65.

30. *Woman's Journal*, July 10, 31, September 16, 1915; Maria Myers, "The Margaret Brent Suffrage Guild," paper prepared for Boston Theological Institute, 1986, in author's possession.

31. *Los Angeles Tidings*, April 29, October 20, 1911. Also see Dowd, "Public Rights of Woman," 312–20; Haines, "Catholic Womanhood," 55–67; Edward McSweeney, "Das ewige Weiblich," *Catholic World* 99 (June 1889): 326–33; *Woman's Journal*, June 1, July 13 1901, July 31, 1904, June 10, 1911, January 25, February 8, 1913; *New York Times*, April 12, October 12, 1915.

32. "Fallacies on Feminism," *Ave Maria* 75 (December 1912): 725.

33. Thomas H. Murray, "Municipal Suffrage for Women," *Donahoe's* 21

(May 1889): 451, 454; *Catholic Citizen* (Milwaukee), quoted in "Notes on Current Topics: The Result in Boston," *Donahoe's* 21 (March 1889): 199.

34. "Ecclesiastical News," *America* 19 (September 7, 1912): 528; *Woman's Journal*, April 11, 1919; *Woman Citizen*, May 10, 1915; *New York Times*, September 13, October 12, 1920; paras. 143–45 of the "Pastoral Letter of 1919," Nolan, *Pastoral Letters*, 244–45.

35. "Woman Suffrage: Editorial," *Catholic World* 107 (April 1918): 136; "Catholic Women at the Polls," *America* 18 (December 8, 1917): 215; J. W. Dawson, "Woman Suffrage," *Catholic World* 112 (November 1920): 145–46; John A. Ryan, "Suffrage and Women's Responsibility," *America* 18 (December 22, 1917): 260–61; "The Duty of Woman Suffrage," *America* 23 (August 28, 1920): 448.

36. "Address of Rev. Joseph Husslein to NCCW" and "Proceedings First Annual Convention and Resolutions Second Annual Convention," both in Proceedings of National Conventions, National Conference of Catholic Women, NCCW Papers, Archives of the Catholic University of America; Daniel M. O'Connell, "Should Catholic Women Vote?" *America* 44 (March 14, 1931): 171–73. In moments of crisis, even the papacy urged women to vote; see Pius XII, "Faith and Life" and "New Daughters," in *The Woman in the Modern World*, ed. Monks of Solesmes (Boston, 1959), 146, 171–73.

37. John F. Piper, "Father John J. Burke, C. S. P. and the Turning Point in American Catholic History," *Annals of the American Catholic Historical Society of Philadelphia* 92 (March–December 1981): 102–4.

38. Williams, *American Catholics in the War*, 116, 135, 127–28, 148; Daniel E. Doran, "The Work of the National Catholic War Council," in McGuire, *Catholic Builders*, 2:273.

39. John B. Sheerin, *Never Look Back: The Church and Concern of John J. Burke* (New York, 1975): 28.

40. Ibid., 63.

41. National Catholic War Council Committee on Special War Activities, *Girls' Welfare*, Reconstruction Pamphlet no. 8, (Washington, D.C., 1919); John F. Piper, *The American Churches in World War I* (Athens, Ohio, 1975), 71, 85.

42. Sheerin, *Never Look Back*, 45; Williams, *American Catholics in the War*, 389–94, 410–32; Marguerite T. Boylan, *They Shall Live Again: The Story of the National Catholic War Council Overseas after World War I* (New York, 1945), 2–33, 61, 72, 133–34; Elizabeth McKeown, "War and Welfare: A Study of American Catholic Leadership" (Ph.D. diss., University of Chicago, 1972), 154–56; Piper, *American Churches*, 149–50; Esther MacCarthy, "Catholic Women and War: The National Council of Catholic Women, 1919–1946," *Peace and Change* 1 (Spring 1978): 23–24; Loretto R. Lawler, *Full Circle: A Story of the National School of Social Service, 1918–1947* (Washington, D.C., 1951), 1–34.

43. John J. Burke, "Special Catholic Activities in War Services," *Annals of the Academy of Political and Social Science* 91 (September 1918): 219; Mad-

den, *Catholics in South Carolina,* 198–99; "Patriotic Meeting of New York Women," *Catholic Charities Review* 1 (May 1917): 156; Williams, *American Catholics in the War,* 215, 233; Maurice F. Egan and John B. Kennedy, *The Knights of Columbus in Peace and War* (New Haven, Conn., 1920), 1: 239, 276, 368, 375–78; Mary Stanislaus Connaughton, *The Editorial Opinion of the Catholic Telegraph of Cincinnati on Contemporary Affairs and Politics, 1871–1921* (Washington, D.C., 1943), 94.

44. O'Brien, who had been educated at a Visitation convent, remained single, as she never met a man her own age who satisfied her intellectually. See Eileen Manning Michels, "Alice O'Brien: Volunteer and Philanthropist," in Stuhler and Kreuter, *Women of Minnesota,* 136–54.

45. Julia C. Walsh, "Elizabeth Nourse: A Reminiscence," *Ave Maria* 49 (May 6, 1939): 51–52; *New York Times,* March 6, October 27, 1921, October 10, 1938.

46. David Spalding, "The Negro Catholic Congresses, 1890–1894," *Catholic Historical Review* 55 (October 1969): 357 n. 63.

47. This bill was originally supported by the NCWC as an emergency measure; see Joseph B. Chepaitis, "The First Federal Social Welfare Measure: The Sheppard-Towner Maternity and Infancy Act, 1918–1932" (Ph.D. diss., Georgetown University, 1968), 87, 142, 219, 293, 340, 343. Also see Agnes Regan, "The National Council of Catholic Women up to Date," in *Proceedings of the Seventh Session of the National Conference of Catholic Charities, September 18–22, 1921* (Washington, D.C., 1921), 217–20; "Sheppard-Towner Program," *America* 26 (December 10, 1921): 182–83; "Lay Councils Join NCWC in Opposing Cooper Maternity Measure," *NCWC Review* 13 (February 1931): 26.

48. Lawler, *Full Circle,* 41–95, 110–95; Abell, *Catholicism and Social Action,* 219–33.

49. Dorothy A. Mohler, "Agnes Gertrude Regan," in *NAW,* 3:128–30; *New York Times,* November 19, 1925, November 4, 1934, September 13, 1937; Dorothy A. Mohler, "Jane Hoey and Agnes Regan; Women in Washington," in Trisco, *Catholics in America,* 209–13; Lawler, *Full Circle,* 47, 66, 70, 84, 96, 111, 116, 121, 207, 210.

50. *Catholic Review* (Baltimore), October 8, 1943.

51. A. Hillard Alteridge, "Women's Work in Wartime," *America* 16 (January 27, 1917): 372–73. Also see "False and True Women," *America* 17 (August 4, 1917): 424; J. V. McKee, "Woman and Child Labor under War Conditions," *Catholic World* 106 (March 1918): 741–51; "Exploiting Women for Profit," *America* 18 (November 3, 1917): 86; Joseph Husslein, "Welfare of the Woman Laborer," *America* 20 (October 12, 1918): 8–10.

52. Richard H. Tierney, "Some After War Problems," *Catholic Mind* 16 (November 22, 1918): 552.

53. Paras. 16, 24, 133, 143 of Bishops' Pastoral, in Nolan, *Pastoral Letters,* 204, 207, 242, 244. Also see Joseph M. McShane, *"Sufficiently Radical":*

Catholicism, Progressivism, and the Bishops' Program of 1919 (Washington, D.C., 1986), 162.

54. Mrs. Michael Gavin, "The National Catholic Council of Women," in McGuire, *Catholic Builders*, 2:371; Elizabeth McKeown, "Apologia for an American Catholicism: The Petition and Report of the National Catholic Welfare Council to Pius XI, April 25, 1922," *Church History* 43 (December 1974): 516.

Chapter 10 — "Lady" Novelists: Twentieth-Century Iconoclasts

1. Esther Neill, "Mary Theresa Waggaman, 1846–1931," in *The Book of Catholic Authors*, ed. Walter Romig (Detroit), 1st ser., 270–76; "Mary T. Waggaman: A Beloved Author," *Ave Maria* 34 (October 10, 1931): 449–53; White, *Era of Good Intentions*, 40–43.

2. Anna T. Sadlier, "Women in the Middle Ages," in Donnelly, *Girlhood's Hand-Book*, 60–61, 88.

3. Anna T. Sadlier's, "Mistress Rosamond Trevor," in Donnelly, *Round Table*, 275–303; "The House of Mystery: A True Story" and "Two Parts of a Letter," both in *Where the Road Led and Other Stories* (New York, 1905), 27–33, 35–42.

4. Agnes Repplier, *In Our Convent Days* (Boston, 1905). Unless otherwise indicated, the account of Repplier is based on Agnes Repplier, *Eight Decades: Essays and Episodes* (Boston, 1912), and George S. Stokes, *Agnes Repplier: Lady of Letters* (Philadelphia, 1949).

5. *Woman's Journal*, December 20, 1908.

6. Agnes Repplier, "The Girl Graduate," in Repplier, *Americans and Others* (Boston, 1913), 99–118; idem, "The Spinster," in Repplier, *Compromises* (Boston, 1904), 170–84.

7. Agnes Repplier, "Woman Enthroned," in Repplier, *Points of Friction* (Boston, 1920), 167–203; Brewer, *Nuns and Education*, 125–27.

8. Repplier, "Woman Enthroned," 187, 198; idem, "Woman and War," in Repplier, *Counter-Currents* (Boston, 1916), 98, 101–6, 116, 135. It was probably this disdain that led her biographer erroneously to interpret her as opposed to feminism (Stokes, *Agnes Repplier*, 167–68).

9. Stokes, *Agnes Repplier*, 23.

10. Agnes Repplier, "Catholicism and Authorship," *Catholic World* 90 (1909), quoted in Schmandt, "Catholic Intellectual Life," 623.

11. Agnes Repplier, "The Novel Reader," *America* 34 (January 23, 1925): 356–57; White, *Era of Good Intentions*, 122–24.

12. *Woman's Journal*, December 20, 1908; Agnes Repplier, "The Eternal Feminine," in Repplier, *Varia* (Boston, 1897): 1–29.

13. Agnes Repplier, "Repeal of Reticence," *Atlantic Monthly* 113 (March 1914): 297–304.

14. Agnes Repplier, "Cost of Modern Sentiment," *Atlantic Monthly* 111 (May 1913): 610–17.

15. For Jordan's life, see Elizabeth Jordan, *Three Rousing Cheers* (New York, 1938).

16. William M. Halsey, *The Survival of American Innocence: Catholicism in an Era of Disillusionment* (Notre Dame, Ind., 1980), 110.

17. Jordan, *Three Rousing Cheers*, 129. These experiences were the basis for the chapter "The Cry of the Pack" in her *May Iverson's Career* (New York, 1914).

18. Halsey, *Survival of American Innocence*, 109.

19. This life-style may explain why she did not become a nun, see "Maria Annunciata," in *May Iverson's Career*.

20. Anna Howard Shaw, *The Story of a Pioneer* (New York, 1915). Also see Jordan, *Three Rousing Cheers*, 320–25; *New York Times*, December 5, 1917, August 13, 1932, and obituary, February 29, 1947.

21. Lucille P. Borden, "Why 'Catholic' Novelist?" *America* 34 (April 13, 1920): 597–98; Arnold J. Sparr, "From Self-Congratulation to Self-Criticism: Main Currents in American Catholic Fiction, 1900–1960," *U.S. Catholic Historian* 6 (Spring/Summer 1987): 218–20.

22. Review of *King's Highway, New York Times Book Review*, November 23, 1941.

23. Halsey, *Survival of American Innocence*, 109.

24. Kathleen Norris, "Religion and Popular Fiction," *America* 34 (March 13, 1926): 525–27. For her life, see idem, *Noon: An Autobiographical Sketch* (Garden City, N.Y., 1925); idem, *Family Gathering* (New York, 1959); and Elinor Richey, "Kathleen Thompson Norris," in *NAW Modern*, 509–11.

25. Louis F. Doyle, "Novels Called Catholic," *America* 35 (August 7, 1926): 403–4.

26. Kenneth Rexroth, "Mrs. Norris' Story," *New York Times Book Review*, February 6, 1955.

27. For support of ERA, see Caroline Babcock to Dorothy S. Granger, May 20, 1946, St. Joan's Society File, National Woman's Party Papers, Library of Congress.

28. Kathleen Norris to the Editor, *Commonweal* 33 (December 20, 1940): 230–31; Wayne S. Cole, *America First: The Battle against Intervention, 1940–1941* (Madison, Wisc.,1953), 108–10.

29. For her life, see the following: Carmen N. Richards, *Minnesota Writers: A Collection of Autobiographical Stories* (Minneapolis, 1951), 90–94; Mary Mitchell, "Margaret Culkin Banning," *Minneapolis Tribune* 1951, in Authors' File, Minnesota Historical Society; dust jacket of Margaret Culkin Banning, *The Vine and the Olive* (New York, 1964); obituary, *New York Times*, January 6, 1982, and her fictional autobiography, *The Will of Magda Townsend* (New York, 1974). Her "Novel and Religion," *Writer* 69 (July 1956): 189–92, also provides insights into her life.

30. Margaret Culkin Banning, *Letters from England: Summer 1942* (New York, 1943), 56.

31. *New York Times*, July 25, 1936, January 18, August 17, 1941; Banning, *Letters from England*, 38–39.

32. *New York Times*, April 23, 1947; Margaret Culkin Banning, "Inquiry into Women's Clubs," *New York Times Magazine*, April 6, 1947, 20, 48–49; idem, "They Raise Their Hats," *Harpers* 171 (August 1935): 356, 361–63.

33. *New York Times*, July 19, 1939, April 8, 1940, January 8, 1943, June 2, 1946; Margaret Culkin Banning, "Women Can Man Machines," *New York Times Magazine*, May 10, 1942, 12–13.

34. *New York Times*, February 22, 1942; Margaret Culkin Banning, *Women for Defense* (New York, 1942).

35. Margaret Culkin Banning, *The Call for Chastity* (New York, 1937). This book, written at the request of the editors of the *Reader's Digest*, was a more complete treatment of an article published in that magazine for which there were twenty-nine thousand requests for reprints only two weeks after its appearance. See idem, "The Case for Chastity," *Reader's Digest* 31 (August 1937): 1–10.

36. Margaret Culkin Banning, "Sex Life after Middle Age," *Reader's Digest* 61 (September 1952): 8–10.

37. Mitchell, "Banning," 90–94. The *New York Times* reviewer seized upon the "unresolvable elements" in the novel as "another argument for birth control" but one in which there was "too much sincerity and sympathy for the Catholic as an individual human being in such an impasse to be dismissed lightly"(*New York Times Book Review*, December 21, 1937).

38. Margaret Culkin Banning, *The Convert* (New York, 1957) and *The Iron Will* (New York, 1936).

39. *New York Times*, April 18, 1943, December 4, 1952; Margaret Culkin Banning, "Filth on the Newsstands," *Reader's Digest* 61 (October 1952): 115–19.

40. Margaret Culkin Banning, "They Raise Their Hats," *Harpers* 171 (August 1935): 360.

41. Page 74. At that time Banning, a divorcée, had not yet met the man who would become her second husband.

42. Margaret Culkin Banning with Mabel Louise Culkin, *Conduct Yourself Accordingly* (New York, 1944), 120, 174–76.

43. Katherine Burton, *The Next Thing: Autobiography and Reminiscences* (New York, 1949); obituary, *New York Times*, September 24, 1969.

44. Katherine Burton, "Woman to Woman," *Sign* 30 (January 1950): 57; (February 1951): 29; (June 1951): 39; 31 (October 1951): 59; (January 1952): 61, and various essays in *Woman to Woman*.

45. Katherine Burton, "On Woman," *Commonweal* 19 (February 23, 1939): 463–65; idem, "Woman to Woman," *Sign* 45 (May 1966): 27.

46. Katherine Burton, "Woman's Place in the World," in *Woman to Woman*, 86.

47. Katherine Burton, "There Is No New Woman," *Marriage* 50 (March

1968): 47–49; idem, *According to Pattern: The Story of Dr. Agnes McLaren and the Society of Catholic Medical Missionaries* (New York, 1946).

48. Mary E. Mannix, *Michael O'Donnell; or, The Fortunes of a Little Emigrant* (Notre Dame, Ind., 1900); Conway, "Individual Catholic Women," 397–98; Driscoll, *Literary Convert Women*, 78–87; Edith O'Shaughnessy, "The True Book of Adventure," in *Fiction by Its Makers*, ed. Francis X. Talbot (New York, 1928), 164; idem, *Married Life* (New York, 1925); Jeffrey M. Burns, "The Ideal Catholic Child: Images from Catholic Textbooks, 1875–1912," Center for the Study of American Catholicism, Working Papers no. 3 (Notre Dame, Ind., 1965).

49. Halsey, *Survival of American Innocence*, 149–50.

50. Clare Boothe Luce, Introduction to Anne O'Hare McCormick, *Vatican Journal, 1921–1954*, ed. Marion T. Sheehan (New York, 1957), x–xi.

51. See columns for September 26, 1942, December 25, 1943, April 15, 1947, March 23, 1948, December 24, 1950, December 26, 1953, in McCormick, *Vatican Journal*.

52. Anne O'Hare McCormick, Introduction to Marion T. Sheehan, ed., *The Spiritual Woman: Trustee of the Future* (New York, 1955).

53. Sandra G. Treadway, "Anne Elizabeth O'Hare McCormick," in *NAW Modern*, 439–40; C. L. Sulzberger, *A Long Row of Candles: Memoirs and Diaries, 1934–1954* (New York, 1969), 95, 1013; Sheehan, Preface to *Spiritual Woman*, xi.

54. Obituary, *New York Times*, September 13, 1966; Halsey, *Survival of American Innocence*, 106; Blanche Mary Kelly, "The Romance of Reality," *America* 28 (November 18, 1922): 104–5.

55. Velma Bourgeois Richmond, "Frances Parkinson Wheeler Keyes," in Mainiero, *American Women Writers*, 2:450–52; Frances Parkinson Keyes, *All Flags Flying: Reminiscences of Frances Parkinson Keyes* (New York, 1922), 185; idem, "Doll House," *Catholic Digest* 25 (May 1962): 100.

56. Barbara H. Davis, "Helen Constance White," in *NAW Modern*, 729–30; *Catholic Citizen*, January 15, 1937.

57. Introduction to Donnelly, *Girlhood's Hand-Book*.

58. Sally Fitzgerald, Introduction to Flannery O'Connor, *The Habit of Being: Letters Edited and with an Introduction by Sally Fitzgerald* (New York, 1979). Also see Sally Fitzgerald, "Flannery O'Connor," in *NAW Modern*, 512–14; Eugenia Kaledin, *Mothers and More: American Women in the 1950s* (Boston, 1984), 129.

59. Quoted in Fitzgerald, "O'Connor," 514.

60. See Flannery O'Connor, *Mystery and Manners* (New York, 1969), 118, 146–52, 157, 163, 170–75, 180, 185, 197, and the following letters in the *Habit of Being:* to Ben Griffith, March 3, 1945, p. 69; to "A," July 20, 1955, p. 90; August 2, 28, 1955, pp. 92, 97; September 15, 1955, p. 103; July 28, 1956, p. 168; July 5, 1958, p. 290; June 27, 1959, p. 338; to John Lynch, November 6, 1955, p. 114; to Margaret Lee, March 10, 1957, p. 209; to Cecil Dawkins, May 19, 1957, p. 221.

Chapter 11 — Between the Wars: Continuing Tensions

1. McKeown, "War and Welfare," 260.

2. *Boston Pilot*, March 13, 1920.

3. Virgil Michel, "The Christian Woman," *Catholic Mind* 37 (May 1939): 669; Lucian Johnson, "On Living Twice," *Catholic World* 131 (June 1930): 261–62.

4. MacCarthy, "Catholic Women and War," 28–29.

5. Felix M. Kirsch, *Sex Education and Training in Chastity* (New York, 1931), 288; Adolph D. Frenay, *The Head of the Family: The Husband and Father: Rights and Obligations Ordained by God* (St. Louis, 1939), 10; also see "Report of the Congress of Catholic Women, 1937," Levis Papers, file 37.

6. *New York Times*, November 21, 1925, April 15, 1929; *Boston Pilot*, April 30, 1938; "Are Women Degenerating?" *America* 35 (January 1937): 299–300; James M. Gillis, *The Catholic Church and the Home* (New York, 1928), 36, 56, 109–12; Grace H. Sherwood, "The Church and the Dignity of Women," *Catholic Action* 14 (July 1932): 12.

7. James J. Walsh, *Sex Instruction* (New York, 1931), 131, 197; Mrs. Francis Slattery, "The Catholic Woman in Modern Times," *Catholic Mind* 28 (March 22, 1930): 124–27; Michel, "Christian Woman," 669.

8. *New York Times*, April 24, 1922, July 18, 21, October 12, 1924, July 18, November 1, 1927, June 24, 1929, February 15, 1930; "Immodest Women's Dress," *Homiletic and Pastoral Review* 30 (November 1929): 171–73. Strictures on sex education were so closely adhered to that Mary Boyle O'Reilly, a graduate of Sacred Heart Academy, did not learn "the facts of life" until she was nearly thirty (Ryan, *Beyond the Ballot Box*, 73).

9. *New York Times*, October 13, 1934, May 11, 1937, June 10, 1948, and her obituary, October 13, 1969.

10. *New York Times*, May 9, 1911, August 5, 1920, December 15, 1927, February 9, 1936, January 8, 1936; "Miss Anglin Tells the Whole Truth," *Commonweal* 14 (June 17, 1931): 189–90.

11. Ralph M. Huber, ed., *Our Bishops Speak, 1919–1951* (Milwaukee, 1951), 41, 42, 263.

12. Joseph V. Nevins, "Education to Catholic Marriage," *Ecclesiastical Review* 79 (September 1929): 249.

13. Burton, *Next Thing*, 178–80; "An Invasion of Rights" in her *Woman to Woman*, 101–4. The book she referred to, Valère Coucke and James J. Walsh, *The Sterile Period in Family Life* (New York, 1933), was written primarily for confessors and asserted that intercourse during nonfertile periods was permissible if it fostered mutual love, one of the ends of marriage, and that the object of sexual relations was preservation of the species, not necessarily children in every family. However, the author urged moderation and suggested abstinence by inviting husbands to "a manly exercise of Christian virtue."

14. Noonan, *Contraception*, 423.

15. J. M. Fleming, "What to Preach," *American Ecclesiastical Review* 59 (August 1918): 166.

16. Nevins, "Education to Catholic Marriage," *Ecclesiastical Review* 79 (September 1929): 246 and (December 1929): 632.

17. Kirsch, *Sex Education*, 454.

18. John W. Riley and Matilda White, "The Use of Various Methods of Contraception" *American Sociological Review* 5 (December 1940): 895; Norman B. Ryder and Charles F. Westoff, *Reproduction in the United States, 1965* (Princeton, N.J., 1971), 186; Hennesey, *American Catholics*, 327; Tomasi, *Italian American Family*, 32, 37; Catherine Moran McNamara interview in June Namias, *First Generation: In the Words of Twentieth-Century American Immigrants* (Boston, 1978), 18. There was a temporary increase in Catholic fertility in the 1930s after Pope Pius XI issued *Casti connubii*, describing the frustration of the sex act as a grave sin. One of the reasons for this pronouncement was his belief that priests were not enforcing the church's prohibitions. See Noonan, *Contraception*, 424; Susan H. Van Horn, *Women, Work, and Fertility* (New York, 1988), 94.

19. Joseph H. McMahon, "The Catholic Woman in Modern Life," *Catholic Mind* 30 (June 8, 1932): 265–68.

20. Rosemary Radford Ruether, "Are Women's Colleges Obsolete?" *Critic* 27 (October–November 1968): 63; Brewer, "Beyond Utility," 102–4; I. J. Semper, "The Church and Higher Education for Girls," *Catholic Educational Review* 29 (April 1931): 215–21; Doyle, *Curriculum at Catholic Women's Colleges*, 44–45, 48–49, 112–19; Sister I. H. M. Mary, "Social Service for College Girls," *America* 65 (May 17, 1941): 261.

21. John F. Fitzgerald to William H. O'Connell, October 20, 1909, O'Connell Papers, 5:3. Not only did Rose comply, but she sent her daughters to the Sacred Heart nuns for higher education, unlike her sons, who attended secular colleges. She later wrote, "I would much rather be known as the mother of a great son or a great daughter than the author of a great book or the painter of a great masterpiece" (Rose F. Kennedy, *Times to Remember* [New York, 1974], 481 and 23, 28, 47, 132, 153). On another occasion she described herself by saying, "I am an old-fashioned wife. I believe what he [my husband] believes; he is right so often" (Gail Cameron, *Rose: A Biography of Rose Frances Fitzgerald Kennedy* [New York, 1971)] 172).

22. Kirsch, *Sex Education*, 298; Semper, "Church and Higher Education" 220, 222; William F. Cunningham, *Pivotal Problems of Education* (St. Louis, 1940), 185–88.

23. Katherine Burton, "Mother Marie Joseph Butler," in *NAW*, 1:272–73.

24. Mary A. Molloy, "A Statement and Purpose and a Pointing of Arms: A Letter to the Members of the Faculty of the College of St. Teresa, February 2, 1928," and "Catholic Colleges for Women: A Paper Presented at the Annual Meeting of the Catholic Educational Association 1914," both in Oates, *Higher Education for Catholic Women*, 338–41, 342–50.

25. Mary Prudentia, "The Dean of St. Margaret's Writes to the Bishop,"

Catholic Educational Review 30 (November 1932), reprinted in Oates, *Higher Education for Catholic Women*, 351–52. In 1906 the Jesuit son of General Sherman encouraged Catholic women's colleges to follow the example of Harvard in its wide-ranging approach to education and thereby no longer cripple "our helpmates and life long comrades" (*Woman's Journal*, August 25, 1906).

26. Edward A. Fitzpatrick, "The Aims of Mount Mary College," *Catholic Educational Review* 36 (January 1938), reprinted in Oates, *Higher Education for Catholic Women*, 175.

27. Lorine M. Getz, "Women Struggle for an American Catholic Identity," in Ruether and Keller, *Woman and Religion*, 3:178–79; Madeleva, *First Seventy Years*; idem, "Scholarship for Catholic Women," *Catholic Educational Review* 30 (January 1932): 32; Mary E. Klein, "Sister Madeleva Wolff CSC, Saint Mary's College, Notre Dame, Indiana: A Study of Presidential Leadership" (Ph.D. diss., Kent State University, 1983), 43, 52. Long before the introduction of graduate programs in theology, Marie L. Points (d. 1931) had been described as "one of the greatest theologians" by New Orleans's Bishop Anthony Blanc (1792–1860). The daughter of a cotton merchant slave owner, Points was a public-school teacher and then the education and woman's department editor of the *New Orleans Picayune*. In the year of his death Blanc drafted her to edit the diocesan paper, *Morning Star*. For years she wrote the news and editorials (from 1909 to at least 1918, every editorial was hers), assisted only by her younger sister (*Morning Star*, April 6, 1918; obituary, *Times Picayune*, September 29, 1931).

28. Grace Dammann, "The American Catholic College for Women," in Deferrari, *Essays on Catholic Education*, 192–93; M. Redempta Prose, *The Liberal Arts Ideal in Catholic Colleges for Women in the United States* (Washington, D.C., 1943), 78, 91, 96–97, 109, 152; Lavina C. Wenger, "Analysis of the Aims of Catholic Women's Colleges in the United States," *Catholic Educational Review* 42 (May 1944): 276–78.

29. Edgar Schmiedeler, "Near Equality with Men: So What!" *Homiletic and Pastoral Review* 45 (October 1944): 11–12; Brewer, "Beyond Utility," 666.

30. Helen M. McCadden, "Women Who Work," *Commonweal* 11 (March 26, 1930): 580–82.

31. Parker T. Moon, "Catholic Social Action," in McGuire, *Catholic Builders*, 2:218; "Women's Work," *Commonweal* 15 (November 4, 1931): 3–4; Elizabeth Spearman, "Educating Our Daughters," *Ave Maria* 40 (August 1934): 225–27; Frederick Fries, "Should Women Work?" *Catholic Digest* 2 (May 1938): 29–31; William J. Benn, "Women Have a Place in Business and Industry but Must Not Surrender Their Place in the Home," *America* 61 (May 17, 1931): 155.

32. Gleason, "Working Women in Oregon," 585–86; *Woman's Journal*, September 2, 1916; O'Grady, *Catholic Charities*, 330–31, 385–86; Catholic Professional Women's Club Papers, file M-962, Archives of the Archdiocese of Boston.

33. Reports of the League of Catholic Women, October 1910–January 1912, May 1912–May 1913, May 1914–May 1915, box 1, files 3–5, and R.J. Haberlin to Monsignor Splaine, November 18, 1916, box 1, file 3, both in League Papers, Archives of the Archdiocese of Boston; *Boston Pilot*, October 5, 1918.

34. In 1937, after marrying W.J.B. Macauley, Irish envoy to the Vatican, she lived in Rome until her death the following year. See New York Times, October 30, November 13, December 1, 1932, and the following by Genevieve G. Brady: "Girl Scouts," *Catholic World* 134 (November 1931): 212–14; "Thing That I Missed," *Commonweal* 13 (December 10, 1930): 155–56; and "Woman and Relief," ibid., 17 (November 30, 1932): 119–20. Also see "Comment," *America* 60 (December 3, 1938): 195; John Tracy Ellis, "Catholic Philanthropy: Building the New American Church," in Trisco, *Catholics in America*, 163–64.

35. Michels, "Alice O'Brien," 136–54.

36. For an excellent biography of Day, see William D. Miller, *Dorothy Day: A Biography* (New York, 1982). Also see Kenneally, *Women and Trade Unions*, 168–71. Much of this section is also drawn from Day's own writings.

37. Dorothy Day, *House of Hospitality* (New York, 1939), 49.

38. *Catholic Worker*, May 1934.

39. Patricia F. McNeal, *The American Catholic Peace Movement, 1928–1972* (New York, 1978), 41–42, 50, 175, 192; Miller, *Dorothy Day*, 314, 332–33, 343, 345, 437–39, 479.

40. *Catholic Worker*, March and May 1942.

41. Catherine de Hueck, *Friendship House* (New York, 1946), 137. For her life, see Romig, *Book of Catholic Authors*, 4th ser., 71–75; obituary, *New York Times*, December 16, 1985; William H. Shannon, *The Hidden Ground of Love: The Letters of Thomas Merton on Religious Experience and Social Concerns* (New York, 1985), 3. Catherine de Hueck, *My Russian Yesterdays* (Milwaukee, 1951), gives some insights into her character.

42. de Hueck, *Friendship House*, 111; *New York Times*, May 8, 1939.

43. Catherine de Hueck, *Dear Bishop* (New York, 1947), 34–35.

44. Thomas Merton, *The Seven Storey Mountain* (New York, 1948), 341–57; Michael Mott, *The Seven Mountains of Thomas Merton* (Boston, 1984), 186–97.

45. Romig, *Book of Catholic Authors*, 3rd ser., 93–99.

46. McNeal, *Catholic Peace Movement*, 20, 23, 32.

47. Ishbel Ross, *Ladies of the Press: The Story of Women in Journalism, by an Insider* (New York, 1936), 142–43; idem, "Marie Mattingly Meloney," in *NAW*, 2:525–26; obituary, *New York Times*, June 24, 1943; Keyes, *All Flags Flying*, 177.

48. "Souvenir Program of the General Bazaar, April 27–29, 1920," box 3, file 4, and Lillian Slattery to Friends, June 9, 1929, box 2, file 10, both in Papers of the League of Catholic Women. It should be pointed out that the Catholic Women's League of Chicago condemned xenophobic Americanism,

defended the rights of foreign born, blacks, and Jews, and asserted that in order to assimilate immigrants United States citizens must first "American- ize" their attitude toward them and recognize that the demand for higher wages and fewer hours was not un-American (Margaret Madden, "Problems of Americanization," *Catholic Charities Review* 4 [January 1920]: 10–11).

49. "Resolutions, 1943," League Papers, box 2, file 17.

50. Lawler, *Full Circle*, 44.

51. Gavin, "National Council of Women," 371, 379–80; Slattery, "Cath- olic Woman in Modern Times," 125–29.

52. *New York Times*, November 19, 1925, November 4, 1934, September 3, 1937; National Catholic Welfare Conference, *The Catholic Woman and Civic Life* (Washington, D.C., 1935).

53. Dorothy M. Brown, *Setting a Course: American Women in the 1920s* (Boston, 1987), 177; Ewens, "Removing the Veil," 273.

54. Oates, "Good Sisters," 178, 183; idem, "Organized Volunteerism: The Catholic Sisters in Massachusetts, 1870–1940," in *Women in American Re- ligion*, ed. Janet M. James (Philadelphia, 1980), 168.

55. Ewens, "Political Activity," 46–51; Getz, "Women Struggle," 3: 202–3.

56. The hospital had been erected pontifically, with the superior under the jurisdiction of the pope.

57. Jeanne M. Lyons, *Maryknoll's First Lady* (New York, 1964).

58. *The American Foundations of the Sisters of Notre Dame de Namur Compiled from the Annals of Their Convents by a Member of the Congregation* (Philadelphia, 1928), 633–48.

59. Cohalan, *Popular History*, 307–8.

60. Henry S. Spalding, *Talks to Nurses: The Ethics of Nursing* (New York, 1920), 90–93, 144–45.

61. Anna Dengel, *Mission for Samaritans: A Survey of Achievements and Opportunities in the Field of Catholic Medical Missions* (Milwaukee, 1945), 21–24; Burton, *According to Pattern; Catholic Citizen*, December 15, 1943. For Dougherty's successful efforts to have canon law changed so that religious women could perform obstetrics, see Margaret Reher, "Denis J. Dougherty, an Unlikely Feminist," a paper delivered at the 1989 spring meeting of the American Catholic Historical Society.

62. Sister M. Loyola, "Women in Medicine," *Catholic World* 157 (May 1943): 163–64; Hugh J. Nolan, "The Native Son," in Connelly, *Diocese of Philadelphia*, 368, 413.

63. Elsie Whitlock-Rose, "Catholic Women in Medicine," *Catholic World* 141 (May 1935): 274. For a survey of Catholic women physicians, see Oates, "Catholic Lay Women," 108–12.

64. Hope Chamberlin, *A Minority of Members: Women in the U.S. Con- gress* (New York, 1973), 40–41.

65. Jean Azulay, "Rediscovered Woman: Ferraro's Forerunner," *New Di- rections for Women* 13 (September–October 1984): 12–13; Chamberlin, *Mi-*

nority of Members, 52–57; Mary T. Norton, "What Politics Has Meant to Me," *Democratic Digest* 15 (February 1938): 19; *New York Times*, March 28, 1926, January 13, 1928, June 17, 1942, and her obituary, August 3, 1959.

66. House, 86th Cong. 1st sess., 105 *Cong. Rec.* 15093 (August 4, 1959).

67. Emily N. Blair, "Many Roads Lead Women Into Politics," *New York Times Magazine*, October 28, 1928, 7, 23; *New York Times*, November 5, 1924.

68. House, *Cong. Rec.* 15096 (August 4, 1959).

69. *New York Times*, July 4, 1940, March 4, June 7, 1943, June 23, 1944, January 4, 1945, February 18, 1947; Mary T. Norton, "Woman in Industry," in Sheehan, *Spiritual Woman*, 88–92.

70. *New York Times*, June 13, 1940, May 1, 1947.

Chapter 12 — The Ending of an Era

1. Guthrie, "Woman's Place," 497–99. For additional comments on women and suffering, see C. J. Woolen, "The Failure of Feminism," *Homiletic and Pastoral Review* 48 (October 1947): 38–39.

2. Mary Bernice, "Training All Out Mothers," *Catholic World* 58 (October 1943): 79–81.

3. "Victory and Peace," Pastoral 1942, in Huber, *Our Bishops Speak*, 112; MacCarthy, "Catholic Women and War," 25; C. J. Stratman, "Casualties on the Home Front," *Columbia* 22 (January 1943): 3, 22–23; Josephine MacDonald, "The Home Page," *Columbia* 22 (January 1943): 15, 24; *New York Times*, April 12, 1942; Thomas W. Tifft, "Toward a More Humane Social Policy: The Work and Influence of Monsignor John O'Grady" (Ph.D. diss., Catholic University of America, 1979), 320–23; "Conserving Home Life of Children in War Employment Urged," *Catholic Action* 6 (April 1942): 4; NCWC Convention Resolutions Pertaining to the Status of Women, 1921–1960, NCWC Papers.

4. Proceedings of the Twenty-second National NCWC Convention, 1944, NCWC Papers, U.S. Catholic Conference, Washington, D.C.

5. Joseph B. Schuyler, "Women at Work," *Catholic World* 157 (April 1943): 27–30; Proceedings of the Twenty-second National NCWC Convention; "Forgotten Woman," *America* 69 (July 31, 1943): 463; J. A. White, "Post War Problems," *Catholic World* 167 (May 1943): 128.

6. "Women in War Industry," *Ave Maria* 56 (July 25, 1942): 99; "Bishop Duffy Deplores Mothers' Wartime Jobs," *Catholic Action* 6 (July 1942): 6–7. These fears were not confined to Catholics. A study undertaken by the Office of War Information concluded that three-fourths of the public accepted the wartime employment of women, but with regret, for females belonged at home and thus should leave their jobs at war's end. Interestingly enough, nearly all of the single women and one-half of the married women interviewed in the same study planned to continue working even when hostilities ended (Office of War Information, "Opinion about the War Time Employ-

ment of Women," Report no. C31, May 29, 1944, RG44, Box E 149, National Archives, Washington, D.C.).

7. Ruth Reed, "Women in War Jobs: A Social Evaluation," *America* 69 (July 3, 1943): 454.

8. Winifred Hayes, "Woman's Place in the Future World Order," *Catholic World* 157 (August 1943): 482–87.

9. Helen C. White, "University Women in War and Peace," *American Association of University Women Journal* 34 (Winter 1944): 67–68.

10. Minutes of the Twenty-fourth Annual Meeting of U.S. Bishops, November 1946, United States Catholic Conference Archives, Washington, D.C.; Sister Mary Bernice, "Nurses Are in Great Demand for Civilian and Military Needs," *America* 66 (December 27, 1941): 318–20; "Medical Heroes," *America* 71 (July 1, 1944): 351.

11. "Women Want to Join for War but Run into Some Skepticism," *Newsweek* 19 (January 12, 1942): 23, 25.

12. *New York Times*, March 22, 1942. A year later, when it was apparent that the WAAC experiment was successful, O'Hara claimed, "The Army and Navy wives put me up to it — their great complaint was that they were not allowed to live overseas with their husbands, but the Government planned to draft women and send them overseas to distract their husbands" (O'Hara to Richard Berlin, March 27, 1943, quoted in Thomas T. McAvoy, *Father O'Hara of Notre Dame: The Cardinal Archbishop of Philadelphia* [Notre Dame, Ind., 1967], 245).

13. Eustace to O'Hara, March 23, 1942, and Thomas A. Mulry to O'Hara, March 23, 1942, Women's Auxiliary Army Folder, Con. A, Box 13, Personal Papers of John F. O'Hara, Archives of the University of Notre Dame.

14. Sometime later the NCWC itself held that women should enter the military only as a last resort and only after ensuring adequate protection for their families (Minutes of the Administrative Board of NCWC, April 14, 1942, Catholic Conference Archives).

15. *Fall River Herald News*, May 18, 1942; *New York Times*, May 19, 1942.

16. *Boston Pilot*, May 16, 1942; "A Neo-Pagan Bill," *America* 66 (April 4, 1942): 714. The others were cited in "Catholics v. WAACS," *Time* 39 (June 15, 1942): 39. One of the most outspoken congressional critics of the corps, asserting it would cast a shadow over the sanctity of the home, was the Catholic senator Francis T. Mahoney (Conn.); see 77th Cong., 2nd sess., 88 *Cong. Rec.* 4090 (1942). Emotional rhetoric has misled at least one historian as to the extent of Catholic opposition; see D'Ann Campbell, *Women at War with America: Private Lives in a Patriotic Era* (Cambridge, Mass., 1984), 27–29. There was not as much criticism of the women's navy (WAVES) and women Marines, as these groups were formed after the WAAC. However, Senator David I. Walsh (Mass.), a prominent Catholic and chairman of the Senate Naval Affairs Committee, delayed legislation authorizing the WAVES until he was persuaded that enlistees would not have their femininity or potential

for motherhood destroyed. The syndicated columnist Drew Pearson referred to Walsh as a "committee of one to protect the purity of American womanhood." See Joy B. Hancock, *Lady in the Navy: A Personal Reminiscence* (Annapolis, Md., 1972), 55; Virginia C. Gildersleeve, *Many a Good Crusade* (New York, 1954, reprint, New York, 1980), 271; *Minneapolis Star Journal*, December 30, 1943; Ruth Cheney Streeter, "History of the Marine Corps Women's Reserve: A Critical Analysis of Its Development and Operation, 1943–1945" typescript, Schlesinger Library.

17. For example, see "Women and War," *Commonweal* 35 (March 27, 1942): 116; "Comment," *America* 67 (April 15, 1942): 507. Catholic opposition to compulsory service remained unswerving. See "Two Important Conventions," *Catholic World* 153 (September 1941): 750; *Catholic Worker*, May 1942; "Potpourri," *Catholic World* 155 (May 1942): 186–87; "Draft of Women," *America* 70 (February 26, 1944): 575.

18. Mattie E. Treadwell, *The Women's Army Corps* (Washington, D.C., 1954), 484; Ann E. Allen, "The WAC Mission: The Testing Time from Korea to Vietnam" (Ph.D. diss., University of South Carolina, 1984), 330 no. 43, 206; Director's Representative and Evaluation Board, Box 189, Women's Auxiliary Army Corps Papers, National Archives. In June 1943 the corps was made an integral part of the army for the duration of the war and six months beyond and was no longer an auxiliary.

19. Louise E. Goeden, "Date with Destiny," *Extension* 37 (April 1943): 14, 42, 48; idem, "Women in Uniform: Work of the WACS," *America* 69 (July 31, 1943): 457–59; "Women at War, by a Catholic WAC Officer," *Sign* 22 (June 1943): 676–77.

20. File 000.3 Army G-1, WAC Decimal File, 1942–1946, National Archives; *New York Times*, June 9, 11, 22, 27, 30, 1943; *New York World Telegram* and *Washington Post*, June 11, 1943; Treadwell, *Women's Army Corps*, 195, 207, 217.

21. *Catholic Review* (Baltimore), July 2, 1943.

22. "WAACS and Rumors," *Sign* 22 (July 1943): 709–10.

23. Mrs. Katherine Nangle to Mildred McAfee, October 19, 1942, GRS-8, Bureau of Naval Personnel, General Correspondence, 1941–1945, National Archives.

24. "Draft of Women," 575.

25. *Catholic Citizen*, January 15, 1944.

26. O'Hara to Richard Berlin, March 22, 1943, quoted in McAvoy, *Father O'Hara*, 245.

27. Ann E. Allen to author, February 21, 1987. According to Allen, most women who joined were unaware of clerical trepidations, and for those who were familiar, it made little difference. An NCWC reporter estimated that over 25 percent of the corps were Catholic (*Catholic Review* [Baltimore], July 2, 1943).

28. Irene C. Kuhn, "The Little Colonel," *Catholic Digest* 15 (January 1951): 1–6; Allen, "WAC Mission," 7–8. For her early years, see folder 11A

in Papers of U.S. Defense Advisory Committee on Women in the Service, Schlesinger Library.

29. Allen, "WAC Mission," 221–22, 245–46, 282–88. Hoisington told an interviewer that if she had been aware of hierarchical opposition to the corps, she never would have enlisted (Allen to author, February 21, 1987). An interesting account of one of the Catholic WASPs (Women's Air Force Service Pilots) is found in June A. Willenz, *Women Veterans: America's Forgotten Heroines* (New York, 1983): 62–63.

30. Allen, "WAC Mission," 27, 84, 113; Minutes of Defense Advisory Committee, November 25, 1952, May 12–14, 1955, and booklets "Builders of Faith" and "Your Daughter's World," in file 4 of Papers of Defense Advisory Committee.

31. Hancock, *Lady in the Navy*, 252.

32. Interview with Mary K. Fitzgerald Phaneuf, December 31, 1985; Isabel Currier, "Frances Sweeney," *Commonweal* 40 (August 18, 1944): 428; idem, "Monument of, for, and by the Living," *Common Ground* 9 (August 1948): 33–41.

33. Nat Hentoff, "My Boyhood Hero: Ms. Frances Sweeney," *MS* 3 (July 1979): 16–18; idem, *Boston Boy* (New York, 1986), 65–73.

34. John Roy Carlson, *The Plotters* (New York, 1940), 273.

35. Hentoff, "Boyhood Hero," 15; idem, "To Be Young and Jewish in Roxbury in the Thirties," *Boston Globe*, September 30, 1985.

36. John F. Stack, *International Conflict in an American City: Boston Irish, Italians, and Jews, 1935–1944* (Westport, Conn., 1979), 131–34; Edward Lodge Curran Clips, George H. Beebe Communications Library, Boston University.

37. Arnold Beichman, "Boston Christian Front–Jews: A Series of Articles," *P.M.*, October 18–22, 1943; Elsie McCormick, "Boston's Fight against Rumors," *American Mercury* 55 (September 1942): 275–81; "Rumor Clinic," *Life* 13 (October 12, 1942): 88–100; John Roy Carlson, *Under Cover: My Four Years in the Nazi Underworld of America* (New York, 1943), 454; Stack, *International Conflict*, 137–39; Casper Grosberg to Hans Kroto, October 11, 1948, Frances Sweeney File, folder I-123, Jewish Community Council Papers, American Jewish Historical Society, Waltham, Massachusetts.

38. *Boston Traveler*, January 19, 1945.

39. Frances Sweeney Clips, Beebe Library; Papers of the Frances Sweeney Committee, file M-541, Archives of the Archdiocese of Boston.

40. After leaving Congress in 1945, Stanley served as counsel to the New York State Employee Retirement System, then as state assistant attorney-general (1955–79), and then resumed private practice; see *Who's Who of American Women* (Chicago, 1985–86), 795.

41. Material on the ERA and Catholicism up until 1945 is based on James J. Kenneally, "Women Divided: The Catholic Struggle for an Equal Rights Amendment, 1923–1945," *Catholic Historical Review* 75 (April 1989): 249–63.

42. Archbishop Richard J. Cushing of Boston, probably about this time, also informed a NWP representative and Granger of his private support of the amendment (Granger to author, December 3, 1987, and Leila J. Rupp and Verta Taylor, *Survival in the Doldrums: The American Women's Rights Movement, 1845 to the 1960s* [New York, 1987], 142).

43. For an account of Catholics and the ERA from the 1950s to the present, see Kenneally, "Question of Equality," 146–51.

44. *New York Times*, August 17, 1941.

45. Rita L. Lynn, *The National Catholic Community Service in World War II* (Washington, D.C., 1952); MacCarthy, "Catholic Women and War," 25–29; Anne Sarachen Hooley, "Catholic Women and Defense," in *Proceedings of the Twenty-seventh Meeting of the National Conference of Catholic Charities, October 19–22, 1941* (Washington, D.C., 1942), 309–14.

46. Helen W. Homan, "Long, Long Trail of Trailers," *America* 69 (July 31, 1943): 457–58; Marilu Colbert, "Youth Inspiration," *Catholic Woman's World* 3 (1941): 29–30; *New York Times*, August 17, 1941.

47. Edgar Schmiedeler, "Are American Women Shirkers?" *Catholic World* 153 (July 1941): 426–29; "Statement on International Order, November 16, 1944," in Huber, *Our Bishops Speak*, 119; Leo J. Kinsella, *The Wife Desired* (Techny, Ill., n.d. [early 1940s]), 148; Harry C. Koenig, ed., *Principles for Peace: Selections from Papal Documents, Leo XIII to Pius XII* (Washington, D.C., 1943), 515; *New York Times*, July 2, 1945; Pius XII, "New Duties," in Monks of Solesmes, *Women in the Modern World*, 127–42.

48. James H. Vandervelt and Robert P. Odenwald, *Psychiatry and Catholicism*, 2d ed. (New York, 1959), 453–54.

49. Mary Mullaly, "Woman and the World," *Ave Maria* 73 (February 24, 1951): 245; A. Durand, "The Christian Ideal of Womanhood," *Homiletic and Pastoral Review* 52 (May 1952): 700–704; Elizabeth Morrissy, "The Status of Women: An Address before the National Council of Catholic Women, September 12, 1948," *Vital Speeches* 15 (November 1948): 55–60; Louis C. Fink, "Salute to the Ladies: Woman Is the Glory of Man," *Family Digest* 10 (April 1955): 51–54; "About Women in *Who's Who* in America," *Social Justice Review* 13 (September 1950): 164; John B. Sheerin, "Mary Most Gracious," *Homiletic and Pastoral Review* 52 (May 1952): 681; idem, "May, Mary, and Mothers," *Homiletic and Pastoral Review* 49 (May 1949): 603–5; Patricia A. Crowley, "Women and Family Life," in Sheehan, *Spiritual Woman*, 72–81; Sheehan, Preface to ibid., xvii–xviii; idem, "Woman's Spiritual Role in Society," in ibid., 153–67; John L. Springer, "Brides Don't Know Enough," *Sign* 42 (June 1963): 8–10; Sister M. Patricia, "Lovely Ladies: The Heart of God's Creation," *Catholic Educator* 21 (April 1951): 394; Dominicus M. Prümmer, *Handbook of Moral Theology* (New York, 1957), 213–14; National Catholic Women's Union, *Proceedings of the Thirty-eighth Convention and Ninety-ninth Meetings of the Catholic Central Verein of America, 1954* (St. Louis, 1954), 163–64; Joseph C. Haley, *Accent on Purity: Guide for Sex Education* (Notre Dame, Ind., 1948), 109; Irving De Blanc, "The

Eternal Woman of 1956," in *Proceedings of the Twenty-eighth National Convention of the National Council of Catholic Women, 1956* (Washington, D.C., 1956), 53–56; Daniel B. Carroll, "The O'Hara Years," in Connelly, *Diocese of Philadelphia*, 432; *Boston Evening American*, May 24, 1956.

50. Carol Jackson, "The Tragedy of the Modern Woman," *Integrity* 3 (November 1948): 5; Dorothy Dohen, *Women in Wonderland* (New York, 1960), 160, 171.

51. Dohen, *Women in Wonderland*, 5; Prümmer, *Moral Theology*, 214; Woolen, "Failure of Feminism," 30–39; Patricia, "Lovely Ladies," 395.

52. Alden V. Brown, "The Grail Movement in the United States, 1940–1972: The Evolution of an American Catholic Laywomen's Community" (Ph.D. diss., Union Theological Seminary, 1982); Getz, "Women Struggle," 216–17.

53. Lydwine Van Kersbergen, "Toward a Christian Concept of Woman," *Catholic World* 186 (October 1955): 6–11. The following essays by Van Kersbergen appear in *Woman: Some Aspects of Her Role in the Modern World* (Cleveland, 1956): "Search for Women's World," "Toward a Christian Concept of Woman," "The Role of Women in Virginity," and "The Role of Women in Motherhood."

54. W. B. Flaherty, "American Feminism a Century After," *America* 80 (December 4, 1948): 234–36.

55. Edwin V. O'Hara, "The School and the Community," *Bulletin of the National Catholic Educational Association*, August 1952, 50–55.

56. Mary Brennan, "Marriage Is a Career," *Catholic Educator* 29 (May 1959): 665–66.

57. Ethel Marbach, "The Eternal Woman," *Catholic Digest* 28 (October 1964): 79–81; Sister Mary Eva, "Femininity Can Be Taught," *Marriage* 46 (September 1964): 24–28.

58. M. Leonita Smith, "Catholic Viewpoints about the Psychology, Social Role, and Higher Education of Women" (Ph.D. diss., Ohio State University, 1961), especially 110–18, 130–32, 142–44, 166–70, 183–86, 193, 203.

59. Haley, *Accent on Purity*, 20; Catholic Women's Union, *Proceedings of Thirty-eighth Convention*, 26, 29, 39.

60. Joseph H. Fichter, *Dynamics of a City Church* (Chicago, 1951), 146, 213–16.

61. John C. Ford and Gerald Kelly, *Marriage Questions* (Westminster, Md., 1963), 201.

62. Judith Blake, "The Americanization of Catholic Reproductive Ideals," *Population Studies* 20 (July 1966): 27–34, 43.

63. Dohen, *Women in Wonderland*, 92.

64. Priscilla O'Brien Mahoney, "The Lady Has a Brain," *Catholic World* 178 (March 1954): 451–54.

65. Abigail McCarthy, "A Threatened Resource: Leadership and Catholic Women's Colleges," *Commonweal* 101 (June 17, 1983): 357–58.

66. *New York Times*, June 12, 1956, May 19, August 4, September 2, October 11, 1959, November 14, 1961, September 29, 1962.

67. "Footnote to Mrs. Luce," *Ave Maria* 115 (April 12, 1947): 451–52. The death of her daughter and the problem of the existence of evil helped lead to her conversion, following six months of instruction from Sheen; see Clare Boothe Luce, "The Real Reasons," *McCall's* 74 (February to April 1947).

68. See Alden Hatch, *Ambassador Extraordinary: Clare Boothe Luce* (New York, 1956); Clare Boothe Luce, Oral History, Columbia University; Wilfred Sheed, *Clare Boothe Luce* (New York, 1982).

69. *New York Times*, May 30, 1926, March 2, 1927, June 6, 1932, obituary, October 7, 1968; Mohler, "Hoey and Regan," 211.

70. Mohler, "Hoey and Regan," 209–13; Jane M. Hoey, Oral History, Columbia University; idem, "Woman in Social Work," in Sheehan, *Spiritual Woman*, 137–52; Kaledin, *Mothers and More*, 84; *New York Times*, April 26, May 13, 1942, April 6, 1948, December 1, 1949, January 25, 1951, November 4, December 9, 1953, January 26, 1956.

71. Hoey, "Woman in Social Work," 137–52.

72. Patricia Murphy, *Glow of Candle Light: The Story of Patricia Murphy* (Englewood Cliffs, N.J., 1961).

73. *Cleveland Press*, January 19, 1924, January 18, 1925; unidentified clippings in scrapbook 11 in Lillian and Clara Westropp Papers, Schlesinger Library.

74. *New York Times*, April 10, 1938; *Cleveland Universe Bulletin*, January 25, 1968; obituary, *Cleveland Plain Dealer*, August 16, 1968; clippings in scrapbooks 11 and 15, and Frank Kulla and Ernest R. Tidyman, "The Ladies of the Ledger," *This Day* 16 (January 1965): 22–23, in scrapbook 12 in Westropp Papers.

75. *New York Times*, September 11, 1952, September, 12, 1955, January 30, 1958.

76. Mary Ellen Kelly, *But with the Dawn, Rejoicing* (Milwaukee, 1959), 681–82.

77. Ethel Barrymore, *Memories: An Autobiography* (New York, 1955); Pat M. Ryan, "Ethel Barrymore," in *NAW Modern*, 58–60; Barbara B. Jamison, 'Ethel Barrymore in Mid-Career at 75, *New York Times Magazine*, August 15, 1954, 32.

78. Sister M. Paraclita, "Making Women out of Girls," *Catholic Educational Review* 55 (March 1957): 155.

79. Margaret O'Connell, "The New Role of the Single Woman," *Catholic Digest* 25 (May 1962): 44–47. As early as 1927 there was a Bethany Conference organization in the Boston Archdiocese, consisting mostly of schoolteachers who met monthly for conferences, benediction, and rosary (Francis X. Weiser to Robert J. Senott, January 11, 1958, Chancery Subject File, Archives of the Archdiocese of Boston).

80. Bulletin for 1948, file 2:12, and Alice M. Johnson, "Report," file 2:25, both in box 2, League of Catholic Women Papers.

81. Jean Holzhaver, "Doing Daddy In: The Feminine Mystique," *Commonweal* 78 (October 18, 1963): 100–103.

82. Garry Wills, *Bare Ruined Choirs: Doubt, Prophecy, and Radical Religion* (Garden City, N.Y., 1976), 59.

83. Jeffrey M. Burns, "American Catholics and the Family Crisis, 1930–1962: The Ideological and Organizational Response" (Ph.D. diss., University of Notre Dame, 1982), 200–207; idem, "Catholic Laymen in the Culture of American Catholicism in the 1950s," *U.S. Catholic Historian* 5 (Summer/Fall 1986): 385–400.

84. Brown, "Grail Movement," 270, 274, 305–7.

85. "The New Catholic Woman," *Ave Maria* 106 (September 1964): 6–10; (November 1964) 14–15.

86. Schmiedeler, "Near Equality," 11–12; Ewens, "Political Activity," 44.

Epilogue

1. For nuns, see Ewens, *Nun in Nineteenth Century*, 1; for Vatican II, see Walter M. Abbott, ed., *The Documents of Vatican II* (New York, 1966), 227–28, 267, 500, 468–69. For a view emphasizing the traditionalism of the encyclical and council on women's issues, see Christine Gudorf, *Catholic Social Teachings on Liberation Themes* (Latham, Md., 1980), 302–12; for the new Catholic woman, see Weaver, *New Catholic Woman*; for a survey of postwar Catholic feminism, see Rosemary Rader, "Catholic Feminism: Its Impact on United States Women," in Kennelly, *American Catholic Women*, 182–97; and for feminist liturgies, see Rosemary Radford Ruether, *Women-Church: Theology and Practice of Feminist Liturgical Communities* (San Francisco, 1985).

2. Carol Felsenthal, *The Sweetheart of the Silent Majority: The Biography of Phyllis Schlafly* (New York, 1981), 27; interview with Elwell in Peter Occhiogrosso, *Once a Catholic* (Ballantine edition, New York, 1989), 213–37.

3. Smeal interview in Cateura, *Growing Up Italian*, 36.

4. For example see Vincent P. Miceli, *Women Priests and Other Fantasies* (Norwell, Mass., 1985), 19–35. Also see the advertisements for traditional communities in *Our Sunday Visitor* and the *Wanderer*, especially in the May 18, 1989, issue of the latter, which gave a post office box after the following notice: "Traditional Order of Sisters. Committed to Community Prayer, Community Life and wearing full religious habit, welcomes recruits with experience or without."

5. See articles by Mary F. Rousseau, Katherine Rose Hanley, Michael Novak, and David Burrell in *Communio* 8 (Fall 1981) on the relations between the sexes, a special issue of that journal commissioned by the American Catholic Philosophical Society. Also see Miceli, *Women Priests*, 3–19.

6. Pars. 217–18 of *Partners in the Mystery*, in *Origins* 17 (April 21, 1988): 781.

7. Ibid., pars. 34, 84, 111; pp. 763, 767, 770.

8. Ibid., pars. 73–75, 121; pp. 766, 771.

9. Ibid., pars. 239–43; pp. 783.

10. William H. Shannon, "The Bishops' Pastoral on Women," *America* 159 (August 6–13, 1988): 84–86.

SELECT BIBLIOGRAPHY

The works listed here have been cited in more than one chapter.

Abbelen, P. M. *Venerable Mother M. Caroline Friess, First Commissary General of the School Sisters of Notre Dame in America.* St. Louis, Mo., 1893.

Abell, Aaron I. *American Catholicism and Social Action: A Search for Social Justice 1865–1900.* Garden City, N.Y., 1960.

Bell, Stephen. *Rebel, Priest and Prophet: A Biography of Dr. Edward McGlynn.* New York, 1937.

Bennett, Helen C. *American Women in Civic Work.* New York, 1915.

Biddle, Ellen H. "The American Catholic Irish Family," In *Ethnic Families in America: Patterns and Variations,* edited by Charles H. Mindel and Robert W. Habenstein, 89–123. New York, 1976.

Bowler, Mary M. *History of Catholic Colleges for Women in the United States of America.* Washington, 1933.

Brewer, Eileen Mary. "Beyond Utility: The Role of the Nun in the Education of American Girls 1860–1920," Ph.D. diss., University of Chicago, 1984.

———. *Nuns and the Education of American Catholic Women, 1860–1920.* Chicago, 1987.

Buetow, Harold A. *Of Singular Benefit: The Story of Catholic Education in the United States.* New York, 1986.

Burton, Katherine. *According to the Pattern: The Story of Dr. Agnes McLaren and the Society of Catholic Medical Missionaries.* New York, 1946.

———. *In No Strange Land: Some American Catholic Converts.* New York, 1942.

———. *The Next Thing: Autobiography and Reminiscences.* New York, 1949.

———. *Woman to Woman.* New York, 1962.

Byrne, Patricia. "Sisters of St. Joseph: The Americanization of a French Tradition." *U.S. Catholic Historian* 5 (1986): 241–71.

Callan, Louise. *The Society of the Sacred Heart in North America.* New York, 1937.

Campbell, Jane. "Women and the Ballot." In *Girlhood's Hand-Book of Woman: A Compendium of Views on Woman's Work — Woman's Sphere — Woman's Influence and Responsibilities,* edited by Eleanor C. Donnelly, 198–200. 2nd ed. St. Louis, Mo., 1905.

Cantor, Milton, and Bruce Laurie, eds. *Class, Sex, and the Woman Worker.* Westport, Conn., 1977.

Caroli, Betty Boyd, Robert F. Harney and Lydio F. Tomasi, eds. *The Italian Immigrant Woman in North America.* Toronto, 1978.

Cateura, Linda B. *Growing Up Italian.* New York, 1987.

Clark, Denis. *The Irish in Philadelphia: Ten Generations of Urban Experience.* Philadelphia, 1973.

Cohalan, Florence D. *A Popular History of the Archdiocese of New York.* New York, 1963.

Conway, Katherine E. *Bettering Ourselves.* 3rd ed. Boston, 1904.

Crews, Clyde F. "American Catholic Authoritarianism: The Episcopacy of William George McCloskey, 1868–1909." *Catholic Historical Review* 70 (1984): 560–80.

Curran, Robert E. *Michael Augustine Corrigan and the Shaping of Conservative Catholicism in America 1878–1902.* New York, 1978.

Deferrari, Roy J., ed. *Essays on Catholic Education in the United States.* Washington, D.C., 1942.

Deshon, George. *Guide for Catholic Young Women Especially for Those Who Earn Their Own Living.* 31st ed. New York, 1897.

Dolan, Jay P. *The American Catholic Experience: A History from Colonial Times to the Present.* Garden City, N.Y., 1985.

Donnelly, Eleanor C. *Girlhood's Hand-Book of Woman: A Compendium of the Views on Woman's Work — Woman's Sphere — Woman's Influence and Responsibilities.* 2d ed., St. Louis, Mo., 1905.

Dowd, Mary A. "The Public Rights of Women: A Second Round Table Conference." *Catholic World* 59 (1894): 312–20.

Driscoll, Annette S. *Literary Convert Women.* Manchester, N.H., 1928.

Dwyer, John T. *Condemned to the Mines: The Life of Eugene O'Connell, 1815–1891, Pioneer Bishop of Northern California and Nevada.* New York, 1976.

Ewens, Mary. "Political Activity of American Sisters before 1970." In *Between God and Cesar: Priests, Sisters and Political Office in the United States*, edited by Madonna Kolbenschlag, 41–59. New York, 1985.

———. "Removing the Veil: The Liberated American Nun." In *Women of Spirit: Female Leadership in the Jewish and Christian Traditions*, edited by Rosemary Radford Ruether and Eleanor McLaughlin, 255–78. New York, 1979.

———. *The Role of the Nun in Nineteenth Century America: Variations on the International Theme.* New York, 1978.

Fénelon, François. *A Treatise on the Education of Daughters Translated from the French and Adapted to English Readers by the Rev. T. F. Dibdin.* Boston, 1806. Reprint. Boston, 1821.

Fox, Mary H. *Peter E. Dietz, Labor Priest.* Notre Dame, Ind., 1953.

Funchion, Michael F., ed. *Irish-American Voluntary Organizations.* Westport, Conn., 1983.

Getz, Lorine M. "Women Struggle for an American Catholic Identity." In *Women and Religion in America: A Documentary History*, edited by Rosemary Radford Ruether and Rosemary S. Keller, 3:175–222. San Francisco, 1986.

Girardey, Ferreol. *Mission Book for the Married*. New York, 1897.

Gleason, Caroline J. "For Working Women in Oregon," *Survey* 36 (1916): 585–586.

Goebel, Edmund. *A Study of Catholic Secondary Education During the Colonial Period up to the First Plenary Council of Baltimore 1852*. Washington, D.C., 1936.

Goodwin, M. B. "Schools and Education of the Colored Population in the District." *Special Report, Department of Education*. Washington, D.C., 1870. 193–300.

Guilday, Peter. *The Life and Times of John England First Bishop of Charleston 1786–1842*. 2 vols. New York, 1927.

Hammond, Harold E., ed. *Diary of a Union Lady 1861–1865*. New York, 1962.

Harper, Ida Husted. *History of Woman Suffrage*, vol. 6. See Stanton.

Hennesey, James. *American Catholics: A History of the Roman Catholic Community in the United States*. New York, 1981.

Herron, Mary Eulalia. *The Sisters of Mercy in the United States*. New York, 1929.

Holworthy, Mary Xavier. *Diamonds for the King*. Corpus Christi, Tex., 1945.

Horgan, Paul. *Lamy of Sante Fe, His Life and Times*. New York, 1975.

Howlett, W. J. *Life of Charles Nerinckx: Pioneer Missionary of Kentucky and Founder of the Sisters of Loretto at the Foot of the Cross*. 2d ed. Techny, Ill., 1940.

———. *Life of the Right Reverend Joseph P. Machebeuf, D.D., Pioneer Priest of Ohio, Pioneer Priest of New Mexico, Pioneer Priest of Colorado, Vicar Apostolic of Colorado and Utah, First Bishop of Denver*. Pueblo, Colo., 1890.

Huber, Raphael M., ed. *Our Bishops Speak 1919–1951*. Milwaukee, Wis., 1952.

Hughes, John. 'Reminiscences." U.S. Documents in Propaganda Fides. Vol. 2, no. 1417, fols 490rv, 492–524. Microfilm. University of Notre Dame.

Ireland, John. "Social Purity: An Address Delivered to the World's Congress on Social Purity, 1893." John Ireland Papers. Microfilmed from Various Depositories by the Minnesota Historical Society, St. Paul, Minn., 1984.

Jacoby, George P. *Catholic Child Care in Nineteenth Century New York*. Washington, D.C., 1941. Reprint. New York, 1974.

James, Edward T., et al., eds. *Notable American Women 1607–1950: A Biographical Dictionary*. 3 vols. Cambridge, Mass., 1971.

Kaledin, Eugenia. *Mothers and More: American Women in the 1950s*. Boston, 1984.

Kenneally, James J. "Catholic and Feminist: A Biographical Approach," *U.S. Catholic Historian* 3 (1984): 229–53.

———. "Eve, Mary and the Historians: American Catholicism and Women," *Horizons* 3 (1976): 187–202.

———. "A Question of Equality," In *American Catholic Women: A Historical Exploration*, edited by Karen Kennelly, 125–51. New York, 1989.

———. "Sexism, the Church, Irish Women," *Eire-Ireland* 21 (1986): 3–16.

———. *Women and American Trade Unions*. Montreal, 1981.

Kennelly, Karen, ed. *American Catholic Women: A Historical Exploration*. New York, 1989.

Klarmann, Andrew. *The Crux of Pastoral Medicine: The Perils of Embryonic Man: Abortion, Craneotomy and the Caesarian Sections, Myrna and the Porro Sections*. New York, 1905.

Landriot, Jean François. *The Valiant Woman: A Series of Discourses Intended for the Use of Women Living in the World*. Translated by Helen Lyons. Boston, 1872.

Lawler, Loretto R. *Full Circle: A Story of the National School of Social Service 1918–1947*. Washington, D.C., 1951.

Leaves from the Annals of the Sisters of Mercy. By a Member of the Order of Mercy. 4 vols. New York, 1889.

Leonard, M., ed. *Immortelles of Catholic Columbian Literature*. Chicago, 1897.

Levis, Rosa Marie. Papers. Schlesinger Library, Radcliffe College, Cambridge, Mass.

Liebard, Odile, ed. *Love and Sexuality: Official Catholic Teachings*. Wilmington, N.C., 1978.

Lord, Robert H., John E. Sexton, and Edward T. Harrington. *History of the Archdiocese of Boston in the Various Stages of its Development 1604–1943*. 3 vols. New York, 1944.

MacCarthy, Esther. "Catholic Women and War: The National Council of Catholic Women, 1919–1946," *Peace and Change* 1 (1978): 23–32.

McColgan, Daniel T. *A Century of Charity: The First One Hundred Years of the Society of St. Vincent de Paul in the United States*. 2 vols. Milwaukee, Wis., 1951.

McDannell, Colleen. *The Christian Home in Victorian America 1840–1900*. Bloomington, Ind., 1986.

McGovern, James J., ed. *The Life and Letters of Eliza Allen Starr*. Chicago, 1905.

McGuire, C. E., ed. *Catholic Builders of the Nation: A Symposium on the Catholic Contribution to the United States*. 5 vols. Boston, 1923.

McKeown, Elizabeth. "War and Welfare: A Study of American Catholic Leadership," Ph.D. diss., University of Chicago, 1972.

Madden, Richard C. *Catholics in South Carolina: A Record*. Lantham, Md., 1985.

Madeleva, Sister M. *My First Seventy Years*. New York, 1959.

Mainiero, Lina, ed. *American Women Writers: A Critical Reference Guide from Colonial Times to the Present.* 4 vols. New York, 1979.

Mindel, Charles H. and Robert W. Habenstein, eds. *Ethnic Families in America: Patterns and Variations.* New York, 1976.

The Mission Book: A Manual of Instruction and Prayers Adapted to Preserve the Fruits of the Mission. New York, 1853.

Mohler, Dorothy A. "Jane Hoey and Agnes Regan, Women in Washington." In *Catholics in America, 1776–1976,* edited by Robert Trisco, 209–13. Washington, D.C., 1976.

Moguin, Wayne, and Charles Van Doren, eds. *A Documentary History of the Italian-Americans.* New York, 1974.

Murphy, Mother M. Benedict. "Pioneer Roman Catholic Girls' Academies: Their Growth, Character, and Contribution to American Education: A Study of Roman Catholic Education for Girls from Colonial Times to the First Plenary Council of 1852." Ph.D. diss., Columbia University, 1958.

National Conference of Catholic Women. Papers. Catholic University, Washington, D.C.

Nolan, Hugh J., ed. *Pastoral Letters of the American Hierarchy, 1792–1970.* Huntington, Ind., 1971.

Noonan, John T., Jr. *Contraception: A History of Its Treatment by the Catholic Theologians and Canonists.* Cambridge, Mass., 1956.

Oates, Mary, ed. *Higher Education for Catholic Women: An Historical Anthology.* New York, 1987.

O'Connell, J. J. *Catholicity in the Carolinas and Georgia: Leaves of Its History.* New York, 1879. Reprint. Spartanburg, S.C., 1972.

O'Connell, William. Papers. Archives of the Archdiocese of Boston.

O'Grady, John. *Catholic Charities in the United States: History and Problems.* Washington, D.C., 1930.

O'Reilly, Bernard. *The Mirror of True Womanhood; and True Men as We Need Them.* 2 vols. in 1. New York, 1881.

Penny, Virginia. *Think and Act: A Series of Articles Pertaining to Men and Women, Work and Wages.* Philadelphia, 1869. Reprint. New York, 1971.

Peterson, Susan and Vaughn Roberson. *Women with Vision: The Presentation Sisters of South Dakota, 1889–1985.* Urbana, Ill., 1988.

Pillar, James J. *The Catholic Church in Mississippi, 1837–1865.* New Orleans, 1964.

Potter, George. *To the Golden Door: The Story of the Irish in Ireland and America.* Boston, 1966.

Power, Edward J. *A History of Catholic Higher Education in the United States.* Milwaukee, Wis., 1958.

Richmond, John F. *New York and Its Institutions 1609–1871. A Library of Information.* New York, 1871.

Rosenberg, Charles E. *The Cholera Years: The United States in 1832, 1849, and 1866.* Chicago, 1947.

Ruether, Rosemary Radford, and Rosemary S. Keller, eds. *Women and Religion in America: A Documentary History.* 3 vols. San Francisco, 1981–1986.

Ryan, Dennis P. *Beyond the Ballot Box. A Social History of the Boston Irish, 1845–1917.* Madison, N.J., 1983.

Sewall, Mary Wright, ed. *The World's Congress of Representative Women.* Chicago, 1894.

Sicherman, Barbara, et al., eds. *Notable American Women: The Modern Period.* Cambridge, Mass., 1980.

Stanton, Elizabeth. C., et al., eds. *History of Woman Suffrage.* 6 vols. New York, 1881–1922. Reprint. New York, 1969. Vols. 1–3, ed. Stanton et al.; vol. 4, ed. Susan B. Anthony and Ida H. Harper; vols. 5–6, ed. Ida H. Harper.

Starr, Ellen Gates. Papers. Smith College, Northampton, Mass.

Trisco, Robert F., ed. *Catholics in America, 1776–1976.* Washington, D.C., 1976.

Walch, Timothy. "Catholic Social Institutions and Urban Development: The View from Nineteenth Century Chicago and Milwaukee." *Catholic Historical Review* 64 (1978): 16–32.

Walsh, Marie de Lourdes. *The Sisters of Charity of New York 1809–1959.* 3 vols. New York, 1960.

Weaver, Mary Jo. *New Catholic Women: A Contemporary Challenge to Traditional Religious Authority.* San Francisco, 1985.

Williams, M. Mother. *Second Sewing: The Life of Mary Aloysius Hardey,* New York, 1942.

Williams, Michael. *American Catholics in the War.* New York, 1921.

Wittke, Carl. *The Irish in America.* Baton Rouge, 1956. Reprint. New York, 1970.

Wood, Thomas O. "The Catholic Attitude Toward the Social Settlement Movement, 1886–1914." M.A. thesis, University of Notre Dame, 1958.

Woodward, C. Vann, ed. *Mary Chestnut's Civil War.* New Haven, Conn., 1981.

INDEX

INDEX